D0871722

MACKENZIE KING AND THE PRAIRIE WEST

ROBERT A. WARDHAUGH

Mackenzie King and the Prairie West

UNIVERSITY OF TORONTO PRESS
Toronto   Buffalo   London

© University of Toronto Press Incorporated 2000
Toronto Buffalo London
Printed in Canada

ISBN 0–8020–4733–5

Printed on acid-free paper

Canadian Cataloguing in Publication Data

Wardhaugh, Robert Alexander, 1967–
Mackenzie King and the Prairie West

Includes bibliographical references and index.

ISBN 0-8020-4733-5

1. Prairie Provinces – Politics and government – 1905–1945.*   2. King,
William Lyon Mackenzie, 1874–1950.   3. Liberal Party of Canada.
4. Federal-provincial relations – Prairie Provinces.*   5. Liberalism –
Prairie Provinces.   I. Title.

FC3242.W36 2000   971.2'02   C00-930339-1
F1060.9.W36 2000

The six cartoons following page viii are from the *Grain Growers' Guide,* which
was owned and published by the Organized Farmers, in Winnipeg, 1908–28,
and are reprinted by kind permission of the *Country Guide.*

University of Toronto Press acknowledges the financial assistance to its
publishing program of the Canada Council for the Arts and the Ontario
Arts Council.

This book has been published with the help of a grant from the Humanities
and Social Sciences Federation of Canada, using funds provided by the
Social Sciences and Humanities Research Council of Canada.

University of Toronto Press acknowledges the financial support for its
publishing activities of the Government of Canada through the Book
Publishing Industry Development Program (BPIDP).

To my parents,
Bob and Ann

Contents

She wouldn't be happy with either.

"In the spring a young man's fancy
Lightly turns to thoughts of love." – Tennyson.

Grain Growers' Guide, 15 March 1922, by Charles Thorson

It looks as though someone will be hurt when the crash comes.

Grain Growers' Guide, 21 June 1922, by Charles Thorson

An Evener Which Does Not Even

Grain Growers' Guide, 2 April 1924, by E.S. Russenholt

Perhaps!

Grain Growers' Guide, 24 December 1924, by E.S. Russenholt

A Bit Late But Riding Hard

Sir Knight (somewhat out of breath): "Od's bodikins! If these two noble chargers perchance seek diverse paths, verily I am undone."

Grain Growers' Guide, 27 January 1926, by Arch Dale

Profiting by Experience

Grain Growers' Guide, 1 November 1927, by Arch Dale

MACKENZIE KING AND THE PRAIRIE WEST

Introduction

The latter half of the twentieth century has been a miserable time for the Liberal party on the Canadian Prairies. What is commonly referred to as the most 'national' of Canada's parties has enjoyed remarkable success at the federal level, maintaining office for the majority of the century, yet it has failed in an area that at one time was considered, alongside Quebec, one of the twin pillars of Liberalism. It would seem that since John Diefenbaker, the 'beloved Prairie son,' captured western hearts for the Progressive Conservative party in 1957, Prairie Liberalism has remained in the doldrums. The governments of Lester B. Pearson and Pierre Elliott Trudeau served to reinforce the already established sentiments that the Liberal party was out of touch with the Prairie region and much more concerned with reinforcing its hold on central Canada. Federal–provincial disputes over resource control between the Prairie governments and Ottawa only exacerbated these views. Ottawa's obsession with the constitution and Quebec separatism has led many westerners to the opinion that both old-line parties are out of touch with their concerns. An occasional breakthrough at either the provincial or federal level has stirred the hope and optimism of the party faithful, but never has it translated into the re-establishment of a genuine base of support.

But the disintegration of Liberal fortunes in the Prairie West began much earlier than 1957. Indeed, by this time, much of the damage to the party had already been done, and the years that followed witnessed only the continuation of a trend that had been ongoing at least since 1935. The objective of this book is to delve into the first half of the century to discover the roots of the Liberal party's collapse, what David Smith has called 'the regional decline of a national party.'[1] This period was dominated by one Liberal politician – William Lyon Mackenzie King. For that reason this enigmatic personality serves as the centrepiece of the study. The plight of the party is chronicled through three decades that witnessed dramatic changes to the region and nation, transformations that would see not only the decline of the party but also the decline of the region.

In contrast to most studies of Prairie politics, which focus on the protest parties that the region produces in abundance, this work approaches western alienation via what Reg Whitaker calls the 'government party' that was coming to dominate national politics with such mastery. It analyses the views and treatment of the Prairie West by Canada's longest-serving prime minister. It traces its way through the myriad 'western' issues – from tariffs to freight rates – in order to explain Liberal policy. It scrutinizes the roles and relationships of key Prairie politicians through such factors as cabinet representation. It explains the Liberal party's never ending quest to defeat the region's tendency toward third party alternatives. Above all, it attempts to explain the position of Liberalism on the Prairies while at the same time helping to explain the place of the region in the nation.

It is the premise of this work that Mackenzie King entered the leadership of the national Liberal party in 1919 with a remarkably sympathetic view toward the Prairie West. Favourable perceptions of the region were common at the beginning of the century and reflected the optimistic belief that the West had a major role to play in national development and prosperity. But King's perceptions were remarkable in that he perceived, and in many mays constructed, a natural affinity between himself and the area. The Prairie West was fertile ground for more than wheat, oats, and barley. The area sported the strongest social reform movement in the nation; in this it was in accord with the young, idealistic Mackenzie King, who saw himself very much in the role of reformer. It would not be coincidence that King would find himself in agreement with the religious, economic, and political sentiments being espoused in the West or that the Farmers' platform of 1919 was almost identical to the Liberal platform adopted that same year. Yet, as so often was the case with Mackenzie King, romantic idealism is difficult to distinguish from pragmatic realism. In the face of the agrarian revolt, the Liberal party that emerged from the divisions of the First World War desperately needed western support. The revolt had to be subdued and the Progressives reabsorbed into Liberal ranks. Not surprisingly, King's sympathies toward the Prairies in the 1920s translated into federal policies directed at regaining that support. In King's view, his government was continuing along Laurier's path of holding the West as one of the main party strongholds. But the wrath of the Great Depression and the onset of the Second World War wrought changes that transformed the relationship between Ottawa and the regions. By the time Mackenzie King retired in 1948, his attitude toward the Prairie West had undergone dramatic transition, and the region had responded in kind. The reasons for the failure of the Liberal party on the Prairies lie buried within the 'Age of Mackenzie King.'

Both Mackenzie King and Prairie Liberalism have received attention from scholars, but the two subjects have never been brought together. It is not the intention here to offer a revisionist interpretation of the ever enigmatic prime minister, nor is this study meant to overturn the work done on the Liberal party in the West. Rather, *Mackenzie King and the Prairie West* is meant to fill one of the many gaps that the official biographies could not handle in any real detail. David Smith has written extensively on Prairie Liberalism, but his emphasis has been on the Saskatchewan Liberal party. He discusses Liberalism throughout the region in a later work but deals strictly with the period after 1957.[2] This book, then, is not meant as a biography of Mackenzie King nor is it meant to serve as a complete history of Prairie politics. Rather, it is a study of the meeting of the two. It is hoped that it offers additional insight into King's career while at the same time providing some understanding of the complex phenomenon that is Prairie politics.

1

In Search of the New Jerusalem, 1874–1919

I believe so strongly that the interests of all classes in Canada depend primarily on the extent and prosperity of agriculture in Canada and in this connection the moral fibre not less than the material well-being of the nation, that I do not think it is possible for the agricultural interests to receive too much consideration from Parliament.

W.L.M. King to H.B. Cowan, 23 April 1914

It is doubtful that the Canadian Prairies played any significant role in the early life of William Lyon Mackenzie King. When King was born on 17 December 1874, the distant interior of the Northwest had yet to feel the full impact of a nation desirous of expansion and development. Canadian interest in the area had prompted the British Crown to purchase Rupert's Land in 1870 from the Hudson's Bay Company, and, after the tension surrounding the Red River Resistance, it was incorporated into the Dominion. Although white settlements were gradually appearing, the Northwest remained a vast expanse of rolling plain and rugged parkland that seemed better suited to the aboriginal nations and the wandering buffalo herds. The march of 'progress' and 'civilization' long anticipated by central Canadians, particularly Ontarians, was only slowly proceeding, but the region did offer great potential for growth. Waves of immigrants from Ontario were swelling the population of Manitoba. The institutions and ideas of European industrial society had come to stay, and Native groups were forced to suffer the consequences. Indians and Métis were pushed further west in search of the declining buffalo herds. By the end of the 1870s, 'the Indians were on reserves, the Metis in disarray, the whites in control.'[1] By the 1880s the frontier-settlement communities of the trading post, the parish, and the hunting group had given way to commercial agriculture carried across the Prairies by the railways and serviced by a burgeoning Winnipeg.

The Ontario of Mackenzie King's birth must have seemed far removed from events in the Canadian West, yet in central Canada, too, the powers of transformation were at work. The traditional rural lifestyle was being forever altered by the forces of industrial capitalism and its partner, urbanization. The changes in society were marked by the new class system, one that was soon characterized by conflict. The populations of the cities rose to new heights; dramatic increases in poverty, crime, prostitution, gambling, and alcoholism were viewed as social vices directly associated with urban life.

Amid the uncertainties of the tumultuous transformation, the Northwest seemed to offer hope for a new future. The area seemed to be vast, open, and empty – a perfect place to found a new, more harmonious society. The popular perception of the interior took on an even more attractive appearance that came to dominate the thinking of an entire generation.

As early as the 1850s a consensus had already taken shape in the minds of expansionists that the Northwest was a land of opportunity – a beckoning agricultural frontier. It would offer an escape from the constraints of industrial society and the pressures of an increasingly urban world. By the 1870s the concerns of the Palliser Expedition regarding the aridity of the southern plains were conveniently replaced by the reports of John Macoun. Expansionists described the area as 'the largest flower garden on the continent,' and the popular image was transformed into a 'fertile garden well adapted to agricultural pursuits.'[2] It was generally believed that the potential of Canada existed within the developing interior: these perceptions 'raised the image of the West to new heights and shattered the last qualifications in the Canadian myth of the garden ... The result was an image of the North West that was more idealistic and optimistic than anything that had gone before, or, for that matter anything that has existed since.' By the early 1880s expansionist writers were viewing the region as 'something approximating an [sic] utopia.'[3] The Canadian West produced its share of heroes to dramatize the new society, as images of the pioneer and the North West Mounted Police glorified frontier life amid the continuing development of eastern urban industrialization. Novelists such as Ralph Connor 'gave immortality to the image of a cultivated utopia in the prairie west.'[4]

Despite the hardships of pioneering, the myths of utopia and frontier survived and prospered in the popular imagination, and the image of a western Garden of Eden came to dominate the period from 1880 until the First World War. In these years the popular perception of the West was characterized by the search for a 'new and better society – the promised land, a garden of abundance in which all material wants would be provided and where moral and civic virtues would be perfected.'[5] The nation was being discussed in terms of a 'New' and 'Old' Canada, of an 'East' and a 'West.' Images in art and literature described the Prairies as a new society, the symbolic land 'wherein the heavenly city might yet be founded.' It was pure and filled with hope, an untrammelled wilderness that represented nature as God had intended, a paradise to be lost or won. The dominant qualities of the region were described as 'youthful,' 'manly,' and 'rugged.'[6] In the words of Stephen Leacock, 'going West, to a Canadian, is like going after the Holy Grail to a Knight of King Arthur. All Canadian families had, like mine, their Western Odyssey.'[7]

The West was also portrayed as a 'liberal' society. It represented the last frontier;[8] according to dominant images, it could offer equality of opportunity and potential for prosperity. Yet, in the popular imagination 'the emphasis upon the individual and his opportunities did not create a society of hard-bitten competitors. Everyone started out equal, according to the ideas of the day, and faced similar tasks. Although material prosperity accrued in private accounts, the social wealth of co-operation and friendliness was shared by all.'[9] Also attached to the symbols of liberalism and individualism was the idea of progress: 'The development of the West, expansionists had promised, would ensure Canada's economic prosperity, enhance its political power, and even allow moral improvement.'[10]

Mackenzie King's early diaries contain only brief mention of the West, but it is logical to assume that his initial views would have been shaped by the prevailing popular imagery. At the same time, his philosophy was becoming imbued with the ideas of reform, which were dominating the social, economic, and political language of the day and which were so evident in Prairie imagery. The youth was always romantically aware of his maternal grandfather's role in reforming Canada's political system through the rebellion of 1837. King believed it was his task to continue the reforming process, 'to better the condition of the poor, denounce corruption, the tyranny of abused power, and uphold right and honoured principles.'[11] He was developing a strong social conscience aimed at the evils of industrialization, and he embraced the movement toward social reform that had been evolving for over a century.

King's undergraduate years at the University of Toronto in the 1890s furthered these sentiments and saw him wavering between a career in the Christian ministry and politics, between his devout piety and his dream of following in his grandfather's footsteps. The intellectual environment provided by the university offered a third possibility. Together they fed King's growing belief that reform could best be achieved through a union of religion, politics, and education. He discovered an interest with and sympathy for the labouring classes through his work at Hull House in Chicago. At the same time, he was inspired by the writings of Arnold Toynbee. Hope for a new, stable society, free from class conflict, Toynbee argued, lay in the formation of a new moral order. Despite King's rhetoric of philanthropy, the realities of social work at Hull House were simply too gruelling and disheartening. His ambition again turned to academe and a possible career as a professor or university president.

King's liberal economic beliefs were strengthened while he worked toward a doctoral degree at Harvard, and his ideas were formed during the great theoretical debate that transformed political economy at the end of the nineteenth century. Like Toynbee he viewed society's arduous pilgrimage along the road of liberal capitalism as being assailed by the vices of class conflict. The rise of trade unionism and of working-class political movements was threatening the social order, already under attack from industrial capitalism. A debate revolved around the question of whether class cooperation or conflict would prevail. Dissociating themselves from the laissez-faire orthodoxy of the past, the new political economists prescribed a positive role for the state and endorsed trade unionism and social reform movements. These movements called for a regeneration of society, a cleansing of the old order, and the formation of new perspectives for the future. King's blending of Calvinism and social reform produced what has been called a 'religious liberalism.'[12] His faith was imbued with the spirit of individual and social moral reform that seemed so apparent in the West.

The period from the 1890s through the 1930s was dominated by the ideals of social reform expressed through the social gospel.[13] The movement was rooted in the search for a new interpretation of religion, and its objectives were couched in the language of the Kingdom of God on Earth, the New Day, the New Birth. In large measure, the popular images of the West spawned a reforming ideal for the social gospel, and the Prairies supported the strongest and most active movement. As Gerald Friesen points out, 'the Social Gospel was progressive, optimistic, and driven by a crusading zeal; it was strongest within the Protestant churches that were strongest on the prairies; it provided the support of the churches and the gospel – crucial elements in that age – for campaigns of social reform and regeneration; it was at the very heart of western Canada's developing sense of mission to the wide world because it came of age with and expressed the ideals of the new west.'[14]

The social gospel was also a dominant feature of King's philosophy. From early youth he was adamant in his religious convictions. On numerous occasions he seriously contemplated entering the clergy, always believing that he had a divinely inspired mission to fulfil. What he believed to be his genuine concern for 'the people' and the progress of humanity led him logically to the social gospel. King agreed with the search for a reformed faith, 'the renaissance of a pure religion.'[15] He was seeking the golden path to Salvation and Redemption, the gates of 'the New Jerusalem.'[16] The influence of Christianity was to serve 'as a motive power in social reform,' and this union of religion and reform resulted in the search for a new society. The old order was being transformed, but the young King was frustrated with the result. He could not understand 'how men are looking into all corners of the earth creating literally a new heaven & new earth & yet nothing new under the sun.' It was, he believed, possible to find the Kingdom of God on Earth. He saw himself as the questing Galahad in search of the elusive Grail: 'It comes back to the truth of the scriptural saying 'Seek first the Kingdom of Heaven, & all these things shall be added unto you' that is what I am striving to do.'[17]

Mackenzie King was aware of the strong influence the social gospel was having in the West, and this coloured his perceptions of the region. His initial impressions were formed by the popular imagery and then reinforced on his first journey across the Prairies in 1903 as deputy minister of labour in the government of Wilfrid Laurier. King's willingness, even desire, to perceive the West as a new society closer to the Kingdom of God became immediately apparent. While travelling he was struck by an otherwise ordinary gesture. A man on the train lent his coat to King, and this act conjured up an idealistic and symbolic response in his diary: 'He lent me his coat, to wear & was as kind as could be. I thought of Christ's words "I was a stranger & ye took me in, naked & ye clothed me." Surely those who will be first in the Kingdom of Heaven are such men as these.'[18] The politician would find that he was often struck by such symbolism, whether real or in dreams, when he was visiting the West.

The geographical traits of the Prairie West took on an element of the sublime. For King, nature was a symbol of the power of God: it reflected the purity, regeneration, and rewarding and punishing power of the Garden of Eden. He searched for 'the great pure world of Nature' because 'all Nature' seemed 'a manifestation of the Divine.' Whenever his early career with the Department of Labour or as labour consultant for the Rockefeller family took him to the West, King remarked upon the powerful force of nature in terms that were saturated with religious imagery. While he could not help but notice the 'monotony' of the Prairie landscape, more often he commented on the 'presence of trees, & water with hills in places' affording 'many glimpses of beautiful land-scape. The presence of many blue flowers on the prairies during the afternoon, of fires at night, and of the brightness of the stars & the vastness of the open spaces were the most attractive features of the day's journey.'[19]

Mackenzie King always placed a romantic importance on agriculture and rural life that affected his perceptions of the Prairies. 'I am con-vinced,' he observed, 'we must consider what is going to help to keep the people on the land first of all. It is sound economics & helpful to the morality and character of a nation.'[20] Within the myth of the West, the pioneers were viewed as simple but morally sound and hard-working individuals. King's idealistic views of agriculture fit into the utopian image of the West and his own search for moral reform: 'I believe so strongly that the interests of all classes in Canada depend primarily on the extent and prosperity of agriculture in Canada and in this connec-tion the moral fibre not less than the material well being of the nation, that I do not think it is possible for the agricultural interests to receive too much consideration from Parliament or placed [sic] in too strongly a position to compel consideration of their demands.'[21]

Working as a government negotiator on the Lethbridge coal strike in 1907, King commented on changes he perceived in the region. The Anglo-Saxon pioneer from Ontario or Britain was being replaced by those emigrating from central and eastern Europe: 'The Indians seemed to be disappearing and the stations and small towns have a different class of settlers than appeared a few years ago.' The result, however, was still a land of opportunity where one noticed 'the great prosperity in this country and of the exceptional opportunity it afforded to all classes who were willing to work.' He was impressed by the region's emphasis on 'labour,' 'the people,' and 'humanity.'

An 'intellectual' supporter of what he termed 'the working classes,' King believed his mission in life was to help labour in its struggle against 'all tyranny and oppress'n & effort to gain better life for the toilers.'[22] As a young boy he remembered reading his grandfather's words: 'Well may I love the poor, greatly may I esteem the humble and the lowly.'[23] As one of his contemporaries has written, 'Mackenzie King was not only on the side of the poor and humble; he believed he was spiritually one of them.'[24] His graduate career at Harvard, his position with the *Labour Gazette*, his service with the Department of Labour, and finally his work with the Rockefellers developed King's thinking to the point where he saw himself as a strong advocate of labour. He believed he was the 'impartial umpire' maintaining the balance between industry and humanity and, if anything, being more sympathetic to the plight of the worker.

This same form of idealistic sympathy for labour was transferred to the Prairie region, and King viewed the pioneering farmers essentially as workers. Western farmers, however, were independent operators and employers of labour who did not usually identify with the working classes. Regardless, in the overall struggle of labour and management, King's romantic views of the West and agriculture led him to equate the West with 'the masses,' while 'the interests' were generally associated with the manufacturing East. Years later, he reflected on the Lethbridge strike, calling it 'the most enlightening experience of those years.' The impact of that strike would remain with the young politician: 'What I saw, at the time, of the desperate plight of a large portion of the Prairie population made an indelible impression on my mind.'[25] Western leaders such as Saskatchewan premier Walter Scott credited King with having 'solved' the strike. As one of King's correspondents put it, 'the people of a great province will be saved this winter from disaster and suffering.'[26] In the mind of Mackenzie King the struggles of the worker and the farmer against the established interests were similar, and both deserved sympathy. Yet this sympathy could be offered only as long as the movements did not exceed the bounds of moderation. His attitude toward socialism is therefore crucial in understanding his later views toward the radicalization of the Farmers' movements in the West.

Mackenzie King may have considered himself a radical but he refused to embrace socialism. In the words of one of his biographers, 'for one whose paramount desire was to help the working man, King still proved singularly impervious to the appeal of socialist arguments directed to the same end.'[27] King admired 'the emphasis ... upon the spirit which the Socialist movement is intended to express' but could not embrace a movement that was 'the opposite of that which admits of private property, and of individuals pursuing, under voluntary association, their own interests in their own way.'[28] Although he acknowledged Karl Marx's contribution and objective, he could not accept his means or analysis of change. For King, the answer to society's social and economic ills lay in reform not revolution. As a 'liberal democrat' he would not accept the inevitability of class conflict, and he distrusted all schemes that threatened to abolish private property and curb individual initiative and freedom.

Within the desire for social reform there remained for Mackenzie King the fundamental principles of nineteenth-century liberalism. 'I find myself,' he wrote, 'becoming ever stronger against govt. action, except for making restrictions, regulat'ns etc. chiefly because of the deteriorating effect it tends to have on human character, giving wider scope for favoritism leading to idleness etc. in those employed, & a favouring sycophancy on the part of those seeking it.' Six months later he would write, 'While my love is mostly for the wkg. classes, I am inclined to believe that it is better for public bodies to leave the matter of ownership etc. alone – I am on the whole opposed to "Socialistic Schemes."' For King, state regulation was beneficial only to check the abuses of private enterprise. While visiting England he had been 'immensely taken' with the cooperative movement as having 'all the virtues claimed for Socialism without its defects.' He did not, however, agree with the socialism or secularism of the Fabian movement in Britain and found it to be 'faithless.' He shared Toynbee's emphasis on moral improvement as being the key to social reform: 'Till the heart of man & his morality has [sic] changed, external changes whatever they be will neither end corruption or misery.' Humankind was not morally prepared for the responsibility of creating a society of equals; socialism, therefore, was too idealistic: 'How impossible it would be, against the ignorance of the age, & the weakness of human nature as it is constituted, to expect men to be governed in their dealings by motives of honor only, a spur to exertion, or all to govern themselves without external function or external corruption. Human nature changes slowly, but until men have changed greatly from what they are today anything like a regime of Socialism is entirely a mistake & impossibility.'[29] The radicalism of labour caused an internal struggle for Mackenzie King in which his personal sympathies had to coexist with his desire to play mediator. His dilemma would extend to the Prairies. The increasing radicalism of the Farmers' movements would clash with his personal sympathies, and he would often find it necessary to fall back on his desire to balance regional interests across the country.

Mackenzie King may have felt a 'spiritual' link with the developing region, but these sentiments would mean little if, as a politician, he did not share the same concerns and advocate the same policies as westerners.

By the early years of the twentieth century the utopian images of the Prairie West had been tempered by the realities of a region being pulled into the political and economic framework of a growing nation. In the face of East–West antagonism and increasing western alienation, particular 'Prairie' issues emerged. Mackenzie King found himself, for the most part, sympathetic to these western concerns.

As late as 1896 the great expectations of the Canadian West were as yet unfulfilled. The area between Lake Superior and the Rocky Mountains remained largely as it had in the era of the fur trade. Manitoba was gradually being settled. By the late 1870s the large influx of immigrants from Ontario were joined by colony settlements including German Mennonites in the Red River Valley and Icelanders on the western shore of Lake Winnipeg. Nominally reserved tracts of land encouraged specific groups to gather in specific areas. In the 1880s and 1890s the region became home to English, Scottish, Hungarian, Scandinavian, German, Romanian, Danish, Finnish, Swedish, Belgian, Russian, Ukrainian, and Jewish communities. But further into the Northwest lay only isolated scatterings of settlement that would provide the nuclei for later expansion. By the middle of the 1880s settlement in the North-West Territories was limited principally to four areas: two concentrations around Edmonton and Prince Albert in the North Saskatchewan River Valley and adjacent parkland belt; along the dry rangeland of the southwest, extending from the Cypress Hills to the foothills of the Rocky Mountains; and throughout the farm district of Assiniboia positioned on the CPR main line between Moosomin and Moose Jaw.[30] The general depression of 1873–96 hindered the hopes of western prosperity. In the words of W.L. Morton, 'the empty West was testimony to the failure of the great hopes of Confederation.'[31]

The roots of western discontent went back to the region's absorption into Confederation. The anger over the purchase of Rupert's Land – feelings that had culminated in the Red River Resistance – became symbolic of the area's relationship with Ottawa. Manitoba's entry into Confederation was itself reason for bitterness. The control of the province's natural resources, which at the time consisted mainly of its unalienated lands, remained in the hands of the federal government to foster development. The railway had to be built and immigrants had to be settled. Manitoba would receive a subsidy in lieu of the resources, but this could not replace the symbolic control that was, according to British tradition, not to mention the British North America Act, an inherent right of responsible government. When British Columbia entered

Confederation in 1871 and Prince Edward Island joined in 1873, they both received full control of their public domain. Yet in 1905 Saskatchewan and Alberta received the same treatment as Manitoba. This exclusion transformed the issue from a provincial into a regional complaint. Westerners justifiably felt they were not on a par with the other sections of the nation.

Mackenzie King found it easy to sympathize with the western desire for control of natural resources. The Dominion Lands Policy was generally viewed as a short-term measure to deal with the rapid expansion of the region. As a result, it was commonly accepted that the claims of the Prairie provinces had what King called a 'moral' basis.[32] The issue fit into his belief that the West had genuine grievances against Ottawa that only a sympathetic government could properly manage.

Ottawa had fostered western development through the National Policy of Sir John A. Macdonald and the Conservative party. The three main elements of the policy – transportation, immigration, and protectionism – all became sources of regional discontent and augmented the belief that the Prairie West was being exploited and manipulated for the benefit of central Canada. The protective tariff, which was the cornerstone of the National Policy, became a lightning rod for westerners' anger.

The tariff, a customs duty levied on imported goods, generated about 60 per cent of Ottawa's revenue in the 1870s.[33] By the end of the decade the tariff for government revenue had been converted to a tariff for protecting manufacturing interests, the vast majority of which were in the East. Most westerners viewed the so-called National Policy as protection for eastern manufacturers against American competition and an assurance that Prairie consumers would remain a profitable market for eastern wares. Nationalist arguments for protecting a young, small, and vulnerable manufacturing sector meant little to the farmer whose produce received no such protection on the international market. Protective tariffs merely ensured that while the price and profits of the farmers' produce were left to the whims of the marketplace, the costs of supplies and the necessities of life were guaranteed to remain high. Whether the tariff plank of the National Policy, or indeed the policy's entire framework, was harmful or beneficial for the West is debatable.[34] Regardless of the economics, to the average westerner the tariff was a manipulative tool of an insensitive, eastern-based government. The party that advocated free trade was guaranteed a good measure of Prairie support.

King's views on such traditionally liberal ideas as freer trade were strengthened by his graduate work at Harvard. Professor Frank William Taussig, in particular, influenced his thinking.[35] After listening to a lecture by Taussig, King claimed to be 'convinced for the first time of the truth of the theory of free trade. We must have regard for conditions in practice. I see the side against protect'n more clearly than ever. This has been a day, if not of political convers'n, at least of conviction.' Journeys into the West further convinced him of the soundness of this issue. 'To my mind,' he wrote in 1907, 'the people have much to gain, by a reduction in tariffs all round.'[36]

Along with tariffs, transportation and freight rates were also sources of debate on the National Policy. Since the early 1880s Prairie residents claimed they paid higher transportation costs than eastern Canada because of a discriminatory rate structure that had become publicly labelled as fair discrimination.[37] The railways argued that because of competition from other rail lines, cheaper water routes in eastern Canada, and the additional costs of carrying the freight north of Lake Superior across the Prairies and through the mountains, the extra financial burden for transportation should indeed be carried by the region. Westerners viewed the railways as a private monopoly that received constant government assistance and then consistently exploited the populace. The Dominion Lands Act of 1872 had provided the CPR with a forty-mile-wide belt of land that ran the length of the railway. The land was to be reserved for sale by the CPR or the government, and, although these provisions were altered in 1873, 1882, and 1894, westerners often argued that the policy obstructed expansion of their homesteads.

In addition, a myriad of problems related to grain handling. Farmers complained, not only about the CPR and its monopoly, but also about the elevator companies and such issues as low grades, short weight, excessive dockage, and unfair prices.[38] The solution, westerners believed, was nationalization or at least regulation of the railways and an equalization of freight rates across the country. In 1897 the West did receive freight rate concessions under the Crow's Nest Pass Agreement. The line of rich mineral deposits in the Kootenays led the CPR to build a spur from its line at Lethbridge, Alberta, to Nelson, British Columbia, via the Crow's Nest Pass, to forestall American competition. The expensive undertaking required additional government assistance. On the Prairies such support was palatable only if freight rate concessions were offered in return. As a result the CPR agreed to reduce its rates by approximately 20 per cent, including those on eastbound grain and westbound settlers' effects. The agreement would eventually become a source of Ottawa–Prairie friction and a bell-wether in freight rate debates.

Mackenzie King shared the westerners' distrust of the CPR and viewed the relationship between the railway and the region as one more example of 'the people' being manipulated by 'the interests.' As labour minister he had witnessed the railway's attempts to exploit its employees, and in 1903 he drafted the Labour Disputes Act, providing for the compulsory investigation of labour disputes. For King it was not mere coincidence that the Crow's Nest rates had been introduced by Wilfrid Laurier's Liberal government. King viewed the agreement as just one of the 'first fruits' of the new government's policy, which represented a break with that of its Conservative predecessors.[39]

As the architects of the National Policy, the Macdonald Conservatives bore the brunt of western resentment against Ottawa. In addition, other thorny issues that arose during the Conservative's long tenure in office fanned Prairie grievances. Political and economic disputes over land boundaries, provincial status, federal financial assistance, railway concessions, and denominational schools dominated relations between Ottawa and the region. In Manitoba the issue of federal disallowance of railway charters to protect the 'monopoly' clause fuelled provincial rights sentiments, which were appropriated by the Liberals.

In contrast, the period that followed 1896, reawakened much of the original optimism that the West would play a significant role in national development. The price of wheat was rising steadily and, amid an immigration explosion, the West was leading Canada into the age of the wheat economy. Farmers witnessed adaptations and improvements to agricultural techniques that established the mixed farm economy and augmented growth and development. By the end of the 1890s, rail lines extended northward from the CPR into the parkland region, thereby opening it up for settlement. The southwestern district of the North-West Territories became cattle country, and many Anglo settlers joined the already established ranchers who had come from the United States. The timing of Laurier's election victory ensured that the Grits would reap the political benefits. When Laurier made his famous remark about 'Canada's Century,' the optimism was founded largely on the potential of the Prairie West. Whereas the region had been 'the repository of hope in the Macdonald years,' it was to be the 'source of wealth in the Laurier era.'[40] Moreover, the West was to be a Liberal region, and to party members such as Mackenzie King this seemed only natural.

From 1896 until 1911 the Liberals held power and built a national organization to rival that of the Tories.[41] The western population quadrupled and two new transcontinental rail lines were constructed. To the westerner discontented with Macdonald's National Policy, the Liberals seemed to offer hope. They were the acclaimed party of free trade, lower freight rates, and provincial rights. The creation of Alberta and Saskatchewan in 1905 under the auspices of Laurier's government not surprisingly ensured that both provinces would begin as Liberal bases of support. But the optimism of the 'Golden Years' was to be short-lived, and even during its most prosperous period the region continued to suffer from sectional handicaps. The boom years convinced the West that it deserved a prominent role in the nation yet highlighted its lack of influence.

From its first years in office, the Laurier government demonstrated its intentions to continue along the path set by the National Policy. It would not prove quick to deal with Prairie concerns such as decreasing the tariff. This recognition sparked the beginnings of an agrarian revolt. Across North America, Farmers' movements were reacting to the dominant position of the manufacturing sector. The Grange, the Patrons of Industry, and the Non-Partisan League were populist movements that entered the Canadian West from the United States in the 1880s and 1890s. Farmers were frustrated with a system that saw their income fluctuating radically with the vagaries of the climate and the international price of wheat. The struggle for survival was made more difficult by a grain marketing system that seemed designed to victimize producers. Agitation against the CPR and the big elevator syndicates led to significant reforms in the Manitoba Grain Act of 1900.[42] After 1901 agricultural discontent coalesced around local Grain Growers' Associations. In their attempts to improve the plight of western wheat growers, the new Farmers' movements devised plans to confront the economic and political system that so directly manipulated their fate.

The Liberal parties on the Prairies observed the increasing influence of the agrarian movement and what was becoming the popular discontent with the entire traditional party system. Survival necessitated immediate action. Unlike the two more recent provinces, Manitoba had a strong Conservative as well as a Liberal base. The Conservatives had dominated the province in the 1880s under the Norquay government, and the Liberals had done the same in the 1890s under Thomas Greenway. From 1900 until 1915 the Tories maintained power under Premier Rodmond Roblin. Both parties recognized the benefits of cooperating with Ottawa at certain times and resisting at others. But the emergence of the Farmers' movements altered the political scene. By 1910 Manitoba Liberals had adopted most of the leading proposals of the organized Farmers, and when the Roblin government collapsed amid scandal in

1915, T.C. Norris and the Liberals were waiting in the wings with a coalition of suffragists, prohibitionists, and farm and labour movements.

The agrarian movement in each of the Prairie provinces reflected the particular nature of that province. In Manitoba what has been called 'crypto-Liberalism' dominated the Farmers' organizations. According to David Laycock this version of Prairie populism 'was a western, rurally inclined, more socially progressive and politically experimental version of Ontario Grit Liberalism.' It emerged from the heavy influence of Ontario immigration into Manitoba and 'marshalled and re-presented prairie symbols and traditions of opposition to central Canada's domination.' The crypto-Liberalism of Manitoba was closest to being a 'disguised Liberalism.'[43]

In Saskatchewan the Liberal base was stronger and the party better organized than in Manitoba, but the provincial government still emphasized its efficient and progressive nature through the language of agrarian reform. The Ontario Grit influence was also apparent, although in Saskatchewan 'one found a greater tendency to supplement or replace radical Grit and Liberal perspectives with British labourite as well as 'republican' ideas of American Jacksonian democracy, Populism, and eventually Progressivism.'[44]

In Alberta an even stronger dose of American populism diminished the strength of the Liberal government and the general influence of the traditional two-party system. The first Liberal government, led by A.C. Rutherford, had been crippled by a railway scandal in 1909–10, and although the party continued in power under Arthur Sifton and then Charles Stewart, Liberal strength was already waning. The province 'was not only subject to more intense sectional feeling than its eastern neighbours but was developing a more radical spirit than the leaders of the organized farmers had yet invoked.'[45]

In 1909 the Grain Growers of the West joined the Grange and the Farmers' Association in Ontario to form the Canadian Council of Agriculture. The Farmers' movement suddenly assumed a national character and was speaking for agriculture as an organized interest. The *Grain Growers' Guide* voiced the Farmers' creed: faith in democracy, hatred of corporate wealth, and distrust of the political system. The movement had not yet entered politics, but its frustration was mounting. 'The time is ripe,' the *Manitoba Free Press* trumpeted, 'for Western Liberals to decide that they will rely upon themselves – and do their own thinking, formulate their own policies and provide their own leaders.'[46]

It seemed that agrarian protest was working. The Laurier government had set the precedent of establishing royal commissions to investigate complaints against the grain trade in western Canada. A commission was set up in 1899 to study the shipment and transportation of grain in Manitoba and the North-West Territories. Another was established in 1906 to investigate farmers' complaints about the inadequacy and injustice of the inspection and grading systems. Both federal commissions were made up almost exclusively of western grain growers, and both studies resulted in prompt government action, albeit each time on the eve of an election.[47] Yet C.B. Macpherson argues that the gains made by Prairie farmers during the Laurier years were not so much due to agrarian protest as they were to the fact that the gains also served eastern capital: 'Until the west was filled up, whatever legislation was needed to promote further immigration and development was needed by eastern capital as much by the western farmers.'[48]

Mackenzie King sympathized with the reformist cries emerging from the West and had no problem supporting some kind of vague crusade against oppression. He was certain the region contained all the elements to become an even stronger Liberal base, but the spectre of radicalism was threatening what seemed a natural progression. Prairie voices warned that the Liberal party needed to move toward reform. Some even resorted to threats. 'Here in the West,' journalist J.A. Stevenson wrote, 'we have all the materials for an efficient Liberalism ... but I tell you frankly, the Western Liberals will not be prepared to work with any enthusiasm for the modern Whiggism which has characterized the party's policy for the last years.' King claimed to be in full agreement. The Liberals could remain true to their traditional spirit of reform and thereby disarm the mounting threat of radicalism: 'I agree entirely with you that a radical policy which will, if carried, mean something of real value to the great mass of the people is what the Liberal party must adopt, and be prepared to advocate as strongly as possible.'[49]

The Prairie West awaited this 'radical policy' from the governing Liberals in Ottawa but instead witnessed the continuation of the National Policy. Between 1906 and 1910 western demands for a lower tariff increased. In 1909 the world price for wheat began a downward spiral while the costs of transportation and supplies continued to rise. Forgotten was Laurier's 1894 Winnipeg declaration: 'I denounce the policy of protection as bondage – yea, bondage; and I refer to bondage in the same manner in which American slavery was bondage.'[50] Instead the prime minister was explaining to the Canadian Manufacturers' Association in Quebec City that western settlers 'will require clothes, they will require furniture, they will require implements, they will require shoes – and I hope you can furnish them to them in Quebec – they will require everything that man has to be supplied with. It is your ambition, it is my ambition also, that this scientific tariff of ours will make it possible that every shoe that has to be worn in those prairies shall be a Canadian shoe; that every yard of cloth that can be manufactured there shall be a yard of cloth produced in Canada, and so on and so on.'[51] In 1907 the Liberals had structured the tariff into the British preferential, intermediate, and maximum set of rates. The Republicans in the United States began to raise their tariff after 1909. The Liberals had to face the realities of office and the sectional interests of the nation. Despite his personal beliefs and sympathies, King was the sitting member for North Waterloo, Ontario, and was prepared, if necessary, to hold the government line: 'I must frankly confess I see great danger in whole tariff negotiations at this time ... The West just now is affording a good market to Eastern mffrs. We are building up an internal development ... & well enough had better be left alone ... We could meet the farmers by tariff reductions in agric. implements. This has been the view I have taken, it is the Ont. view I believe, & is in national interest, as well as interests of Govt.' He believed that it would be 'questionable' to injure the interests of the manufacturers.[52]

The Liberals were under pressure from agrarian interests. Laurier's western tour of 1910 was met by repeated demands for such incentives as federally operated grain terminals to regulate handling. When the prime minister expressed a willingness to discuss the matter further, the result was a march on Ottawa by over 800 representatives of the western grain growers and eastern agrarian interests, an event that would become known as the Seige of 1910.[53] The government successfully negotiated a reciprocity agreement with the United States in 1911. Later the same year the Liberals staked their future on an election on the issue. Mackenzie King was relieved to be able to return to his own personal stance as he once again advocated what he believed to be the proper liberal position: 'Agreed the party should think of the consumer primarily, not look to the mffr'r, get after the combines & trusts, not look to them for support. Go in for increase of the British Preference & show up the selfishness of those who were waving the flag as a pretext in the Reciprocity campaign. Look to the West & not a few interests in Montreal & Toronto for results.'[54]

In reaction to the Liberal move toward reciprocity, the railway and manufacturing interests argued that the deal would destroy the growing system of east–west trade. Led, ironically, by Laurier's former western

lieutenant, Clifford Sifton, a group of Liberals also took up the nationalist arguments, bolted the party, and moved to support the Conservatives.
In the election of 1911 the Tories, wrapped in the flag and calling for 'No
truck or trade with the Yankees,' were victorious. The nationalist appeals
had had an effect in Sifton's province of Manitoba, but in general the
Liberal defeat was instrumental in breaking the West's faith in the
traditional parties. 'The defeat of reciprocity in 1911,' Morton claims,
'was the first act in the agrarian revolt of Western Canada.'[55]

Both parties suffered a loss of influence throughout the region, but
the Conservatives, the party that had defeated reciprocity, would pay
most heavily. The Liberals could pose as the 'martyr of reciprocity,' a
stance that was to be 'rewarding.'[56] Prairie Liberals warned their party
that for the region to become the 'Gibraltar of Liberalism' the struggle
for lower tariffs had to continue. King observed the lessons from 1911
and was satisfied that the seeds of an eventual Liberal revival had been
planted. But Sir Wilfrid Laurier had also learned from the defeat. 'Our
best course,' he informed the younger politician, 'is to follow as we have
commenced – a revenue tariff – appealing to the common sense of both
producers and consumers ... we must convince every class of the community – farmers, manufacturers, consumers and producers – that we are
enemy to none, friend of all and that we want justice for every one.'[57]

Laurier had made Quebec the main bastion of Liberal support, and
that province favoured protectionism. His successor would have to hold
this stronghold. King recognized the wisdom in his mentor's tutelage
and carefully studied the art of brokerage politics that would later become his trademark. He was personally sympathetic to the plight of the
Prairie populace and strongly believed in the liberal principle of freer
trade. In a nation of diverse interests, however, such sympathies and
beliefs would not necessarily translate into policy. He understood the
manufacturing sector's desire for protection and the influence of this
industry in central Canada. It was admirable to take a stand on an issue
but, as the election of 1911 had shown, rarely was it worth defeat. 'I had a
feeling, while in Quebec,' King noted, 'that certain of our friends there
were likely to be more concerned about keeping the tariff where it is than
effecting any modifications of it. Under the circumstances it has seemed
to me the part of wisdom not to be involved in any discussion of this
subject just at this time.'[58] He remained convinced that 'the West is right
in wanting freer trade,'[59] and if the opportunity arose, he would act. In
the meantime he was prepared to justify Laurier's tariff for revenue, and
westerners were advised to remember the obstacles to full reciprocity:

One has also to remember that Canada has had a protective tariff now for a number of years and is alongside of a Nation whose industries are very similar and which have been built up by the aid of protection. To alter a fabric of this kind without injuring legitimate vested interests is a difficult task, and changes as radical as those suggested by some of the members of the Canadian West ... if put into force would only retard in the long run the attaining of the goal to [sic] freer trade which is their ultimate aim and which may come in time, though not for many years.[60]

If reducing tariffs would take time, King was sure to remind the West that its hopes lay with the Liberal party. Yet, to Prairie residents, Liberal support meant the usual sacrificing of their interests upon the altar of eastern appeasement. 'Unless the Liberals can be depended upon to reduce the tariff very considerably,' the *Grain Growers' Guide* announced, 'there is no advantage in returning them to power.'[61] It was becoming evident that in the years following 1911 the Liberals were going to have increasing difficulty maintaining their western support. With the Farmers' movements already waiting in the political wings, such support seemed even more unlikely.

There may have been a storm brewing in the West, but from his home in Ontario Mackenzie King was able to continue weaving his already favourable impressions of the region into his overall design for the future. He felt akin to the reforming impulse of the area, at least at the intellectual level, and began to contemplate a Prairie seat in Parliament. In Saskatchewan the provincial Liberals had erected an impressive party organization that seemed to be weathering the Farmer storm. The position of the party at both political levels made the province particularly alluring, and to add to the appeal, Laurier himself had sat for the district. King's early years in politics had already demonstrated the difficulty of finding a safe seat: after being elected in North Waterloo in 1908, he had lost the riding in 1911. He wrote after his defeat that if he could not win a seat in Ontario he would 'go to Saskatchewan.' Western Liberals were not quite so encouraging. 'I received today a letter from Martin of Regina,' King recorded, 'offering me his seat there, but expressing doubt as to the wisdom of opening it or transplanting an eastern man west.' King found the notion of being labelled an 'eastern man' unacceptable: he believed he would make a suitable, if not ideal, western representative. If such regional prejudice existed, he was certain he could soon overcome it simply 'by getting around among the people.'[62] Some Prairie Liberals reinforced King's belief about the desirability of a strong relationship between King and the region. 'Your ideas,' one correspondent wrote, 'on national subjects are much [more] in accordance with the spirit of the West than of old conservative Ontario.'[63] Mackenzie King preferred to heed this advice over more lukewarm assessments: 'More & more Saskatchewan seems to me the best province for my purpose.'[64]

Any thoughts of re-entering politics were put on hold by the onset of the First World War, an event that would have a marked impact on the development of the West, the Liberal party, and the career of Mackenzie King. Reversing the trends in declining agricultural expansion and prices, the war propelled the region's economy from the recessionary state it had collapsed into after 1912. The wheat economy was booming, with the price of wheat nearly tripling its prewar value. Yet, as John Thompson has warned, one should not be lulled into the belief that the war years simply brought 'a period of prosperous expansion for Western agriculture.'[65] The more lasting economic gains were not made on the Prairies but in the industrial sectors of central Canada. The western farmer responded to Britain's increased demand for wheat by depending even more heavily upon this one cash crop. The costs of production were rising and so too was the farmers' reliance on credit. Moreover, prairie cities had never fully recovered from the prewar recession. After the war Westerners would come to blame the economic situation on the developmental policies of Ottawa, which had encouraged rapid, if not reckless, wheat production, while maintaining debilitating transportation and freight rate policies. Not surprisingly, western farmers continued to organize throughout the war. In 1917 Thomas A. Crerar, president of the Winnipeg-based Grain Growers' Grain Company convinced its Albertan counterpart, the Alberta Co-operative Elevator Company, to combine and form the United Grain Growers, a farmer-owned cooperative with its own elevators and marketing facilities. The Saskatchewan Co-operative Elevator Company refused to participate.[66]

The war emergency brought a new level of intervention by Ottawa into the wheat economy. In December 1916 the federal government used its wartime emergency powers to confiscate all the wheat remaining in storage. Britain had demanded the action to compensate for disruption to Australian and Argentinean wheat exports to Europe. As a result of the government's action, the Winnipeg Grain Exchange suspended futures trading. By 1917 a Board of Grain Supervisors was established to control the industry.[67] In 1919 the supervisors were replaced by a wheat board. Although this level of government intervention was welcomed by most farmers, it was not to outlast the emergency conditions. By the 1920 crop year, the open market system was restored. Many farmers would associate the prosperity of wartime sales with government control of marketing, and they continued to militate for a permanent wheat board.

Mackenzie King spent the war in the United States working as a labour consultant for the Rockefeller family. These years provided him the opportunity to write *Industry and Humanity*. This book, which was published in 1918, serves as the most comprehensive account of his early philosophy. The treatise laid out his plan for social reconstruction in the postwar era, with an emphasis on avoiding industrial disputes. Its rhetoric was shaped by the ideology of reconstruction and the 'swelling currents' of the social gospel.[68] 'Can we not begin anew,' King wrote, 'this time with belief in Divinity, and accepting some law which evidences a divine order, seek out the rules of conduct and methods of organization which accord with the principles it suggest?' With the proper cooperation between social groups, he preached, 'it is not alone a new dawn Labor and Capital may summon forth; they can create a wholly new civilization.' The work demonstrated King's reforming brand of liberal philosophy, arguing that the emphasis on individual freedom had to be tempered by concern for all humanity.[69] It found a generally receptive audience in western Canada, and throughout King's career Prairie residents would often remind him of the book's message.

During the war years, events were unfolding in Canada that would have a profound effect on the future of the Liberal party as well as Mackenzie King. The conscription crisis of 1917 not only tore the fabric of French–English relations but also split Canadian Liberalism. 'The war blew up the old party structure of Canada,' Morton writes, 'already groaning under the stresses which the particularism of Quebec and the agrarian sectionalism of the West had imposed upon it.'[70] Laurier's refusal to accept conscription and join the new Union government headed by Conservative Prime Minister Robert Borden, maintained French-Canadian support for the Liberal party in the long run but lost it the immediate support of English Canada. For the most part, western Liberals jumped aboard the Union bandwagon to ensure Canada implemented a policy of conscription and maintained a 'united' war effort.

The desertion of the Prairie Liberals was not based solely on the issue of conscription. Regional concerns dominated much of the discussion and were set against a general sentiment that the party was too much under Quebec's domination. The desire for a 'western bloc' to influence the party was very much in evidence. Although the controversy over coalition did not single-handedly destroy party fortunes in the region, it was the last straw for many Prairie Liberals and did serve to widen the breach between eastern and western members. 'I told Sir Wilfrid himself,' the editor of the *Manitoba Free Press*, J.W. Dafoe, wrote as the election of 1917 approached,

> that the course he was taking meant defeat at the polls and the absolute ruin of the party ... If we had an ordinary party fight in Western Canada the Liberals would easily have carried 45 out of 57 seats. As it is, there are strong probabilities that when the final returns are available it will be found that there is not a single supporter of Sir Wilfrid Laurier elected west of the Great Lakes. This is what happened to the party in that portion of Canada in which, before the question of compulsion arose, Liberal opinions were most strongly held.[71]

While the majority of Prairie Liberals supported Union, enough Laurier loyalists existed to cause division within the provincial Liberal parties. In Manitoba the loyalists would become known as the 'Diehards.' In Saskatchewan the Liberal cabinet was split into factions dominated by key personalities. The Unionist faction was led by J.A. Calder, one of the influential founders of the party organization known as 'the machine.' In 1916 Calder was seen as the likely successor to Premier Walter Scott, but in October 1917 he entered the Union government as minister of immigration and colonization. W.M. Martin, another Unionist supporter, became premier. The Laurier faction was led by W.R. Motherwell, who resigned from the Martin cabinet in 1918.[72] The Alberta Liberal government was also crippled by the crisis when Premier Arthur Sifton abandoned office to join the Union government. The party would never recover.

The crisis also dealt a blow to the Liberal press in the region. The all-powerful *Free Press*, owned by Clifford Sifton, led the battle from Winnipeg in support of conscription and coalition. When there was an attempt at a western Liberal convention in 1917 to determine the position of Prairie members, Dafoe argued that the 'Liberal machine' went out and 'captured' the delegates, with the result that the convention was 'strongly pro-Laurier.' In reaction, 'the Free Press turned all its guns upon the convention as not representing Western Liberalism.'[73] In the general election of that year, the Prairies returned forty-one Unionists and only two Liberals.

The cause of the federal Liberals had not been aided by the presence of a French Canadian as party leader. Deteriorating relations between French and English Canada after the conscription crisis had fuelled negative appraisals of Laurier in the West. Although Mackenzie King had remained loyal to his party's leader, both he and Laurier agreed that 'the West would not support a French Canadian Leader.'[74] J.W. Dafoe had been expounding these sentiments in Manitoba since 1915: 'This is one Canadian province in which the name of Sir Wilfrid Laurier has never been one to conjure with.'[75] Laurier's death in early 1919 seemed to present an opportunity to rebuild Prairie support, but the party had emerged from the war deeply divided. The national and regional divisions in the party, which would be a festering wound for years to come, would present a major challenge for the next leader. In the words of Gerald Friesen, 'the rift ... was never bridged completely and contributed to the decline of federal Liberal fortunes on the Prairies.'[76]

The end of the war heralded the return to traditional partisanship. Despite the hopes of many Prairie members that the Union government could maintain its coalition nature, the dominant Tory elements were making their presence felt. As Friesen points out, 'for a group that had been elected with such widespread support on the prairies in the late autumn of 1917, the Borden Unionists had frittered away their advantage with remarkable dispatch.'[77] Already Dafoe was complaining that the government had fallen under the control of 'old Conservatives who could not bring themselves to realize that it was a coalition government' and who 'looked upon their Liberal colleagues as brands plucked from the burning who were thereafter to be good Tories like themselves.' Such a party would 'not get very far in the west.'[78] With the Unionists showing themselves as true blue Tories, and the Liberals as loyal to the French-Canadian Rouge tradition of Laurier, the disgruntled westerners continued their search for new alternatives.

The Union government was faced with the need for revenue in the postwar economy and inevitably it sought to satisfy the protectionist desires of its eastern representatives and Tory ideologues. The budget of 1918 brought 'little relief to the west and, if anything, only made more evident how different were the economic interests of central and prairie Canada.'[79] Westerners welcomed the proposed nationalization of the Canadian Northern Railway, but the Crow's Nest rates remained suspended. In the face of wartime inflation, freight rates had actually been increased a week after the election of 1917. Government controls on food and fuel received harsh criticism in the West for not taking into account the economic difficulties of the Prairie farmer. At the same time, the West's growing demand for more democracy and accountability in government ran up against rule by order-in-council.

Not surprisingly, it was the tariff issue that broke the coalition. After the budget speech of 1919 promised only minor reductions in the tariff, Minister of Agriculture T.A. Crerar and eight other western Liberals bolted the government benches and crossed the floor of Parliament to sit as private members. The coalition was disintegrating, the government was returning to its Conservative roots, and Crerar saw the writing on the wall: 'Privately I am convinced that there is nothing to hope for from the Union Government in the way of any real progressive measures, especially on the tariff. The old Tory influences dominate and I see little prospect of any change on their part from the protectionist policies of the past.'[80] As J.E. Rea points out, Crerar was 'never a consistent partisan.' He was a Liberal, but 'his Liberalism ... was defined as much or perhaps more by his view of the political alternatives as by faith in the Liberal party.'[81] His experience in the Union government convinced him this coalition was not a viable alternative either. Crerar's stand was heralded by Liberals across the Prairies as 'the barometer of Western opinion.'[82] The region had been awaiting tariff reduction for many years and had lost faith in the promises of both traditional parties.

Crerar's exit from the Union government once again exerted pressure for a new national party with a strong base in western Canada. But differences of opinion were already emerging among Prairie leaders, demonstrating that while there existed a regional desire for a western-based party, there were varying provincial views as to its nature. The differences among the three provinces were becoming increasingly evident and would serve to complicate politics in the region. The Farmers' organization in Alberta was proceeding along the lines of an occupational movement whose radicalism was setting it apart from groups in the other two provinces. In Saskatchewan the agrarian movement had a broader appeal that thus far was successfully being appropriated by the Liberal party. In Manitoba there seemed to be little organization and no real threat to the more established parties.[83]

Despite the divisions, by July 1919 the Farmers' movement in every constituency of Alberta and Saskatchewan had passed resolutions calling for the nomination of candidates before the next federal election. This vague and disparate movement was coming together under an umbrella of populism that obscured its many divisions. Although fragile, the new-found unity of the Farmers' movement was a threat to the two-party system. A majority government – whether Liberal or Conservative – was by no means a certainty in the coming election, a state of affairs that worried not only the traditional parties but supporters of the Farmers as well. 'How,' Dafoe asked, 'are we going to get out of this mix-up a government that can steer the ship through the storms of the future?'[84]

The demand for a Farmers' party to take direct political action continued to mount. The agrarian revolt reflected the diminishing role of the farmer in Canada, which by the end of the war was a significant industrial nation. The defensive reaction of the agrarian classes was to take the offensive. They argued that a 'New National Policy' was required, that Ottawa should adopt measures designed to stimulate agriculture. In November 1918 the Canadian Council of Agriculture, representing the organized Farmers, had drawn up a platform. It proposed the abolition of the tariff on many raw materials, on all foodstuffs, and on certain machinery; a reduction in the tariff generally; the acceptance of the old reciprocity agreement with the United States; an increase in the Imperial preference; direct graduated taxation on personal and corporation income; inheritance taxes; assisted land settlement for veterans; extended organization of cooperatives; public ownership of coal mines and public utilities; and a number of miscellaneous political reforms, such as the initiative, referendum, and recall, proportional representation, abolition of patronage, reform of the Senate, and the repeal of the Wartime Elections Act.[85] In general the platform reflected western concerns.

Prairie discontent was intensified by the onset of a postwar recession. Expectations that the old order had finally collapsed during the war, to be replaced by a new era of hope and progress, were quickly dispelled. This was particularly evident in the West, where hopes of reform had been greatest. Disappointed expectations helped to germinate the seeds of radicalism. Labour turmoil erupted in May 1919 with the Winnipeg General Strike. The working-class movement in western Canada may have been smaller than in central Canada, but it was more radical, pushing for reform and even revolution.[86] Thus, the Canadian labour movement was divided on regional lines, with western unions tending to be more interested in independent labour politics and more militant than their eastern counterparts.[87]

Mackenzie King did not comprehend the full significance or nature of the brewing agrarian protest but he was well aware of the dangers in labour unrest. He had come to admire the organization of international unionism as reflected in the American Federation of Labor, but he disliked its tendencies toward agitation. Instead King emphasized the importance of moderate leadership.[88] He had been in England at the time of the Winnipeg General Strike, but his brief comments upon the event reflected his sympathies: 'I think fundamentally the right of collective bargaining was at the basis of the strike, and that the greater readiness on the part of some of the employers to meet with representatives of Organized Labour some time ago would have prevented the growth of feeling of which advantage was taken when the strike came on ... So far as the Government was concerned, its action was belated and of little real help in the situation.'[89] The failure of the strike and the urban labour movement to establish an acceptable and effective political alternative shifted the onus onto the burgeoning agrarian protest movement. To King, both the Labour and Farmer movements were similar – they represented the impetus for reform that had been forced outside the bounds of moderation by a reactionary government.

The death of Sir Wilfrid Laurier in January 1919 forced the Liberal party to contemplate its future leadership and direction. The national leadership convention of 5–7 August was the first of its kind in Canadian history. It was organized by Laurier Liberals who were determined to maintain party control while reintegrating lost Unionists. An appeal was made to the organized Farmers to send representatives,[90] but with the arrangements and machinery firmly in the hands of Laurier Liberals, reconciliation was unlikely.

Four candidates contested the leadership. D.D. McKenzie and W.L.M. King were Laurier Liberals, while G.P. Graham's loyalty was questionable, and W.S. Fielding was a Unionist. At forty-five, King was the youngest of the candidates: his three opponents were all over sixty (Fielding was seventy). Of the four, only Fielding seemed to have the experience and charisma to be prime minister. The old veteran, however, was lukewarm about the leadership. The anti-conscriptionist sentiment in his home province of Nova Scotia along with that of Quebec, as well as his own protectionist views, made him question his potential to reunite the party.

Premier W.M. Martin of Saskatchewan had initially been considered a contender for the leadership, 'chiefly because of a vague desire that the Liberal party should seek its new leader from the West,'[91] but in the end he decided not to run. The premier was in the midst of a struggle to save his own Liberal government, and this necessitated preventing the Farmers from directly entering politics. His government was consulting the Grain Growers' organization on legislation, and efforts were being made to bring its members into government. The provincial Liberals were taking pains to dissociate themselves from those in Ottawa. When it came time for Saskatchewan to select its delegates to the leadership convention, the Martin government did everything in its power to send a contingent favourable to the Farmers. 'Let me make myself clear,' the premier told a party gathering in Saskatchewan. 'While I believe that a re-organized Liberal party with a progressive platform is the best medium of expression for western opinion, I do not intend nor do the people of Saskatchewan intend to slavishly follow the Liberal party nor any other party.'[92] King conceded Martin's Prairie appeal but was confident he would have little chance, even if he had decided to run, due to his loyalties during the war: 'Martin will have a strong influence and is a practical politician. But he was a "unionist." If it comes in the Convention to Unionist Liberals versus Laurier Liberals, the choice will be Laurier.'[93]

The uncommitted delegates at the convention came mainly from the provincial organizations that had supported the Union government. 'These Laodiceans,' MacGregor Dawson notes, 'were mostly from the West.'[94] Some Prairie leaders such as Crerar refused to attend but were cautiously hopeful that the gathering would avoid 'the old reactionary spirit, that has for years largely pervaded the Liberal Party, and stifled the national aspirations for real Liberalism.' This would be difficult because this spirit was 'still strong in the Councils of the Party.' If it could be accomplished, however, it was believed the West could 'remake' the party.[95] The genuine liberal elements would come together and the reactionaries would be forced out.

The varying stances of the delegations from the Prairies reflected the positions of Liberalism in the respective provinces. Manitoba's Liberal forces were uncommitted, and for good reason. The split in the party over the 1917 crisis ran deep, and its implications were only just being felt. The *Free Press* had supported Union, and no one was sure where its support was now headed. To make matters worse, the Farmers' movement in the province remained an unknown quantity. The delegation led by Premier Norris came to the convention as a group, free to dissociate itself from the party if an undesirable platform were adopted. The sentiments of Dafoe, who supported Fielding and a revitalization of the party 'with an advanced radical programme,' carried considerable weight. Fielding was a protectionist, but he seemed 'the only man in sight' who could lead a reunited party, because there was little chance of anyone who opposed conscription being successful in the West. Neither Dafoe nor Crerar regarded Mackenzie King as a possibility. If Fielding were selected and a platform drafted that was 'so radical' it would 'drive out' all the 'eastern reactionaries,' the Liberals would gain the support of the farmers' movement and have a chance in the next election. Otherwise, 'nothing could prevent the inauguration of a western radical party.'[96]

The convention was a testing ground for Canadian Liberalism, and observers like Crerar were watching closely.

Saskatchewan's delegation reflected a widening breach in the province's Liberal forces. The division remained between a significant Laurier faction and the Unionists who held the premiership. The breach was enhanced by the perceived need of the provincial government to appease the Farmers. As a result, despite Martin's efforts, Saskatchewan sent a delegation that would split on the leadership vote. Crerar was under the impression that the Saskatchewan representatives would oppose the Laurier Liberals,[97] but he was underestimating this faction in the province. Those who had remained loyal to the chief, such as W.R. Motherwell and J.G. Gardiner, would support King. 'Fielding wasn't going to live long anyway,' Gardiner later explained. 'I supported King and I told Motherwell that he was going to win ... I felt he would come back full of new ideas for the party.'[98]

The Alberta delegation travelled from the province where the Farmer storm was most threatening. A mixture of populisms containing radical democratic ideologues, crypto-Liberals, and left-wing social democrats was gaining credence.[99] The Liberal government of Premier Charles Stewart somehow had to demonstrate sympathy to this array of agrarian protest and look to Ottawa for a party leader who could do the same. Any connection to an unfavourable federal party could prove disastrous at the provincial level. Saskatchewan and Alberta members made a strong effort to bring about unity in the western delegation in an attempt to have a low-tariff plank implemented.[100]

The convention platform reflected the need to conciliate and attract the many wavering elements both within the Liberal party and the nation. In particular the West had to be won. Resolutions on the tariff were aimed directly at inducing the region, as well as rural Ontario, to return to their Liberal allegiance. The resolutions called for the lowering of duties on the necessities of life and supplies used in natural resource industries. The British preference was to be increased to 50 per cent of the general tariff, and the desire to resurrect the reciprocity agreement of 1911 was reaffirmed. Resolutions on Canadian autonomy, and in particular on labour and industry questions, were in accord with the spirit of reform and showed 'the hand of Mackenzie King' in their framing.[101] To critical westerners, however, the much-anticipated tariff resolution did not go far enough. It called for reform but did not repudiate the principle of protection.

It soon became evident that the convention could not select a leader suitable to the discontented West. In the two main contenders the region saw contradictions. Fielding was a Unionist who had held to his conscriptionist convictions, but he was also a protectionist and of the old guard. King, on the other hand, was young and filled with reforming ideas, but he had been in the United States when other Canadians had been forced to make sacrifices during the war, and had supported the position of Laurier and Quebec. Regardless of the convention's choice the western Liberals, dominated by the Unionists and the increasingly influential Grain Growers' Associations, were going to be disappointed. Many in the West had already made up their minds as to the nature of the federal Liberals. To westerners like Dafoe, the party was in a divided, chaotic state with little hope for the immediate future. 'I do not see how,' he observed, 'these various tendencies can be merged into a single party. If apparently common ground upon which they all can stand is discovered at Ottawa, will the resulting party be anything more than an organized hypocrisy dedicated to getting and holding office?' The editor asked Crerar whether in his judgment it was possible for the Liberals to draft a platform that would head off the third party movement. He answered that 'it would be difficult.' Dafoe concluded 'that regardless of what the liberals do at Ottawa, there will be a farmer's [sic] movement in western Canada.'[102] The roots of western alienation were running so deep that unless the main parties made considerable concessions to the region, discontent was inevitable, and the agrarian revolt would continue unabated. 'Such a movement,' Crerar remarked, 'with the three Provincial Governments behind it, would carry ... practically every seat in the three Prairie Provinces.'[103]

It is not known how the western delegates voted at the 1919 convention. Dawson contends that it was 'generally agreed' that 'the West split fairly even [sic].'[104] W.L. Morton, on the other hand, quotes the Globe in arguing that King received only a following of the 'Old Guard' from Alberta, while Saskatchewan 'almost solidly,' and Manitoba and Alberta in part, gave Fielding their vote. It seems likely that the western Liberals, like the other delegates, voted mainly according to their stance in 1917. King had 'no connection with the West, where he was comparatively unknown,' and to many he was merely an 'eastern' attempt to balance the 'western' platform.[105] On the first ballot King received 344 votes, Fielding 297, Graham 153, and McKenzie 153. On the second ballot King received 411 votes, Fielding 344, Graham 124, and McKenzie 60. Graham and McKenzie then withdrew, and on the third ballot King was selected leader with 476 votes, while Fielding received 438.[106]

Mackenzie King was selected leader of the Liberal party for several reasons, but his loyalty to Laurier was the main factor. As the *Montreal Gazette* reported, the gathering was a 'Laurier convention' that would 'stampede' any 'defectors.' There was a 'light in the window,' but those 'returning to the fold' would first have to do 'penance.'[107] King had questioned Laurier's strategy on the Union government, but he was sure to remind Quebec delegates that he had remained loyal. The rumours that the chief had personally handpicked King as his successor, whether accurate or not, also had aided his bid. His relative youthfulness and apparent commitment to a more radical philosophy needed to rejuvenate Liberalism may have added to his appeal, but in reality 'few Liberals realized King's inner thinking.'[108] He was not well known to the convention, so the main consideration remained his stance in 1917. He was, however, the party's best hope, however slim, of winning the Prairie West.

The journey ahead for the new Liberal leader could hardly have been more arduous. The party and nation had suffered bitter divisions. 'I think any person who holds office now or any time during the next five years,' Dafoe mused, 'is entitled to a measure of sympathy. It is going to be demanded of him that he do things that cannot be done; things that are mutually contradictory and destructive; and whatever he does he will have more critics than friends.'[109] Dafoe and his powerful Prairie newspaper would be two of those critics.

By the time he was selected as party leader, Mackenzie King had convinced himself that he was particularly suited to represent the West. He would work to represent all Canada's regions, but he claimed a unique connection to this area. It fit into what he saw as his divine mission to reform the nation. 'A political leader,' King wrote, should 'be a true servant of God helping to make the Kingdom of Heaven prevail on Earth. This is what I love politics for.'[110] Above all he saw the Prairies as the natural mainstay of the new Liberalism and himself in the vanguard of these ideals. Perhaps the party had failed the region in the past, but the new leader was confident that he understood the concerns that were spawning its discontent, and more importantly, that he sympathized with them. There would be no need for radical third-party alternatives. The Liberal party was still dominated by older easterners such as W.S. Fielding and Sir Lomer Gouin, but King would fight to defend and advance the western position, and in doing so secure his position as leader. Together, Mackenzie King and the Prairie West would revitalize Liberalism. It was time to bridge the gulf of 1917 and bring the region home to its Liberal roots.

By 1919 Mackenzie King had constructed an image of the Prairie West that conveniently coincided with his political objectives. This image was undoubtedly based on romantic perceptions of the region, rather than on actual knowledge and understanding of the area's concerns, and it certainly reeked of political opportunism when placed alongside the Liberal party's need to regain Prairie support. If the party and its new leader were to be successful, their best hope lay in winning the West. But the temptation to label King's views of the Prairies as mere opportunism is dangerous. It is difficult to ascertain King's precise perceptions of the Prairies because he was far too cautious to articulate strong regional biases. Instead, what emerges from an understanding of his early think-ing, when pieced together with subtle comments from his diaries and letters, is a complex mixture of genuine sympathy, self-deception, and political expediency. King's western sympathies served a definite prag-matic purpose, but it must be understood that he believed them to exist. They would influence his handling of the region, and in 1919 the West was witness to a new Liberal leader who seemed intent on meeting its demands. Westerners were only too aware that they held considerable sway in the national scheme, and Mackenzie King would now have to offer more than the romantic aspirations of a central Canadian. He would have to prove to western delegates returning from the convention that he was not merely 'the puppet of Quebec' and the Laurier faction that had so dominated the party.

2

Following Phantoms, 1919–1921

Mr. King was very discreet in his references to the political movements in the West which are outside the old party lines ... He may have had hopes that some kind of an official alliance could be entered into by which there could be a division of constituencies in Western Canada, but, if so, he will by now have abandoned them if he has the faculty so necessary to a successful political career of seeing things as they are and refusing to follow phantoms.

J.W. Dafoe to Clifford Sifton, 10 November 1920

Mackenzie King's career has been characterized by the struggle to maintain national unity. This struggle is usually associated with a continuation of Laurier's quest to maintain both Quebec support and harmony between French and English Canada. Yet, in the early years of King's leadership, Quebec was firmly in Liberal control; the threat to national unity came from the Prairie West. Upon acceding to the Liberal leadership, King was forced to bring his idealistic perceptions of the West to terms with the political realities of regaining the region's support. The obstacle was the agrarian revolt. One of King's most remarkable political traits was patience: he would certainly need a considerable store to somehow return the frustrated Prairies to the Liberal fold. Nonetheless, he never doubted that he was the man for the job: 'I have not the slightest doubt that it will be mine to link together Liberals, Farmers & Labor, and form a really progressive party in Canadian affairs.'[1] This arbitration process would become one of the greatest challenges of King's career.

Reaction in the West to the choice of the leadership convention was generally sceptical, but King chose to hear only the voices of support, usually coming from the Laurier loyalists. This minority agreed that their new leader should enjoy a special relationship with the region, and they were prepared to allow him a chance to show his mettle. One western supporter wrote: 'Young Canada is looking for someone to trust, for an appeal to heroism for the sounding of a high note of idealism + purity in politics ... You may safely trust yourself to the great moral current which has set in all over the world.'[2] He was succeeding the 'grand old leader' but would usher in a 'new Liberal Party.'[3] For his part, King saw his relative youth as an essential attribute in breathing new life into the party and nation. Laurier had opened the West, and King believed it was his task to develop it. Even the *Grain Growers' Guide* seemed prepared to give him a chance. 'In regard to Mr. King,' the voice of the agrarian revolt announced, 'there is undeniably one thing which appeals to the imagination in the fact that he is the grandson of William Lyon Mackenzie, who was four score years ago for democracy in Canada.' Further, the spirit of the rebellion in which King's grandfather was so prominent a leader has 'much in common with the movement of the organized farmers today as a fight against privileged interests for justice and for equal rights.'[4] From Manitoba the new leader was informed that his selection had been received 'with very general satisfaction,' except by those considered 'the Tory element of the Liberal Party.'[5] Unfortunately for King, this 'Tory element' consisted of the Unionist Liberals who dominated Prairie Liberalism. Their response would not be so positive.

Mackenzie King's idealistic and naive perceptions of the Prairies were immediately put to the test when it came to dealing with the growing farmers' movements. He claimed a sympathy for these manifestations because they were 'a people's movement & as such the truest kind of Liberalism.'[6] Unfortunately, he noted, the Farmers had become radicalized and would now have to be tempered with conciliation. He viewed their entry into politics as unnecessary because the nation's politics were encompassed by the Liberal and Conservative parties, which already espoused the two fundamental philosophies of Western democratic thought. 'There is an attitude,' King wrote, 'which is the direct opposite of Liberalism, and that is Conservatism. Liberal and Conservative forces will always be opposed in the nature of things.' A third party had no place and would inevitably pull support away from one of the two groups: 'Instead of any group being able to count upon the support of a great party to ensure the reforms and desires of the armies of progress, we will see a number of factions destroying each other in the face of a common hereditary foe.' Because the Farmers were liberal in philosophy, the losses would be felt by that party. Both Farmers and Liberals would suffer as their vote was split; in the end the third party would either disintegrate or return to its roots. 'You may be perfectly sure,' King warned, 'that it will be a matter of only a very short time before ... [the Farmers] encounter a formidable opposition, which will either destroy their influence altogether or drive them for refuge back into the arms of the parties to which they naturally belong.'[7]

King's attitude toward socialism and the concept of class struggle shaped his opposition to the third party's radical tendencies. Liberalism, and the Liberal party as its vehicle, had to represent the interests of all groups, and had to transcend the concept of class. If most farmers considered themselves a class, it was a 'class' based on occupation, not on a Marxist analysis of ownership of the means of production. King rejected the notion that his party could not represent their interests. They were 'class organizations under false characterization.'[8] Class conflict occurred, he believed, because divisions were being highlighted rather than obscured. King's career as labour mediator had trained him to work to bridge these growing divisions and demonstrate that class cleavages were not necessary. At present he believed the Farmers were blinded by their sudden rise and influence, but eventually they would 'come to realize that as a class organization it is going to be impossible for them to succeed, and that their real hope lies in maintaining a close alliance with the political party which is broad and progressive enough to promote principles and policies similar to their own.'[9] There was little doubt to which group King was referring. 'The Liberal party,' he asserted, 'all along has been fighting the battle of the farmers. That will remain an essential part of its work through the years to come, so long as it remains a Liberal party. It is well, I think, that the farmers should never lose sight of this.'[10]

If a new party and leader were not enough evidence that the Liberals were prepared to accommodate the West, King considered that the convention platform should have dispelled all doubts. It was not mere coincidence that the Liberal platform mirrored the Farmers' platform adopted by the Canadian Council of Agriculture. 'The Liberal party has fashioned a programme in which the Farmers have every reason to believe,' he noted. 'It is their battle, in no small measure, that Liberalism has undertaken to wage.'[11] The *Grain Growers' Guide* had praised the convention for redrafting the party program in 'the new progressive spirit of our day' and admitted it was 'well nigh impossible to distinguish between the platforms.' It seemed the Liberals 'had been so anxious to meet the wishes of the farmers wherever it was possible so to do, that they had adopted the very wording of some of the planks in the farmer's platform.'[12] Mackenzie King had raised his colours, and as far as he was concerned they were the same as those in the Prairie West: '"United we stand; divided we fall" ... The enemy's only hope lies in creating divisions between those who should be rallying around the one standard.'[13]

Western journalist J.A. Stevenson was willing to praise the convention and platform as being 'very radical,' but he made one essential observation about King's relationship with the region. Despite all the moves to accommodate the Farmers, the Liberal leader was still 'singularly ignorant of the extent and power of the agrarian movement.'[14] The Farmers' revolt, when combined with the divisions created by the 1917 crisis, created a remarkably complex political scene on the Prairies that western leaders would have difficulty understanding or handling. For Mackenzie King the situation was next to impossible. Gradually, he would be forced to realize that he had little understanding of agrarian discontent, agriculture, or, for that matter, the Prairies themselves.

At best, the reconciliation of the Liberal party with the Prairie region would take time. Western frustration had been simmering for years. The scepticism toward the traditional political system had been deepened by the experiment of Union government. Just as there was nothing King could have done at the convention to bring the Farmers back on side, he had no chance as leader of immediately winning their support. 'There is no question,' one Prairie Liberal wrote, 'but that the farmers are going to be in the saddle for the next three or four years.'[15] Westerners unanimously echoed these sentiments. While there was hope for the future, the present was determined: 'The people of the West ... have completely lost confidence in the old political parties, and ... nothing that the Liberal party can do, at least in the immediate future, can restore that confidence.'[16]

A strategy had to be formed in the meantime to deal with the brewing agrarian revolt. The plan would encompass King's Prairie sympathies, his expedient need for western support, his opposition to class movements and third parties, and his overriding goal of national unity. Compromise and conciliation always remained at the core of this approach and would be employed whenever possible. 'I hope that our Liberal friends will not lose heart,' he wrote, 'but, by showing every sympathy to the farmers in the aims which we have in common, do their part in enabling the farmers themselves to see the wisdom of maintaining the friendliest relations with the party which, ever since it has been formed, has been the one to champion their cause.'[17] Patience was King's considered reaction: 'Time will have its effect on these "sectional" movements. Two parties in the end will be necessary & I shall win the Leadership of the Liberal & other radical forces, thru being true to Liberal principles.' He was confident the Union government was 'doomed completely' in the West, and 'whether the Liberal party will survive the Farmer Labor combination depends on our conciliatory attitude.'[18]

The first issue to be resolved was the threat of three-cornered contests and the resulting split in the Liberal vote. The federal party had to decide whether to oppose Farmers' candidates by nominating Liberals or to treat the Farmer as a species of Liberal and not contest the riding. The issue was already furthering the divisions among western Liberals. The Laurier loyalists opposed any conciliatory gestures toward 'the traitors of 1917,' many of whom had been drawn into Farmer ranks. The Unionist Liberals were adamant in warning the federal party that to oppose the agrarian movement was to commit suicide in the region. Mackenzie King did not have long to ponder, however, as a series of by-elections demanded immediate action.

It was quickly decided that the best course would be for the Liberals to seek candidates who had the support of both groups. The representative need only declare opposition to the Union government and approval of the Liberal platform. If the seat were won, the member was to support appropriate resolutions on the tariff, agriculture, reciprocity, and taxation, and was to make it clear that the Grain Growers and Liberals were united on these matters of western concern. The strategy, of course, was to have only one candidate challenge the Conservatives in each riding. If the Grain Growers' candidate were first in the field, then he was not to be opposed by a Liberal.[19] On the other hand, the federal Liberal leader could not have it appear that his party was merely succumbing to the Farmers. 'You speak ... of my policy being not to oppose any Farmers' candidates,' King corrected a Manitoba party member. 'There has evidently been some misunderstanding of my attitude, if such an impression has gone abroad ... I have as a matter of fact, been urging our friends to get Liberal candidates into the field before any other candidates were put up.'[20] King was pushing to have Liberals nominated before the Farmers could act, in order to avoid the dilemma completely.

The federal by-election for the Saskatchewan constituency of Assiniboia in October 1919 became the testing ground for Liberal support in the West. According to the Liberal leader, the by-election was 'the most significant of any of the eight elections which are being held.'[21] When King learned that the Grain Growers had called a convention for 25 September to select a candidate, he urged Premier Martin to beat them to the punch and have a Liberal, acceptable to both groups, nominated as quickly as possible. The precedent of the Glengarry–Stormont by-election in Ontario had shown that if the Farmers selected their candidate first, the opportunity of having an acceptable Liberal nominated was lost. 'Had it been possible for our friends to hold their convention first,' King claimed, 'there appears to be no doubt whatever that the Farmers would have been agreeable to allowing the Liberal nomination to stand and not enter the field.'

King's immediate plan was to have a Liberal convention called and a candidate placed in the field, but he was prepared if necessary to compromise. The Liberal government in Saskatchewan was struggling to keep afloat amidst the wave of Farmer popularity, and any sign that the premier stood in opposition would have spelled his demise. 'It will never do for the Liberal party in this province to get into conflict with the Grain Growers [sic] organization,' Martin warned King. 'Speaking generally, the Liberals and the Grain Growers stand on a very similar platform and there is no doubt in my mind but that the majority of the Grain Growers are friendly disposed towards the Liberal party.' Martin advised King to take his conciliatory approach one step further and refrain from opposing the Farmers even if they placed a candidate in the field after the Liberals. There would be only one result if it came down to a contest: it would 'ruin the chances of the Liberal party in the province for several years to come.' The situation had taken on a 'serious character,' and a 'serious mistake' had to be avoided. For Premier Martin there was only one path to follow: 'The main thing in Assiniboia is to see that someone is elected who is opposed to the present Government – whether he calls himself a Grain Grower or a Liberal makes very little difference.'[22]

While King was being advised by the provincial Liberals not to oppose the Farmer candidate, the federal Liberals in Saskatchewan reacted by calling their convention for 11 September. At the meeting they went against King's desired strategy and postponed nominating their candidate until after the Grain Growers' convention. The day after the Farmers' gathering on 25 September, the Liberal convention reconvened and W.R. Motherwell accepted the nomination.

At the time, Motherwell was the most influential of all western Liberals. He has been credited with the discovery of the dry farming technique of summerfallowing and had been one of the founders of the Territorial

Grain Growers' Association in 1901. Motherwell entered the Liberal provincial government of Walter Scott at the time of Saskatchewan's inauguration in 1905, serving as minister of agriculture until 1918. But he was also the leader of the Laurier faction in the province. Motherwell had become deeply embittered over the 1917 crisis and had resigned from Martin's cabinet in 1918. The official reason was a policy disagreement over the teaching of foreign languages in schools, but the resignation signalled a 'larger disenchantment.' Motherwell was disgusted that Martin was keeping a distance from the federal party. The Grain Growers had been overjoyed to see their old mentor's resignation, viewing it as the loss of an 'old style politician' from a 'political clan' that was 'steeped in partyism.'[23]

As a founder of the Territorial Grain Growers' Association, Motherwell admitted to being 'naturally sympathetic' to both the Liberal and Farmers' platforms but he had become the type of 'extreme Liberal Partisan' that Dafoe described as characteristic of Saskatchewan.[24] He favoured opposition to the Farmers in order to force them back into the fold, and he believed that allowing them to stand unopposed was an admission of surrender and defeat. 'I, in common with thousands and tens of thousands of Canadians,' he trumpeted, 'fought for these Liberal principles long before there was a Grain Growers [*sic*] organization hoped or dreamed of.' Motherwell agreed with the logic of Martin and King that to have three-way fights was to divide the Liberal vote and possibly allow a Unionist Tory the victory. They differed, however, on whether this sacrifice was justified. 'There would appear,' he argued, 'to be nothing but an actual object lesson in such an eventuality that would help to drive home to the farmers of this province the unfortunate results that were bound to follow their advent into the political arena at this time. Therefore it would be better in the end, and for the future, for us to fight in Assiniboia and lose out, to even a Tory, than not to fight at all.'[25]

Premier Martin immediately wrote King to denounce Motherwell's nomination and to point out that O.R. Gould, the Grain Growers' candidate, should have been acceptable to the Liberals: 'I have no hesitation at all in saying that this is a most serious mistake. It is most embarrassing as it is contrary entirely to what we think should be done and I do not think that Mr. Motherwell has any chance at all of being elected; in fact, from information we have, I am quite satisfied that he will be hopelessly defeated. You can readily understand what a serious effect this will have on the future of the Party in this Province.' The premier lobbied King to intervene in order to avoid the impending disaster.

'There is only one course to pursue,' he pleaded, 'and that is to use every endeavour to get Mr. Motherwell to retire from the field.'[26]

In October King conferred with J.A. Robb and T.A. Crerar and agreed with the 'unwisdom' of the situation. He would attempt to have 'the withdrawal of Motherwell from [the] present campaign.'[27] If this occurred, Crerar agreed that the Grain Growers' candidate should make a declaration that he was against Union government and in favour of certain planks in the Liberal platform. The support of the Grain Growers would be gained and Motherwell could be nominated in his home riding of Saltcoats. These plans were scuttled when Motherwell refused to withdraw. King did not fully recognize the severity of the impending defeat and was not prepared to push the issue. Instead, he admired Motherwell's fighting spirit: 'Motherwell has put some of his own money into the fight & is ready to sell a flock of sheep & use proceeds for the cause if necessary.' It was decided he was 'too good a friend not to help, even if defeat certain.' The federal party sent financial aid, and Liberals went West to participate in the campaign.[28]

The results of the by-election proved Martin correct and served as a valuable lesson on the political dangers of the agrarian revolt. They also demonstrated King's weakness in Prairie affairs. Motherwell 'charged into the arena with more vigour than discretion' and was defeated by a majority of over five thousand votes, thereby losing his deposit.[29] 'The party has suffered seriously from the ill-advised fight,' one Liberal mourned.[30] Three-cornered contests simply had to be avoided. At times the party would be obliged to surrender the field to the Farmers, but such a course, in the long-term, would be less damaging than splitting the vote. Walter Scott recognized King's weakness in western affairs and recommended that in the future the new leader should not 'give advice hastily' without having first procuring advice from 'dependable' men.[31]

The contest also demonstrated that Saskatchewan's position as a Liberal stronghold was vulnerable. King was informed that Martin was under increasing pressure to support the Grain Growers and was prepared to bend. The disaster at Assiniboia undoubtedly made matters worse. 'Premier Martin has thrown in his lot with [the Farmers] as he is convinced that in them lies the hope of the West,' one Saskatchewan Liberal observed.[32] King's relationship with the premier indicated a growing breach between provincial and federal branches of the Liberal party. When King requested aid in strengthening the federal party's organization in Saskatchewan, Martin was evasive. Any federal attachment, even in the traditional stronghold of Saskatchewan, was now a political handicap. According to the premier, the need for Saskatchewan Liberals to avoid being associated with Ottawa was preventing the provincial organization from selecting its six members to sit on the National Liberal Committee to be formed in December. The committee, also known as the National Council of Fifty-Four, was a federal initiative designed to rebuild the party's organizational structure. In an attempt to involve the premier in the process, King requested that Martin personally appoint some of the Saskatchewan representatives. The premier refused. Despite this rejection, King continued to assume that Martin would himself represent the province on the committee, blindly ignoring the premier's repeated warnings to the contrary. Finally Martin made his refusal absolutely clear: 'I have intimated to you on two previous occasions that it was impossible for me to remain a member of the ... [committee] and I am today forwarding you my resignation.'[33]

King resented Martin's stance, refusing to accept his explanation that any federal connection in the West would be political suicide. Instead King placed the blame solely on the 1917 division. 'Martin ... would have been satisfied only with Fielding's selection as Leader,' King sulked. 'Clearly the Liberal Unionists do not wish to coalesce with the Laurier Libs if it can be avoided.' When the two leaders met in the early months of 1920, relations remained tense. 'Felt from his attitude that there was little in the way of friendliness towards me,' King recorded. 'He went so far as to say his govt. might find it necessary to come out & support the Farmer's party ... I felt I could not trust him.'[34] It was clear that King would receive little cooperation from the Liberal governments on the Prairies in his quest to regain western support.

In October 1919 the United Farmers of Ontario (UFO) surprised the nation by winning provincial office. The victory demonstrated that the agrarian revolt would no longer be content to pressure the traditional parties for particular policies but was going to participate directly in the process. If the Liberals and Conservatives harboured any notion of avoiding battle with the Farmers, the UFO victory was sobering indeed. The entry of the Ontario movement into politics also forced the Prairie organizations to reconsider their own strategy. Suddenly the sectional revolt against eastern exploitation was broadened to a reaction of the entire agricultural industry. The Farmers could now raise their sights to the possibility of a more national campaign.

The Farmers were under considerable pressure to enter politics in Saskatchewan, while the provincial Liberals sought desperately to demonstrate that they could effectively represent agrarian interests. In May

1920 Premier Martin responded to the suspicion that his government was still too friendly toward the federal Liberals by publicly announcing that henceforth his activities would be confined solely to provincial matters.[35] In the legislature the government increasingly ignored party labels. Farmer representation was increased when C.M. Hamilton and J.A. Maharg joined the government and ardent Liberal W.E. Knowles was dropped. 'It is plain the Martin Govt has capitulated completely to the Grain Grower's [sic],' King observed. 'It is all a matter of treachery.'[36]

The federal Liberal leader was distressed by the attitude of the Martin group, but the Saskatchewan situation was made even more troublesome by the position taken by the Motherwell faction. J.G. Gardiner, an up-and-coming Liberal stalwart who was becoming well known for his intense partisanship, was following in Motherwell's footsteps. After working for his mentor in the Assiniboia disaster, he continued to advocate opposition to the Farmers. The Liberals were the rightful defenders of agrarian interests, as far as Gardiner was concerned, and there would be no compromising this position. Liberal weakness in the West was due to 'the inactivity' and poor organization of the party. The Grain Growers, he believed, were 'backed' by the Conservatives, and the Liberals would have to 'carry the banner against all opposition.' He criticized the 'so called leaders' of his own party for 'standing aside,' arguing that 'fear of the enemy can never win a victory.'[37] Gardiner echoed Motherwell's complaint that in the West loyalty to party and principles seemed to be 'taking an extended holiday.'[38]

The situation of the Liberal party in Manitoba was even more depressing. 'You invite me to be frank in stating my views,' a despondent party member wrote to Andrew Haydon, federal Liberal organizer. 'To be frank one must be brutal. Your question implies that there is a Liberal party here. There isn't.'[39] The election of 1917 had cut the electorate of Manitoba adrift from its traditional political affiliations, and long after King's selection as party leader the division in the Liberal party remained. The breach aroused long-term controversy and bitterness in Manitoba, more so than in any other province. Those who had remained loyal to Laurier never stopped believing they were the 'stalwarts of Liberalism,' while the Unionists had shown their Tory colours.[40] After 1919, the 'Diehards,' as they were becoming known, viewed all other groups in the province as disguised Conservatives. The Farmers were not seen as the vanguard of a genuine agrarian revolt but rather as one more 'plot' hatched by the traitorous Unionists. The Farmers 'are steadily and effectively getting control of the Grain Growers [sic] Associations,' one paranoid Diehard told King. 'Conservatism, standing on its own legs is dead in the West, but travelling under some other euphemism it is a very lively corpse, indeed it is running the west in every particular.'[41] King was warned not to expect support from T.C. Norris's provincial Liberal government because it was backed by the Unionist group. Norris, it was argued, was 'scared stiff of the farmers,' and if King went to Manitoba he would not even be extended the usual social courtesies.[42] As in Saskatchewan, the Unionists favoured cooperation with the Farmers while the Diehards advocated opposition.

If there were some possibility of Farmer–Liberal cooperation in Manitoba and Saskatchewan, there was virtually none in Alberta. The national Farmers' movement was becoming divided between the Manitoba wing of crypto-Liberals led by T.A. Crerar and the Alberta wing of radicals led by H.W. Wood. The latter, with its primarily rural, western American intellectual roots, advanced a 'co-operativist, anti-capitalist perspective on questions of economic and political power.' It rejected partisanship and insisted on 'funtionally co-ordinated delegate democracy leading into a group government.' Its radical stance was distinguished by a non-British parliamentary conception of democratic representation.[43]

At a meeting of the National Liberal Organization Committee, the Alberta representatives indicated that the province would not be able to raise the funding required of them by the federal party until King himself came to the province and 'served to arouse and revive Liberal interest.'[44] It was only a matter of time before King would have to brave the storm and head west for a speaking tour. The region was moving into open revolt against the party system, particularly that dictated by Ottawa, but the Liberal leader was confident that once westerners came to know and understand his message, the fury would diminish. Prairie voices were generally more cautious. Although both Unionist and Laurier Liberals agreed that King eventually had to go west, they did not concur on the timing of the journey. Some of the Laurier rump told their leader to come as quickly as possible because he would have 'immense influence in quieting the unrest'; others claimed the results would not be very tangible.[45] The Unionist groups believed the tour had to be shaped around the sensibilities of the provincial governments. King was informed that Alberta support for the United Farmers' movement was on the wane and that he should wait until its popularity had diminished further. Both the Saskatchewan and Manitoba groups wanted the tour delayed until their elections were over.[46] Mackenzie King was annoyed and could not believe that his presence would jeopardize the situation. Despite his personal wish to undertake the trip immediately and prove his critics wrong, in the end caution prevailed. After pondering the tour late in 1919, he conceded the majority opinion and delayed until 1920. This way he could satisfy the bulk of Prairie Liberals and also follow his own strategy of avoiding being drawn into possible controversy with the Farmers.[47]

One of the keys for the Liberals in regaining the support of the region was the press. As the sole medium of communication for a large, widely scattered rural population, the press was in a powerful position to influence political sympathies. The Unionist Liberals in Manitoba had found a powerful ally in the *Free Press*. The newspaper, which as everyone admitted exerted 'an immense influence in the west,' was hostile to both the Diehards and Mackenzie King.[48] In Saskatchewan the party could usually count on the support of the *Regina Leader*, the *Moose Jaw Times*, and the *Saskatoon Phoenix*. After 1916 the *Prince Albert Herald* switched loyalties and was supporting the Liberals after the Borden government had failed to offer a senatorship to the area. Throughout the region the Liberals dominated the control of the ethnic press, including Icelandic, Norwegian, Swedish, Ruthenian, German, Hungarian, and Hebrew papers.[49]

The problem was that the majority of the western papers, like the party members, had supported the Unionists. 'The provincial governments of Manitoba and Saskatchewan are ... afraid of the Unionist press,' one Manitoba Liberal informed King, 'and they may well be afraid. The Winnipeg dailies and the Grain Grower's [*sic*] Guide could knock the props from under the Norris Government in one month, and the urban press of Saskatchewan and the Guide could do the same to the Martin Government.'[50] King recognized the lack of a friendly press in the region as a 'most serious want.'[51] He had no doubt the *Free Press* should be on side. Its owner and editor were prominent Liberals yet, along with the *Grain Growers' Guide,* it was doing everything in its power 'to prevent any accommodation being reached by the Grain Growers and the liberals.'[52] The *Free Press*, like the region, would have to be returned to its roots.

After only months as Liberal leader, Mackenzie King was being forced into some alarming conclusions about his relationship with the West. He had seriously underestimated western scepticism toward the traditional parties and, as a result, the miserable state of Prairie Liberalism. The Farmers were a more formidable force in the region than he had first assumed. The breach of 1917 had severely divided the western Liberals, and this division was making victory over the Farmers even more of an impossibility. Prairie Liberalism was in such a mess that much of the best talent remained outside party ranks. There was no 'Prairie lieutenant' to handle the region as a political unit, as Laurier had possessed in Clifford Sifton and then Frank Oliver. Although Motherwell was the senior-ranking western Liberal, the Assiniboia disaster had been an accurate measure of his value. He was respected for his long service to the party, but as one western Liberal indicated, 'his political sagacity is not equal to his administrative ability.'[53] The former premier of Saskatchewan, Walter Scott, reinforced these views: 'A splendid man, but was always a mere infant regarding elections or political management.'[54] Mackenzie King was sympathetic toward the region's plight, but this alone would not translate into support. As King now admitted himself, when it came to the West, he was 'completely in the dark as to what is best.'[55]

The Liberal leader hoped the situation was at least beginning to improve, but early indications in 1920 were not favourable. The National Organization Committee indicated that the region was in a 'tempest tossed condition.' The Grain Growers continued to ride strong in Manitoba and Saskatchewan, while Alberta was in such an uncertain state that it was impossible to produce an evaluation.[56] When Andrew Haydon went to Winnipeg in November to discuss organization, much of his effort was 'wasted in idle argument.' The lack of finances coming from the area further hindered party prospects.[57]

Federal Liberals could at least take solace in the state of Conservative fortunes in the West. Prime Minister Robert Borden retired and was succeeded by Arthur Meighen. The change in leadership, along with the protectionist budget of 1920, reinforced the Union government's Tory nature. Meighen, who had served as solicitor general in Borden's government during the war, was the author of the Wartime Elections Act, which in 1917 deprived many 'foreign' Prairie immigrants of the franchise. With the selection of Meighen, the Union government was clearly not about to win support in the Prairie ethnic communities. The economy, meanwhile, was further hindering western support for the federal government. Near-drought conditions existed on the southern Prairies, a situation worsened by a decrease in overall grain production and a price collapse in world grain markets.

If the two traditional parties could not deal effectively with western issues and concerns, a third alternative would be necessary. The organized Farmers led by Crerar committed themselves to independent political action and became the National Progressive Party.

The Prairie West had to be convinced that Mackenzie King sympathized with its plight and, more importantly, was prepared to act on these sentiments. In Parliament the Liberal leader offered speeches that glorified agriculture and the rural lifestyle. He lamented that industrialization was forcing the people from the country to the city and producing 'a great plutocracy and aristocracy combined on the one side, and men decaying and villages and rural life deserted on the other.' Agriculture was directly associated with the morality of the nation. 'What we want,' King argued, 'is a bold peasantry; what we want is men who love the soil, who love contact with nature. We need them ... if we are to maintain our human society in a proper degree of strength and vigour.'[58] The agricultural interests had to be defended. 'I am determined,' he wrote in his diary, 'the Liberal Party shall stand true to the farmer's interests for it is only by developing our agricultural wealth that Canada will ever become a great & prosperous country.'[59]

Mackenzie King was also coming to realize just how crucial the West was to his leadership. He had won the convention narrowly. Moreover, while the Unionists certainly doubted his abilities, the Laurier group from Quebec who had seen to his victory held little more confidence. The most powerful of the Quebec members, Sir Lomer Gouin, had supported W.S. Fielding. The younger King was forced to work closely with older easterners who disagreed with much of his 'radical' thinking. In particular, the two most influential members of the party, Fielding and Gouin, were protectionists who opposed the western stance on railway regulation, freight rates, and the natural resource transfer. They accepted King's leadership only grudgingly and it was generally recognized that Gouin's attitude was 'not far removed from open contempt and defiance.'[60] King concluded that Gouin's Montreal group was prepared to 'fight the farmers' and did not 'think much of Crerar.' 'Hoping for an alliance of Ont & Quebec against the West,' they wanted 'as little said on the tariff as possible.'[61] Prairie support would be an obvious weapon to disarm this eastern bloc. Although King had no choice but to recognize the influence of these political veterans, he disliked and distrusted their policies as well as their standing in the party. He would have to be patient and bide his time until his leadership was more secure before he could advance his own positions more strongly. Already he was looking to the younger members from Quebec, led by Ernest Lapointe, to become his French-Canadian advisers.

If King were going to survive as Liberal leader long enough to turn his Prairie sympathies into action, the West would also have to be patient – an unlikely scenario. The Laurier years had created the notion that Quebec controlled the party, and the selection of the new leader only furthered this impression. King was seen as too weak to control these forces and 'terrified lest the French-Canadian majority in his party may throw him overboard.' As a result, many westerners believed he would go to any lengths to 'placate' the 'Quebec reactionaries' even if this meant sacrificing western interests. Western journalist J.A. Stevenson was quickly losing faith in King, partly for this reason: 'The Liberal party led by him is now sunk to the level of a localized faction. It has ceased to be a nationwide party and its hopes for a recovery of that status are dim. It lives on the memory of dead and departed heroes, it allows its elder statesmen too much influence.'[62] Caught between both groups and accepted by neither, Mackenzie King was out in the cold.

The Liberal performance in the budget debate of 1920 demonstrated the dangers of King's balancing act. The primary issue of concern for the West remained the tariff. Fielding moved an amendment advocating a reduction in the tariff on food as well as the implements of production necessary to the development of Canada's natural resources. Nonetheless, promises of tariff reduction seemed 'much more guarded than ever before.' As far as the West was concerned, King was following the path of his predecessors by sacrificing his principles and catering to the whims of the central Canadian manufacturers. 'No Liberal leader ever makes a public speech now without announcing that he is not a free trader, never has been and never expects to be,' Liberal journalist R.J. Deachman complained. Gone were the 'savage onslaughts' on protection made in the past by such Liberal stalwarts as Sir Richard Cartwright. Westerners were weary of a 'Liberalism full of apologies' and no longer put any stock in the justification that, because the party had defended regional interests in the past, it was deserving of support in the present and future. The West was already pointing to inconsistencies between the party's 1919 platform and its actual practice. Fielding's speech on the budget was seen as 'a defense of bounties and protection' that was 'so vague and uncertain that it might be canonized by the Pope and prove acceptable to the Devil at the same time.'[63]

King consoled himself with the knowledge that the Meighen government was positioning itself as the defender of protectionism. In the long run this could only bring the Farmers and Liberals closer together.[64] The Farmer groups had come under strong attack from the Meighen Tories, and King believed this made them recognize that 'their lot is necessarily with the Liberals.' He informed Prairie critics that, as party leader, he had no choice but to consider the interests of his colleagues and the rest of the nation for that matter. If the West were so anxious for the party to represent its interests, there was one certain way to ensure results: 'When it is remembered that so far as representation of the West in Parliament is concerned, practically all of those who are men of Liberal thought and feeling have for the time being either identified themselves with the Unionist Party or withdrawn themselves into a separate group, is it perhaps not to be wondered at that you fail to hear the note of Western Liberalism as clearly sounded from the Liberal benches in Parliament as is to be desired.'[65]

In the autumn of 1920 the Liberal leader at last prepared for his western tour. Although the record of the unpopular Union government would be emphasized, the central plank of the tour would be cooperation between Liberals and Farmers.[66] He decided to have a relatively small party accompany him, including younger Liberals who were not so associated with the bitterness of the past.[67] But the tour would demonstrate the sceptical nature of Prairie opinion toward the King Liberals and the continuing dissension caused by the events of 1917. Regaining the West would prove much more arduous than the Liberal leader first envisioned.

The tour commenced in Alberta. There, King's optimism, along with his particular ignorance of the province, convinced him that his presence was already alleviating division: 'There are some jealousies here over Unionist control from Edmonton vs Liberal from Calgary, but all agree that this visit is helping to lessen feeling.' The organization was 'in poor hands, – everything disorganized' but he was confident the Farmers' movement was on 'the wane' and the Liberal forces 'reuniting.'[68] The trip was also demonstrating that King's romantic perceptions about the region remained intact. The rhetoric in his diary was filled with symbolic and religious imagery. The West had indeed become the manifestation of the New Jerusalem that contained the hope for progress, reform, and salvation:

> Looking out of the window just as the train left Calgary I saw the most glorious sun rise I have ever seen in my life – nothing like it have I ever seen. The horizon was like a sea of liquid gold with a wonderful light all over it. The richest colours blazed forth in all directions across the sky. There were liquid greens & violets & azure colours, but a golden glory thro' all. I thought of the New Day, the New Social Order. It seems like Heaven's prophesy of the dawn of a new era, revealed to me.[69]

Regardless of the idealistic perceptions and apparent optimism, time would show just how out of touch King was with Alberta sentiment.

The Liberal leader's optimism was tested during the remainder of his journey. The so-called party stronghold of Saskatchewan offered a reception that shocked Mackenzie King. As part of their attempt to win the support of the Grain Growers, the provincial Liberals refused to greet the federal leader publicly in Regina. King was all for cooperation, but he was incensed that the party would go to such lengths to win Farmer support. 'What a miserable type of Liberalism,' he responded in his diary. When called upon to speak at a private gathering of the party with the premier in attendance, King 'opened up pretty strongly' against Martin for his public behaviour. 'Altogether,' he recorded, 'it was an outburst & a bomb, but while it made Martin a little incensed, [it] did good. It cleared the air.'[70]

Manitoba was in a state of 'discord,' with divisions widening rather than narrowing. The struggle between the Diehards and Unionists (or 'Free Press' Liberals as they were often known in the province) was so divisive that they were in reality two parties. The groups could not coordinate any schemes of organization and continually bickered over which one represented the 'official' party. The Diehards claimed the Unionists were 'usurping authority' by refusing to acknowledge the former's representatives or conventions.[71] The Unionists, meanwhile, were demanding that party affairs be taken out of the hands of 'the coterie in Winnipeg.' They granted the Diehards 'considerable credit' for maintaining an organization throughout the difficult years of the war but argued that this wing 'cannot forget 1917.' Conceded one Unionist, 'I admit it is hard to do. But we have not only got to forget, but to forgive a lot, in the interests of the party.'[72]

The Diehards were completely uncompromising. They opposed not only the Unionists but also the Progressives, the *Free Press*, and the Norris government. When the premier began to court the Farmers' party after the victory of the UFO in 1919, the Diehards vehemently displayed their opposition. They were furious when Norris arranged to have Tom Crerar restrain his Progressive followers in the provincial field in return for Liberal support at the federal level. The opposition to cooperation seemed justified when Crerar failed to keep the Farmers from the provincial field. In June 1920 the Norris government went to the polls. Despite the self-imposed separation from the federal party, it was denied a majority. 'Practically every Laurier Liberal in the province voted against Norris for his unfaithfulness,' the Diehards complained. By 1920 frustrated Liberals from many factions were calling for a complete reorganization of the party and for stronger leadership. They felt like 'sheep having no shepherd.'[73]

Mackenzie King could not have agreed more and believed he would become that uniting force. 'Here in Winnipeg,' he wrote, 'one feels that politically the people are without a shepherd.' The loyalty of the Die-hards was admirable, and King shared their admiration for Laurier, but their refusal to compromise went completely against his strategy. The personnel, he noted, also left much to be desired. The Liberal cause was 'in the wrong hands,' with 'many of those most prominent' being 'discredited citizens.' King could find little cause for optimism: 'The whole atmosphere is other than encouraging ... Organization all gone to pieces.' These impressions were reinforced when he left Winnipeg to tour the province. 'There had been little or no organization of any kind ... ,' he recorded. 'Manitoba is far from encouraging, neglect, dissatisfaction & indifference everywhere.'[74]

The only sign of encouragement for the province came from a meeting between King and the Progressive leader, T.A. Crerar. Topics of discussion included cooperation in the upcoming federal election or even fusion to be conducted before the contest. King indicated his willingness to form a 'union of progressive groups' and, according to King's diary, Crerar agreed that generally it was better to have an open alliance before the elections, as long as western issues would be paramount.[75] Crerar and A.B. Hudson emphasized the 'need of going slowly,' as their following was 'difficult to handle.' By the time he left Manitoba, King was certain he had made considerable progress: 'This means we have concluded our trip by the leaders of the progressive forces coming together & planning a joint campaign. What greater triumph or finer ending could there be to the Western trip ... It has been successful beyond all anticipations.'[76]

J.W. Dafoe's account of the meeting differed in tone and substance, and was probably closer to reality. Crerar, according to the *Free Press* editor, placed Mackenzie King in the 'Liberal end' of the party and believed his sympathies and outlook were progressive, but he had 'no belief in King's capacity for the successful leadership of a party.' Dafoe believed that, if King were hoping for 'some kind of an official alliance' that would share western constituencies, he was 'following phantoms.' Dafoe was certain there would be no alliance before the next election. Any proposed coalition would alienate the non-Liberal sections of the populist Farmer party. The agrarian movement would show itself not to be just a group of 'Liberals in a hurry,' as King believed them to be. Dafoe was confident a fusion after the election was more practical. This would allow the Farmers to maintain their identity throughout the contest and then deal with the Liberals from a position of power. A fusion would very likely be necessary for the successful formation of a government. Once the coalition began to articulate its liberal policies, the Tories and radicals would be forced out and a truly 'Farmer–Liberal Government' would emerge. Dafoe believed that Crerar, along with Ontario Premier E.C. Drury, would be able to command the support of the 'liberal' Farmers and turn the movement into 'the Liberal party of the future.'[77]

At best, Mackenzie King's first tour of the Prairie West as Liberal leader was given mixed reviews. Although he had 'improved his personal position considerably because ... he is now known personally to a very considerable number of Western people who have heard him speak,' the results were not as 'triumphant' as he believed. 'I find no traces of any wild enthusiasm over his platform performances,' Dafoe remarked. 'So far as putting the official Liberal party back upon the political map is concerned, the trip, if it was designed for this purpose, was a failure.'[78] The West welcomed King's message but not his leadership or his party: 'Liberal views were never so universally held in western Canada as they are today,' the *Free Press* warned. 'And official Liberalism was never so weak. There is Mr. King's problem.'[79]

The impression had also been left that King favoured a Liberal–Farmer coalition as the 'only chance' for a 'sure future.' On three separate occasions between November 1920 and February 1921, he proposed an open coalition to Crerar and Premier Drury of Ontario to be worked out before a general election. He was anxious to 'combine' forces, and at one point considered offering Crerar 'a 50:50 deal' if the Progressive leader could unite his forces and 'divide' the seats with the Liberals.[80] 'I have been seeking to make that alliance a feature of the relations of the parties in the country,' King wrote at the end of 1920, 'I think we are not very far apart.' Neither side, he believed, would have to sacrifice its identity.[81] In the early months of 1921 King reiterated the desire to maintain close relations until a fusion occurred. King was already pondering a possible name for the alliance, and in February made the suggestion once again to Crerar: 'I asked how Liberal-Progressive wd do for a coalition name ... Crerar clearly was impressed with my suggestion of a Progressive Liberal alliance.'[82] As Dafoe had assumed, however, the Progressive leaders were not prepared to entertain a coalition until after the election results were known. They did not wish to risk their movement while it was still in the ascendancy.

In 1921 another by-election tested Liberal support in the West, this time in Alberta. The United Farmers of Alberta (UFA) were boasting that

Medicine Hat housed their largest organization of any constituency in the province, and the Liberals announced they would not put forth a candidate. King later received information from the same Alberta Liberals, advising the opposite strategy. They argued that conditions had changed in the province, that the Farmers were on the decline, and that a Liberal candidate should now be nominated.[83] But the lesson of Assiniboia loomed large: with King's urging, the party refrained from entering the contest. On 27 June Robert Gardiner, the UFA candidate, won the seat by an unparalleled majority of 9765 votes. The landslide demonstrated just how out of touch the Liberals were with provincial sentiment. There was little chance of cooperation with the 'radical' Farmers of Alberta, and the movement certainly was not waning. The Medicine Hat result made it clear that Liberal fortunes were not improving on the Prairies but rather were declining. 'The Liberal party's chances rest in Quebec, the Maritime provinces and British Columbia, together with what can be accomplished in Ontario,'[84] Alberta Liberal J.R. Boyle concluded. Even the federal Progressive leader was shocked by the magnitude of the victory. 'It was more like a crusade than like an election,' Crerar observed.[85]

In July Premier Charles Stewart and the Liberal government in Alberta had to face the rising storm in an election. The United Farmers of Alberta were swept into office under Herbert Greenfield. Despite the portents of the Medicine Hat result, Mackenzie King was still taken aback by the defeat of the provincial Liberals, who had held office for sixteen years. The victory gave the Farmers' movement 'an impetus ... greater than it has had anywhere else,' he recorded. King had denounced 'the shortcomings and fallacies of class and group movements,' and now a party based on these principles had been elected in Alberta.[86]

As the general election of 1921 approached, a change was occurring in King's strategy with the Farmers. His selection as party leader and conciliatory attitude had not provided the expected results in the West. With little to show for his efforts in that region, King shifted his concern to ensuring the preservation of his party's identity as well as to appeasing his eastern colleagues and more reliable bases of support. His previous suggestions of a Liberal–Progressive coalition were replaced by an invitation for the Progressives to join the Liberals. King justified his shifting ground by harping on the 'selfishness' of the Farmers, which had resulted in more Liberal animosity toward them than toward the Tories in Ottawa.[87] He denied that he was turning his back on the West and bowing to eastern pressure. It was only natural, he argued, that Liberals and Progressives should unite to defeat the government, but there would be no 'sacrificing the principles for which Liberalism and the Liberal Party stand.' Rather than emphasizing Progressive appeasement, King was now pointing to situations where the two groups could not cooperate: 'Wherever ... the Farmers continue to insist upon separate action on their own part, on a class basis, it will be the clear duty of Liberals and the Liberal Party to place in the field candidates who will stand as Liberals representing no one class, but all classes alike.'[88] Three-cornered contests were still to be avoided, but Liberals were to be nominated in as many ridings as possible. 'I have been trying in Saskatchewan, Alberta & Manitoba,' King indicated, 'to have candidates put in the field for moral reasons if for no other – to make the front of Liberalism strong across the continent.'[89] Finally, in the face of Quebec pressure just prior to the election, King denied any intention of uniting with the Progressives. Crerar claimed to be 'at a loss' over the apparent and sudden reversal.[90]

Another feature of Liberal strategy in the election campaign was to avoid commitments on tariff policy. Pressure from central and eastern Canada, and the powerful Montreal wing of the party in particular, was strongly advising King to leave the tariff alone. 'I shall keep sympathetic with farmers, but adopt a middle course as between Protect'n & Free Trade,' the Liberal leader decided.[91] 'To my mind it is not only utter folly, but quite wrong, to talk of Free Trade in Canada with conditions what they are at the present time.'[92] The campaign would follow the lines of the Laurier–Fielding approach, which included a revenue tariff with incidental protection. King did not believe the nation could do away entirely with revenue from the customs tariff and raise all the required revenue by direct rather than indirect taxation. Throughout the campaign he would emphasize that neither the Liberals nor the Farmers were actually advocating genuine free trade: 'They stand for freer trade, not for free trade ... they aim at freedom rather than at restriction in matters of trade ... they would reduce rather than increase the burdens of taxation.'[93]

Arthur Meighen, meanwhile, was attempting to use the Liberal platform of 1919 to persuade the eastern manufacturers that the Grits were indeed pushing free trade. King had been defending himself and the party against these charges since the opening of Parliament in 1920, and the debate continued throughout the campaign. 'The issue, so far as the Liberal party's attitude on the tariff is concerned,' King argued, 'is not and never has been in this country, between free trade and protection; it has been between a tariff imposed primarily for purposes of protection, and a tariff imposed primarily for purposes of revenue.'[94] The prime minister found the Liberal position to be meaningless: 'Those words are just the circular pomposity of a man who won't say what he means. He might as well say he favours a perambulating tariff, or an atmospheric tariff, or a dynamic tariff.'[95]

Party strategists bolstered King's confidence by arguing that the West would 'throw the tariff to the winds' if the government introduced a satisfactory pooling and freight rate policy.[96] The Liberal leader had to avoid a railway policy that might be construed in the West 'as our looking with favour upon a possible C.P.R. Monopoly,' but 'friends in Ontario' were most anxious that the question of government ownership be avoided.[97] The Montreal Liberals were of one mind with King's Ontario 'friends' on the issue of the nationalization of the railways.

The question of the wheat board was another issue in the West, but because the region was so divided on how to proceed, King could avoid making promises. The federal government had created the Canadian Wheat Board to dispose of the 1919 crop, but in 1920 the act establishing the board was not renewed and open market trading recommenced on the Winnipeg Grain Exchange. As Gerald Friesen points out, 'the dramatic collapse in wheat prices in 1920, just as Canada returned to the private grain trade, was at the root of farm protest for the next decade.'[98] But there had long been fundamental disagreement among the Prairie provinces over the handling of grains. Saskatchewan was pushing for some form of either national marketing of the western grain crop or national support of a cooperative plan. Manitoba and, to a lesser extent, Alberta were advocating the free market. These differences existed among western Liberals and Progressives alike, so the issue would cause King little immediate harm. The Liberal leader attempted to avoid cleavages by turning the emphasis onto the Unionist record.

It was only too apparent in western Canada that the Liberal party, despite its rhetoric, was still catering to the East. The situation in Alberta during the campaign mirrored that of the Medicine Hat by-election, and Mackenzie King's retreat from western incentives only made matters worse. According to party stalwart J.R. Boyle, while the Liberals were in a better position than the Conservatives, it would not be 'wise' to expend very much money or energy attempting to win the West. Conditions across the Prairies were depressing, Boyle stated bluntly, but 'in so far as Alberta is concerned, I would not think that we have a fighting chance.'[99] There was little hope for King's strategy of friendly cooperation. Alberta Liberals did not view the majority of Farmers as kindred spirits, and they agreed with the decision to avoid coalition. Believing that the Farmers would soon see the 'folly' of their ways, and that 'the lost sheep' would all be 'back in the fold,'[100] Alberta Liberals wanted King to fight the Farmers in every constituency.[101]

But according to other party members from the province, the Farmers were a result and not the cause of Liberal difficulties. The main problem, blamed on the division of 1917, was that there was no organization. When A.L. Sifton was premier, the party had been kept strictly under his control. When he 'turned traitor' by supporting the Union government, his machine had gone with him, leaving the Liberal party 'helpless.'[102] During a campaign swing through Alberta, King shed much of the optimism he had displayed on his tour of the province in 1920. Just a year after that tour, he claimed there were as many divisions within the party as there were between Liberals and Progressives. 'There is a regular feud here, & no forgiveness,' he recorded.[103] According to C.B. Macpherson, the Liberals never stood a chance from the outset. Unlike Saskatchewan, the desire for non-partisan politics established in the territorial days never disappeared. As a result, the provincial Liberals failed to build an organization, and the railway scandal of 1910 destroyed any hopes of doing so. The demand for a business-like government dominated the period after 1910, and the elections of 1921 would serve as 'the culmination of ten years of mounting anti-party feeling.'[104]

In Saskatchewan Mackenzie King decided to take a more aggressive approach to the Progressives. There had been a snap provincial election called for early in 1921 as W.A. Martin moved to take advantage of his strong position with the Saskatchewan Grain Growers' Association. The Liberals went so far as to have their members run simply as 'government' candidates. The result was a 'government' sweep with a smattering of 'Independent supporters of the Martin Government.' The Farmers were delighted 'because now they had a number of non-government MLAs to represent them plus a government that appeared to be as much theirs as any on the prairies.'[105] As the federal election approached, W.R. Motherwell reported that the premier was not to be trusted: 'Martin will continue pussyfooting, until he is quite convinced which of the two opposition parties are going to have the ascendency in Canada.'[106] His government was 'desperately afraid' to antagonize the Farmers and was attempting to appease them by cooperating in the federal contest. At the same time Martin was indicating that he would not take part in the campaign but would 'regard himself as a Western man.' He advised King to 'forget all about the West.'[107] Motherwell had learned his lesson in

Assiniboia and, while he opposed fusion, he was now prepared to cooperate in 'looking for some honourable basis upon which we can get + fight together.'[108] Jimmy Gardiner, on the other hand, continued to urge King to have Liberals oppose the Progressives in every constituency. He pointed to the experience of 1917 as evidence of what happens when 'Liberal sentiment is cast aside in order that some preconceived idea of what is best might ride triumphantly over everything else.'[109] Mackenzie King hoped to find some middle ground between the Martin and Gardiner groups, but personally he felt 'betrayed' by the provincial party.

The situation, however, was changing. Saskatchewan Liberals acted upon King's last-minute aversion to Progressive cooperation by reidentifying themselves as Liberals and rebuilding the organization. Three-cornered contests would be avoided, but Liberals were nominated where possible. Suddenly, in the last days before the vote, Premier Martin began openly attacking some planks in the Progressive platform. He indicated that 'party government' was 'the only workable system' and mocked the emergence of the Progressives, which, he claimed, had 'resulted in the appearance of the largest number of carpet-baggers ever scattered over these prairies.' Several days later, Martin endorsed Motherwell's candidacy in Regina. The Farmers, to say the least, were stunned. Farmer representative J.A. Maharg resigned from the provincial government, arguing that its position on the federal election violated his original terms of entry. Martin branded Maharg's resignation as hypocritical. Did the farmers not stand for a separation between federal and provincial politics? Why should the provincial government support the federal Progressives any more than the Liberals?[110]

By the end of the campaign Liberals and Progressives were quarrelling openly in Saskatchewan, and the Martin group had returned its support to the federal party. 'The man in Saskatchewan that the Progressives are after hot foot these days is Premier Martin,' Dafoe observed.[111] Progressivism in Saskatchewan was proving less durable than in either of the other two Prairie provinces. The stronger Liberal base had survived the Farmer offensive through Martin's timely compromise. Saskatchewan was slowly returning to its position as the nation's second most powerful Liberal stronghold. This move was the only optimistic sign for party resurgence in the West.

The interparty battle raged on in Manitoba throughout the campaign, but the vacillating position of the King Liberals on coalition served as the death blow. The Diehards were adamant about fighting the Progressives on every front and were overjoyed when King rejected fusion. They were placing candidates in as many constituencies as possible and went so far as refusing to concede a seat to the popular Progressive Robert Forke, despite the fact that he was 'an old and tried Liberal of the highest standing.'[112] The Free Press group was recognized by the national organization as the official party in the province.

Although the federal party had now rejected coalition, it still needed to maintain cooperation with the Progressives. Dafoe was angry. He claimed that the Diehards were of 'no political significance' other than to make the 'Liberal impotence still more marked.'[113] For the most part they represented only one section of the Winnipeg Liberals and had no influence in the rural areas. When planning his campaign swing through the province, King was advised to take both Unionist and Laurier Liberals with him to maintain the appearance of balance.[114] Regardless, Manitoba proved a hostile environment. Many of the Free Press Liberals did not even want King to visit the province, and he described it as 'the worst mix-up of any place in Canada.'[115] Despite the antagonism, he met with both 'factions' and tried to 'pour oil on troubled waters.' In the end the best King could do was avoid offending either side. 'Factions as irreconcilable as in Ireland,' he noted in frustration.[116]

The reaction of the western press to the Liberal campaign was predictable. 'Mr. King showed what Liberalism ought to be,' the *Grain Growers' Guide* reported, 'what, theoretically, it is, and it is just because the official Liberal Party failed to measure up to the very standards set by Mr. King that it finds itself very largely a discredited political body. What Mr. King has to say about Liberalism is interesting, and to some extent important, but both the interest and the importance are modified by the degree to which reasoned assent is given to the principles and policies he laid down, by the principal men in his party.'[117] John Dafoe was convinced that, prior to the leadership convention, the party had had no strength in the region, and the situation had not changed: 'Laurier had destroyed it [the party] in 1917 and Mr. King has not been able to revive it.'[118] J.A. Stevenson continued to emphasize Quebec domination: 'What we are going to be in for is pseudo-Liberal administration, of which King may be the nominal head but Gouin will be the moving spirit.'[119]

The federal election of 6 December 1921 proved dismal for Prairie Liberalism. The government of Arthur Meighen was defeated and King's party won office, but it was the first minority government in Canadian history. The electorate returned 116 Liberals, 65 Progressives, 50 Conservatives, 3 Labourites, and 1 independent. Not a single Liberal was elected in Alberta. Motherwell was the sole representative from Saskatchewan, and Manitoba returned only one Liberal as well. The Progressives had swept the Prairie provinces, winning thirty-nine out of a possible forty-three seats, and in doing so denied King the opportunity to form a majority government.

If there had been any doubt as to Quebec's domination of the party before the election, there was none after. For the first time since Confederation, the Liberals won all sixty-five seats in the province. This posed distinct problems for King. While he certainly appreciated the support, his distrust of the Montreal Liberals had only grown during the campaign. Their pressure had altered his desired strategies dealing with coalitions, tariffs, and railways, and, as a result, had diminished his western appeal. He had taken seriously the rumours that Gouin and several others of the group were considering an alliance with the Conservatives. In fact, King had gone so far as to request public expressions of loyalty.[120] Still, the overall battle had been won and the Liberal leader would now have to divide the spoils among his generals.

The Progressive movement had aggressively forced its way onto the national scene, and Mackenzie King would have to deal with the disgruntled West from the prime minister's office. This posed new difficulties. The first of these was the formation of the cabinet. With only a minority government, he had no choice but to turn to the Progressives for support, yet at the same time he had to manage pressures being exerted by the eastern sections of his own party. There was absolutely no possibility of coalition. 'I had thought this out carefully,' King recorded, '& felt a coalition was not in interest of country ... better to face the inevitable at once.'[121] He was confident that the Liberals had won enough seats to proceed without sharing power. If the Progressives wished to be represented in cabinet, they would have to do so as Liberals.[122] King assumed they no longer harboured notions of coalition and were prepared to negotiate upon this basis.[123]

Having rejected coalition, Mackenzie King believed he could still continue his quest for western support. There was no doubt that his dealings with the region had been an eye-opening experience, and some frustration had crept into his original optimism. Indeed, this sentiment had been displayed in a letter to his brother just twelve days prior to the election: 'This wretched Progressive movement will alone be responsible for the failure to secure a really effective democratic government in the next parliament, should such prove to be a consequence of the divisions in the three-cornered contests. You will observe that I am beginning to deal a little more sharply with this aspect of affairs.'[124] But while his frustration was mounting, compromise remained the logical strategy. Until he won the Progressives back to Liberalism, the position of the party, not to mention his own leadership, remained precarious. An alliance with the Prairies was essential for future political success. His sympathies with the region remained, and he swore not to allow 'the West to become isolated.' His goal would still be an 'alliance with the rural elements as the solid foundation of the Liberal party through the years to come.' The government of Mackenzie King would count on 'the people' rather than 'the interests' while working to eliminate the notions of 'East and West.'[125]

When it came to cabinet formation, the Progressive leaders were invited into the government but the influence of the eastern members could not be ignored. Ontario Liberals had been engaged in both provincial and federal battles with the Farmers' movement and were in no mood for generous treatment. A Liberal faction from Quebec City, led by Ernest Lapointe, Jacques Bureau, and Henri Béland, was flexible in its attitude on the tariff and favoured accommodating the Progressives. The Montreal Liberals, led by Sir Lomer Gouin, Walter Mitchell, and Rodolphe Lemieux, were associated with financial, transportation, and industrial enterprises, and were much less willing to compromise.[126]

The preliminary cabinet list drawn up by King and Andrew Haydon was undoubtedly an attempt to reach out westward and included T.A. Crerar, A.B. Hudson, W.R. Motherwell, and D.M. Marshall to represent the Prairies. It leaned heavily toward the agrarian interests and low-tariff Liberals. King wanted to convince the Progressives that their presence would counterbalance that of the strong protectionists – Gouin, R. Dandurand, W.C. Kennedy, and W.S. Fielding. On 9 December he was prepared to make his first overtures to the Progressives, and Crerar was invited to meet Haydon in Winnipeg. Before that meeting could take place, King met with Lapointe, who indicated that Gouin would be hostile to the idea of bringing in the Progressives and that the only way to succeed would be to provide the Montreal group with more influential posts than first intended. If King wanted to absorb the Progressives, therefore, he had to provide the Montreal faction with extra incentives. King wished to strike a deal with the agrarian leaders as quickly as possible to strengthen his position vis-à-vis the Gouin group.

Four meetings took place between Haydon and Crerar. The Liberal emissary made it clear from the outset that the Progressive leaders were needed in cabinet to 'free' the government from the 'domination by the Montreal interests and any reactionary influences' within the Liberal party. Cabinet positions, Crerar responded, would not be enough to placate the West: 'measures' were more important than 'men.' The discussion then turned to matters of policy, with Crerar and Hudson putting forward a list of conditions that reflected the usual western concerns – tariffs, resources, freight rates, and railways. Crerar wanted four cabinet positions given to the Prairies, including one Progressive from Alberta, and he proposed that Hudson receive the influential justice portfolio. He also pronounced on the acceptability of King's preliminary cabinet list: Motherwell was unsatisfactory; C.M. Hamilton should be the Saskatchewan representative; Charles Stewart should represent Alberta. Before any deal was finalized, Crerar indicated that he would have to meet with his western followers, a meeting scheduled for 20 December in Saskatoon.

On 14 December Haydon received King's response to the Progressive proposals. The tariff could be adjusted according to the proposed Liberal amendment to the 1921 budget; that is, the government would repudiate the principle of protection and call for a reduction in the costs of living and implements of production. Negotiations for the resources transfer would be commenced, but the discontinuance of the annual dominion subsidy in lieu of the resources would be part of the settlement. The questions of freight rates, reciprocity, and railways would be considered, but no commitment was given. Finally, King was not prepared to consider more than one minister for each of the western provinces.[127] Motherwell would have to represent Saskatchewan, and both Hudson and Crerar from Manitoba could enter the cabinet if the Alberta Progressives would give one of them a seat.

After consulting with the Manitoba Progressives a third time, Haydon informed King that they were not satisfied. The tariff amendment was 'altogether too indefinite to make progress.' Substantial general reductions and a free list of agricultural implements, extended according to the Liberal platform, were required. The freight rates remained a 'burning question' and were of 'vital importance.'[128] The resource question would require a transfer and settlement to replace the subsidy. The Prairies deserved four positions in cabinet because future redistribution would provide the region with more seats.

King believed 'Crerar was making a mistake and asking too much ... that he should have faith in men proposed [and] not exact conditions.'[129] There would be no further concessions. 'Can only consider taking representation from Progressive party into cabinet on same basis as representation from ranks of Liberals,' King wired Haydon.[130] The

Liberal leader was under immense pressure from the Quebec members, and time was running out. He advised Haydon, Crerar, and Hudson to come to Ottawa immediately. While Crerar agreed, he indicated he first had to receive the support of the Saskatoon gathering. King responded that he could not wait until 24 December when Crerar would arrive, and he arranged for Hudson to come without delay. Premier Drury of Ontario would also come to Ottawa. Along with Hudson, they would receive the telegraphed report of the Saskatoon proceedings from Crerar.

Mackenzie King was confident the western negotiations were proceeding well, but before any Progressive delegation could depart for Ottawa, pressure was exerted on Crerar, Drury, and Hudson that would dramatically alter their negotiating position. On 17 December Crerar met with J.W. Dafoe to review the week's developments. The *Free Press* editor had been confident that unless King offered coalition there would be no chance of the Progressive leaders even contemplating entering the cabinet. Sir Clifford Sifton agreed with Dafoe that the Progressives would have to refuse King's attempts at absorption and leave him to 'the Liberal antiques who are now congregating at Ottawa.' They were suspicious of the new prime minister's overtures and argued that the result would be an eastern-dominated government: 'The Liberal party would in effect be a Quebec and Nova Scotia party with a Rump from the rest of the Provinces ... They should sit at the head table and the Farmers organization should take whatever crumbs that are offered to them.'[131] By refusing to join the cabinet without coalition, the Progressives would maintain their identity and soon become the vanguard of liberal ideas.

Dafoe was consequently surprised to learn that the Progressive leaders were considering entering King's cabinet without the guarantee of a coalition.[132] He immediately set out to follow Sifton's advice of forming a united front and warning them of the dangers. 'Once they are in without anything more definite than that,' Sifton wrote Dafoe, 'the Progressive party as a political force comes to an end.'[133] Without a coalition he predicted that 'the Progressives will share the fate of the Liberals who went into the Union Government, with the absolute certainty that if the Progressive movement stays alive the followers will turn upon the leaders who have gone into the Government and regard them as having betrayed their principles.'

The pressure on Crerar mounted when Drury indicated in a telegram that he had come to the same conclusion and did not believe his following would allow him to enter the cabinet: 'Am of opinion that for sake of future progressives should guard against absorption by liberals. If alliance or coalition formed should be conditional on King professedly accepting fundamental parts of progressive platform and leaving Gouin bloc out of Cabinet. This I think he is prepared to do – political continuity of progressives should also be assured. Fear I cannot accept invitation.'[134] The Progressive strategy once again turned to seeking a coalition, and Hudson set out to convey the terms to King. On 20 December, at the same time Crerar was meeting with his supporters in Saskatoon, Hudson would be arriving in Ottawa.

The pressure on Mackenzie King in the meantime was aimed more at altering the cabinet slate than preventing the Progressives' entry.[135] There was actually less resistance to the Farmers than first anticipated.[136] The problem for King was that proposed changes to the slate were altering the intended low-tariff complexion of the cabinet and jeopardizing the Progressive negotiations. There was 'a very real danger that the original "purity" of this body which had seemed so attractive to Western eyes, would become gravely compromised and the Progressive leaders would then find it increasingly difficult to enter the Cabinet themselves or to justify their entrance to their followers.'[137] King wanted to cement an agreement for the entry of the Progressives before his bargaining position was placed in jeopardy by eastern pressure. Prior discussions with Drury had indicated that the Ontario premier had a strong interest in joining the cabinet, and King was as yet unaware that Drury's position was changing. The question of a coalition, raised by the premier, was rejected by King: 'Once he spoke of Progressive–Lib. alliance, but I was emphatic in saying that it must be straight Liberal Govt.'[138] The question, as far as King was concerned, had been laid to rest.

On 19 December Haydon arrived in Ottawa and, ignorant of the recent changes in the Progressive position, he provided an optimistic report. The Prairies would have to be given four ministers, though Motherwell could probably be included in this group. Even if Crerar refused to enter the cabinet, it appeared Hudson would come in. There was no knowledge that the coalition proposal had re-emerged as a factor or that Drury had decided to stay out. The situation looked positive, and King was proud of his efforts to battle the eastern interests and ensure Prairie representation: 'Haydon says my attitude was a surprise to the Western men, they never really believed I could be other than with the "big interests."'[139]

On 20 December, with the arrival of Hudson in Ottawa, the coalition question was suddenly thrust to the forefront of the negotiations. Crerar had received the support of the Saskatoon meeting as long as a coalition was formed. King was surprised and disconcerted by the sudden reemergence of the issue. He told Hudson that he could not contemplate coalition, that the Progressives would have to enter the cabinet as Liberals. If they refused, it would create a 'serious' situation of having the West unrepresented. It was preferable to 'accept the verdict of the people than "bastardize" the Liberal Party.'[140] Alberta Liberals Frank Oliver and Charles Stewart were consulted later that day and emphatically opposed a coalition. The next day the Liberal–Progressive negotiations were further threatened when Drury arrived from Toronto to inform King that his followers had refused to release him from provincial responsibilities until after the next election. The Ontario premier reaffirmed his support for coalition but also suggested to King that Crerar and Hudson should enter the cabinet regardless.

By noon of 21 December it appeared that King's desire to bring the Progressives into cabinet had failed, but the situation improved when a telegram arrived from Crerar that provided his version of the Saskatoon meeting. The western Progressive members had decided unanimously to retain their identity as a party and give independent support to 'progressive' legislation, but the meeting had also given 'tacit approval' for any Progressive member to enter the government.[141] Crerar would meet with the Progressive MPs from Ontario on his way to Ottawa. King was optimistic 'the Rubicon has been crossed and that the gulf between East and West has been bridged.' He was relieved when Hudson indicated that the tariff should not present any obstacles and the issues of main concern were the railway rates and the natural resources: 'I don't think the latter will be difficult of solution, the former may be hard to do in terms but can be done in Council. – Hudson said Tariff was a matter of attitude.'[142]

On 24 December the leaders of the Liberal and Progressive parties met for the first time since the election. King was confident he deserved western support due to his refusal to bow to Montreal pressure.[143] King presented Crerar with the offer to join the cabinet as a Liberal: 'I said that to promote national unity & inspire confidence and good will ... I was willing to consider taking into the cabinet representatives of the movement, himself and others he might name, but would be prepared to do so only on the understanding that they came into a Liberal Government on the same basis as others invited. I would not discuss coalition, nor on line of policy.' Crerar refused. Once again the situation had changed. In Toronto he had met with his members from Ontario and had found them to be unanimously opposed to the entrance of any Progressive. 'Crerar met me quite frankly,' King recorded, 'by saying that he would like to come in, he thought it would be the right thing to do from one point of view ... [but] he now felt he was not free to come for the present at least ... He hoped that it would be possible to come in a little later, that if I would keep this in mind he also would & would do all he could to bring the Lib's & Progressives together in the House.'

Crerar tried to reassure King that, despite his party's refusal to join the Liberals, it did not intend to become the official opposition. It would maintain its identity as a party and provide the government independent support so long as the legislation was progressive. King argued that the West would be left out of the councils of government, and he ushered a veiled threat: with no Progressives in cabinet it would be more difficult to offer incentives to the west. Nonetheless, he was confident that the Farmer cause would 'suffer' and its followers would be absorbed into Liberal ranks.[144]

In the end, western representation was left to Motherwell and Stewart, but neither was capable of filling the role of western lieutenant. Stewart had lost in Alberta, and a 'safe' seat would have to be found in Quebec. King would have preferred a Manitoba representative, leaving Alberta isolated for its failure to elect any Liberals: 'We were under no obligation to give Alberta representat'n. She must accept situation as she had made it.'[145] Crerar was not pleased to learn that since the Winnipeg negotiations the cabinet slate had been considerably altered. Low-tariff men such as Marshall, McMaster, Drury, Hudson, and himself were out, and Graham, Lemieux, and McKenzie were in. Clifford Sifton was under the impression that King had been more prepared to adhere to Crerar's cabinet suggestions, but 'the Montreal element had got to work ... and practically put the pistol to Mr. King's head, forcing an alteration of King's proposed list of Members.'[146]

The 1921 cabinet negotiations were critical for Mackenzie King's relationship with the Prairie West. Although they failed, they had been doomed from the beginning, and, as Norman Lambert, the secretary of the Canadian Council of Agriculture, noted, 'blame cannot be fairly placed on the head of Mr. King or Mr. Crerar.'[147] While both King and Crerar believed the other should have been stronger in commanding his following and more willing to compromise in his negotiations with the other party, both were negotiating from positions of weakness. If not for eastern pressure King would have attempted a coalition before the election. When this pre-election coalition appeared unacceptable to the Progressives, he worked to win a straight Liberal government. Having only a minority government, he sought to have Progressives in the cabinet, but would not consider a coalition. Likewise, the Progressives were not prepared to surrender their position after the election. It was Sifton and Dafoe who correctly analysed the reaction of the Progressives. Crerar, Hudson, and Drury had all been prepared to enter the cabinet as Liberals. Crerar interpreted the meeting at Saskatoon as giving him 'tacit approval' to enter the government, but it is doubtful he could have carried the Alberta group. The attitude of the Ontario Farmers toward King and cooperation, never mind coalition, had been manifest as early as the Stormont-Glengarry by-election in 1919: 'We intend to fight every election that comes across. The farmers here have nothing whatever to do with the aspirations of Mackenzie King as representative of the farmers.'[148]

The negotiations did, however, demonstrate some positive signs for King's party on the Prairies. The Progressive leadership had indicated a willingness to enter the cabinet as Liberals if western issues were satisfactorily addressed. While King had failed to absorb the movement, he was aware that the opportunity still existed and could be pursued in the future. The new prime minister believed he had demonstrated his sympathies with the Prairie West and had gone as far as possible to have the region represented. His government now depended on Progressive support, and this fact alone would ensure that these attentions continued. But the failure of the negotiations left the West feeling dissatisfied and at the mercy of Quebec. From Montreal, Kirk Cameron wrote Crerar: 'The general opinion here is that our friend King has delivered himself into the hands of the Montreal crowd that from now on, they will control the whole situation.' The western response to King's efforts was mixed. He had demonstrated an 'attempt at a rapprochement' but had 'not had the courage and strength to carry it through.'[149] If he had offered a coalition and policy assurances to the Progressives, he would have largely solidified the region. He would have lost the Gouin group and strengthened his own leadership, but Quebec would not have abandoned the Liberals altogether because there was nowhere else to turn. The province certainly would not have embraced Meighen's Tories, and there was no sign of turning to a nationalist group. Until Mackenzie King rid his government of the Laurier leftovers and demonstrated he was not the puppet of Quebec, his position in the West would remain weak.

3

Belling the Cat, 1922–1924

Those members of the Liberal party who found themselves more or less in
sympathy with the views held by the Progressives ... told King ... that if he did not
'get' Sir Lomer it was only a question of time until Sir Lomer would 'get' him.
They told King that it was quite obvious that Sir Lomer Gouin regarded himself
as the real head of the administration ... There is a possibility of a definite
understanding being reached between the Government and the Progressives ...
Gouin's disappearance from the government and from parliament is, I understand, the first essential ... I don't think King has the courage to 'bell the cat.'

J.W. Dafoe to Clifford Sifton, 11 July 1922

As prime minister, Mackenzie King would have his western sympathies,
whether genuine or contrived, put to the test, and he would be expected
to turn rhetoric into action. It would not be enough to point to the
platform of 1919 as evidence of Liberal concern for Prairie issues. He
would have to walk the political tightrope. Thus far the balancing act had
entailed catering to Quebec while maintaining at least the possibility of
gaining western support. Now it would necessitate a more aggressive
stance on western issues. The problem was that King's position was far
from secure. The eastern elements that dominated the party viewed the
Progressives with a mixture of distrust and contempt. Although the
westerners had refused the mantle of opposition, they held the balance
of power in Parliament. They in turn viewed the eastern Liberals with
suspicion. To convince the West that the government was not dominated
by Quebec, Mackenzie King would have to exert more of an influence in

his own party. The situation was aptly summed up by Andrew Haydon in a letter to King:

> The Party cannot live in the long future unless it can hold the West. It will continue to hold the East. The holding of one end of the country and losing the other is just the opposite to a national viewpoint and real Canadianism, which after all is the only thing worth fighting for. I know how strongly you feel this way. I take the liberty of suggesting that you might show a bit of 'the big stick' in some of these things. Macdonald was Master of his Administration. Laurier was very much so. You have to be also.[1]

Many questioned whether King's leadership could withstand the test of time needed to bring the Prairies on side and thereby counter the eastern influences. T.A. Crerar did not doubt that King was sympathetic to the West but thought he lacked the 'strength of purpose.' The prime minister did not seem prepared to risk losing some of his eastern support to make western gains. 'To my mind,' Crerar noted,

> Gouin is the boss of the administration. He gives the impression of having great reserve power ... he sits in his seat, with his square head and determined jaw, alert and keen, he impresses you as a man of strong purpose and determined will. His outlook on public life is the outlook of the Montreal financial transportation and manufacturing interests ... It seems certain that the situation cannot last any great length of time. The Government is divided and there are evidences of a cleavage behind it.[2]

The prime minister was well aware of his precarious situation: he would have to tread carefully. Talk of ousting him had temporarily subsided, and Gouin had issued a declaration early in the parliamentary session that 'the Liberal party has one chief and one chief only.'[3] The statement of loyalty was belated but appreciated nonetheless by a nervous King. He would have to tolerate Gouin's influence and patiently deflect his threats of resignation when government decisions were unfavourable. King hoped Gouin's following would gradually decline and be replaced by the younger and more liberal members from Quebec including Lapointe, Power, McMaster, and Cannon. Still, many in the party remained unimpressed with King's leadership and suspicious of his sympathy to the Progressives.

The prime minister's problems were not confined to divisions between eastern Liberals and western Progressives. Even after the election, the

Laurier and Unionist factions across the Prairies remained bitterly divided. King recognized the Free Press group of the Manitoba Liberals as the official party and continued to show his distaste for the Diehards. 'I regret that some of our friends in Manitoba,' he wrote, 'do not seem to appreciate that by divisions in our ranks we may never expect to make any progress. We have come to a day when reconciliation and not recrimination must be the rule.'[4] Premier Norris, meanwhile, informed King that a provincial convention held in April had been 'a wonderful success.' The premier naively indicated that the gathering had 'successfully ironed out any difficulties that may have developed between the two wings of the Liberal party.'[5] The defeat of the Norris government at the hands of the United Farmers a short time later would come as no surprise to anyone familiar with Manitoba Liberalism. Provincial Liberals, in their attempts to walk the line between the federal party and the Farmers, had ended up alienating both.

In Alberta cooperation between Liberals and Progressives remained impossible. The Liberals refused to believe the Progressives could be absorbed and instead awaited their anticipated disintegration. They blamed the up-start movement for their province's miserable showing in the federal election. 'The farmers were simply fanatical on class representation and have succeeded in isolating the West,' one angry party member told King. But already party officials were claiming to have noticed 'a great accession to the [Liberal] party ranks since Election Day.'[6] They attempted to assure the new prime minister that the province could be won back. '"Father Forgive them, they know not what they did,"' H.H. Christie wrote. 'The western farmer is driven to almost any insane act ... He is unaccountable for his actions at present.'[7]

Prairie Liberals desperately sought a means to revive their party. The 'ethnic' communities of the region seemed logical bases of support, albeit ones that required more attention. The immigration boom fostered under Laurier had given the party a strong foundation in the resulting communities. The disfranchisement of 'enemy aliens' by Meighen and the Union government had only increased the anti-Tory sentiment. 'There is no doubt at all that the large foreign elements in Western Canada are and ought to be Liberal,' Manitoba's E.J. McMurray informed the prime minister. He claimed these people were 'more Liberal in the true sense of the term than any other section of the country ... These elements are the first to be won to us and gradually we can win the West over.'[8] They were 'by instinct' Liberal and 'deeply attached' to Laurier, whom they looked upon 'as the Moses who brought them out of the wilderness to the land of promise.'⁹ Mackenzie King shared this perception, and the ethnic groups on the Prairies were further subject to his romanticization:

> While dictating [enroute by train from Prince Albert to North Battleford during the 1920 western tour] I heard a band at one of the stations and on going to the platform found a number of Ruthenian settlers, about 70 or thereabouts who had come to the train to serenade. One of them told me that they had all been deprived of their votes last election, but would be solidly Liberal once given the vote again. One feels the ludicrousness of that kind of autocratic behaviour towards these pioneer settlers on the plains – pure Prussianism, nothing more. This was quite a touching scene in the small isolated village on the plains, snow flying & winter approaching with all its dreariness.¹⁰

Western Liberals were also very concerned about the lack of a Liberal press and organization. In Saskatchewan, where the provincial Progressives had been neutralized as an effective alternative, Liberals blamed their poor electoral showing on internal party divisions and inefficient organization. 'The destructive force has come from within ourselves,' western Liberal J.G. Turgeon claimed. 'It is the result of decay, which in return is the result of lack of activity.' Liberal organization had never been strong in the West, but the creation of the Union government had caused it to be 'absolutely cut off.'¹¹ King listened to the western calls for a Liberal press, and while he agreed with the necessity, he too believed 'organization is our real weakness.' Finances to establish western newspapers could not be contemplated when the western branches of the party had insufficient funds even to support the national headquarters of the party.¹² He blamed the region's 'lack of organization' on its 'looking to Ottawa' and the federal party.¹³ Mackenzie King would become infamous for his shifting the burden of organization onto others and then blaming them for its failings.

For the government to survive, Liberal overtures to the Progressives had to be resumed immediately. 'The hope of the future of Liberalism in Canada,' King told J.R. Boyle, 'lies in the West ... It is inevitable that we should lose some of our following in Eastern Canada as the years go by and what is lost in the East must be more than overtaken in the West.'¹⁴ Long before the House met, the prime minister and his party worked to gain indirect assurances of support from Progressive members. Less than a fortnight after being named minister of finance, W.S. Fielding wrote to

Crerar requesting the western position on the government's program. The Progressive leader replied with a list of Prairie concerns: reductions in the tariff and freight rates, reforms in the banking system, transfer of natural resources to the Prairie provinces, reciprocity with the United States, consolidation of the government-owned railways, and others. Fielding's 'desire for co-operation' would prove to be a token effort.[15] The two men differed to such an extent on the tariff issue that the possibility of the gesture having any substantial impact on ensuing policy was unlikely.

When Parliament opened on 8 March 1922 the Progressives sat on the speaker's left, providing a fair indication of their political leaning. Mackenzie King was fairly confident he had their 'good will,'[16] but continued support would depend upon the government's record, and in particular its adherence to the platform of 1919. The Progressives expected the Liberals to falter and King to justify the failure through having to satisfy eastern protectionists. Many Progressives wished to see such a crisis divide the party and purge it of these 'conservative' influences. 'Governments often become more conservative in office, but I never knew one which became more radical,' J.W. Dafoe mused. 'The Liberal Government at Ottawa has got to move a long distance to the left before it can make any worthwhile appeal for support in Western Canada.'[17]

It was not long before the difficulty in appeasing both the Montreal Liberals and western Progressives surfaced. In April, Ontario Liberal Andrew McMaster introduced a motion to prevent cabinet ministers from holding directorships in business corporations. The policy would find sympathy with the Progressives, who wished to see politics purged of its corporate interests, as well as many Liberals who had initiated the same motion a year earlier while in opposition. The chief offender this time was Sir Lomer Gouin, who held directorships in fourteen major corporations.[18] The King government voted against the motion and found itself in the uncomfortable position of being aligned with the Tories against the Progressives. The incident confirmed western suspicions that the Liberals were just as subservient as the Conservatives to the 'big interests.' It also demonstrated that, when forced to choose, King would cling to his Quebec supporters and sacrifice his professed principles. For the prime minister it was a no-win situation. In the end he had helped defeat the motion, but Gouin, and the party in general, had been embarrassed nonetheless. 'I seem to have run counter to or offended the Montreal group at practically every turn,' King brooded. 'First one then another, the very men I must do my utmost to placate. I have little hope of being able to hold them, they do not *belong* to the Liberal Party, but I do not want to give them cause for complaint or offense.'[19] His need to strengthen his leadership, when combined with his political philosophy and Prairie sympathies, pushed him in one direction while his instincts for survival pushed him in another. If the storm could be weathered, King believed he could consolidate his position in the future. Gouin's influence, like that of the Progressives, would have to be neutralized. Dafoe was doubtful, meanwhile, that King had the courage to 'bell the cat.'[20]

Although the program of the new government was directed at many western issues, it did not go far enough to satisfy the region. The wheat board remained a contentious topic, but for most Canadians it was a local Prairie issue that would result in higher prices for flour and bread. Crerar, who was philosophically opposed to compulsory marketing, recognized the pressure from the West and pressed the new government to re-establish the board on a permanent basis.[21] The prime minister, responding to a recommendation of the Commons' Agriculture Committee, introduced enabling legislation allowing any two of the Prairie provinces to establish their own wheat marketing agency.

King's early career with the Department of Labour had seen him advocating a stronger role for the state in the economy.[22] The idea of a wheat board also played into his sympathy for the individual farmer as opposed to the speculators, such as the Winnipeg Grain Exchange: 'There is no doubt that Western farmers [are] at the mercy of speculators & it is a national duty to save them from such a crisis.'[23] Yet, as with so many of his approaches to Prairie issues, ignorance and caution precluded strong action. Mackenzie King knew nothing about the wheat business and was not prepared to pursue an aggressive policy that would ensure the re-establishment of a board. In the end, Alberta and Saskatchewan passed legislation to set up their own board but Manitoba refused to join them. The more easterly province experienced an earlier harvest and the grain moved soon enough for the farmers to take advantage of the new crop prices. The Alberta–Saskatchewan scheme collapsed completely when no competent or willing individual could be found to run the agency.[24] For the next ten years the government's role in the grain industry was 'played in low key.'[25]

The King government also introduced legislation that proposed a cautious immigration policy and urged the United Kingdom to lift the cattle embargo, both of which found support with the Progressives. The Liberals could not, however, adopt a satisfactory course on the crucial issues of natural resources, railways, tariffs, and freight rates. The wheat board could be delayed due to division among the Prairie provinces; the same could not be said for these other regional concerns.

Mackenzie King had promised immediate action on the transfer of the Prairie provinces' natural resources. King admitted that the western provinces had 'a certain moral claim,' and noted that Canada as a whole was benefiting at the expense of the region. There was no doubt that, in principle, control of natural resources resided with the provinces. The problem lay in ironing out a compensation package. As far as the federal government was concerned, any agreement would also have to consider that the Prairie provinces had benefited from previous Dominion expenditures.[26] King met with all three provincial delegations in April, but by the second meeting in November he realized each would have to be handled separately. Their situations were simply too different.

In April the Manitoba delegation had been led by T.C. Norris; by November the premier's office was occupied by John Bracken of the United Farmers of Manitoba (UFM). Bracken, who was not a politician by nature, had been reluctant to accept the premiership in the wake of the UFM election victory. Prior to being vaulted into politics, he had been the principal of the Manitoba Agricultural College. His approach as premier would be pragmatic, non-partisan, and businesslike. While in office the Norris government had agreed to attempt a negotiated settlement of the natural resources issue. If this proved impossible, arbitration would be requested. In April Premier Norris had made it clear that the dominion would not be let off the hook merely by balancing receipts and expenditures from Crown lands. Manitoba had become a province thirty-five years prior to Saskatchewan and Alberta, and it demanded compensation for this period. Much of the province's lands had already been used by Ottawa, and Norris would not ignore the 'indirect abundant fiscal returns from its immigration and free homestead policy.'[27]

In November, the Bracken government submitted a basis of adjustment that included the return of the unalienated resources and the continuance of the subsidy in compensation for lands already alienated for dominion purposes. The proposal was rejected by King, and the federal government then advanced several of its own methods of adjustment. Manitoba would receive its unalienated resources and a cash payment possibly totalling two or three years of the subsidy, but the subsidy itself would be discontinued. Another federal proposal included the discontinuance of the subsidy, the return of the unalienated resources, and an accounting of receipts and expenditures in respect of dominion lands, as well as a consideration of certain alienations of land made for purposes outside the province. None of these proposals were acceptable to Manitoba. Because the two parties lacked enough common ground to go to arbitration, the possibility of referring the question to the Judicial Committee of the Privy Council was raised.[28]

The prime minister also dealt with a new premier when it came time to negotiate with Saskatchewan. Martin's stance against the Progressives in the federal election campaign paved the way for his departure from the premier's office. On 5 April he was succeeded by a former Grain Grower and manager of the Saskatchewan Co-operative Elevator Company. Although a Liberal, Charles Dunning was popular with the Farmers and ensured that cooperation would remain the strategy at the provincial level. The new premier praised Ottawa for setting the precedent of at least meeting with the Prairie delegations and, more importantly, in admitting that the resource issue had to be settled without reference to the eastern provinces. In the past, he noted, 'the Prairie Provinces have been placed in the position of, in reality negotiating with the other Provinces of Canada.' Discussions with previous governments had been complicated by claims that any new conditions offered the West would entitle the East to compensation. King hoped to avoid this stumbling block by having the Prairie provinces surrender their subsidy. He argued that whatever gains the dominion government had received from the western lands were fully balanced by the costs expended in their management.[29] Dunning disagreed. The return of the unalienated resources would not be compensation for what had already been lost. Prince Edward Island had entered Confederation with its public domain already alienated, and as a result received a subsidy as well as its resources.[30] The premier did admit that at present the dominion was paying more for the administration of Saskatchewan's resources than it was receiving in revenue. As a result, while the province wished to be rid of its 'colonial status,' it was not as anxious as Manitoba and Alberta for the transfer. 'That is the serious part of the whole situation,' King wrote. 'The Dominion is being taxed in perpetuity, a subsidy which will continue to increase, & has reached the point where it is costing more to administer than to give up control.'[31]

The United Farmers had taken office in Alberta in 1921 under Herbert Greenfield. The premier generally agreed with the positions taken by Manitoba and Saskatchewan. The value of the alienated resources, even including that prior to 1905, could not be overlooked. He suggested the appointment of an independent tribunal to establish an accounting.

Although King responded with the same proposal offered Manitoba, including the equivalent of three years' subsidy, Greenfield was not satisfied. Despite the desire of the Alberta government to gain control . over coal and oil deposits, no agreement could be reached.[32]

Prime Minister King was relatively sympathetic to the Prairie positions on the resource issue, but from the outset opposition appeared in the forms of Gouin and Fielding, who resisted all proposals for western compensation. When the cabinet discussed the matter in April, King recorded that he 'could get nowhere with Fielding who is like a dog in the manger ... You would think Alberta was out to rob N.S.' The prime minister was 'exasperated' during the November meetings when some members of the cabinet reversed their positions on promises made in April. Gouin was 'obdurate' and 'all for postponing, doing nothing etc. ... I pointed out their attitude was putting me in a false light and I was unwilling to be "humiliated" by any going back on what had already been agreed.' The issue became so heated that a potential breach appeared in the cabinet. As King recorded, 'I opened fire pretty strongly ... I said I wd not stand for procedure of that kind, would follow out pledges given the electorate in good faith or leave it to others to carry on the Government, if individuals could not agree with policy decided upon they could withdraw from Government. It was the farthest I have gone at any time.'[33] It was becoming apparent that either King or Gouin would have to go, and it would likely be a western issue that would spark the powder keg.

The old problem of railways seemed a good possibility. During the war a number of rail lines had been threatened by bankruptcy; as a result the government was forced to take over thousands of miles of track. Legislation had been passed in 1919 authorizing the operation of these lines as one system but, when the Meighen government left office, no action had yet been taken. Although the Liberals had endorsed nationalization of the Grand Trunk in their platform, they hesitated taking action. The public generally favoured nationalization, with support strongest on the Prairies. The CPR feared the competition of a government-backed rival and had placed its confidence and powerful support in the Montreal bloc of the Liberal party. King, however, was determined to use the railway issue to distance himself from the domination of the CPR and the Gouin group, to portray his own convictions and sympathy toward the Progressives, and to demonstrate his adherence to platform pledges. He hoped that by forming one large system under the same management, the national railway could be competitive. Despite lukewarm support in both cabinet and the House, in the end Parliament passed the legislation to form a government-owned transcontinental rail system.

The other rail issue of concern to the West was the fabled Hudson Bay line. Some Prairie farmers, most particularly in Saskatchewan, had long dreamed of a direct link to the bay as a shorter and cheaper route in moving their goods to port. Proponents of the scheme, including W.R. Motherwell, argued that the line would not only save on transportation costs, it would eliminate monopoly evils, avoid losses accrued in shipping grain over foreign rail from Buffalo to New York City, encourage rural immigration, develop resources, and hasten the return of prosperity to the West.

The desire for the rail link went back to the earliest days of settlement. When the Dominion Lands Act was originally drawn up, it contained a provision for a grant to ensure the construction of such a line. Laurier had pledged his support to the project in 1908 and construction was started, only to be suspended in 1911 when the Tories came to power. After an investigation into the feasibility of the route, construction was recommenced. In 1917 the demands of war once again halted the process and the project had remained on hold ever since.

The King government had to proceed cautiously with the issue to avoid complaints from the other regions that the West was being offered preferential treatment. Easterners were quick to denounce the 'romantic' and 'extravagant' project as 'simply throwing good money after bad.'[34] Westerners responded that a conspiracy hatched by Ottawa and the CPR was intent on maintaining western traffic over the main lines. The government was voting yearly amounts to be spent on maintaining and repairing the existing track but no new construction was being undertaken.

The real test for the King government would be tariff policy. Westerners were not optimistic when W.S. Fielding was appointed to finance. Their judgment proved correct, as he continued to guide policy along the path he himself had set in the Laurier government from 1896 to 1911. Despite the prime minister's assertion that protection was a 'mistaken policy in nat'l interest,'[35] Fielding clung to conventional fiscal principles and espoused balanced budgets through increased revenue from tariffs and new taxes. While he sounded out possibilities for reciprocity with the United States and opened trade negotiations with a number of countries, changes to the tariff were to be insubstantial.

The free trade Liberals were actually forced onto the defensive when Fielding brought down the budget of 1922. 'If the Budget is to be regarded as the final attitude on the trade question of the Liberal party,' Andrew McMaster observed in an obvious search for justifications, 'it is absolutely unsatisfactory. If it is to be regarded merely as the first movement towards lower tariffs, to be followed without undue delay by other movements in the same direction, it can be accepted and defended.' Fielding's budget reflected the dominant position held by the high-tariff Liberals. 'We must frankly recognize the fact,' the finance minister informed King, 'that in matters relating to the tariff there is much difference of opinion, I might even say conflict of opinion, within the ranks of our own friends.' The already suspicious and sceptical Progressives were provided ample ammunition with Gouin's statement that he advocated 'a reasonable measure of protection' and Fielding's indication that he had never approved of the tariff section of the 1919 platform.[36] The divisions within Liberal ranks and the deviations from the platform forced the prime minister to argue that the convention of 1919 did not actually bind the party to an immediate set of pledges; rather, it served instead as a chart that set the direction. King once told journalist Bruce Hutchison that detailed platforms were objectionable because they 'gave the other fellow something to shoot at.' According to Hutchison, the prime minister 'had reduced his platform to a series of resounding generalities which the most skilled marksman could not hope to hit.'[37] Once more the Progressives were witness to the Liberal party wavering on clearly outlined promises, and as usual it seemed to be the western issues that were expendable.

Freight rates also remained a central issue for the West in 1922, especially in the face of declining wheat prices and the return of Australia and Argentina to the market. The need for a declared policy on the Crow's Nest Pass Agreement dropped the sensitive issue directly onto the lap of the King government. The special rates on western grain and flour, and on a number of eastern miscellaneous commodities, had been suspended in 1919 for three years by order-in-council. They would become operative again on 7 July 1922 unless Parliament intervened. Yet the issue would produce inevitable controversy, providing the opportunity to raise other rate grievances held in check by the war. It was readily apparent that a more equitable rate structure was required, but to accomplish this without jeopardizing the financial position of the railways was next to impossible. Moreover, any reductions of Prairie rates would also reopen rate grievances in the Maritimes and British Columbia.

King knew little about railway issues and even less about freight rates.

He entered the debate armed only with his romantic sympathy for the western farmer, his distrust of the CPR, and his desire to bolster his position against the railway's ally – the Gouin bloc. After discussing the issue with Sir Clifford Sifton on 8 April, he became convinced that the Crow's Nest rates should be restored. The situation seemed one more example of eastern financial interests manipulating the Prairie producer, and King realized the political harvests to be reaped through a settlement. His standing would improve in the West and the Progressives would be weakened. 'I believe in letting the Railway lose some of their profits & help along the consumers,' he recorded in his diary. 'I favour the Crow's Nest agreement coming into effect and will work to that end.'[38] This sentiment was voiced in Parliament on 4 May: 'I have been through the Canadian West on two or three occasions of late, and I may say frankly that I have been impressed with the absolute necessity for a reduction in freight rates if that part of our Dominion is to develop as it should.'[39]

Party divisions, along with King's insecure leadership, led the prime minister to avoid the controversial subject as long as possible. The speech from the throne barely mentioned the question. Like so many others, the issue divided the Liberals into two camps, with the Montreal bloc and its allies generally favouring the CPR position and the others supporting reimplementation of the agreement. The cabinet decided to ask the House to refer the question to a special committee, which could hear testimony from the railroad executives as well as other interested parties. King expected the committee to recommend a restoration of the rates even though he had allowed several Liberals to be placed there who favoured the CPR position.[40] Westerners, always suspicious of the CPR and its inordinate influence, were not so confident. 'I expect the Crow's Nest Pass business to put a chasm between the Liberals and the Progressives which will never be bridged,' J.W. Dafoe wrote Clifford Sifton. 'I thought King's speech in Parliament supporting the motion for a committee rather significant as indicating his preference for what he calls a broad national view, but which is in reality nothing but acceptance of the C.P.R. contention.'[41]

The committee rejected a Progressive proposal for the revival of the rates and instead approved a report favourable to the railways. Intent on fighting until the bitter end, the Progressives prolonged the session well past the 7 July deadline. The cabinet erupted into a battleground between the King and Gouin factions. The committee was recalled on the pretext of receiving new evidence, resulting in an amended report. The agreement was to be suspended for another year, except for the section on grain and flour rates, and it would be possible to extend the suspension an additional year if desirable. The railway commission in due course ordered a reduction in rates on a number of basic commodities. Mackenzie King had won a victory, but he soon learned that gains for the West were being credited to the western Progressives. The 'impression' was that the partial acceptance of the Crow's Nest rates had been offered 'reluctantly,' and only due to the struggle put forward by the Progressives. As a result, Crerar was able 'to successfully claim all the glory.'[42] The episode made the prime minister even more determined to absorb the Progressives into the Liberal party.

Mackenzie King's first session as leader of the House did not bode well for the need to restore Prairie faith. The Progressives came away from Parliament with an even greater suspicion of the power that the 'big interests' wielded in Liberal councils, and the sentiment was not confined to the third party. 'We are such good Liberals,' R.F. McWilliams from Manitoba complained, 'that we are unwilling to continue compromising with those who call themselves Liberals but are quite as Tory in their real views as Arthur Meighen and we would welcome a split which would take a considerable section of the Montreal and Toronto Liberals over where they belong.'[43] The prime minister's response offered little satisfaction. 'Any Government in office can never satisfy its friends,' he told T.C. Norris, 'and because of its necessary assertion of authority whether farmer or Liberal is bound to come to be viewed by many of the more radical elements in the community as conservative, if not reactionary in character.'[44]

Despite unfavourable conditions in the first several years of his mandate, King never abandoned the possibility of having Progressives enter the government. Discussions took place with Crerar in the summer of 1922, yet the same obstacles remained. The prime minister could not put any more strain on his support from the Montreal bloc, and Crerar could not consider entering a cabinet with such a group in the dominant position. An issue in foreign affairs, meanwhile, did at least serve to bring the Liberals and Progressives closer together.

In September 1922 a critical situation for the British Empire developed around the Turkish Straits. Although peace had been signed with Turkey in 1920 through the Treaty of Sèvres, the agreement had not been ratified by the British and it was repudiated by the new Turkish nationalist government. The Greeks were defeated in the area and the French withdrew. The British suddenly found themselves the sole defenders of

Constantinople, Chanak, and the neutralized zone about the straits. The advance of a victorious Turk army seemed imminent. British Prime Minister Lloyd George desired an effective display of imperial unity and expected support from the dominions. A message was sent informing them of the situation and requesting a military contingent. Before the Canadian government received any communication, the British government informed the press of the invitation. Much to Mackenzie King's annoyance, he learned of the invitation only when a journalist asked what response Canada would offer. The prime minister viewed the presumptuous attitude of the British government as one more example of 'the imperial game,' but, true to his nature, the crafty politician was already seeking possible gains from the dilemma. There was no doubt that Arthur Meighen's Tories would support imperial centralization and the sending of a contingent. 'Remote as the connection may appear,' King noted, 'the Near East situation seems to me to illustrate in the clearest possible manner the need for the closest kind of union between the Progressives and ourselves.'[45] He was 'confident' the Progressives would advance the cause of Canadian autonomy and align themselves with the Liberals. 'It is the time now to bring them into the Government,' King trumpeted. At a meeting of the cabinet all except Gouin agreed to the prime minister's suggestion to invite Crerar to Ottawa for consultation. The two leaders met in late September, and Crerar demonstrated his complete agreement with King's position. While granting that the crisis necessitated cooperation, Crerar made it clear that neither he nor A.B. Hudson would enter a government alongside Gouin. Yet King did not see any chance of 'crowding' Gouin out because his 'good will' and 'word with big interests would be helpful.'[46]

The Chanak Crisis was alleviated on 29 September when an armistice was signed with Turkey. The need for a Liberal–Progressive union passed, but the implications of the incident were not lost on King. There were common planks to Liberalism and Progressivism that transcended regional divisions: 'It has demonstrated ... that in matters of real fundamental concern our interest is a common one, and that unity of action is essential to secure our common end in the face of our common foe, the jingo-tory-militarist. I believe we have found the basis on which the Progressives of Western Canada may be brought into real accord with the Liberals of the Province of Quebec and other parts of the Dominion.'[47] Progressive support on Chanak served to forestall criticism that the government's policy was solely a reflection of the isolationism and anti-imperialism of Quebec. Conservative attacks on the Liberal policy, along with Meighen's 'ready, aye ready' speech, indicated the alternative. The crisis also provided a crucial boost to King's leadership. Yet, while the prime minister could harp on about Liberal-Progressive unity, nothing would bring Crerar and Gouin together. Once again the Progressive leader had refused to join the government, and the West was again witness to the prime minister siding with Gouin.

Several weeks after Chanak, Crerar gave up the leadership of the Progressive party. The primary reason was personal, and he also wished to devote more time to his business interests, but it was no secret that he was discontented with the movement's direction. He was also distraught at the plight of the Prairie West and pessimistic about future policy, regardless of whether the Progressives held the balance of power or not. In the words of *Maclean's* columnist J.K. Munro: 'Nobody knew better than Crerar that with Sir Lomer Gouin helping the little grey Nova Scotian [Fielding] to make his budget any concessions in the tariff wouldn't yield enough money to buy a Christmas box for the hired man.'[48] Crerar had resigned from Borden's government when its direction went against western interests; he resigned as Progressive leader when the King government seemed to be headed the same way. Robert Forke, another crypto-Liberal from Manitoba, was chosen as his successor.

King, who saw Crerar's resignation as a sign of Progressive disintegration, welcomed the leadership change.[49] Forke was a weaker leader and more willing to cooperate with the Liberals. 'Was delighted to hear tonight that Robert Forke has been chosen leader of Progressives,' King wrote. 'This means complete co-operation.'[50] Toward the end of the year, two Ontario Progressives joined the Liberals, providing the government a majority in the House, but these optimistic signs were offset by the defeat of the Liberal government in Manitoba at the hands of the United Farmers. If Progressive strength had been weakened in 1922, Mackenzie King's struggle was far from complete. Unless some critical event convinced the Progressives to come on board, the prime minister would have to rely on policy initiatives to win the West. Yet the struggle within the Liberal party made such initiatives exceedingly difficult.

The transfer of the natural resources remained a promising possibility. Negotiations continued between Ottawa and Alberta throughout 1923, though discussions with the other two provinces were stalled. A stalemate had been reached with Manitoba, while Saskatchewan was simply not very interested in the issue. Both Alberta and Manitoba hoped to profit from the transfer through provincial control of such unalienated resources as minerals, timber, and water-power sites. The proposed replacement of the subsidy with the resources did not provide Saskatchewan with the same incentive.

Although Alberta wished a quick settlement to the old issue and was prepared to forgo the present subsidy, Premier Greenfield wanted compensation for alienated resources. He also advanced the idea of compensation for land that had been provided to subsidize the railways prior to the creation of the province in 1905. King refused to consider conditions that predated the province and reiterated his offer of the unalienated resources plus a continuation of the subsidy for three years. Greenfield warned that Alberta was asking for considerably less than what it would receive if a complicated and lengthy accounting took place. The province would consider the dominion offer only if a subsidy continuance of ten years were offered.[51] Once again the issue was placed on hold.

There was no avoiding other Progressive demands. While the prime minister personally favoured such reforms as the use of the alternative vote in single-member districts and the proposal for proportional representation as a means to avoid three-cornered fights, Quebec opposition again proved formidable. The most divisive issue, as usual, proved to be the budget. During cabinet discussions in early March 1923, King proposed an increase in the British preference. His views seemed to have general acceptance, but in the weeks that followed Sir Lomer Gouin, H.S. Béland, T.A. Low, J.A. Robb, and J.H. King put up steady opposition against significant tariff reductions of any kind. As far as King was concerned, his low-tariff ministers were not proving forthright and standing by their principles. W.R. Motherwell and Charles Stewart in particular were proving inadequate to defend Prairie interests. The prime minister was in danger of once again bowing to eastern domination. In early April he urged a 20 per cent discount on preferential duties: 'Mr. Stewart was not equal to backing up the suggestion with vigour, Lapointe said practically nothing & Graham was silent ... It was difficult therefore to expect much ... I spoke out strongly against increase of duties & need to introduce legis'n that wd. help people on the land. It always comes back to where we receive our support.' When King again took up the issue two days later, he could secure only a few supporters and found himself out of sympathy with most of the cabinet. He was not prepared to precipitate a crisis. When the tariff came before the Liberal caucus on 12 April, it was clear the party was going to 'stand pat.'

The protectionist wing, which had successfully blocked King's advances, took the offensive in the third week of April by pressing for specified increases in the tariff. This time the prime minister stood his ground: 'I spoke out strongly against considering any increases, unless Br. preference conceded. Sir Lomer fought against the latter, also Low, but I carried my point, tho' not for a large amount. Sir Lomer talked of resigning etc. Murdock was very outspoken about the big interests. I let the Cabinet see I was determined to head in the right direction.'[52] Five days later, when Fielding attempted to win support for a tariff on food, King was strongly opposed and carried all of the cabinet except Gouin. By the time the discussions were complete the prime minister was frustrated. He saw no way out of the dilemma:

> No one appreciates more keenly than I do the ills and evils of protection ...
> I confess, however, that the more thought and study I give to these prob-
> lems the less I find in the way of helpful constructive suggestion, despite all
> the criticism and denunciation of conditions as they exist. The trouble with
> our whole economic order is that the minute one attempts to alter estab-
> lished institutions in some fundamental particular one discovers conse-
> quences wholly unforeseen, and often more serious in their possible out-
> come than the evil it is being sought to remedy.[53]

When he brought down the budget of 1923, Finance Minister Fielding left the tariff virtually untouched. Insult was added to injury for the West when he intimated that the existing tariff was as fair and reasonable as circumstances would permit. The Progressives immediately banded together in opposition, joined by Andrew McMaster and A.B. Hudson in voting for Forke's amendment, which demanded implementation of the Liberal and Progressive platforms. The damage to Liberal fortunes in the West could hardly have been greater. 'It would be folly for me to attempt to minimise the effect of Mr. Fielding's statement regarding [tariff] stability contained in the Budget Speech,' Saskatchewan Premier Charles Dunning told King. Tariff reduction had become 'the principal basis' of organization and the hopes for a Liberal revival in the region. The Progressives had used Liberal insincerity as their base, and they would now point to the 1919 promises and the current budget 'as proof of that insincerity.' The influence and electoral power of western Canada was increasing, Dunning warned, and if the Liberal party wished to remain even 'a factor' in the region, it had to demonstrate it was 'sincerely a low-tariff party and give evidence of that by performance when in power.'[54] Even Laurier Liberals from the West were beginning to lose faith in Mackenzie King, as one letter from the disgruntled so aptly indicated:

I am a Liberal – one who supported you in the Convention at Ottawa ... We went to Ottawa in 1919 to reconstruct the Liberal party ... We had read your books – we were proud of your heredity and thought we would see a renaissance of the Liberal party under a new man of Liberal outlook and one who would stand for the principles of true Liberalism against its enemies within the party ... You chose for your Finance Minister the same man in the same position who helped betray the party under Laurier. You chose as Minister Mr. Gouin who was not in sympathy with the platform laid down by the Convention which elected you to your responsible office ... You at best gave us a two and a half per cent performance of a one hundred per cent promise.[55]

The prime minister could plead for patience and argue that he had little alternative at present, but the Progressives were not listening. Any possibility of sympathy for King's predicament was even further diminished with the decennial revision of the Bank Act. The Progressives were urging federal assistance in scaling down farm debts and obtaining easier credit. To this end they brought forward an array of proposals when the revision was referred to a standing committee. This move toward reform was met head-on by a combination of Liberals and Conservatives who quickly countered the radical ideas, with some support from the moderate wing of the Progressive party. Despite the division in the Progressive ranks, the Liberal government emerged once again as being just as conservative as the Tories.

If there was any sign of hope for Mackenzie King on the Prairies in 1923 it was in Saskatchewan. The Liberal party in the province, while suffering from the same divisions that plagued Liberalism across the nation, had thus far survived the Progressive assault. The provincial highways minister, Jimmy Gardiner, had taken over J.A. Calder's old party apparatus and fine-tuned the organizational machine to perfection. Gardiner, whose anti-Progressive sentiments had not wavered, was serving as Motherwell's 'Saskatchewan Agent.' But Premier Dunning was not yet prepared to jump back into bed with the federal party. The process of disarming the Farmers was not yet complete, and the premier was not prepared to risk his government. He took additional steps to mollify the Farmers by asking the Saskatchewan Grain Growers' Association for copies of their convention resolutions, presumably as a guide for future policies.[56]

Although provincial by-elections in the summer of 1922 had demonstrated the continued strength of his government, Dunning was the first to admit that the western situation for the federal Liberals remained unpromising. Fielding's budget statement had done 'great harm'; the King government was at 'a lower ebb' in Saskatchewan than ever before. Dunning had 'succumbed' to the pressure of Gardiner and W.R. Motherwell, and allowed a stand to be taken against the Progressives in the Moose Jaw federal by-election of April 1923. The premier, who was never comfortable with the decision, did not take part in the campaign, which culminated in Liberal defeat and embarrassment. The Moose Jaw rout convinced Dunning to follow his own judgment and appease rather than fight the Progressives.[57] The contest seemed to provide impetus for the Farmers to enter provincial politics in Saskatchewan. A provincial Progressive party was formed in the autumn of 1923, apparently to oppose what was deemed the growing relationship between the King and Dunning governments. The premier responded by announcing that it was a bad thing for a provincial party to be 'bound hand and foot' to any federal party organization. His government would not become the 'donkey engine' of the King Liberals.[58] For the time being Dunning would pursue the policy set by Martin, but King was heartened that the premier was intent on gradually restoring the link between the provincial and federal parties. However, Dunning was determined to control the evolution of this link. Gardiner had commanded the forces working for the federal candidate in Moose Jaw, and the provincial party consequently shared the 'stigma of defeat.' In the future Dunning demanded that he be kept fully informed as to King's western plans. He would 'guide' the federal party in 'matters affecting the West.'[59]

The prime minister was thrilled to receive Dunning's observations, even if they came in the form of criticism. They were certainly preferable to a break with Ottawa. Both Motherwell and Charles Stewart were proving incompetent western advisors; King hoped to manoeuvre Dunning into this role. He was popular among Liberals and Progressives alike and had a solid reputation in the other two Prairie provinces. The premier was not ready, however, to embrace the King government publicly. A close relationship between Ottawa and Regina, he argued, would 'at this time mean our defeat Provincially.'[60] Even Jimmy Gardiner agreed that it was becoming increasingly difficult to defend the policies of the federal government. Ottawa had to be careful not to 'isolate the West' as punishment for the last federal election. 'Self preservation, if nothing else,' Gardiner warned, 'should now dictate a policy favourable to the West.'[61]

Self-preservation was not something on which Mackenzie King usually needed counsel. He would attempt to atone for his western record. A select committee was established to study agricultural conditions and look into the question of ocean freight rates. A royal commission on the marketing of grain was also appointed. The campaign to revive the wheat board had failed, and Prairie farm organizations were now attempting to determine whether a pooling system would provide a suitable recourse.[62]

The pooling idea seemed simple and straightforward. It would eliminate the traditional evils of the trade through by-passing the middlemen. Farmers would receive the same price for the same grade throughout the crop year. The unpredictable and fluctuating market would also be avoided. The pool would create a single large common fund and distribute the net returns after the entire crop had been marketed. In the autumn of 1922 Aaron Saprio, 'the messiah of the pooling movement,' came north from the United States to spread his message in the Canadian West. He received encouragement from the Grain Growers' locals as well as the *Grain Growers' Guide*. Crerar put his United Grain Growers Company (UGG) behind the idea. The prime minister had been impressed with the cause but not enough to provide Sapiro with requested government guarantees for a line of credit. A speaking tour by Sapiro witnessed the spread of the pooling idea 'like an evangelistic wild fire.' Still, the movement was not without its divisions. The entire wheat marketing question had already demonstrated its potential to split the western farmers.

From the inauguration of the pooling idea, a debate was sparked between the opponents and proponents of compulsory marketing. In July 1923 the Canadian Council of Agriculture met to consider the issue. Crerar proposed a regional voluntary pool based on short-term contracts. His company, the UGG, would offer its elevator network, its selling agency, and its financial strength to get the organization off the ground Support for compulsory, rather than Crerar's voluntary, pooling was building in Saskatchewan, and representatives for the Saskatchewan Co-operative Elevator Company refused to comply with Crerar's proposal. Yet, the Saskatchewan Farmers' movement was divided. The provincial section of the Farmers' Union of Canada (FUC) was antagonistic to the cozy relationship that had long existed between Grain Growers' Association and the provincial Liberals. The FUC was equally antagonistic to the UGG and the Winnipeg Grain Exchange. As a result of the animosity and ideological dispute, three separate and voluntary pools were organized, although they did combine to form a Central Selling Agency, which had a seat on the Winnipeg Grain Exchange.[63]

Prime Minister King was content that the appointment of several commissions, along with the direction of the pooling movement, had successfully headed off the marketing question. He continued his western incentive program by promoting the consolidation of the railways, by agreeing to complete the Hudson Bay Railway, and by submitting a construction program of railway branch lines. While these proposals together provided the semblance of a solid western agenda, they produced few tangible results. For too long the populace had been waiting on promises; only concrete measures would satisfy its demands. In the meantime King was receiving complaints from the Maritimes and British Columbia that his government was already too concerned with the Prairie West. If the government were going to sacrifice support elsewhere, it had to have western gains to balance the losses.

Early in 1923 the prime minister offered Progressive leader Robert Forke the portfolio of immigration; again the attempt to absorb the third party failed. The Progressives remained dissatisfied with the cabinet composition, and these doubts only increased when King brought in the protectionist E.M. Macdonald to appease the Maritimes. The Progressives viewed the move as another example of the government falling under the influence of the 'interests' and becoming indistinguishable from the Tories.[64] Andrew Haydon warned the prime minister that his reputation was falling into a 'reactionary position.' Although Haydon acknowledged that, Macdonald would be a capable minister, his entry served to 'divorce the West further than from where it is now.'[65] Since Manitoba remained without cabinet representation, Haydon recommended appointing A.B. Hudson. In an unexplained move, King instead filled the vacancy by appointing E.J. McMurray solicitor general. McMurray, who had only mediocre political ability, was one of the leaders of the Diehard Liberals in Winnipeg. The appointment would only further antagonize the Progressives and prevent unity among Manitoba Liberals.

The 1923 Imperial Conference offered Mackenzie King a reprieve from domestic problems and another opportunity to use foreign affairs to improve his standing in the party and nation. To have the government's position more fully represented in the western press, J.W. Dafoe was invited to accompany the Canadian delegation. Although the editor's dislike of King was apparent, Dafoe had been impressed by the prime minister's stand on dominion–imperial relations.[66] Still, he remained sceptical: 'I must say that I have very little confidence in King. I am afraid his conceit in his ability to take care of himself is equalled only by his ignorance and I should not be surprised if he should find himself trapped.'[67] The prime minister would not go so far as to have a Progressive in the delegation but he did arrange with Forke to provide advice if cabled.

The Imperial Conference of 1923 became one of the crowning glories in Mackenzie King's career. Not only did the autonomists stave off the advances of imperial centralization, but the Canadian prime minister played a leading role in the defence. Dafoe was impressed: 'As for King, my regard for him has perceptibly increased by what I saw of him in London. He is an abler man than I thought; he has more courage than I gave him credit for.' Still, it would take more than one conference, however important, to win over the sceptical editor. Although Dafoe would admit that King had 'many excellent qualities for public life,' he did not believe he possessed 'the equipment for leadership for times such as these.' If the party were purged of its 'reactionary' influences, Dafoe felt that King could remain leader: 'In the right setting and with the right men behind him, King would be a not unacceptable party leader.'[68] Dafoe might be prepared to accept King as Liberal leader, yet that acceptance could hardly have come with more qualifications.

For his part, Mackenzie King was well aware of the advantages to having the *Free Press* and its editor on board, and he believed the support could become the key to ensuring Liberal–Progressive cooperation.[69] In case the prime minister had missed the point, other westerners were there to emphasize its importance. 'As you know Mr. Dafoe has not been friendly either to your Government or to yourself, so that his praise is all the more valuable,' R.F. McWilliams wrote. 'He is undoubtedly the greatest individual force in this Western country and has at his hand an unrivalled instrument for moulding public opinion in the West.'[70]

Once King was back home, it became apparent that Liberal fortunes would not be quick to change. While in London King had been persuaded, against his better judgment, to open the Halifax constituency in a by-election, only to have the seat lost to the Conservatives. At the next cabinet meeting King chastised his ministers for not following his advice. His scorn was clearly aimed at the old guard. The West was becoming increasingly crucial to strengthen his position, and he would act even at the risk of cabinet division. 'I am inclined now to take the bold course and link up at once with the farmers,' he told his diary. A 'break' and realignment of the party would occur, but party lines would eventually be restored. 'I am convinced we need to unite the East and the West,' King wrote. The entry of Crerar into the cabinet would be a 'means to that end.' King was now talking of the same 'fusion' that Dafoe had been advocating since 1919: 'This good may come of it, it may force a union with the progressives sufficiently strong to give us a substantial majority on which we can count. For this I am grateful.' In cabinet the prime minister outlined his plans to appeal to the moderate Progressives, including serious attempts to bring Crerar to Ottawa. King's 'firmer' stance was greeted by the silent assent of his colleagues.[71]

On 4 December W.S. Fielding suffered a paralytic stroke that would force his retirement. After a subsequent cabinet meeting Sir Lomer Gouin informed King that his physician insisted he also give up public life, although there is little doubt that Gouin's increasing alienation from the government contributed to his decision.[72] In one instant the composition and posture of the cabinet, the government, and the leadership were altered. At the same time the opportunities for gaining Liberal support in the West markedly increased. 'It is apparent that the Liberal party in Canada has come to the parting of the ways,' Saskatchewan Liberal G.W. Sahlmark remarked with anticipation.[73] If the government was losing two of its ablest parliamentarians and the cabinet two of its sharpest minds, at least King would be rid of the two most obstructive thorns in his side. Since the budget speech, the stock of the Liberal party on the Prairies had been at a low point. Westerners hoped that changes in the Department of Finance would lead to Liberal revival.[74]

Mackenzie King hoped the retirements would provide the final inducements to the Progressives. Two cabinet positions would be opened, and the third party could no longer demur on the basis of Gouin's presence. When the Liberals lost another by-election, this time in New Brunswick, the urgency of the situation increased. Western gains were essential in the face of eastern losses. 'I think the time has come now to cut the Gordian knot to sever this [Montreal] connection and bring the Liberals and the Farmers together,' King recorded.

> Fielding & Sir Lomer have both now gone. It remains to readjust ... [We should] consolidate the Liberals & Progressives to make a strong party now with two years of office to prepare for appeal & to get back to two party lines. I do not want to lose Quebec support, much less incur active opposition of powerful financial & mffg. interests, they are against us anyway at heart, & we might as well have the fight in the open. If I can be sure of a straight alignment that will bring strength, I shall endeavour to reconstruct at once.[75]

The prime minister's desperation was matched only by that of western

Liberals. 'I fear we have been busier over post-mortems than anything else,' Manitoba Liberal J.F. Kilgour confessed. It would require a great revitalization 'to reanimate our valley of dry bones.' Liberalism was 'dead'; it would be resurrected only if the people were convinced they were not following 'a will-o'-the-wisp.'[76] The Progressives had received credit for any western concessions, however minor. J.G. Turgeon informed King that cabinet reconstruction would be only the first step: the prime minister needed an influential western lieutenant to deal first hand with Prairie concerns.[77]

It remained uncertain at the end of 1923 whether the cat had been belled in time to save Liberal fortunes in the West. During its first two years in office, the King government had continued the Laurier precedent of making sympathetic noises toward the Prairies while remaining committed to Quebec. Mackenzie King had not proven master of his party, and western offerings were meagre at best. Even if the region recognized King's Prairie sympathies – and there were ample reasons to doubt them – these were meaningless if they did not translate into action. With the weakening of the protectionist wing providing the opportunity, King's reservations were now gone. The path was clear to bring the West on side.

4

The Angels on Side, 1924–1926

The angels are certainly on the side of Willie King. He has a finer opportunity now than he had in 1921, and I hope he will be equal to it. I am beginning to think that probably he will measure up to his opportunities this time.

J.W. Dafoe to J. Willison, 17 September 1926

With Lomer Gouin and W.S. Fielding gone, Mackenzie King moved immediately to shore up his position in the West. If the Liberal party were to be successful, there would have to be a shift in emphasis away from Quebec, and central Canada in general, and toward the Prairies. Once again westerners cautiously waited to see if the policies would match the rhetoric. The prime minister was given another chance to prove his mettle but, with an election approaching, it was by no means certain that the 'angels' would be on King's side.

Thomas Crerar and Charles Dunning were invited to Ottawa early in 1924. Despite Crerar's resignation from the Progressive leadership, he remained an influential member of the movement and the one who was most friendly with the Liberals. Dafoe believed that Crerar had a 'good deal of confidence in King as a man of fundamentally sound principles who wants to do right.'[1] The prime minister also had, from his 1921 talks, Crerar's implied willingness to enter the cabinet when conditions proved favourable. Dunning, in the meantime, had been rapidly rising in political popularity since he had succeeded W.M. Martin as Liberal premier of Saskatchewan. King was aware of the impotence of his two present western ministers and recognized the value of both Dunning and Crerar. It was not coincidence that the prime minister had no Albertan in his sights. It was, rather, reflective of King's stronger relationships with the two more easterly provinces and their Liberal parties. To King, Alberta was a province swept up by a radical Farmer movement that had yet to come to its senses.

The prime minister met with the two westerners in January to discuss their possible entry into the cabinet. Crerar reiterated the traditional list of western concerns. More specifically, he requested the finance portfolio for himself, with Dunning replacing W.R. Motherwell as Saskatchewan representative and A.B. Hudson replacing E.J. McMurray from Manitoba. Dunning assumed the seemingly selfless stance of being more interested in western policies than cabinet reconstruction as a means of disarming the Progressives, since it was this strategy that had allowed Liberal survival in his province. Mackenzie King was impressed with the Saskatchewan premier. 'I confess,' he recorded, 'I formed a high opinion of him, of his mind & attitude. He is a stronger saner & sounder man than Crerar.'

Dunning was a deceivingly straightforward type of politician whose emphasis on sound and efficient administration often disguised a powerful ambition. Privately he advised King that perhaps Crerar was not suitable for finance because he was 'not a good administrator, too visionary.' Ironically, considering Dunning's later health problems, Dunning claimed Crerar was 'lacking the physical health, likely to weaken under close application.' The prime minister agreed, admitting he did 'not like Crerar's bargaining spirit.' The Manitoban was informed that his proposed cabinet changes could not be met immediately and that, for the present session, it would be better to have finance filled by an easterner. But Dunning had played a fine Caesar, refusing the crown while displaying his ambition, and King was already considering him for an eventual change in the finance department.[2] Although the premier was hesitant in abandoning his secure position as head of the Saskatchewan government to join a battered federal ship, he did indicate his interest in eventually moving to national politics. Crerar, who became frustrated with the discussions, believed the prime minister was being too cautious and concerned with his own survival: 'I am afraid that one of King's difficulties is that he is not able to distinguish between good advice and poor advice, and that he has scarcely anyone whom he can take into his confidence, and whose advice he seeks. He has a lot of faith in his own star, but keeps his eye so intently on it that he may miss seeing the pitfalls at his own feet.'[3]

For the moment, changes were made to cabinet personnel that reflected not so much a shift in influence from East to West as from Montreal to Quebec City. James Robb took over as acting minister of finance and Ernest Lapointe replaced Gouin as minister of justice. Despite the urging of the Montreal wing, Rodolphe Lemieux was passed over, and P.J.A. Cardin was appointed to marine and fisheries. While no changes were made to western representation, King discussed the issue with Lapointe and stressed the need to include Dunning. King hoped that the premier could facilitate Liberal–Progressive cooperation, restore Prairie Liberalism, and curb the region's radical tendencies:

> The people of the three Prairie Provinces are undoubtedly naturally Liberals ... My view is that permanent Liberalism in Canada must eventually include the Western Farmers. Liberalism has a right to them and that is where they surely belong, but I personally am without much hope of a successful and happy Liberal Family until this [Liberal–Progressive] breach is healed. It is no doubt true that the Westerners have in some ways gone to extremes and have forgotten that they must, in a country of such varied interests as ours, be ready to compromise ... I believe that if Mr. Dunning were there it would inspire almost universal confidence among the rank and file of the Westerners ... I believe they would have confidence that Mr. Dunning with his experience and recognized sagacity would have a very steadying and perhaps restraining influence on any unduly radical tendencies in the West.[4]

Provincial delegations from the Prairies also met with the prime minister in January 1924 to discuss the natural resources question. The United Farmers of Manitoba premier, John Bracken, requested that his province receive rights to at least a portion of the resources pending a final solution and transfer. He was after the unsold school lands and moneys from their sale, which the dominion was holding in trust for educational purposes. King immediately rejected the offer, annoyed that Bracken was attempting to depart from previous negotiations and solve the dilemma 'piecemeal.' The whole question, he argued, had to be fully resolved and then submitted to both levels of government.[5] Dealing with the controversial issue serially would only allow opposition from the other areas of Canada additional opportunity to block the legislation. More importantly, such a process would raise the ghost of the Manitoba Schools Question: there would be an instant debate over what share the Catholic schools would receive.[6] King may have been annoyed, but Bracken was frustrated. 'After five years of almost continuous negotiation upon the

Natural Resources Question absolutely no tangible results have yet been achieved,' he complained. If the School Lands question could not be resolved through discussion, Bracken concluded, 'there would seem to be no hope of settling anything by that method.' Arbitration would be necessary.[7]

The Alberta negotiations, meanwhile, were more successful. The United Farmers of Alberta premier, Herbert Greenfield, was prepared to accept a transfer without an accounting if the dominion would pay six years of the subsidy rather than the three offered by Ottawa and the ten suggested by the province. King once again refused. He wished to avoid a lengthy and costly accounting but would not pay more than a three-year subsidy.[8] Later in the year Greenfield informed Ottawa that the Alberta legislature had authorized him to accept the dominion's offer for the transfer on the basis of an accounting since 1905. A fixed sum in lieu of an accounting could be accepted, but only if the King government offered a better settlement than its proposed three-year subsidy, as provincial estimates were indicating that this was not sufficient compensation. With pressure mounting for a settlement, King responded to Greenfield's offer of an accounting by immediately pushing ahead and hiring J.S. Ewart as the dominion legal adviser.[9] Eastern opposition to a transfer deal had become largely irrelevant because the federal government was not giving up an asset but being relieved of a liability. In all three provinces, the administration of the natural resources in the last ten years had cost substantially more than the total revenue received.[10]

In February King attempted to take advantage of his strengthened position in cabinet by outlining some initiatives in a draft of the throne speech. There was, he noted, a 'warm discussion' on whether to include a special reference to the tariff. A paragraph was framed that referred to a reduction of taxation on implements of production, which King's 'Western friends wanted & rightly so.' The cabinet 'swallowed' the initiative, something that, according to King, would never have been possible with Fielding and Gouin. The prime minister admitted to feeling 'a greater freedom' and was hopeful 'the west is now coming our way.'[11] Others were still sceptical. 'I do not see a chance in the world in Western Canada for the Ottawa government at the next election,' Dafoe claimed. 'Meighen, simply by virtue of being in opposition will probably stand better in the West than King.'[12]

Winning the West still relied heavily on ensuring Progressive support, and the prime minister's optimism was bolstered on 27 February when he met with Robert Forke. The Progressive leader was informed of the government's new line that was intended 'to get East and West united.' The duties on such items as agricultural implements would be reduced if the Progressives would be 'half decent in their support.' The length to which King would go, of course, depended on the strength of that support. While he was prepared to sacrifice some eastern support for western gains, the prime minister would not 'fall between two groups.' According to King, Forke was 'wholly sympathetic & friendly & promised to do all he could.' Since the beginning of January the prime minister had been informed that the Progressives 'were ready to cooperate with the Govt. in an open manner ... I feel a greater freedom with Gouin & Fielding gone, will be able to take my own natural course.'[13] After the Progressives voted solidly with the Liberals on the throne speech, King was elated. It was 'a great victory,' he trumpeted, 'a splendid beginning.'[14] As usual the real test would be the budget, on which the Progressives were frequently consulted to ascertain their views.

Although the strength of the Progressives was not going to dissipate completely before the next election, there was a possibility the group could be transformed into an element of the Liberal party. The problem was separating the moderate Progressives from the radicals. Dafoe observed that 'if some magician could only make the necessary shift,' moderate progressives would be 'quite content to serve as a sort of Western wing' of the Liberals. But no one had succeeded in bridging the gap between the two parties.[15]

Increasingly apprehensive as budget day approached, Mackenzie King was nonetheless hopeful his gamble would pay off. Yet, as he told Forke, he would not continue 'trying to meet the West' unless the efforts were reciprocated.[16] Already the party had gone 'farther than the country or members expect' on tariff reductions, and King expected a 'cleavage' as a result. The Ontario and Montreal members would be 'aggrieved,' and three or four of them would possibly abandon the government.[17]

When the budget was brought down, the government's financial position was aided by the general improvement in economic conditions: the finance minister was able to announce a surplus for the first time since 1913. Tax reductions naturally increased the budget's popularity but interest centred around the tariff. Customs duties were reduced or abolished on equipment used in primary industries and on material used to manufacture that equipment.[18] The prime minister was delighted by the reception of the government's first moves toward freer trade. 'We have done the right thing,' he assured himself, and 'the House have [sic] responded.'[19]

The Progressives supported the budget and, according to King, were 'surprised in that it goes farther than they had anticipated.' He hoped rural Canada would respond and the disintegration of the Progressives would commence: 'We have constructed a bridge which will help to unite East and West, and to bring the Progressive party across into our ranks ... I really believe it will be, as I wrote Robb, an epoch making budget in the history of the Liberal party.' Mackenzie King was convinced he had answered the call and measured up to the challenge: 'I am happy that I have been true to Liberal tradition, true to the platform of [the] 1919 Convention, true to the pledges I gave the electors in 1921 and true to the people – the producers and consumers. Had Fielding or Sir Lomer both or either remained in the Cabinet we could never have done what we have done. I have had my own way from the start, and have carried every point for which I have fought.'[20]

The budget did receive widespread western support. Meighen and the Conservatives attacked the budget, affirming their position as the party of protection. Four protectionist Liberals voted with the Conservatives against the government, and Walter Mitchell, who was not in the House during the vote, resigned his seat in protest. Many of the Progressives wanted more substantial reductions on tariffs for the necessities of life, and J.S. Woodsworth introduced such an amendment. This move widened the breach within the Progressive movement. A month later what became known as the Ginger Group was formed when ten of the Ontario and Alberta radicals broke away with two Labour members. Yet, King had won the confidence of the moderate Progressives. Moreover, the break in the Progressive movement seemed to open the way for a Liberal resurgence in the region. 'Our Liberal friends thro' Western Canada are put once more at the head of the procession,' he crowed, and the path had been paved for the two groups to come together.[21] From Saskatchewan, Premier Dunning warned that 'the appetite of Western Canada for tariff reduction is almost unsatiable [sic]' and that the Progressives would attempt to convince the electorate that any concessions had come as a result of their pressure. On the whole, however, there could be no doubt that King's government had 'increased its stature' on the Prairies. Dunning's commentary to King on the budget performance differed markedly from that of the previous year: 'So far as one can gather the policy of the Government has put new heart into a great many Liberals and has had an effect upon former Liberals who in the past few years have been Progressive ... The general condition, therefore, is much more hopeful than when I saw you last.'[22]

The West expected the Liberal government to continue along its aggressive new line, but King was cautious. Although his position in the cabinet was certainly stronger, he still had to mediate divergent interests, many of whom believed the government had already gone too far. The prime minister's caution inevitably slowed the pace of new and expected initiatives. Senate and electoral reform, particularly popular with the Alberta Progressives, came to nothing in 1924, and the branch line program, which had been defeated by the Senate in 1923, also once again ground to a halt. Meanwhile, the proposal to proceed with the Hudson Bay Railway bogged down in the usual eastern opposition. In April King met with a Prairie delegation – the 'On to the Bay' Association – who advocated the fabled rail route, and while he was favourably impressed,[23] the results were intangible. G.H. Haney of Saskatchewan wrote an open letter to the prime minister in the form of a poem, entitled 'The Way to the Bay':

With the uttermost farthing ground out of the West,
    Ere she lands her vast crops at the sea,
You haven't a dime to spend on the line
    That will make this great prairieland free.
To our plea for 'The way to the Bay,' Mr. King,
    You reply with a curt – 'N.S.F.'
But you've money to spend on a tapering tower
    That may mark your political death.
We will not desert the old flag, Mr. King,
    Or the Empire that mothers the world,
But you'll build us the line to the Bay, Mr. King,
    Or – there'll be a new banner unfurled.

You tell us the Senate sits hard on this scheme,
    And we know that in this you speak true,
But we've tired of the tricks of the barnacle crowd –
    We look, not to them, but to YOU.
YOU were given command of the fair ship of State,
    To direct without favor or fear
But you're letting the forecastle pilot the craft
    With the sequel that wreckage is near.
Then give us 'The way to the Bay,' Mr. King,
    Ere the tide of secession up-rolls,
Or we'll show you the way to the hay, Mr. King,
    When our chance comes again – at the polls.

You willingly father the Vanceboro line –
A matter of ninety odd miles –
And the buying of hotels in La Belle Paris
Evokes nothing harsher than smiles.
You've doubled the payroll on government jobs –
That is, your predecessors and you –
But YOU are the man on the job, Mr. King,
And YOU get the blame – only you.
You subsidize private-owned ships, Mr. King,
While our own lie awash at the quays;
Could you not send these idlers up into the Bay
To carry our wheat o'er the seas?

You could if you would – and you will, Mr. King,
Or we'll cut this Dominion in twain;
And on whom, do you think, when the history's writ,
Will fall ignominious blame?
On you, Mr. King. You are seized of our case;
You know that we pay through the nose
For every dam'd thing, both forward and back,
From the grain we produce to our clothes;
You know that it costs us a third of our crop
To land it at old Liverpool –
So give us 'The way to the Bay,' Mr. King –
Be the BOSS, use the old Golden Rule.[24]

While there was no denying that the budget was a positive sign for the West, it would have to be a harbinger of things to come if the good will of the region were to be retained. It would not produce the instant results King expected. Crerar believed the prime minister regarded the region as a sort of 'sulky child that will soon get over its sulks.' He was on 'Olympus, looking upwards,' Crerar wrote, 'and a person in this position is often in danger.'[25]

The West was waiting anxiously for the federal approach to the postponed Crow's Nest Pass rates as an indication of the government's true standing. Mackenzie King did nothing. The Crow's Nest Pass Act of 1897 had been suspended after the war. In 1923, only some parts of the act were restored. The full act was allowed to come back into effect on 7 July 1924, and the railway companies retaliated by restoring the rates only for those points that were on the lines of the Canadian Pacific in 1897 when the original agreement was made. This action meant that recently settled areas would pay more than those along the original lines. For their part, the railways argued that the agreement rates were too low to cover the cost of moving goods. Their restoration would lead to increased rates in other regions to offset losses. As Blair Neatby points out, Mackenzie King was 'still baffled by the problem.'[26] King knew intervention in any direction would be unpopular in some quarter, so he delayed. The initiative was left to the provincial governments to appeal to the Board of Railway Commissioners and, if necessary, the Supreme Court of Canada. Confident that the railways would not continue their 'obvious discriminations' and 'injustices,' King expected the board to take action. He was concerned, however, that the Prairie provinces would not 'fall in line' if the decision was not in their favour.[27] In August the board began hearings on the discriminatory rates. Its judgment, issued in October, asserted that, under the Railway Act, the board had the authority to override the Crow's Nest Pass Act of 1897. The board revoked the rates on all commodities except grain and flour moving east from the Prairies, restoring those in effect prior to 7 July.

The timing could hardly have been worse. The decision was declared while King was in the midst of a western tour to convince the region of Liberal sympathy and sincerity. The meetings had been well attended, and he was basking in the tariff reductions while playing down Progressive claims for credit. Anticipating a favourable decision, he was even claiming credit for the restoration of the Crow's Nest rates. The prime minister discussed the opening of the Peace River district in Alberta, the construction of the Hudson Bay Railway, and the development of natural resources. 'Indeed,' he indicated, 'all these so-called Western policies appeal very strongly to me, and I believe we can sweep the country on them.'[28]

In Manitoba King was courted by both wings of the Liberal party. He was improving his relations with Clifford Sifton, J.W. Dafoe, and the *Free Press*, much to the disgust of the Diehards. 'To-day [the *Free Press*] hates the Liberal party, including yourself, with an implacable hatred,' Diehard A.M. McLeod claimed, 'and its aim is to destroy your government and to smash you. It has no principles, but its guiding prejudice is hatred of Liberalism and Liberals, and it is moving Heaven and earth to get you and your government in its power – simply to use you both for its own purposes and then to throw you in the discard.'[29] King obviously disagreed, believing the recent friendly tone of the *Free Press* indicated 'a sort of preparation to come over.'[30] The Winnipeg-based Diehards were also adamant that the federal party end its courting of the Progressives, whom they referred to as 'intensely jealous' and much like a group of 'western broncos.'[31]

King had grown tired of the bickering and the uncompromising attitudes. Throughout the province he met with leading Liberals of the 'Unionist persuasion,' privately wishing that the party organization was controlled by them, rather than by the Diehards, who had once again been recognized as the official branch of the federal party under King's cabinet minister E.J. McMurray. The Free Press group represented 'many influential & powerful interests' and, according to King, were of 'an entirely different stamp than those who have gained control.' He admitted to feeling ashamed of those surrounding McMurray, and could not help noticing that his presence in cabinet was injuring attempts to win the confidence of the Free Press group. A.B. Hudson refused to appear on the prime minister's platform with the Diehard leader. Yet publicly the prime minister spoke of the need to sink differences, and he apparently believed the gulf was closing.[32] Dafoe, who was much more in touch with the situation, disagreed. King's desires for party unity, though admirable, remained 'pious aspirations.'[33]

In Saskatchewan the prime minister was reassured that when a successor could be found, Dunning would enter the government and take the portfolio of railways. The premier was less friendly in public: neither he nor any of his ministers took part in the official reception tendered King or appeared on the platform at the Regina meeting. Although the slight angered King, he swallowed his pride in order to maintain good relations with Dunning. He continued to urge Progressive–Liberal cooperation, arguing that the timing was even more crucial because of a resurgence of the Conservatives and the approach of an election. The Regina *Leader* responded with the assertion that

> whether or not that union of Liberal and Progressive forces which Mr. Mackenzie King so earnestly desires is effected before the next general election will depend more upon what happens at the forthcoming session of parliament than upon anything he can say in the West at this time or on the eve of an election ... There is a desire in the West for a rapprochement if it can be effected without sacrificing the interests of the West; but we are equally convinced that no such union can be brought about except by concrete evidence that Mr. Mackenzie King's professions of friendship for the West are sincere.[34]

Whatever the view of the media, Liberal–Progressive cooperation was not going to be found in Saskatchewan. With Dunning looking to make an exit to Ottawa, Jimmy Gardiner would be the likely successor, and his antagonism toward the Progressives was common knowledge. 'There is only one attitude to take toward the Western Progressives,' he reiterated to King, 'and that is to recognize in them the real opposition to your Government. If I had to make a choice tomorrow between voting and working for Progressive or Conservative candidates, I would have no hesitation in saying I would support the Conservative.' According to Gardiner it was the Progressives who were denying King a working majority, who were reaping any harvests sown by the government, and who were opposing the Liberals in the West. He believed his party in Saskatchewan was in a position 'to clear the Progressive movement from this province.'[35]

In the middle of King's western tour, the railway commission delivered its decision. Immediately, all eyes turned to the prime minister. If he hoped for any credibility in the region, he would intervene and overturn the decision. Yet, the Prairie West was to be disappointed, and King was left grappling for justifications. His thoughts on the issue, expressing what he would ideally 'like' to do, were reminiscent of his romantic perceptions of the Prairies. 'Personally I feel strongly like suspending the decision,' the prime minister noted boldly in his diary, 'but with difference of view in the cabinet, and the ministers scattered, think it on the whole wiser to accept situation as it is and await the "justice" of it till a more favourable moment.' He constructed a hypothetical scenario in which he would meet with the cabinet on his return from the West. The agreement would be judged out of date and a new rate structure would be devised by the railway commission, favourable to the Prairies. Going to the country on this policy, he would orchestrate a victory and a government dominated by westerners that would 'ensure stability & security for the next five years.' The government would be able to move away from the tariff and make the issue a fight of 'people vs. special interests,' particularly against the railways, which were 'purely selfish in the last resort.' King found himself turning to a theme that would become a future favourite: 'Supremacy of [Parliament] must be maintained even over the Courts of the land.'[36]

As usual, the cautious King prevailed while the bold King was confined to the pages of his diary. 'The situation as I saw it in the West is one thing,' he explained to Gardiner, 'and the situation as we face it in our Parliament is another.' Regardless of how much one wished to take the Prairie position, conditions in the rest of Canada had to be considered:

'Like all difficult situations which politics present there must be a point somewhere at which a proper balancing can be effected.'[37] Western scepticism was confirmed by the tactics of evasion and claims that the issue would require study before action was taken. 'Any good impression' left by King's early speeches on his western tour, Crerar noted, had 'entirely dissipated.'[38] An appeal to the Supreme Court was once again left up to the provincial governments, and western Liberals reacted immediately. The budget had seemed to indicate 'a most desirable strengthening of the Government's hold upon the confidence of the West,' a Manitoba Liberal wrote. This was now 'disastrously shaken.' Regional sentiment was causing 'grave concern to all who have seen its temper' and the conviction was growing that it was due to the 'acquisitive and parochial spirit of the East.' Calls went up again for a western lieutenant 'of the calibre of Dunning.'[39]

At year's end, Mackenzie King pondered his past record and future prospects. 'Our party has reached a high point in the confidence of the country,' he recorded. 'We are I think just at the parting of the ways. We can go on & up if we do the right thing on the Freight Rates case, or we can give the Progressive Party a new lease on life.' Additional western concessions would certainly cause controversy in cabinet. After a meeting in December King noted that he could 'not recall a stormier session in Council, more division of feeling strongly expressed.' Debate now focused around allowing the Supreme Court to decide if the railway commission had the right to upset Parliament's restoration of the rates. Because of the prime minister's insistence, on Christmas Day the cabinet authorized an order-in-council aimed at restoration. King was both relieved and jubilant: 'It has been the most difficult question in the cabinet thus far. I can feel that my judgement for better or for worse has prevailed, I believe it is for the better.'[40] The rates would be in effect until the Supreme Court ruled on the decision of the Board of Railway Commissioners.

Proud of his accomplishment, the prime minister expected western approval. 'I hope our reinstatement of the Crow's Nest Pass rates though belated to a degree which I personally greatly deplore,' he wrote Gardiner, 'may not be without its effects in depriving our Progressive friends of any kudos.' The defender of Parliament's supremacy was now attempting to convince his western supporters that he had gone as far as possible: 'I should like to have gone further and compelled the removal of all discriminations, but I can see where there is a real doubt as to the right of the power of the Governor-in-Council to take so far-reaching a step, which amounts in reality to assuming in its entirety the functions of the Railway Commission in matters of rate making.'[41] The question of the authority of the Railway Commission had gone before the Supreme Court of Canada, which announced its judgment in February 1925. The court ruled that the railway commission had no power to ignore the original 1897 act. The rates restored by the order-in-council were confirmed, and the way was open for a comprehensive national revision of rates with an amendment of the Crow's Nest Pass Act as a central feature. The railways wanted the commission to provide the revision, but the Prairies were much less trusting, and King himself did not believe the commission alone should carry the task of a comprehensive revision.

In May the government brought down its proposals. The commission was directed to make a complete investigation of freight rates with equalization as its guide. It was also instructed that the maximum rates on grain and flour then in force under the Crow's Nest Pass Act should not be exceeded and should be applicable to all points on all western lines, both present and future. The Conservatives opposed the special treatment for the West while the Progressives claimed the region had not been provided enough security. It was evident that King's settlement flew in the face of equalization by giving special consideration to the West, but past pledges, he argued, could not be ignored. The government was dealing with a 'condition, not a theory.' Theoretically, freight rates should be set by the railway commission. A condition existed, however, that for many years had provided the region special protection. The government now had to consider that condition along with the consequences of altering it.[42]

The commission ruled in September that only the Crow's Nest rates on grain and flour moving eastward would be enforced, and it later extended these rates to the same commodities moving to parts of British Columbia. Thus, while the West lost its preferred rates on other commodities, the Crow's Nest rates on the two most important items were confirmed, and they now applied to all railway lines on the Prairies. The issue was a victory for King, one that he believed should produce electoral rewards, yet the West viewed it as a grudging concession that was becoming characteristic of the government. The region was not confident that Mackenzie King was intent on defending or advancing its interests.

The budget of 1925 confirmed this sentiment when it contained only minor changes. The promises to appoint an advisory tariff board announced a year before were again extended. King was surprised to discover that a trade agreement Finance Minister Robb had concluded with Australia contained tariff increases as well as decreases. He refused to accept the deal as it stood, so none of its provisions were included in the budget. 'The more one sees of the effect & workings of a protective tariff,' he wrote, 'the more one sees the extent to which it is an evil and a curse.' He blamed Robb for the blunder because he was 'too Tory and protectionist by instinct and not a big enough man for the position.'[43]

Once again the strategy for gaining Prairie support came to rest on cabinet reorganization. 'We can only hope to win as we carry the West,' the prime minister wrote in July, 'and we can only carry the West as we are a Liberal party in name and fact.' Growing 'tired' of dealing with 'the two groups' in cabinet, King continued to indicate a lack of confidence in his ministers. 'There is need of new strength and blood,' he wrote. In May the discredited E.J. McMurray had been asked to resign because his law firm owed money to the failed Home Bank. When the government decided to compensate depositors for their losses, it was obvious that McMurray's personal affairs made his position in the government an embarrassment, and King jumped at the opportunity to prepare his exit. The presence of McMurray, who had always posed difficulties in cabinet, had hindered any chances of unifying the Manitoba Liberals. When pressure began to mount for his resignation, the minister made an 'exhibition' of himself, 'talking about being "assassinated," a conspiracy of "Crerar, Hudson, Dafoe" etc.' The whole episode confirmed King's view that the Manitoba organization had fallen 'into the hands of the wrong lot in Winnipeg.' It was little wonder, he wrote, that 'the best thinking Liberals want little or nothing to do with them.'[44] The exit of the Diehard brought immediate reaction from his following, who saw the gesture as one more example of King betraying the loyalists of 1917. 'I feel that you have served notice on the old guard that our work is not appreciated,' N.T. Macmillan wrote, 'and perhaps we should fade away and let others take on the fight.'[45]

By the summer King's doubts about the cabinet were increasing: 'I felt that Cabinet was very weak, lamentably weak in fact – really nothing to grip to. Many like barnacles rather than fighters.' He was looking to changes that would appeal to the Prairies. Charles Stewart could be moved to the Senate while W.R. Motherwell could become the lieutenant governor of Saskatchewan.[46] Complaints of corruption within the Department of Customs and Excise and the portfolio's inept handling by its minister, Jacques Bureau, indicated the extent of the cabinet's weakness.

The results of the Saskatchewan election in June 1925 came as a breath of fresh air to the prime minister. The Dunning Liberals won fifty-two of the sixty-three seats. Mackenzie King, depending upon Quebec and Saskatchewan as the twin pillars of Canadian Liberalism, viewed the victory as evidence that his brand of national Liberalism could appeal to diverse constituencies: 'It seems to me that in the circumstances of Quebec and Saskatchewan being alike so largely Liberal, we have one great essential to national unity. If we can find the things which the men of French Canadian descent have in common with the settlers of the plains, and base our policy upon this common ground, we need have no fear as to what the result will be at the extremities or near the heart as I assume Ontario would like to consider itself.'[47]

The election was further evidence that Dunning remained prime cabinet material, the obvious choice for regional lieutenant. He was popular in the East as well as the West. The premier met with King in August and displayed interest in joining the cabinet, probably as the minister of railways. Discussions also dealt with the entry of Crerar as the Manitoba representative and J.E. Brownlee, the attorney general in the UFA government, as the Alberta representative. Crerar's popularity had been damaged by his involvement in the failed Home Bank, but he was still the best choice to represent the province. As for Dunning himself, the prospects of the upcoming federal election were by no means secure and he preferred to await the results before leaving his post in Saskatchewan. He explained that popular opinion in the province was pressuring him to stay and that the solidarity of the provincial party would be impaired if he abandoned the government.[48] Annoyed, King concluded that Dunning was 'a *safety first* man in politics.'[49] Changes to western representation were again placed on hold. Dunning would wait, Brownlee was too involved in provincial politics, and Crerar was undecided as to his future. King could rely on Dunning for support in the general election and as his 'chief lieutenant in the West,' but it was not clear whether this would be enough.

With no western cabinet changes, King had no choice but to look east. The government had to be strengthened before an election, and the 'sustained courting of the West now seemed unlikely to produce striking Liberal gains.' In the meantime, 'his obsession with the west had weakened the party in the east.'[50] The Conservatives were hammering away at the Liberals in the East, arguing that the decreases in the tariff had forced factories to close. The result was more protectionists in the cabinet[51] and a further weakening of the government's image on the Prairies. Despite the prime minister's misgivings, J.A. Robb was raised to full status as minister of finance. 'For all King's blustering,' Blair Neatby notes, 'he had nonetheless been influenced by the need for support in eastern Canada. His hopes were still for Liberal gains on the prairies but, at the last moment, he had hedged his bet.'[52]

In the 1925 general election campaign Mackenzie King hoped the record of the government would be enough to secure victory. He pointed to a balanced budget; reductions in taxation, the national debt, and the tariff; and increases in the British preference. He promised that the Liberals would push to tighten railway expenditures and to hold the line on the tariff. In Ontario he indicated 'that nothing in the nature of free trade would be possible, for however it might appeal to some men in the west, it would breed discouragement and discontent in this part of the Dominion, and therefore would make for divisions, instead of harmony.'[53] In the West he argued that protection threatened national unity, and he again gave the Hudson Bay Railway a cautious endorsement. The region was warned to send members to Ottawa if its concerns were to remain a priority. No action had been taken in 1925 on such promises as Senate reform and the alternative vote in single-member constituencies, so the prime minister again indicated that reform to the Senate was in the works. A dominion–provincial conference would be called to discuss the issue. The 1925 campaign was based around the notion that only Liberal policies were national policies; only the Liberal party was a truly national party.

Prairie Liberals wished to delay an election until 1926. It was still too soon, they argued: recent gestures toward their region had not yet countered the effects of the previous several years. The party had 'struck bottom' in the West and was just beginning to move 'on the upward grade.' Manitobans urged the government to introduce constructive legislation while postponing the election until the following year.[54] The prime minister was warned that if an election were held at present, it was doubtful Crerar or Hudson would be candidates. Dafoe believed that King would fare better in the West than Meighen, but the Progressive threat remained. 'If Mr. King is allowing himself to be lulled by these stories of Progressive disintegration and the certainty of Liberal triumph,' the editor warned, 'he is preparing a disaster for himself.'[55] Manitoba Liberals, who were not uniting sufficiently to ensure anything like an effective organization, were 'still fighting [the] 1917 election.'[56] King pleaded for someone who was not 'blinded by the passions of the past' to take control of party affairs. He told F.C. Hamilton that 'we must cease to think, let alone speak of Conscriptionists, anti-Conscriptionists,

Progressives, non-Progressives, and the like ... The lesson has been a hard one for the West to learn.'[57]

The thought of an election struck fear into Alberta Liberals. If King were deciding to go to the people based on the expectation of a break-through in this province, 'then for God's sake don't,' J.A. Clarke warned.[58] The Liberal organization was described as a 'disreputable broken down political machine' that was confined to Edmonton and Calgary. The provincial UFA government was holding strong, seemingly unshakeable in rural areas. Any disgruntled UFA supporters at both the provincial and federal levels were not following King's expected route and moving into Liberal ranks. Instead they were moving to the Conservative party.

Only in Saskatchewan was the situation slightly promising. King was again impressed by Premier Dunning, who campaigned vigorously for the federal Liberals. The prime minister was given permission by cabinet to tout Dunning as the one who could be 'counted upon as a Western Minister.'[59] But the differences in Liberal support among the Prairie provinces could not have been more pronounced. The question was whether Mackenzie King would recognize the differences as legitimate reflections of regional diversity or merely assume that with better leader-ship, organization, and candidates the other provinces would soon fol-low Saskatchewan's lead. Despite Ottawa's support for Progressive–Liberal cooperation across the Prairies, there were still thirty-two three-cornered contests. Although the Progressive threat was diminishing, in 1925 it remained enough of a force to play a critical role in the results.

When the ballots were counted on 29 October, Liberal representation fell from 116 to 101 seats in a 245-seat House. To make matters worse, Mackenzie King, along with eight other ministers, lost their seats.[60] The Conservatives more than doubled their representation, winning 116 seats, seven short of a majority. Only 24 Progressives were returned, compared to 65 in 1921. Two independents and two Labour candidates completed the list. According to Neatby, 'eastern Canada had punished King for his preoccupation with the prairies.'[61] In contrast to Quebec, which returned sixty of sixty-five Liberals, the Maritimes sent only six of twenty-nine, and Ontario elected an embarrassing twelve of eighty-two. The party did better in the West, winning one seat in Manitoba, fifteen in Saskatchewan, and four in Alberta, while maintaining its three seats in British Columbia. The Tories gained seven seats in Manitoba, and three in Alberta, but remained shut out in Saskatchewan.

The western results and the decline of the Progressives, in particular, were some of the few bright spots for Mackenzie King: 'The progressives have killed themselves, thank God for that, they have bought their own rope, and put it around their own necks and tightened it themselves, they are done for now.'[62] Yet it was not quite that simple. While the strength of the movement had declined, its power in the new House of Commons was even greater than before. The Progressives – now dominated by the radical group – again held the balance of power, and no government could stay in office without their support. Since the Conservatives had won the most seats, the governor general, Lord Byng, hinted that King should do the honourable thing and resign. The prime minister, aware that Meighen would have great difficulty securing Progressive support, decided instead to maintain power and meet the new House.

The uncertain situation renewed speculation about the Liberal leadership. King's popularity, even inside the party, reached an all-time low at the end of 1925. He held 'very little confidence' and received much of the blame for the election results. If the vote carried 'any measure of chastisement,' R.J. Cromie wrote in the *Vancouver Sun*, 'that chastisement was directed, not at Liberalism, but at the inaction and vacillation that have characterized Mackenzie King's exposition of Liberalism.'[63] Despite some minor gains, Prairie Liberalism remained in a pathetic state. Some party members were still hopeful that a western party would unite with the low tariff members in the East. Such an amalgamation, it was argued, would best be led by Dunning.[64]

It has been argued that T.A. Crerar, J.W. Dafoe, A.B. Hudson, Edgar Tarr, Jimmy Coyne, F.O. Fowler, and H.J. Symington, often referred to as 'the Winnipeg Sanhedrin,' set out to replace King with Dunning: 'In the back of the minds of the Winnipeg group was the notion of a Dunning–Lapointe joint leadership somewhat on the order of the Baldwin–Lafontaine Reform ministry of pre-Confederation days.'[65] Despite the dissatisfaction with King, the 'plot' never materialized into anything more than angry grumblings in the face of the poor election results. Dafoe believed King was not necessarily the 'right man for the present emergency,' but he recognized that an attempt 'to swap horses at this moment would probably be fatal.'[66] T.A. Burrows, another prominent Manitoba Liberal, echoed the same concerns. It would be a 'dangerous policy to swap horses crossing a stream,' he wrote. A suitable alternative would have to be secured before commencing 'any agitation against King.'[67] Crerar was also in complete accord.[68] Dunning was aware of the discussions and agreed that 'King was a terrible load and that he should go.' Nevertheless he felt that action would be taken only if the initiative came from the Quebec wing. He wanted to avoid 'even the appearance of a conspiracy.'[69] In the end the episode, which 'scarcely merited the dignity of being called a plot,' never left the realm of rumours. Dunning would play Caesar but not Brutus. 'Palace revolutionaries,' Neatby points out, 'must be made of sterner stuff.'[70]

To hold power when the House met, Mackenzie King would need the support of all the Liberal members as well as twenty others from among the twenty-four Progressives and two Labour members. The most partisan of Liberals could no longer deny the necessity of courting the Progressives. Yet, according to Robert Forke, although the Progressives were anxious to avoid another election, not to mention a Conservative government, their support was by no means guaranteed. He was confident in holding the Liberal support of those from Manitoba and Saskatchewan; the Alberta group remained in question. The long-time UFA sage, Henry Wise Wood, believed the government should be supported only so long as highly controversial measures were avoided.[71] It seems likely that Forke was also hoping that the Liberals would hang on long enough to have Dunning replace King in the leadership.[72] While Forke and Dafoe advanced coalition as the only means of keeping the Conservatives out of office, they were not harbouring false hopes about its viability. The prime minister, confident that Progressive strength had already peaked, seemed intent on the strategy of cooperation.[73] Now, when the movement had 'all but completely disappeared in every province of the Dominion but two,' was not the time for fusion.[74]

If cabinet reconstruction had been a recurring theme of King's first term in office, it was even more of a necessity after the election, and the prime minister informed eastern members that it would 'depend' upon the West.[75] 'The more I think of the Ministers I have had round me,' King noted, 'the less I find them worth ought as "generals."'[76] A few days after the contest, Dunning reversed his earlier decision to remain in Saskatchewan and decided to enter the federal government. Charlie Stewart reported to the prime minister that the premier had been offended at not being officially invited into the cabinet immediately after the election. An apologetic King sent Dunning a message, indicating the enthusiasm of the entire caucus at having him enter the government. He was expected to aid the West by ushering in a new era of low tariffs.[77] Personally, Mackenzie King welcomed the westerner's arrival with 'immense relief.' Dunning's present value to the teetering government far outweighed any threat he posed to the leadership. The timing was crucial and, as King informed the Saskatchewan politician, 'it would almost look so far as you are concerned, as though the gods had staged the proceedings.' Charles Dunning would become the centrepiece for a new Liberal government as well as party hopes in the West.[78] 'I have thought it well,' King observed, 'to regard Mr. Dunning as the keystone of the arch in the West.' His relations with the Progressives would make him of 'utmost service.'[79] Western opinion soon reinforced the decision. 'Premier Dunning in this western country is hailed by Liberals and Progressives alike as the future hope of the Liberal Party for the Prairie Provinces at Ottawa; one meets this hope expressed in every quarter. He has proved himself in Saskatchewan and if he goes to Ottawa he may accomplish something like what Sifton did after 1896.'[80]

King loyalist Andrew Haydon was sent west to discuss details. It was agreed that the Saskatchewan premier would call a provincial session immediately and come to Ottawa as soon as it prorogued, probably late in January. He would take the portfolio of railways and canals because at present he lacked the experience necessary for finance. Dunning approved of King's intentions to reorganize the cabinet by bringing in such Progressives as Premier Bracken of Manitoba and the newly chosen Premier Brownlee of Alberta. He doubted, however, if King could actually convince the two politicians to enter the government.

The prime minister was also considering bringing Jimmy Gardiner into cabinet as the minister for immigration and colonization. Although this move would provide Saskatchewan with three ministers, King believed that Motherwell could be pressured into accepting the lieutenant-governorship. Dunning had received most of the credit for the Liberal survival in the province after Martin but Gardiner was master of the organization. Much of the party's misfortune in the West was blamed on poor organization, and King saw a wealth of possibility in the young, aggressive politician. There was no doubt that he was a solid party man. 'If the day has been saved to Liberalism in Canada,' the prime minister told Gardiner in the election aftermath, 'it is becoming increasingly apparent that it is Saskatchewan that has saved it ... I am looking forward as you know, to seeing you enter the larger sphere of politics and to your cooperation in the work of organization of adjoining Provinces as well as your own.'[81]

Any attempt to bring both Dunning and Gardiner to Ottawa would cause what had become a bitter feud to surface.[82] Dunning had emerged from the 'Martin faction' of Saskatchewan Liberalism, which had supported Union in 1917, favoured breaking from the federal party when convenient, and fostered close ties with the Progressives. Gardiner, on the other hand, was a 'Motherwell man.' Personality conflict added to the animosity between the two men, and they quite simply disliked each other. They had clashed over the Assiniboia by-election in 1919. During that contest Dunning had even threatened to campaign against the Motherwell–Gardiner forces.[83] When Dunning succeeded Martin as premier in 1922, Gardiner's star was rising and he was mentioned as a possible leadership candidate, but his stand against the Farmers made this impossible. Although Gardiner did become minister of highways in Dunning's government, this occurred because Gardiner's skill at organization could not be ignored. His relationship with Motherwell remained strong and he had become the federal agriculture minister's Saskatchewan agent.

Inside the same provincial caucus Dunning and Gardiner had to work together, so, for political reasons, their relationship remained civil. They corresponded with 'cool politeness.'[84] Both, however, were ambitious and competitive; in the relatively small arena of Saskatchewan politics it was inevitable that their personalities would clash. Gardiner's aggressive and combative nature usually placed him in the role of instigator. He never stopped believing that Dunning was a conniving opportunist who was not a Liberal at all.[85] He would allude to rumours that his rival had even opposed the Liberal party in the elections of 1904 and 1908; Gardiner believed that Dunning would have sought the Conservative leadership if he had failed to obtain the Liberal post.[86] For his part, Dunning handled the quarrel in a manner reflective of his personality and politics. He avoided confrontation whenever possible, pursuing his ambitions in a more subtle manner. A very personable figure, he was noted for his ability to command respect, even among his enemies. Regardless of his actual feelings, he treated Gardiner with 'unfailing courtesy.'[87]

If both were summoned to cabinet, their rivalry could become troublesome, particularly when it came to handling the West. After meeting with Haydon, Gardiner was invited to Ottawa for further discussions. Although Gardiner expressed his desire to become a federal minister, King was disturbed by his attitude toward Dunning: 'The day's conversations have disclosed an unfortunate bitterness between Dunning & Gardiner, over the possibility of both going to Ottawa.' Dunning knew that Gardiner's ambition would eventually take him to federal politics, yet with Progressive relations holding such a high priority at present, he preferred to have him remain in the province. Gardiner would later recall telling Haydon that Dunning was not a Liberal and that the prime minister 'dare not depend on a man like that.'[88] Gardiner made certain to warn King of Dunning's personal reasons for not wanting a rival in Ottawa. Noted King, 'He thinks Dunning is very ambitious, and that he wd conspire against myself for the Leadership of the Liberal Party.'[89] On his deathbed thirty-odd years later, Gardiner claimed that in fact he told the prime minister to take Dunning to Ottawa rather than leave him in Saskatchewan because in the larger political arena he would do less 'harm.'[90]

In the end King had little choice but to keep Gardiner in Saskatchewan. Given Gardiner's antagonism toward the Progressives, Dunning was clearly the best choice for regional lieutenant. For his part, Gardiner was angry at having his ambitions checked, and he was furious that the news was delivered by Dunning, the man who had been chosen over him. Despite his disappointment, Gardiner moved quickly to consolidate his position. Dunning's desire to have C.M. Hamilton as his successor did not prevent Gardiner from being selected premier. Once in office he was determined to bridge any remnants of the federal–provincial breach commenced by Martin and fostered by Dunning. The move to Ottawa would come and in the meantime Gardiner's new position would be used to aid the fortunes of Liberalism at all levels.[91] It did not take long for the new premier to purge the party of Dunning's influence. The *Western Producer* predicted – accurately, as it turned out – that Archie McNab and J.A. Cross, 'as Dunning men,' would not remain in the cabinet. Dunning angrily told a *Free Press* reporter that the purge was a 'personal affront.'[92] Back in Ottawa, Vincent Massey, a minister without portfolio in the cabinet, recognized Dunning's ambition and his desire to keep Gardiner at bay. 'This is selfishness on Dunning's part,' King responded, 'desire to get the stage for & credit to himself.'[93] If he faltered as Prairie lieutenant, Gardiner would be waiting in the wings.

In contrast to the abundance of cabinet material in Saskatchewan, Alberta posed problems. Despite King's lack of satisfaction with Charles Stewart, Dunning had no desire to 'knife' the Alberta representative, so he remained in cabinet. Stewart was steadfastly opposed to a fusion of Progressive and Liberal forces or to the entrance of Progressives into cabinet. In time he was confident the movement would disappear.[94] Unlike King, Stewart was well aware that, in contrast to Manitoba, the Alberta group did not consist of crypto-Liberals. Indeed, each Prairie province had its own unique brand of Progressivism that mirrored the distinct nature of the area. Consequently, a single 'western strategy' was doomed to fail. For the present King decided that while Stewart would remain, Alberta was to be 'left to Dunning to do as he thinks best.'[95]

Manitoba also posed difficulties. Premier Bracken was unwilling to come to Ottawa, and Crerar was still too involved with his business affairs to re-enter politics. King had to be content with informal indications that both Crerar and Forke would possibly enter the government at a later date.[96] Although King suggested J.S. Woodsworth as a possibility, Dunning thought the socialist would be more trouble than he was worth.[97] Despite the limited success, Dafoe was moderately impressed by King's attempts at increased western representation.[98]

In the early months of 1926 the King government worked furiously to ensure Progressive support. Attempts to have the third party participate directly in the preparation of the throne speech were thwarted by too much division in the ranks. Robert Forke offered his support as long as the speech did not contain anything offensive, but rumours persisted that cast doubt on his ability to deliver the Alberta group. The prime minister collected suggestions from Andrew Haydon, who had discussed the throne speech with Dunning and Dafoe on his western trip. Tariff policy, it was argued, would now provoke less controversy. Improving economic conditions had weakened the argument that the postwar recession had been caused by high tariffs, and both Dafoe and Dunning now suggested stability. Mackenzie King, however, continued to view the tariff as central to maintaining Progressive support, and he 'intended to wave it like a red flag until western eyes saw nothing else.'[99] If the Meighen Tories could be pressured into an even more protectionist stance, it would be that much easier to convince the West of Liberal sympathy. As a result the speech again contained a recommendation for a tariff advisory board. The Board of Railway Commissioners was to maintain a western bias regarding freight rates. The Hudson Bay Railway was to be completed 'forthwith,' and it was announced that the natural resources would be returned to Alberta. Because the support of the Alberta Progressives was essential, King finally took action on the resource agreement that had sat moribund since 1924. The province was having financial difficulties, and the return of the resources, which included mineral wealth, would provide control over coal and oil deposits.

The speech also contained a section on immigration and land settlement. A vigorous immigration policy was still widely perceived as necessary to develop the nation. Agricultural immigrants seemed the desirable newcomers to bring more unsettled land under cultivation. But these views were more representative of eastern Canada, and westerners became increasingly resentful toward the immigration issue. It appeared as though Ottawa were more prepared to offer financial aid to immigrants than to those already farming. In response to pressure from the West, and Alberta in particular, the last session had resulted in the government authorizing long-term, low-interest farm loans totalling ten million dollars. The bill faced stiff resistance: Meighen had dismissed the action as an election bribe, Forke had viewed the terms as insufficient, and the Senate had voted against the legislation. The new session brought renewed promises of generous availability of rural credits to reduce the costs of farm production.[100] Overall the prime minister was pleased: 'Our policies as outlined in the speech from the throne have evidently made a strong appeal to Western Canada. From now on we should continue to gain strength in that part of the Dominion.'[101]

Despite the western bribes, the position of the Progressives remained uncertain. Forke was willing to support, even join, the government to keep it in office. Indeed, he agreed with the suggestion to have the Progressives sit on the government side of the House, but the UFA members remained intent on asserting their independence of both major parties. Their strategic position would be employed to pressure the government in power. Once in Ottawa the Progressives asked both King and Meighen for outlines of their legislative programs. While they remained ambivalent in their support, Meighen's unwillingness to 'purchase' their votes led them closer to the Liberal camp.

After the government survived the first division in the House on Meighen's amendment to the throne speech, Prime Minister King moved to consolidate his position. He met with a Progressive delegation, led by Forke, and suggested it name a committee to meet with the cabinet and agree on a plan of cooperation. King argued that he would not carry on without an 'assurance' of cooperation and a plan that was 'open & above board.'[102] He indicated a willingness to adhere to Forke's suggestion of having two Progressives enter the cabinet. This proposal pleased Dafoe, who informed King that if the Progressives refused, the *Free Press* would cease supporting the movement. But Mackenzie King was under no illusions. He did not expect the Progressives to enter the cabinet; indeed, he was actually counting on their refusal. The cabinet was 'not keen' on the idea but would accept it if the Progressives agreed. Either way King would emerge smelling like a rose. 'By having made the offer and having it declined we are in the best of positions,' he observed.[103] As expected, Forke proved willing but the Alberta Progressives refused.

At the beginning of the 1926 session Mackenzie King did not have a seat in Parliament: he had lost his seat in North York. Yet King was already tempering the defeat by the prospect of finding a safer seat elsewhere. North York was increasingly becoming a suburban extension of Toronto, which favoured higher tariffs.[104] After the election, some twenty Liberals had offered the prime minister their constituencies, but few of these suited his requirements. Although he briefly pondered a Quebec seat, such a move would destroy Liberal efforts in the West and his inability to speak French would be embarrassing. Ideally, he was seeking a safe Prairie riding, giving consideration to Long Lake, Saskatchewan, and Athabaska or Wetaskiwin, Alberta.[105] 'The West having so long refused to come to King,' Morton writes, 'King was at last going to the West.'[106]

On 15 January 1926 Charles McDonald, the sitting member for Prince Albert, Saskatchewan, resigned his seat to make way for the prime minister.[107] The constituency lay in the province's parkland on the edges of the western fertile belt. After the initial setback of the CPR choosing the southern rather than northern route across the Prairies in 1881, Prince Albert had overcome its economic handicaps by becoming a major lumbering centre for the province. Fishing, trapping, and ranching were included in the area's list of industries, and it possessed considerable potential for mineral exploration. It was, however, primarily an agricultural district. Although the riding was Tory by tradition, and had been the only seat in the province to go Conservative in 1911, it was now solidly Liberal. The Progressives had held the constituency in 1921, but by 1925 the agrarian 'fever' had 'run its course.'[108] The riding seemed a perfect choice for King: 'In deciding on P.A. the safety of seat & possibility of [acclamation] were deciding factors, also that it was preferable not to run in Prov. of Quebec. – This, too, might help to unite East & West & with other 2 leaders in West wd better ensure our keeping our hold there.'[109] The organization of the Saskatchewan Liberals was particularly impressive. 'With an organization approaching this in other provinces,' the prime minister commented, 'we could sweep the country.'[110]

Premier Gardiner, who was promising victory in Prince Albert, sent in his army of organizers. The local Conservatives abstained from entering the by-election, and the Progressive organization agreed to support the Liberal program. Some members of both parties refused to abandon the field, however, and a Tory farmer, D.L. Burgess, was nominated as an independent to oppose Mackenzie King. On 15 February 1926 the prime minister won the riding with a vote of 7925 to 2299. The victory, he was certain, would be a major step in shoring up Liberal support in the region. 'Undoubtedly your candidature there is good strategy,' one westerner wrote, 'for it will unquestionably get the three Western Provinces ... in closer touch with you.'[111] King was delighted to enjoy 'the more intimate contact with Western Canada.' Together with Dunning he believed they would 'accomplish a great deal for the Canadian West, and Saskatchewan in particular.'[112]

Mackenzie King felt he was forming that 'natural' bond with the region and becoming a 'spiritual westerner.' The magnitude of the Prince Albert victory, along with the fact that Charles McDonald had surrendered the seat without asking anything in return, caused King to wax romantic about the Prairie populace. He claimed to have met a Mennonite minister in the riding who 'said his people voted for me not only for political reasons but because they "loved" me for what I had done for them. It was a very beautiful beginning in my new relationship – I should like above all else to be of real service to these pioneers of Western Canada.' McDonald had shown himself to be a 'knight errant full of good cheer ... happier than if the conquest had been made by himself.' At a dinner given in honour of McDonald and F.N. Darke (who had surrendered his seat to Dunning), and attended by Saskatchewan Liberal MPs, King felt a previously unknown sense of belonging. He described the members as 'a fine lot of men, with high ideals & noble purpose, very different to the selfish easterners ... the consequence of their having learned the spirit of sacrifice & service in helping each other in earlier days, being thankful because their hearts had learned the secret of happiness.'[113] If the prime minister's Prairie sympathies had been diminished by his years in office, they received a new lease on life with his representation of a western riding. The question was whether a Saskatchewan seat would be seen in Alberta and Manitoba as representative of these provinces' interests.

Although the choice of Prince Albert had been an expedient one for King, and allowed him to indulge his romantic aspirations, it also carried benefits for the riding. T.C. Davis, the provincial Liberal MLA immediately informed the prime minister of the riding's 'shopping list,' which included rail connections, road construction, and a national park.[114] By May King was reaping rewards for his new constituency. He was determined to deliver the national park that had been proposed for the Prince Albert area in 1921. His desire to establish the park was announced at a cabinet meeting on 12 May: 'If I can bring this about and I will – that will be a real achievement for Saskatchewan & particularly Prince Albert, a fine memorial for years to come.'[115] The official word on King's intention to establish the park was sent to Davis ten days later.[116]

Back in Parliament Meighen again attempted to defeat the government. The Conservative leader proposed an amendment expressing regret that the policy of protection had not been adopted to increase employment in Canada and benefit farmers and other primary producers. Even the Progressives who had voted for Meighen's first amendment voted against the second. King's troubles, however, were multiplying. The government was on the defensive against Tory MP H.H. Stevens's full-scale attack on the customs department. The corruption that had come to characterize the department had not been cleaned up with the banishment of Jacques Bureau to the Senate. The new minister, George Boivin, had done little to improve the situation. The Progressives would soon have to decide whether to support the government in the face of a scandal or to condemn the corruption and defeat the Liberals, thereby allowing the Tories into office. When the House adjourned on 5 February, the Progressives supported the government pledge to investigate the charges. That same day the prime minister and a Liberal committee met with the Progressives. King claimed to be 'delighted to see the closeness of the relationship.' He believed the perilous situation had brought both groups 'to a consciousness of our nearness to defeat in the face of a common enemy.'[117]

The budget of 1926 lowered the tariff on automobiles and reduced income taxes. It received western applause; unfortunately for King its offerings were credited to the vulnerable position of the government. While the Liberals were winning some Prairie favour, the fear of the protectionist Conservatives rather than genuine approval of the Liberal program was proving the main incentive. If westerners wished to avoid the fall of the government and the handing over of power to Meighen, they had to advocate the path of least resistance. 'A Tory party in power in Ottawa,' Crerar claimed, 'would mean a discontented West.' In defence of his increasing support for King, he could only ask, 'What is the alternative?'[118] He congratulated the prime minister on the budget, while T.A. Burrows noted that it had 'struck the popular idea as far as the West is concerned.' A.M. McLeod described it as 'the best we have had since 1897. It is not only good statesmanship but good politics and it faces the rising sun of liberalism.'[119] The fear of Meighen was certainly stampeding the Manitobans into King's camp.

The reaction in Alberta was not so positive. When the province was forced once again to await the promised transfer of its natural resources, the issue was used to challenge the King government. Although the transfer agreement had been announced and the legislation drafted, the question of school lands proved to be a sticking point. The Autonomy Acts of 1905 had included certain guarantees for separate schools, with the resources now in question including lands set aside to finance schools. Both governments had hoped to leave religious sensitivities undisturbed by not drawing attention to this aspect of the agreement. As justice minister, Ernest Lapointe decided the resource transfer would have to include a statement that the separate schools would continue to be administered in accordance with the original federal act. Agreeing at first, Premier Brownlee then changed his mind. To avoid the old school issue reappearing, the original guarantee for separate schools would have to be put to the courts. By mid-June the issue was threatening Liberal–Progressive cooperation. A western Conservative MP motioned for a vote of non-confidence based on the government's failure to transfer the natural resources to Alberta. The Alberta Progressives tried to persuade the prime minister to introduce the legislation without waiting for the decision of the courts. King refused due to the inevitable opposition of the French Canadians. When it came time for the vote, he threatened that if the government did not receive the support of the House, he would ask for a dissolution and an immediate election. The Alberta group had previously given its support to the Saskatchewan Progressives on the issue of the Hudson Bay Railway, so King was worried the 'free lances' would now return the favour. When the votes were tallied, the government carried the division by five votes. 'The Progressives certainly did nobly and saved the day for us,' he wrote. 'We have made a slip over the resources matter & [are] justly open to criticism.'[120] Yet King's minority continued to hang precariously in the balance.

The very next day matters came to a head. The government had agreed to Progressive requests for a Farm Loan Board as well as an amendment to the Canada Grain Act that would force private elevator companies to serve the wheat pools and ship the grain to terminal. The Senate defeated both measures. Far more serious, however, was the completion of the report of the Special Committee on the Department of Customs and Excise. The department was riddled with corruption; what was worse, members of the government had known of the situation but done nothing. The Tories attempted to loosen the already tenuous support of the Progressives by proposing a motion that included a censure of the present minister of customs. The fate of the government depended on Progressive member D.M. Kennedy, who was on the reporting committee. If he supported the Conservative motion, the official Parliamentary report would censure a member of the government. King used the threat of an election and a probable Tory victory to pressure Kennedy to withold his support. Although Kennedy relented and defeated the motion, he then introduced one of his own, describing Boivin's conduct as 'unjustifiable.' This was almost as damaging for the King government. Kennedy's motion also criticized four members of Parliament, one of whom was a Conservative. After considerable negotiation with Progressive members, King managed to have the motion defeated.

As the final vote on the report drew near, King found the French-Canadian members ready to defend Bureau and Boivin, even if it meant calling an election. 'Much was said of not sacrificing Boivin,' King recorded, '& there was a "damning" of Progressives and Kennedy in particular.' In cabinet he argued that the government would have to concur in the report of the customs committee because rejection would drive the Progressives into opposition and defeat the government. The French Canadians were reluctant. 'All this,' King commented, 'because of its reflection on Bureau. The Fr. Can. wd do anything for one of their number. This mentality on these matters is wholly diff't from the Anglo Saxon. There is something fine in its chivalrous side, but from the point of view of morality it is open to question.' The prime minister blamed Bureau for the predicament and thought he might have to resign from the Senate. King was perceptive enough to understand that Parliament was 'determined to have a scapegoat,' and he was willing to provide an offering.[121]

On 22 June the chairman of the Special Committee on Customs reported to the House. After considerable debate, a Conservative-backed amendment was moved by a Progressive. It combined Stevens's criticism of the government with J.S. Woodsworth's recommendation of a judicial inquiry. The result of such a vote would once again censure the government. The debate ended prematurely when King requested an adjournment to consider tactics. He intended to have Parliament dissolved and an election date set. Much to King's surprise, the governor general refused to comply. Governor general Lord Byng had thought it improper for King to maintain power in 1925 when the Conservatives held more seats; he now believed that Meighen deserved the chance, and had the constitutional right, to form a ministry.

On 28 June, after Mackenzie King resigned to avoid censure, a stunned Arthur Meighen was invited by the governor general to form a government. The difficulty for the Conservatives was that if any members accepted a portfolio in the new government (which involved accepting a minister's salary), they would immediately have to vacate their seat and contest a by-election before returning to the House. As soon as he became prime minister, Meighen himself had to vacate his seat; if he named his other ministers, the new government would be deprived of its best debaters and, more importantly, the votes needed to maintain power. This problem was avoided by the unusual tactic of not assigning any portfolios. Meighen appointed seven ministers without portfolio to serve as acting heads of the government departments. These men would not receive a minister's salary and therefore would not have to resign their seats to contest by-elections. Now leader of the opposition, King found unexpected success in attacking Meighen's 'shadow cabinet.' A vote of non-confidence proposed by J.A. Robb carried by one vote. When the Conservative government collapsed, Prime Minister Meighen, unlike King, was granted a dissolution and election, thereby setting the stage for the Liberals to campaign on the 'Constitutional Issue.'

Mackenzie King did his utmost to make the constitutional question the central issue of the 1926 election. The death of George Boivin during the campaign weakened the Tory attempt to maintain the focus on the customs scandal. Regardless, western Canada showed more interest in the tariff, freight rates, and the Hudson Bay Railway. Nonetheless, with the very real threat of a Conservative victory, the Prairies were a much more hospitable environment for the Liberals. 'All agree,' King recorded, 'that outlook in West is entirely different from what it has been for many years past.'[122] The recent parliamentary session had further divided and weakened the Progressives, and the crypto-Liberals were returning in mass to the fold.

In 1925 the Conservatives had elected seven members in Manitoba. This time Liberals and Progressives joined forces to crush the Tories. J.W. Dafoe was crucial to the alliance, and his public editorials and private influence set the tone. Although his fear of a Conservative victory had prompted Dafoe to action,[123] the Liberals were simply relieved to see the editor and his paper on side. No constituency in Manitoba nominated rival Liberal and Progressive candidates; in six constituencies the two associations nominated a joint candidate. Robert Forke, who had resigned as leader of the Progressives after the party had split over the customs committee report, became a joint candidate.

Mackenzie King was delighted by the cooperation. It seemed the culmination of all his efforts to rebuild the Liberal party, not only in Manitoba, but in the West. He found 'a great change from 1925 & still greater from 1921,' and took 'much pride' in the united effort.[124] Manitoba Liberalism had suffered from the split of 1917 and the Progressive upsurge of 1921; the election of 1925 had been the first contest since 1917 in which Liberal candidates had reappeared in many constituencies. If the reorganization process was slow, it was showing results by 1926. Crerar was also pleased: 'The Liberal campaign has been infinitely better handled all around than it was a year ago; that is certainly true of Manitoba for there could not have been fuller cooperation between Progressives and Liberals than has existed in this fight. As you know, I have always believed that Western Canada, especially the prairie provinces, could be made a stronghold for Liberalism for the next twenty-five years and I think that very substantial progress in this direction has been made in this campaign.'[125] King was so spurred on by the confidence and enthusiasm of Manitoba Liberals that he made a trip out to Portage-la-Prairie, Meighen's home riding, in the hopes of having the Conservative leader defeated.[126]

There was, however, one particular note of dissatisfaction echoing from the province. Party members were tired of hearing the federal party praise the organization in Saskatchewan, and they would not tolerate their western neighbour receiving credit for success in Manitoba. 'There appears to be some heartburning here over the apparent tendency at Ottawa to treat Manitoba as the "little brother" of Saskatchewan,' A.B. Hudson complained. The province had not been 'placed under the direction' of neighbouring Liberals, despite the beliefs of some federal members. Manitoba organizers had spoken with those from Saskatchewan but, given the stark differences between the provinces, it was quickly realized that nothing could be done other than having Dunning and Gardiner make a few speeches. Any outside interference in the present or future, Manitoba organizers argued, would only disrupt the Liberal–Progressive unity that had finally developed.[127] They also suspected that King was manoeuvring to replace Dunning with Gardiner as his western lieutenant. According to J.W. Dafoe, the anti-Progressive Gardiner seemed to be 'carrying on a knifing campaign against Dunning, both at Ottawa and in Regina,' and 'he is encouraged in this attitude by King, who is apparently also jealous of his new lieutenant.'[128]

In Saskatchewan the ever-partisan Gardiner continued his battle to defeat all non-Liberals. Despite King's urgings that the premier not fight the Progressives, Gardiner justified his tactics by pointing to his record in having both federal and provincial Liberals elected. Regardless, the prime minister was painfully aware that of the six Progressives who had been elected in Saskatchewan in 1925, three had supported the Conservatives during the session. He could at least take satisfaction in the state of his own constituency. 'These are real people,' he wrote while campaigning in Prince Albert, '& it is a joy to work for them. They are the makers of

Canada & I have tried to have them realize this and that they are writing Canadian history.'[129] After a brief visit to Prince Albert, he returned to Ottawa, letting the local organization manage the campaign. Future prime minister John Diefenbaker was nominated as the Conservative candidate in King's riding and immediately set out to redirect public attention away from the constitutional issue and back to the customs scandal.

Alberta remained the western Achilles heel. A provincial election in the summer had further aggravated the differences between Liberals and Progressives. When C.R. Mitchell resigned as leader of the provincial Liberals, replaced by J.T. Shaw, closer relations seemed possible. Premier Brownlee soon dashed these hopes by discouraging any interparty rapport. Provincial Liberals were left to suspect the UFA of Tory favouritism.[130] 'Brownlee pretends to be liberal in his leanings and friendly to you and the Liberal Party,' one Albertan warned King. 'He is the most unblushing hypocrite in political life to-day.'[131] During the campaign the federal UFA MPs severed their connection with the Progressive caucus and indicated they would maintain their identity strictly as United Farmers of Alberta. Charles Stewart, who was incapable of wielding influence with the UFA, had little more control over the Liberal organization in the province.[132] King noted 'a sort of helplessness on his part in the whole situation.' The prime minister's office received report after report reiterating the contention that the Alberta brand of Progressivism was anything but Liberal. For his part, Mackenzie King shrugged off the advice and held to the belief that the province was as Liberal as the rest of the Prairies. Brownlee could be brought on board as an ally; the situation was nothing more than the result of a lack of organization and leadership. 'It is tragic to see a great province like Alberta go by the boards for lack of leadership,' King observed, 'it is really solidly liberal in the true sense of the word.'[133] Still, King was prepared if possible to omit Alberta from his campaign itinerary and spend more time in Ontario. In the end he was persuaded to tour all the provinces.

Mackenzie King emerged victorious from the election of 14 September 1926 with his leadership strengthened and the Progressives in disarray. The Liberals gained 15 seats to win a total of 116, still leaving them short of a majority. Yet the party's position was bolstered by the election of twelve Progressives, ten Liberal-Progressives, two Independents, and three Labour members, all of whom could probably be relied upon for support. Even the eleven UFA MPs were more likely to favour the Liberals than the Tories. The Conservatives won ninety-one seats in total. The Prairie results were particularly gratifying for King. In Manitoba the Liberals gained three members and the Liberal-Progressives won seven, while the Conservatives lost all seven of their seats. Saskatchewan added one Liberal and one Liberal-Progressive. Although Mackenzie King defeated John Diefenbaker by only 131 votes in the city of Prince Albert, the vote in the riding as a whole favoured the prime minister over his Tory rival 8933 to 4838.[134] In Alberta the Liberals lost two rural constituencies to the UFA but both a Liberal and a Labour candidate stole urban seats from the Tories.[135] 'The angels are certainly on the side of Willie King,' Dafoe remarked. 'He has a finer opportunity now than he had in 1921, and I hope he will be equal to it. I am beginning to think that probably he will measure up to his opportunities this time. It was certainly a Mr. King that I knew nothing about who has been performing in the last two months.'[136]

In explaining their victory the jubilant Manitobans gave little credit to the constitutional issue. According to A.B. Hudson, the work of the *Free Press* was the single most important factor, followed closely by Liberal–Progressive harmony. The dominant issues remained freight rates, the Hudson Bay Railway, and the tariff. The customs scandal seemed to be forgotten.[137] The real possibility of facing a Conservative government brought a flood of praise and support for Mackenzie King. His western speeches were described as impressive, his campaign 'vigorous and dignified.' All agreed he emerged from the fight much stronger than when he entered. 'King is now strongly entrenched,' Crerar noted.[138] If the sceptical Dafoe was in any way representative of Prairie sentiment, the prime minister had finally succeeded in winning the cautious support of the region. 'My regard for King has gone up a good deal since July 1st,' the *Free Press* editor admitted. 'The way he handled himself in the House and the admirable campaign which he has carried on suggest to me that there is more to him than I have been inclined to think there was. He certainly now has a magnificent opportunity and if he fumbles it his blood be on his head.' Crerar's verdict announced that the crypto-Liberals of Manitoba were now on King's side: 'Personally, I think that the Liberal party today is closer to the standard of real Liberalism ... than it has been at any time in fifty years.'[139]

As usual, changes to the cabinet proved less drastic after the election than King envisioned. With no alternative, Stewart remained the representative from Alberta. The only change in Prairie representation was the entry of Robert Forke as minister of immigration and colonization. At first the prime minister wanted the former Progressive leader to move into agriculture, having heard that Forke privately preferred this department. 'If the matter is pressed forward I shall probably have to ask

Motherwell to take another Department,' King admitted. Charles Dunning was suggesting that Gardiner come to Ottawa in Motherwell's place. Although the prime minister was also considering summoning the Saskatchewan premier, once again the move would have to wait. Gardiner was seen as 'the ablest and best of all the men in the West,' but at present keeping him and Dunning in separate 'orbits' remained the best strategy. In the meantime the elderly Motherwell would be kept on as a gesture to placate Gardiner. When King had informed the premier that Motherwell would possibly have to take another portfolio so Forke could have agriculture, Gardiner's ingrained hatred of the Progressives surfaced. He pushed to have Forke accept either immigration or the interior.[140] In the end he became the minister of immigration.

By 1926 Mackenzie King's efforts to win the Prairie West were bearing fruit. The agrarian revolt had largely run its course, and its political manifestation had all but disintegrated. Most of the original Liberals within the Progressive movement were back on side, whether due to King's strategy, the failings within the third party, or the fear of the Conservatives. The prime minister had passed through some turbulent times but had emerged in a stronger position in the party and nation. In the West, Saskatchewan and Manitoba were reasons for optimism.

But the region's lack of homogeneity posted danger signs for the King Liberals. While Saskatchewan's Liberal base seemed genuine enough, Manitoba's apparent unity disguised deeply entrenched party divisions. In addition, despite not winning any seats, the Conservatives had won an impressive proportion of the popular vote. Liberal hopes meanwhile remained fixed on the eventual 'return of common sense' in 'radical' Alberta, Yet the indications were bleak. If Mackenzie King had increased his party's stature on the Prairies, the support was tenuous. To maintain that support would be a formidable task that would involve keeping 'western' issues in the forefront.

From the standpoint of the Prairie West, the danger signs were much more ominous. Since the days of Laurier the region had held centre stage in the nation's development. As early as the First World War, this position was beginning to shift as economic and geo-political factors transferred the emphasis back toward central Canada. Vernon Fowke's work on the national policy and the wheat economy, though dated in many ways, perhaps best illustrates this change. Fowke argues that the altering situation could be seen even in the details of Ottawa's handling of royal commissions and agricultural policy. Prior to 1920, royal commissions were employed to educate the public and to put protest on record.

Farmers played a crucial role in conducting the commissions. They often headed or served on the committees; their views were solicited and heeded. For the most part, the commissions responded to the concerns of the industry. Agricultural conditions changed after the First World War. The problem, according to Fowke, was the 'cumulative and deep-seated shrinkage in the rate of population growth and industrial expansion in the Atlantic economy ... Canadian agriculture, in turn, was faced with overseas markets which instead of steadily expanding now threatened permanently to contract.' When farmers found themselves in a situation that seemed desperate, agrarian protest increased. Wary governments appointed more commissions, 'but it was obvious to them that farmers could no longer be entrusted with the task of prescribing remedies for their own condition.' Instead persons would be selected who would not jeopardize the economic situation or threaten vested interests. 'That governments were genuinely at a loss to know what to do about agriculture in this period,' Fowke concludes, 'there can be no doubt.'[141]

Even the popular perception of the Prairies was changing. 'In the decades after 1920,' Gerald Friesen observes, 'when urban standards and urban technology dominated cultural works, "rural" became a synonym for backwardness.' Industrialization and its accompanying partner, urbanization, seem to have been responsible for this transition. At the same time the Canadian community was becoming 'more than ever plagued by French–English tensions, and as preoccupied by regional problems in the Maritimes as in the West. The era of farm supremacy was over. The agrarian myth was forgotten.' The shift was evident in works of literature, such as the novels of Robert Stead.[142] With the weakening of the agrarian revolt, the region was now reluctantly returning to the traditional parties. The Progressives had lost the balance of power, and westerners would be left wondering if this meant the pandering of Mackenzie King had come to an end.

5

Leaving the Plough in the Furrow, 1927–1930

I felt a good deal of exasperation over King's performance in leaving the plough in the furrow, when there was a great need for it to be ploughed through to the end, and going off on a political adventure.

J.W. Dafoe to D.A. McArthur, 7 October 1930

By 1927 it seemed that the Liberals had regained their foothold on the Prairies. Mackenzie King, however, was taking no chances. Although the influence of the Progressives had waned, they were still a potentially dangerous force. The battle with the third party movement had left its scars; for the remainder of King's career an element of distrust coloured his attitude toward the region. The prime minister was pleased with his party's standing, but he was not yet prepared to lay down arms. His attempts to neutralize and absorb the Progressives merely changed venues: after 1927 efforts were directed toward the Farmers at the provincial level.

Mackenzie King believed that Manitoba was the crucial theatre in the war against Progressivism and was essential in returning the West completely to the two-party system. The province, therefore, would receive special attention from Ottawa. Meanwhile, the onset of economic prosperity would allow the King government to act on western concerns and bolster Liberal fortunes throughout the region. Yet the durability of Prairie support was problematic. Western scepticism toward Ottawa had been submerged, and it would remain below the surface as long as times were good. If times proved difficult, however, there was no guarantee the region would not abandon the traditional parties, once again placing King's dream of a Liberal West in jeopardy.

Mackenzie King's career to date had demonstrated the naivety of his Prairie perceptions. Even his own personal experience made it clear that, while he could romanticize rural life, he had no real understanding of agriculture. He had developed a series of properties at Kingsmere in the Gatineau country, which he used as a retreat from Ottawa. His first investment was a farm, but as Bruce Hutchison so aptly notes, 'typically enough, where another man would have plunged with shovel and pick into the earth, King flung open the doors of his farmhouse to sit alone at a broken table and compose a speech ... The farmer's physical love of the earth he never felt.'[1] Yet by 1927 'he still maintained the illusion that Kingsmere was a farm.' An attempt to raise sheep turned quickly to failure, with King 'perturbed' to learn the difficulties and challenges attached to livestock. The 'farm' was assailed by threats of fire, prowling dogs, livestock diseases, and fencing and grazing problems. By the end of spring 1928, King had become doubtful about continuing with livestock and thought it better to confine himself to gardening. 'The farm has been a mistake, a costly experiment,' he wrote in November, 'with more worry than pleasure & undue publicity.'[2] The 'lovely pastoral scene' had to be abandoned, and 'the gentleman farmer gave way to the country squire,'[3] a role for which Mackenzie King was better suited.

While the prime minister was a failure at farming, he carried himself with the air of an experienced parliamentarian who seemed able to handle the complexities of agricultural issues. He had gained a mastery over his cabinet, and for the first time the Liberal party was united and secure in office.[4] The nation was also prosperous. The postwar recession had finally ended, each successive year offering increased national production and income. King's government had kept its expenditures to a minimum and reduced tariffs and taxes. The policies of fiscal restraint and balanced budgets were working; there seemed no reason to alter them. 'It is the most prosperous period of our history as a country,' King recorded. 'Even the "golden" era of Sir Wilfrid's day ... is not to be compared with the present for prosperity.'[5]

If the Prairie West would never again see the 'golden era' of Laurier, after 1924 rising wheat prices did at least give reason for optimism. Many farmers, borrowing from the banks to expand their operations, became caught up in a frenzy of speculation. These expansions usually involved buying into the new technology – tractors, combines, and trucks – that was revolutionizing agriculture and increasing the size of farms. While many farmers continued to rely heavily on wheat, other grains such as oats and barley also became popular. This was particularly the case in

Manitoba, where diversification was the rule. Mixed farming increased in popularity, most notably in Alberta.

The prosperity was evident in government. Attention was finally paid to the Hudson Bay Railway. As promised, with Parliament passing impressive yearly grants to the project, the line was extended to the newly constructed Fort Churchill terminal. The budget of February 1927 came and went with little opposition. The usual controversy over the tariff was avoided by postponing any changes until the Tariff Advisory Board had conducted its investigations. Income and sales taxes were reduced, and other minor taxes either reduced or eliminated.

The appointment of the Duncan Commission to investigate discontent in the Maritime provinces also reflected the prosperous times, and its report received careful scrutiny from the West. In studying Maritime grievances the commission pointed to the inequalities of Confederation and recommended that the federal government subsidize the less prosperous areas of the nation. Ottawa planned to increase Maritime subsidies by more than $1.5 million, and reduce freight rates by 20 per cent, with the federal government carrying the weight of the railway losses. If Maritime grievances were to be treated so sympathetically, and times were so good, it seemed only proper that Ottawa should also settle some long-standing Prairie complaints.

While Saskatchewan shared in the general prosperity, Prince Albert enjoyed the additional advantage of serving as the constituency of the prime minister. Despite some delays, plans for a national park were proceeding, with King's influence speeding the process along.[6] On 24 March 1927 the park was established by an order-in-council. The prime minister knew that such a project would bode well for the party, as well as his own fortunes, in the constituency, province, and region. 'The Park is going to be a grand thing for Prince Albert,' T.C. Davis observed to King, 'but, the benefits to be derived therefrom are going to be of greater benefit to the Province as a whole than to Prince Albert alone. It is going to preserve in perpetuity a great playground for the people of Saskatchewan ... The people of Prince Albert and the people of Saskatchewan as a whole, will bear an eternal debt of gratitude to you for the great interest that you have taken in this Park.'[7] As minister of the interior, Charles Stewart had James A. Wood, the proposed park superintendent, visit King at Kingsmere to receive the prime minister's 'blessing.' Wood received the appointment and, with Davis's advice, King began to distribute park patronage.[8]

The construction of the Shellbrook–Turtleford branch line was seen as one more example of what the prime minister could offer the constituency. Although there had been talk of an alternative eastern line from Prince Albert to Hafford, which would link the area to Saskatoon, the people had long been pushing for a western line to open up transportation into the area and connect the general district with the city of Prince Albert. It would also serve as a connection to the Edmonton line and an adjunct for the Hudson Bay Railway.[9] 'I venture to say,' King wrote, 'that there will be difficulty in discovering any constituency in Canada which from the point of view of public works, has received as much in a little space of time as Prince Albert. This, of course, is as it should be.'[10]

The Liberals were not alone in attempting to catch the eye of the western voter. In October 1927 the Conservatives chose a new leader in Winnipeg at their first leadership convention. The conference was held on the Prairies in an attempt to revive party fortunes in the region; moreover, the new leader, Richard Bedford Bennett, 'had the advantage of being a westerner.' As the only Tory elected in the region in 1926, he seemed the last hope in an area where Conservatism was 'almost bankrupt.'[11] However, Arthur Meighen had also represented a western riding, in this case Portage-la-Prairie, Manitoba, and his political positions were rarely shared by those in the region. Likewise, western Liberals viewed the selection of Bennett, the millionaire protectionist, as a gift-horse and guarantee that Tory hopes would remain unfulfilled: 'King surely must have horseshoes and rabbits' feet hanging all round his person,' Crerar remarked.[12] For his part, King dismissed any notion that Bennett could gain western support or even that he was a westerner. He had been transplanted to Calgary from New Brunswick, and the region would never accept his traditional Tory views. Of course the prime minister rejected any notion that he was at least equally unqualified to call himself a western representative.

Increasingly, King's western gaze focused on Manitoba. Prairie support in Ottawa, as the election of 1926 demonstrated, necessitated the union of Liberals and Progressives. Manitoba had offered up such a union in the last election. Now firmly in power, the prime minister promoted fusion at the provincial level. If the Farmers were absorbed provincially as well, he would be confident of the long-term support of the region. At the time, Alberta was an anomaly that would either follow Manitoba's lead or be whipped into shape by the Saskatchewan machine. The first step in Manitoba would involve dealing with the United Farmer government of John Bracken.

Any chance of a provincial coalition was unlikely as long as the Diehard and Free Press factions of the Liberal party remained at each other's throats. Despite the bitter opposition of the Diehards, discussions with Premier Bracken were initiated in March 1926 through Ralph Maybank, president of the Manitoba Federation of Young Liberal Clubs. The timing could not have been better: Bracken, who feared he was losing the Conservative element of his populist UFM government, was pondering a new coalition. He considered asking prominent Liberal judge H.A. Robson to enter the government as attorney general, and possibly raised the matter with him, but nothing definite materialized.[13] The Diehards were furious: they viewed coalition as a sure way of allowing the Farmers to absorb and control the Liberals. At a provincial Liberal convention in November 1926 the course to be taken 'caused a very sharp difference of opinion' between the Free Press group, which supported the Liberal overtures, and the Diehards.[14]

The Diehards received the full support of Jimmy Gardiner's forces. The Saskatchewan premier aided in the selection of Robson as the new leader of the Manitoba Liberal party in March 1927 and immediately set about convincing him that 'there is only one way to eliminate the Progressives, and that is by defeating them.' Gardiner had no doubt that 'Bracken is traditionally a Tory and not a Liberal.'[15] The reaction of the Free Press group was initially favourable to Robson's selection because it was believed that he favoured fusion. This quickly changed. The new Liberal leader issued a statement to the press indicating that his party was 'entirely free from alliances' and that both class and group government were unacceptable in Manitoba.[16] He began informing King that the federal party was too friendly with the Progressives: 'I do not like the way our Dominion members fraternize with the members of the Manitoba Farmer Government,' Robson complained.[17] Gardiner also recognized the influence that Crerar and the Free Press Liberals were wielding in Ottawa. They certainly seemed to have the sympathetic ear of the prime minister. Cooperation with the Progressives was, according to Gardiner, 'too big a price to pay for the friendly attitude of the Free Press.' He believed that the Progressive 'problem' was no stronger in Manitoba than Saskatchewan, and that it could be treated with the same 'cure.' It required a strong dose of organization and leadership. After five years of discussion and negotiation, the country was 'absolutely tired of anything that savours of coalition or compromise.'[18] The Saskatchewan premier used the weak-willed Robson to interfere in the Manitoba situation and create obstacles to any proposed fusion. Three days after the leadership convention Robson wrote his mentor, 'I do not want the slightest slip in our connection ... We understand each other and know the situation ... please don't hesitate to do or suggest anything you see fit and *don't wait for us.*[19] Crerar soon became alarmed by the influence that Gardiner was wielding over Robson. 'I think that Gardiner is giving evil counsel to Robson and his friends,' he told Kirk Cameron.[20]

The Manitoba provincial election of the following summer further exacerbated the split in the party over the issue of coalition with the Progressives. Robert Forke warned King that the antagonistic attitude of the Diehards, who were 'more anxious to defeat Bracken than to defeat Conservative Candidates,' could have only an unfortunate effect on the national fortunes of the Liberals.[21] Although the UFM again won the contest, Robson admitted that 'avowed' Tories had gained seats due to the Liberal division. He justified the sacrifice, arguing that the Diehards had successfully weeded out disguised Conservatives from Bracken's party and thereby deprived the government of 'too much Tory influence.' The 'curbing of the Progressive undercurrent' was more important than the election of a few Conservatives: 'We can handle the Tories any time but Progressivism is dangerous.' Robson was annoyed that, during the campaign, prominent members of the federal party had worked toward cooperation. This attitude, he warned King, would create problems when it came time for a federal contest.[22]

Gardiner admitted openly that his Saskatchewan Liberals had participated in the fight against the Bracken government. It was Ottawa's 'surrendering attitude,' and not opposition to the UFM, that had cost the Liberals votes, he argued: 'Had we had the unqualified support of the Federal Liberals, Bracken would not be in power in Manitoba today without a union with the Liberals in control.' The Saskatchewan premier was not pleased that his influence in Manitoba was being undermined from Ottawa. He accused members of the Manitoba and Alberta governments of attending Conservative conventions in Saskatchewan 'to make trouble.' It was only in 'self defense,' he claimed, that both Farmer governments had to be defeated, and if the national party continued to 'line up' against the party faithful, Liberalism in the West was doomed. Amidst his complaints Gardiner could not resist the temptation to throw out an attack against his arch-nemesis, Charles Dunning: 'I am growing tired of having the political situation in the west in the hands of a man who treats us like a group of school boys.' It would even be better, he claimed, to have the situation back in the hands of Charlie Stewart.[23] Jimmy Gardiner was working to increase his stature as the most influential Prairie Liberal. As usual, Dunning seemed to be blocking the path.

Crerar was at his wits' end. Bracken was finally in a position where he needed increased Liberal support, yet Robson's stance against coalition, along with the 'invasion' of Gardiner's workers, had allowed a Conservative revival.[24] Obviously Robson's selection as leader was a mistake, and he would have to go. The Free Press Liberals began to advocate his appointment to a vacant post on the Manitoba bench while the Diehard group urged the appointment of E.J. McMurray to the position.[25]

Mackenzie King was also frustrated. Surprised by the still-simmering bitterness of the anti-Progressive sentiment, he could not understand why the Diehards did not realize the benefits to be gained through cooperation. The Liberals would not be in power at Ottawa, he assured Gardiner, if not for the two groups working together. But rather than subsiding, the resistance to cooperation was forming a united front in both Saskatchewan and Manitoba. To make matters worse, Gardiner remained at odds with Dunning. The premier jealously defended his 'orbit,' suspiciously observing his rival's every move. He perceived the unseen hand of Dunning everywhere, using his position in Ottawa as regional lieutenant to meddle in western affairs. Such an attitude, King believed, was 'unfair & bitter ... Jealousies are at the bottom of it.'[26] King believed he could use Dunning as more of a national representative than strictly a regional one. The prime minister informed Gardiner that Dunning had no intention of controlling the West; indeed, Gardiner himself was wanted in Ottawa 'for that very purpose.'[27] Gardiner's ascendancy to the position of western lieutenant continued despite his anti-Progressive stance. He would not be brought into the cabinet, however, until King was certain that cooperation between Liberals and Progressives was no longer crucial and his value in the region outweighed that of Dunning. Meanwhile, King was left with the impression that 'the Western situation is anything but a happy one.' Charlie Stewart still had 'no grip' on Alberta, and Manitoba had 'no leadership in Forke.'[28]

By August 1927 Gardiner was warning King that a new danger had appeared in Saskatchewan that could threaten not only the provincial Liberals but the federal party as well. There was growing popular hostility toward non-Anglo-Saxon settlers as well as the government policies that encouraged immigration. The Liberal machine in the province had come to achieve such mastery because it maintained the support of both the organized farmers and the 'ethnic' groups. Now, it found itself 'in the unhappy position of trying to pacify one and protect the other.'[29] The ethnic division was exacerbated by religious differences: the public perceived the province as overwhelmingly Protestant and the immigrants as Catholic.

Up to this point the Liberals had shown little real concern over the gathering storm. The schools question had been put to rest with the Autonomy Acts of 1905 and later amendments in 1918. The ethnic communities still resented the actions of the Union government during the war to disenfranchise 'enemy aliens.' It is not surprising that the ethnic communities maintained their Liberal allegiance amid the agrarian revolt, particularly considering the heavy Anglo-Saxon bent of the Saskatchewan Grain Growers' Association. While W.M. Martin and Charles Dunning had been concerned with winning the Progressive vote and were less friendly to ethnic groups, Gardiner was intent of following the traditional 'liberal' – and increasingly unpopular – path of protecting minorities. Critics argued that government policy ought to be to 'Canadianize' immigrants, but that this objective was jeopardized by a steady flow of central European immigrants and declining numbers from Britain. The provincial government could argue that immigration was a federal responsibility, at least until the natural resources were transferred, yet this defence merely led critics to throw the Gardiner and King Liberals into the same lot.

By 1927 the Ku Klux Klan had come west from Ontario to spread propaganda and discredit the Liberal party for what it perceived as its close relationship with Roman Catholics.[30] The old schools question provided ammunition, and the Klan also took advantage of discontent aimed at the federal Railway Agreement of 1925. The Liberal act had allowed the CNR and CPR to recruit European immigrants and transport them to Canada without fulfilling the usual government regulations. For example, the railways were ignoring a requirement that would have prevented the entry into Canada of migrants from the 'non-preferred' nations of southern and eastern Europe without guaranteed permanent employment as domestic servants or farm hands.[31] The King government was blamed for the high numbers of foreign immigrants, including many Catholics, still entering the West. T.C. Davis complained that the KKK was 'breeding dissension' in Prince Albert. The prime minister merely shrugged off the attacks. 'It is rather interesting to discover,' he told Gardiner,

> that at a moment when our Government is being attacked in a by-election in North Huron through the medium of an anonymous pamphlet entitled 'Mackenzie King and the anti-Catholic Alliance' an active propaganda such

as that to which your letter refers should be gaining headway in Saskatchewan on the nature of our alleged Roman Catholic affiliations and sympathies. What you are face to face with is, I think, only the spreading to Western Canada of the influence of the Orange Order as the electioneering nucleus of the Tory Party.[32]

In addition to new threats, Mackenzie King continued to grapple with old issues. In 1927 at the first Dominion–Provincial Conference, the Prairies and Maritimes allied themselves to demand concessions from Ottawa. The western premiers supported the contention that the Maritimes deserved greater subsidies. In return, the Maritime premiers agreed that the Prairie provinces should have control over their natural resources as well as receive continued subsidies from Ottawa. With the central provinces offering no serious objections to negotiations for control of natural resources, the prime minister agreed to reopen the issue. The path to resolving the long-standing question appeared to be cleared at last.

Notwithstanding the good will on the resources issue, one source of contention at the conference would in the future become a particular sore spot between Ottawa and the West. Relief payments to the unemployed, traditionally handled by the municipalities and provinces, were rising, and the decline of seasonal employment was becoming a serious issue. As farm labour was replaced by machines, the Prairie unemployment rolls lengthened. While the other premiers discussed the causes of unemployment, Premier Brownlee of Alberta pointed directly to immigration. Premier Bracken of Manitoba went so far as to suggest that the tradition of poor-law relief was inadequate and that Ottawa would have to take some responsibility. In the past, federal assistance had been only a temporary measure to meet conditions arising out of the war and the return of enlisted men to civilian life. As far as King was concerned, circumstances had not arisen to justify federal contributions to either the provinces or municipalities. Hoping to avoid any expense to the federal treasury, he maintained the traditional belief that responsibility for relief payments rested with the local authorities. The claim of western premiers that the 1925 Railway Agreement was only adding to the problem fell on deaf ears. In fact the agreement was to be renewed by Parliament in 1928.[33]

Yet overall, the West tended to share the optimism of King, who was pleased with the events of 1927. The *Grain Growers' Guide* had taken on a new, positive tone when discussing the prime minister. The government had 'done well' and had 'gained prestige,' the western journal noted at year's end. King was exhibiting 'rare political sagacity'; 'his position never looked surer than it does today.' The *Guide* hinted that King might be on his way to join the ranks of Macdonald and Laurier as a 'great' prime minister.[34] Such praise reflected western prosperity as well as the desire to prevent Conservative inroads. The journal had long reflected the Progressive character of its Manitoba origins.

If the throne speech were any indication, western optimism was only going to increase. The speech referred almost exclusively to Prairie issues. The government claimed that steps were being taken to handle the administration of immigration in a more effective manner so as to prevent the increase of unemployment. The Hudson Bay Railway was progressing well. A settlement of the natural resources question seemed imminent: Mackenzie King announced to the House that the dominion would now negotiate on the basis of returning the resources while at the same time continuing the subsidies.

Three weeks after the session began, the finance minister presented his budget. James Robb boasted of a surplus totalling more than $50 million, again as a result of increased revenues and restricted expenditures. Although the prosperity allowed the opportunity to reduce taxes, King was concerned that such reductions would force the government to rely increasingly on the tariff for revenue. He favoured lowering the tariff because it would be 'the more truly Liberal policy.'[35] The Tariff Advisory Board had recommended increases on some items and decreases on others, but the prime minister insisted in cabinet that only decreases should be contemplated. Despite cabinet's agreement with King's position, the prime minister feared Robb's protectionist nature, noting that some of the finance minister's changes were 'more protectionist than they appear.'[36] The budget debate seemed to justify these suspicions. Robb was forced to admit that in the complicated reclassification of tariff items some of the rates had actually been increased. The United Farmers of Alberta MPs in particular attacked the changes as inadequate, with the *Grain Growers' Guide* now reflecting the same sentiments: 'Careful scrutiny of Mr. Robb's fifth budget during the past few weeks finds it less attractive than at the time of its introduction. It is not so much the actual provisions of the budget as what it portends for the future that is ominous. Tariff changes were so few and so complicated that no one yet can estimate their effect.'[37] The prime minister was disturbed. While he was certain that large-scale reductions would come in the future as long as the boom continued, he wanted something to offer in the meantime. At the end of the session he was planning to frame the next budget to 'compel all the West to vote with us.'[38]

As the session progressed it soon became apparent that the immigration problem, and not the tariff, was now the immediate concern of Prairie representatives. Even if the federal government could avoid accepting responsibility for unemployment, immigration was a joint dominion–provincial responsibility. In Manitoba, Premier Bracken was arguing that, because new immigrants and out-of-province workers were taking the jobs of local residents, Ottawa should help cover the costs of resulting unemployment. Even if the Prairies could absorb the newcomers, increased farm production would only lower prices for produce. The labour movement was also opposed to immigration on the grounds that jobs were being lost. While King agreed that 'the problems of immigration and unemployment are so interlocked that they are incapable of separation,' he knew that the eastern parts of Canada would oppose direct aid to the West. The Maritimes had always complained that they had received little benefit from money expended by Ottawa on immigration. They argued that since the West received the benefits, it must also assume the obligations.[39] It was the manufacturers and railways that most favoured increased immigration to increase the consumer population. The government, therefore, had to be careful to placate both the opponents and proponents. It attempted to disarm criticism by indicating that immigration from Britain had increased. The department of immigration attempted to reassure the House that it was working closely with the provincial governments to ensure that excessive entry was not taking place and increasing unemployment problems. Despite pressure from the British government for Canada to adopt more settlement schemes, thereby alleviating unemployment problems in Britain, King was intent on holding the line.[40]

Continuing prosperity allowed Mackenzie King to offer additional incentives to his own constituency. Prince Albert was experiencing 'a period of development unequalled even in the so-called boom days.' The value of construction in the city as well as the number of homesteads reached new heights, and a second period of intensive mining exploration was underway. The *Prince Albert Herald* announced that the city had 'crossed the threshold into a new era of progress and expansion'; it had at last become the 'the Gateway of the North.'[41] In May 1928 the prime minister informed T.C. Davis that Parliament had just passed a vote for the construction of three public buildings in the constituency. He noted proudly that half the funding going to Saskatchewan was in his riding, concluding that 'I have done my "duty" by the riding.'[42] According to the prime minister, the new buildings, in addition to the railway and park appropriations, indicated that King was 'doing pretty well by the constituency of Prince Albert.' Initially, he appeared to be 'most anxious' to showcase his role in securing the new buildings: he directed that the laying of the cornerstones should coincide with his upcoming visit to open the national park. On second thought, he felt such publicity might be excessive: it could 'attract the attention of other constituencies to the fact that so many appropriations have been made for a constituency all at once.'[43] Local Liberals responded to King's efforts. To show their 'appreciation,' the riding would present him with a cottage in the park.[44]

During the summer, progress was made on the natural resources issue. Confessing to feeling 'ashamed' of his government's 'continuous procrastination,' King wanted to finalize the transfer agreements.[45] Manitoba was seeking to foster economic growth by exploiting its resources, especially the mineral deposits being developed around Flin Flon. Bracken, who had expected prompt action after the rhetoric surrounding the Dominion–Provincial Conference, was becoming impatient by January 1928. After two formal conferences, numerous informal interviews, and continuous correspondence, the prime minister had suggested arbitration, but no action had been taken. Yet, in the meantime, the claims of the Maritime provinces had been dealt with by the Duncan Commission 'in the most prompt and generous manner.'[46] Moreover, Alberta had just recently received lower freight rates on coal moving to Ontario, and Ottawa was reimbursing the railways for their losses. Soon the Maritimes would also receive the same lower rates on their coal moving to Ontario.[47] Manitoba, Bracken indicated, was not requesting special bonuses, subsidies, or freight rates, merely the arbitration of its case under an agreement made nearly six years ago. King explained that, while arbitration was indeed the necessary route, there were objections to sending the question to the Privy Council. Everyone wanted to avoid the possibility of raising the schools question.[48] Before arbitration could take place, Ottawa wished to reach an agreement on the terms of reference as well as the tribunal to which the matter would be referred. Bracken travelled to Ottawa in July to make one final attempt to settle the issue, or, if this failed, to agree on the terms of arbitration.[49]

The natural resources issue was further complicated by the political situation in Manitoba. Liberals of both the Diehard and Free Press persuasion described the condition of the provincial Liberal party as 'a deplorable state of disintegration and division ... with no apparent prospect of extraction therefrom.'[50] King was well aware that he could not dismiss the situation as simply a local dilemma. 'National parties in

Canada are federal in structure,' Neatby notes, 'and local disputes would affect federal fortunes in Manitoba.'[51] The procrastination of the federal government on the resource question was damaging the provincial Liberals, and Liberal leader H.A. Robson was just as anxious as Premier Bracken to see the matter solved.[52] 'Our relations with the Bracken Government are satisfactory,' Robson told King, 'and Liberals and Progressives should present a united front when occasion demands. But there must be progress in the resources matter or this amalgamation will fail to prevent heavy Tory inroads.'[53] The issue was becoming 'a very great impediment to Liberalism,' and Robson was having to support Bracken to prevent him from attacking the Liberals federally. The premier suggested to King that coalition in the province would have a much greater chance of success if the issue were settled.[54] The prime minister took up the question in cabinet with renewed vigour.

His efforts seemed to be rewarded: coalition was again on the table in Manitoba, and some of the younger Liberals now thought it a mistake to have joined 'with the old crowd' against Bracken during the last campaign.[55] A committee representing both wings of the provincial Liberal party was established to recommend federal patronage. By appointing former Liberal premier T.C. Norris to the Board of Railway Commissioners, King was able to remove a bitter Diehard from the scene while still appeasing the demands of the group. Ever since Norris had been manipulated and defeated by the Free Press Liberals at the beginning of the decade, the Diehards had been pushing for some form of compensation for the former premier.

By the spring of 1928 the path to cooperation and the settlement of the resource question was cleared when Robson indicated a willingness to work with Bracken.'[56] Further obstacles to coalition were removed when, after receiving a lecture from King, Jimmy Gardiner promised to fall in line by ceasing to influence Robson. By April the prime minister was hopeful: a Liberal was to go into Bracken's government 'as a sort of lynch-pin' to unite the two groups. 'We will never have Western Canada,' King echoed his old battle cry, 'till Libs and Progs are together as one party.'[57]

The atmosphere was friendly when King and Bracken met in July to discuss the resource transfer. Both leaders were anxious for an agreement and both favoured a coalition. The prime minister confessed to 'feeling ashamed' at Ottawa's continual procrastination on the resource question. He noted that Bracken was 'very nice' in characterizing the ongoing negotiations as 'disclosing great tolerance on both sides.'[58] Although Manitoba would receive its unalienated resources as well as the subsidy, there remained the question of compensation for resources alienated prior to the granting of the subsidy. King suggested that the issue of compensation could be hammered out privately, while a royal commission would educate the public and justify the method of agreement. The Manitoba government could, in the meantime, begin administering its resources and carry out its program of mineral development. The schools question, however, remained a bogey. Both sides agreed that the provincial government would continue the schools system as before; the problem was in announcing the policy. When the school lands were transferred along with the resources, Roman Catholics in Manitoba could possibly object to not having a specific guarantee of the existing system. Any special mention of a guarantee, on the other hand, might also result in a public outcry. In the end it was agreed that the issue would not be mentioned.

The Manitoba delegation was pleased with the conference results, so pleased in fact that King felt 'a bit nervous & agitated' and thought that perhaps he 'had gone too far.' He admitted to not knowing the subject well enough and instead acting according to what seemed 'the right & fair thing.' The dominion could perhaps have negotiated a less costly deal, but King claimed to be assailed by the justice of the matter: 'It is a mistake for Ottawa to be controlling & administering western lands, & it is a losing & costly business as it stands and we should get rid of it all just as soon as we can.' Ernest Lapointe, who obviously did not share King's guilt, protested that indeed the dominion had been too generous. The minister of justice argued that Ottawa should have avoided any declaration that the resources rightly belonged to Manitoba, and instead should have inserted a clause making the settlement subject to the interests of the eastern provinces.[59] Lapointe's protests increased King's misgivings that too much had been surrendered, and he worried once again that after Bracken had returned to Manitoba, controversy over the school issue would still erupt.[60] Some minor changes in wording were made to the agreement. Yet, in the end, King's sense of justice prevailed, and he rejected Lapointe's urging to 'hold back & do nothing, postpone the whole matter.' The West deserved its natural resources; any further delays would only injure the Liberal party. The issue was also being used to unite Liberals and Progressives in Manitoba. A settlement in this province could possibly open the door to agreements in the other Prairie provinces, and King planned to use the issue to cement the region's support. After rereading the proceedings and correspondence, he claimed to feel 'humiliated at the way we have procrastinated in this matter.'[61]

To Mackenzie King the summer of 1928 must have seemed like the crowning achievement in his efforts to re-establish Prairie Liberalism. In August, to open the national park, he made his first journey to Prince Albert since the 1926 campaign. There was little doubt that he viewed the project as his personal reward to his riding. 'What a privilege,' he recorded, 'to be able as P.M. to make a gift of this kind to one's constituency, to a Province & to one's country.' The opening ceremony, surrounded by the sublime scenery, caused King's romantic notions of the West to come flooding back. 'It was a great & beautiful surprise,' he wrote when viewing the park, 'like walking into a golden land of promise.'[62] The citizens' committee presented the prime minister with a cottage overlooking Lake Waskesiu; he spent his first and only night there on this trip. The cabin would become a patronage tool placed at the disposal of distinguished guests; even when King visited the constituency, he would stay elsewhere. Because he never concerned himself with the cottage's upkeep, one of his most loyal constituency workers, Jack Sanderson, ended up being burdened with the maintenance costs. King would later at least compensate Sanderson for his efforts by bequeathing him the cottage.[63] The cabin would prove a revealing symbol of the prime minister's relationship with the area.

Mackenzie King hoped to cap off the successful year by also agreeing to terms with Alberta on the resource transfer. On 23 November the Turgeon Commission was established to inquire into the Manitoba transfer. In mid-December the prime minister met with delegates from Alberta. Premier Brownlee wished to avoid an appeal to the Privy Council and a possible schools question. Instead he suggested that Ottawa maintain the school lands in trust until the agreement was finalized. Alberta would receive the present subsidy and unalienated resources, as well as the right to appeal if Manitoba received additional compensation. King responded that he could not legislate on a contingency.[64]

Despite the failure to reach an agreement with Alberta, King was pleased with the discussions. He continued to believe that his western policies were deserving of support and was mystified by Alberta's reaction to them. Some Liberals in the province were reassuring him that their breakthrough lay just around the corner. The federal government was popular, they argued, and the prime minister's performance at the 1926 Imperial Conference along with the yearly reductions of the national debt and taxation were ensuring success. At the same time the population was growing dubious as to the merits of Farmer government.[65] A more accurate picture was painted by another Liberal from the province,

Joseph Clarke. 'All is not well with this party in Alberta,' he wrote. Local members could offer no solution, but if something was not done, Clarke warned, 'we will fare worse in the next election than we did in the last, and God knows that was bad enough.' Reports indicated that the long-term suspicions of the UFA being more Tory than Liberal were proving accurate. A 'working alliance' was now being discussed between the two groups. Even King was forced to the conclusion that the Alberta Progressives were anything but Liberal.[66] The confusing situation only furthered his belief that a reliable and efficient western advisor was essential. Although Charles Dunning was obviously not fitting into this role, it was still assumed that one influential Prairie Liberal should be able to hold the entire region's support.

The 1929 budget offered few tariff reductions, despite the prime minister's promises of the previous year. The government was now faced by American threats to increase duties against Canadian agricultural goods, and dramatic reductions could prove embarrassing if the American tariff were raised. James Robb once again reported increased revenues and a record surplus. The sales tax was again reduced. The reaction of the West was reflected in the words of the *Grain Growers' Guide*: 'In its tariff features the budget is strictly of the stand pat variety.'[67]

King feared the divisiveness of the tariff issue as well as its potential to provide the Progressives with a new lease on life. While the support of the Liberal-Progressives in Ottawa was secure, the groups continued to quarrel in the three Prairie provinces. The time had come, he decided, to advance cooperation even to the point of using threats. The western situation was 'far from what it should be,' he warned T.A. Crerar. The American tariff situation had brought the government to a 'critical juncture.' King claimed to be 'anxious not to yield to the protectionist sentiment of Ontario.' Such a stance would require western support and, in particular, the unity of Liberal and Progressive forces. The same warnings were issued to Jimmy Gardiner. Tariff revision hinged on avoiding a split in the anti-Conservative forces.[68] Federal pressure toward increased cooperation would include such incentives as a generous settlement of the natural resources question, changes in western cabinet representation, and even direct intervention into the coalition negotiations in Manitoba.

The coalition issue in Manitoba by 1929 had become inextricably intertwined with the resource transfer. The Turgeon Commission reported in May, recommending the existing agreement as well as additional compensation for the resources alienated prior to 1905. Complicated calculations produced a figure of $4.5 million. Yet with both Bracken and King prepared to accept the report, another development was now bedevilling provincial politics. The transfer agreement was to return control of water power to Manitoba, and the premier had negotiated a lease with a private firm, the Winnipeg Electric Company, to develop hydroelectric power at the Seven Sisters' reach. The move caused considerable controversy, sparking a debate over private versus public ownership. Moreover, because the resource transfer had not yet been concluded, the federal government had to make the final decision about allowing the contract to go to a private company. The proposed transfer agreement stated that until control of resources had changed hands, Ottawa's administration would be 'in accord' with the province's 'wishes.'[69] Although Mackenzie King had no problem with Bracken's deal, the minister of the interior, Charlie Stewart, was disturbed by the public outcry in Winnipeg and was more hesitant. Regardless, the lease was issued. The local Conservatives denounced Bracken's abandonment of public ownership and accused the premier of collusion with the Winnipeg Electric Company in return for campaign funds. While a provincial commission found no evidence of corruption, its admission that the government members had acted thoughtlessly, along with the resignation of two ministers, damaged the reputation of the government.

The weakened state of Bracken's government forced him again to consider fusion with the Liberals. Robson had already been complaining to King that Ottawa's delays over both the Seven Sisters and the resource transfer were injuring Liberal fortunes in the province. A local by-election in T.C. Norris's old riding of Landsdowne saw Bracken and Robson endorse a joint candidate, Donald McKenzie. The Liberal leader's stand was openly challenged by many of the Diehards, but McKenzie won the traditional Liberal seat. By March 1929 Bracken was negotiating behind the scenes to have Robson enter his government as attorney general.[70]

The Free Press group, fearing he would back out at the last minute, did not trust the vacillating Robson. King was advised 'to judiciously take a hand' in order to prevent any hope of a coalition slipping away.[71] If the Bracken government were defeated in the Legislature by Liberal votes, J.W. Dafoe warned, the province would be lost to the party both provincially and federally. The editor sensed a willingness on behalf of the Diehards to 'knife' the government regardless of the consequences, and it seemed doubtful that Robson would be strong enough to resist such a move. Dafoe appealed for King's support, suggesting that the dilemma in Manitoba was the federal situation of 1926, only reversed. This time the

Progressives needed the Liberals. The Federal party had to convince the Diehards that the Liberals had no chance of winning provincial office even if the Bracken government fell. The Diehard view was 'hopeless nonsense,' Dafoe scoffed, 'expressed strongly by a small but dwindling minority'; the group simply would not learn from past mistakes. After ten years and five elections in Manitoba, the record spoke for itself. Of the four political campaigns where the Liberals had run candidates against the Progressives, all had been disasters.[72]

Mackenzie King exerted all his influence to convince Robson that the time for coalition was at hand. With the Bracken government shaken, the time was opportune to gain a fusion on Liberal terms. Any division in the anti-Tory forces would allow the possibility of Conservative victory and would injure federal Liberal forces as well as the party in Saskatchewan. Yet rivalry between the Liberals and Progressives seemed to be increasing rather than subsiding. 'This is the temper that presages disaster,' Dafoe warned. He did not believe Robson would enter a government with Bracken as premier. King was informed that as long as Robson remained Liberal leader, there was no hope for cooperation or party prospects. The Diehards were refusing to follow Ottawa's suggestions, and the prime minister found it necessary to write very direct letters to those involved:

> I believe that in every sense of the word it marks the parting of the ways as to the future of Liberalism in your province. We are in power in Ottawa today because I have from the beginning refused to listen to those who told me that the Progressives should be fought rather than won to our side ... Federally ... we shall need the Progressives as never before, and no where will they be needed – if the tariff is to be shaped in accordance with the wishes of the West – than in Western Canada. As a matter of fact, we at Ottawa are really fighting the battle of the West in the matter of trade policy. I think our friends in the West owe it to us to help us in that endeavour.[73]

Despite King's admonishment, the Diehards took the opportunity to show King that his strategy of cooperation was a failure. The Liberals had supported the Progressives on Seven Sisters and were now tainted by the same scandal. The Bracken government might remain in power temporarily; without a coalition its future was questionable.

In early March 1929 federal intervention reached its zenith. Immense pressure was exerted upon Robson to form a coalition and serve as attorney general. Such an amalgamation had the support of A.B. Hudson; Dafoe promised the full backing of the *Free Press.* King had Thomas Taylor, the 'party trouble shooter,' working in Winnipeg for the federal Liberals. Taylor was to report directly to Senator Andrew Haydon, using the code name 'Longbury.'[74] At an initial meeting, Taylor emphasized to Robson the importance of coalition for both federal and provincial party fortunes. The Liberal leader seemed willing to move toward coalition if he could receive the support of the provincial convention later that month. Bracken was indicating a willingness to take Robson and another Liberal into cabinet and to call the new party the Liberal-Progressives. When Taylor again met with Robson, however, the Liberal leader had been in consultation with his own group and was hesitant. He wanted to check in with Gardiner. 'I thought the only thing to do,' Taylor informed King, 'was to tell him that if he had anything to do with Gardiner during the negotiation for a union, it would not be to his advantage and I also told him frankly that it appeared that every time Robson and Gardiner had conversations upon Manitoba politics, it was to the disadvantage of the Liberal Party ... It is quite pitiful to think that Mr. Robson really seems considerably afraid of what Gardiner will think if he goes in with Bracken.'[75]

Taylor also journeyed to Regina to speak with the Saskatchewan premier and urge the necessity of coalition. Although Gardiner was set in his views, Taylor hoped that he could be pressured into staying out of the matter. At the meeting Taylor was disappointed but not surprised to find him 'diehard' in his position. Gardiner was prepared to help only if Bracken would agree to retire in a year and turn the leadership over to Robson.[76] 'You cannot trust James G. Gardiner in his attitude upon Manitoba politics,' Taylor warned King, 'although he feels that he, better than anyone else in Canada, knows the situation here.' In the next several days, the weak-willed Robson was further influenced by the Diehards, notwithstanding Taylor's attempts to 'protect' him from undesirable influences. 'Robson is a vacillating character,' he noted, 'and although at times he is stubborn, his general makeup is one of extreme weakness and almost anyone can sway him to any point of view whatsoever, so I propose to be with him as closely as possible between now and the convention so that no more people will get to him to make him any more pessimistic than he is.'[77]

Even with Taylor's influence, by 12 March all of King's efforts had 'fallen to the ground.' Stating that Ottawa was 'interfering' and 'exaggerating' its importance, Robson turned against fusion. He charged the federal party with 'using him as a tool.' Despite attempts to keep Taylor's presence and mission secret, the Diehards had become aware of Ottawa's actions. With Robson's refusal to cooperate, the federal Liberals had to place their hopes on the upcoming convention. There was a chance that the Free Press group could sway the moderate and undecided portion of the party to push for coalition. Taylor was left to pack the convention with favourable delegates. In the days immediately prior to the gathering, even Gardiner was pressured by King into sending Robson a letter asking him to accept the post under Bracken. The Saskatchewan premier, warned not to divert Robson from this path, responded by demonstrating the trait that Mackenzie King most valued in him – loyalty.[78]

It seemed King's pressure had paid off. At the 19 March convention Robson, while opposing any precipitate action, indicated a willingness to consider amalgamation. A negotiating committee was established to consider policy; in the meantime the Liberals would support Bracken in the Legislature.[79] King was delighted: 'From word received tonight the Liberal Convention at Winnipeg has fulfilled our highest hopes in bringing together Liberals & Progressives in that province. In other words a fusion of the two parties. It has taken a lot of manoeuvring, but Gardiner has played his part well and the pressure put on from Ottawa has worked like a charm.'[80] He was informed that such Diehards as E.J. McMurray remained opposed to amalgamation but, in view of the prime minister's attitude, had agreed to remain silent. The situation, however, was still 'of a highly explosive nature.'[81]

As in the past, cooperation proved illusory. Within a short time the prime minister was again receiving antagonistic correspondence from both sides. Bracken and Robson met to discuss fusion, but the premier's prestige was recovering and the idea was again put on the back burner. Bracken was well aware that his party was in the stronger position and that the Liberals had little choice but to offer support in the face of a possible Conservative victory. To an extent his position was also obstructed by the more Tory members of his own cabinet.[82] The Liberals were in a mess. It was reported that the attempts at fusion had created 'more bitterness in the Liberal ranks than anything that has occurred in the Party since the schism of 1917.' The Diehards, who claimed to be 'the root and stem' of the party, accused King of watering 'the leaves' while allowing 'the roots ... to dry up.' The intervention of the federal Liberals had been so blatant that even the most ardent of the Diehards could not help feeling betrayed: 'The Free Press like the Prodigal Son came back home. There are some of us who feel very much like the elder son in that famous parable.'[83]

Throughout the coalition discussions, the prime minister, not surprisingly, maintained a guise of neutrality and non-intervention in provincial affairs. 'I personally have had little or no concern in the Provincial situation,' he claimed, 'apart from its possible bearings on the future of our Party in the Federal arena.' Within cabinet King did not find it so necessary to temper his attitude or actions. While he 'hesitated' saying anything that might be 'interpreted' as interference, it was undeniable that provincial and federal politics were 'inextricably interwoven.' The prime minister also noted that 'little by little' the federal Liberals had been regaining the invaluable support of the *Free Press*.[84]

On 26 June 1929 the dominion and Manitoba delegations met and agreed to the report of the Turgeon Commission. The province's sixtieth anniversary, 15 July 1930, was agreed upon as the official date of transfer. In Saskatchewan Gardiner's partisanship had always made King's task in dealing with the resource matter easier. Gardiner had met with the prime minister in February to request an increase in the subsidy as well as its continuation, since more lands had been alienated in Saskatchewan than in the other Prairie provinces. King agreed, conceding that because the province did not have the same mineral wealth it did warrant a greater subsidy. The problem was that if Saskatchewan received an increase, the agreements with Alberta and Manitoba would have to be renegotiated. Discussions remained particularly amiable, with the two leaders agreeing to await the other agreements. Gardiner was finding that the flames of religious animosity being fanned by the KKK were also influencing the resource situation. Some critics alleged that there was an understanding between the federal and provincial governments whereby the sale of school lands was intended to benefit Roman Catholics. Such allegations, Gardiner charged, were attempts 'to create a feeling that the Liberal party is controlled absolutely by the Province of Quebec.'[85]

By the fall of 1929, Gardiner was no longer premier. Surprisingly, the Saskatchewan Liberal government had been defeated that summer by a Progressive–Conservative coalition under J.T.M. Anderson. In the aftermath, observers agreed that, while the desire for change and criticism of the Gardiner machine had been partly responsible for the defeat, the main cause had been religious bitterness. Amidst increasingly heated debates on the merits of immigration, Ottawa was being accused of deliberately populating Canada with Roman Catholics. The provincial Liberals were accused of catering to the Catholics on the schools issue, and the federal Liberal reliance on Quebec support only made the charges more difficult to avoid. In typical Gardiner style, 'the little

Napoleon of the prairies'[86] had charged into battle with the KKK, but to the public it seemed he was defending Catholics.

For Mackenzie King, political failures could usually be blamed on leadership and organization. In this case he believed the Gardiner–Dunning feud had been partly to blame for the defeat. The premier had brought on the election despite the advice of Dunning and the federal Liberals, who were still in session and could not lend their aid. 'Gardiner was too cocksure,' King complained.[87] Local Liberals warned the prime minister to stay away from the province and allow religious animosities that had been 'fanned to fever heights' during the election to 'cool off.' When King did visit Saskatchewan during a western tour in the autumn, he avoided the resource question and made no effort to see the new premier. He was assured that the election result had not been a revolt against Liberalism nor would it influence a federal election. In a letter to King, G.C. Porter, a Winnipeg Liberal, opined that 'there is no "uprising of the people" against your government, no matter WHAT the Opposition may say.' Nonetheless, he was warned that a Farmers' movement based around the wheat pools was 'in process of birth' – many Liberals were 'more afraid of it than of anything that has appeared upon the horizon for a long time.'[88]

The resource question posed no difficulties when King reached Alberta. An agreement in principle had been reached, the prime minister was prepared to increase the subsidy as the provincial population increased, and a final conference in Ottawa was arranged for the end of the year. Yet also on the agenda was the issue of cabinet reorganization. King had paid very little attention to the province due to the miserable state of Alberta Liberalism and what he saw as the confusing nature of its Progressive movement. Now he hoped to solve Alberta's lack of cabinet representation by securing the presence of Premier Brownlee – the only Albertan who could 'bring any strength' – in his government. If King was aware that majority opinion placed Brownlee and his United Farmer government more in the Conservative camp than the Liberal, he was ignoring that view. More likely, he was out of touch with the Alberta situation and merely assumed that such opinions again reflected uncompromising Liberals refusing to accommodate Progressives. Charles Stewart had fought the UFA as Gardiner had fought the Progressives in Saskatchewan, but by November King was hopeful that Brownlee and the federal minister were coming to some form of agreement. King did not take to the Alberta premier, whom he met during the 1929 western tour: 'He is a dour sort of person, wrapped in mystery, not too frank.' Despite these impressions, Brownlee was approached about joining the cabinet. While indicating that he was indeed a Liberal, he intimated that he was not politically ambitious. The condition was added that upon joining, he would want the right to resign if he disagreed with policy. 'This is a poor sort of beginning,' King recorded, 'it shews a wrong attitude.'[89] The prime minister decided to wait until after the provincial election the following year before possibly trying Brownlee again.

Having no idea how to clear up the Liberal mess in Alberta, King continued to advance fusion. Local party members were infuriated during the visit when the prime minister publicly hinted at coalition. The suggestion caused division within the provincial party: while the executive named a committee to investigate the possibility, a large meeting in Edmonton repudiated the notion. Alberta Liberal organizer W.R. Howson attempted to convince King that Brownlee had no intention of cooperating with Liberals at any level. The UFA premier was exploiting the situation by playing both sides of the fence. The provincial Liberals would not 'sell out' the party faithful for an advantage that would 'never be realized.' Party leader J.W. McDonald pointed to the 'confusion' in Ottawa regarding the relationship between the UFA government and the federal Progressives. King tried to diffuse the situation by indicating that his thoughts of coalition were aimed only at the federal situation. With the recent and very direct intervention in the push for a Manitoba coalition, however, the Alberta Liberals were justified in their suspicions.[90]

James Robb died while King was touring British Columbia. While the loss of the finance minister would certainly be felt by the cabinet, it also simplified western representation. King had disliked Robb's protectionist leanings, and Dunning was waiting in the wings. Neatby argues that the prime minister 'did not like Charles Dunning,'[91] but this seems a bit of an exaggeration. If the westerner had been heralded as the likely replacement to King, his value as a Prairie lieutenant had overshadowed all threats, and the prime minister would never forget the risk Dunning had taken when he joined King's weakened government in 1925. Dunning's arrogance, self-pity, and hypochondria raised King's ire; yet the prime minister was always highly critical of those around him: 'Dunning has two distinct sides (as we all have) one a very nasty one, a lack of background tradition etc. which discloses itself in situations, another the makings of a fine man.'[92] In 1929 he was very aware of Dunning's merits as finance minister, including his ability, energy, experience, and most importantly, his 'Western (free trade) point of view.'[93]

It is important to note that King was also already moving to replace

Dunning with Gardiner as his main Prairie advisor. The necessity of placating the Progressives was gradually diminishing, so Gardiner's presence in cabinet would no longer cause great division. Moreover, as finance minister, Dunning would have increasing difficulty representing and organizing the West. The portfolio was seen more as a 'national' department, its preoccupation largely with eastern business interests. King was also impressed by Gardiner's organizational skills.[94] With Dunning's popularity diminishing in the West, he was seen less as a Prairie representative.[95] On King's return through Regina, the prime minister discussed cabinet changes with Dunning. He was sworn in as finance minister on 26 November 1929.

Efforts to bolster western representation were followed up on the return trip through Winnipeg. Robert Forke had not helped the Manitoba situation, and western criticism of the immigration department had only diminished his reputation. Again King had his sights set on T.A. Crerar returning to politics and finally joining the cabinet. Although the former Progressive leader had expressed interest on the tour's first pass through Manitoba, he wanted a more important portfolio than immigration. Dunning's move to finance opened up railways and canals. Crerar also wanted a 'free hand' with party organization in Manitoba, and King agreed that he would have responsibility for the province.[96] An official offer of the railways portfolio would have to await King's return to Ottawa so the matter could be discussed in cabinet. Annoyed with the delay, Crerar remained suspicious that the prime minister would attempt to manoeuvre him into a minor portfolio. King assured him that he had never contemplated any other department. The reason for the delay was that the Quebec members were 'a little sensitive' over having 'lost' the finance portfolio to the West. King did not doubt their willingness to have the department of railways retained for the Prairies, but it would still ease the tension if the decision were made only after consulting them.[97] The cabinet changes pleased the prime minister. While he was sorry to see the departure of the gentlemanly Forke, the strength of Dunning in finance and Crerar in railways would more than offset the loss.[98]

In mid-December the final agreement for the transfer of the natural resources to Manitoba was signed. King was disappointed when Brownlee of Alberta hesitated to accept the subsidy in perpetuity as full compensation for lands alienated since 1905 and instead requested an investigation by a royal commission. Manitoba had been provided with over $4 million in cash as a result of a commission's ruling, and Brownlee believed Alberta should also receive cash compensation. It was explained that the money offered Manitoba was intended to place the province on par with the other two Prairie provinces when they entered Confederation, yet Brownlee argued that much more of Alberta's lands had been alienated by Ottawa, particularly for the railways. Despite the premier's resistance, King still hoped he would soon enter the cabinet. He was, at any rate, 'superior to Mr. Stewart.'[99]

The change in Saskatchewan's government dramatically altered that province's resource negotiations with Ottawa. King had been warned that, with Gardiner out of office, harmonious relations were at an end. Premier Anderson would want a commission established 'to make the people believe that they are going to get more,' and also to create an issue for the next election. The prime minister believed that the best thing would be to get agreements signed with Alberta and Manitoba and then pressure Saskatchewan to come to terms. Anderson, who came to Ottawa, rejected the intention to deal with the province on the same basis as Alberta. The purchase of Rupert's Land and the North West territory in 1870 had given Ottawa administrative powers, he argued, not control of the western lands. They were, therefore, held in trust and an actual 'transfer' was not necessary. When the provinces were created in 1905 the issue should have been settled according to the dictates of the British North American Act of 1867, not the 1872 Dominion Lands Act, which was assumed to have converted the trusteeship into ownership.[100] The premier demanded compensation for all the resources alienated by the federal government since 1870. 'Anderson is here to make trouble, not to make an agreement,' King concluded. 'I feel annoyed at Gardiner's letting his province get into such hands.'[101] The prime minister refused to treat the constitutional position of Saskatchewan as 'the subject of general misconception for more than half a century.' Anderson responded that his province could not be treated the same as Alberta because their resource wealth differed. Still, King pushed for equal terms.[102] Anderson also rejected the suggestion that two members of the Turgeon Commission also sit on the new committee.

After further discussions with the other two premiers, King suggested that Anderson's claims for additional compensation be referred to the Supreme Court and, if necessary, the Privy Council. The appointment of the royal commission for Saskatchewan would have to be postponed until the courts gave their decision, but if they agreed with the province the amount would then be decided by the commission. King was confident, however, that Anderson would lose in court. Further meetings with the Saskatchewan delegation in March 1930 would be a token effort. With the other agreements signed, King was confident Saskatchewan would be put in the position of partisan procrastinator, 'where the present Govt. can do us no harm and only bring reaction upon itself.'[103]

The agreements with Manitoba and Alberta were signed on 14 December 1929. 'This completes the real autonomy of these two Western provinces,' King crowed. The prime minister believed that the agreements, concluded with Progressive governments, were an indication of good relations. 'It should help to bring closer Lib & Prog forces,' he concluded.[104] Neatby calls the transfer agreements probably 'the major achievement' of the government's third administration. Solutions to the old problems had been found because King was 'a talented negotiator' and because 'he was ready to be generous.' He had placated the Maritimes with more subsidies and prevented the emergence of a schools question. The confidence of provincial leaders such as Bracken and Brownlee had been maintained.[105] King certainly viewed the agreements, and his role in their fruition, in this way, and there is no doubt they were important for the Prairie region. The problem was that the final settlements were met more with a sigh of relief than hearty congratulations. As far as the Prairie West was concerned, Ottawa deserved no praise for finally providing the region its due.

While in Ottawa, Bracken and King had the opportunity to discuss the Liberal-Progressive situation in Manitoba. Robson was obviously an obstacle to fusion that had to be removed. A wide range of advice was emerging from the province, much of which blamed Bracken for blocking coalition. King admitted to finding the situation 'somewhat baffling.' Any chance of cooperation had been officially ended by Robson and by the end of December the Federal government appointed the Liberal leader to the provincial court of appeal.[106] 'That ends him as leader of Lib. Party in province,' King wrote, '& with Crerar in here means Progs & Libs become one in Manitoba. That is an achievement.'[107] It also ended any notion of coalition for the next several years.

The general economic prosperity was allowing Mackenzie King to make offerings to the Prairie West that he assumed would translate into votes in the next election. While the Wall Street Crash of 29 October 1929 was certainly disconcerting, the Canadian prime minister was not overly worried. He was in Winnipeg at the time, and his speech indicated that the nation had no serious difficulties on the horizon.[108] The crash was viewed as a temporary setback. The difficulties that were beginning to appear in the West were seen as inevitable products of the cyclical pattern of boom and bust. The Prairie farmer remained committed to wheat production, despite increasing calls from experts for diversification, not to mention quotas and embargoes introduced by some importing nations. The field crop acreage was expanding without adequate attention to soil conservation. In addition, much of the farmers' capital was borrowed at fixed charges.[109] Although more wheat had been planted in 1929 then ever before, a drought in June had reduced the yield to little more than half the record crop of 1928, and to below the average for the decade. The 1928 price of wheat had been the lowest in five years, yet some of the crop remained unsold. The combination of a small crop and a poor price led the pools to hold back on sales until prices increased. As the new crop year of 1930 commenced, the pools promised farmers a good initial payment of one dollar per bushel. Within months of the October Crash the Winnipeg wheat market was so depressed that the credit of the pools was in jeopardy and their representatives turned to the premiers of the three Prairie provinces for financial support.[110] The collapse of the pools in 1930 caught the provincial governments, the chartered banks, and the farmers in the financial debacle.[111] Still, the prime minister promised that the problems would be short-lived and the same policies of fiscal restraint and balanced budgets would provide the nation with the prosperity it had enjoyed in recent years.

Despite the increasing severity of unemployment, King continued to maintain that the issue was out of his hands. It was 'a matter for individuals in the first instance; between municipalities and the people living within their bounds, in the second instance; next between the provinces and the citizens of the respective provinces; and only finally a matter of concern [but not responsibility] in the federal arena.'[112] Until such a state of emergency developed that individuals, municipalities, and provinces could not cope with the situation, unemployment would not be an issue for which Mackenzie King felt any responsibility.[113] When a western deputation on unemployment arrived in Ottawa on 26 February 1930, he immediately concluded it 'was clearly a Tory device to stir up propaganda.' In his efforts to justify the government's position, he convinced himself that the cities rather than the more predominant rural areas were demanding action.[114] 'I long for the fresher & cleaner atmosphere of the prairies & the West,' a pressured King recorded. 'Cities are ruinous of what is best in civilization.'[115] He found himself in the House in April refusing demands that Ottawa accept some of the responsibility for relief payments and claiming that there was 'no evidence in Canada today of an emergency situation which demands anything of that kind.' Under pressure from Conservative attacks, King felt increasingly that the demands for federal intervention were mere partisan ploys. Therefore, he answered with an equally partisan response. Ottawa would not give 'a five cent piece' to the provincial Tory governments for 'these alleged unemployment purposes.'[116] For the usually cool and calculating King, such an overtly partisan statement regarding dominion–provincial relations was out of character and the opposition took full advantage. The 'five-cent speech' would become a rallying cry for the upcoming federal election and glaring evidence that Mackenzie King had become complacent in office.

The 1930 budget was delayed until after the Easter recess because of the possibility of an election as well as the threat of an increased American tariff. Although the prime minister had already decided to meet any increases in the American tariff with increases in the imperial preference, he did not wish to provoke the United States until he was able to analyse their legislation. The Smoot–Hawley tariff bill, which had been delayed in 1929, was passed by the U.S. Senate in March 1930. It contained the highest duties ever imposed against Canadian agricultural goods. Once the House of Representatives agreed to details, the final bill would place a virtual embargo on many agricultural imports. In the face of a tariff war, King wanted to avoid an election until the following year. Such a delay would also allow him to attend the Imperial Conference scheduled for autumn of 1931.

Yet, if an election were postponed, the Liberals would be vulnerable to criticisms that their tariff policies were dictated by Washington. The King government could gain a step on the Conservatives by anticipating the passing of the American bill and raising duties against the United States as well as increasing the British preference. The lowering of the tariff on British goods would also smooth the path toward the Imperial Conference. If the economic situation continued to deteriorate, any delay could prove fatal. By mid-February Dunning was told 'to get a real budget in readiness.' A week later King learned that electoral prospects in the Prairie West were questionable due to the world wheat surplus.[117] He hoped that a solid budget introduced by Dunning, his Prairie lieutenant, would more than compensate for any dissatisfaction in the region. 'When our budget comes down almost all else will be forgotten save the Government's record,' he mused confidently.[118] In the West, however, there was a fear that Dunning and Crerar were also becoming complacent in office and less prone to defend Prairie issues.[119]

Western opinion cautioned King to delay the election. An immediate contest should be called only if the Liberals were 'itching to get out of office,' one party member noted. They would be subjected to 'one of the worst trimmings in the West ... that they ever received.' The Manitoba Diehards believed King's recent interventions in their province meant trouble. The Liberal party was heading into the next campaign 'weaker than it has ever been in its history – weak because there is no driving, vital organization of fighting Liberals behind it.' Instead there were crypto-Liberals, such as Crerar, in positions of influence.[120] King also received advice from Dafoe against an election. Instead of noting its contents, the prime minister was more impressed by its 'fine spirit' and 'truly friendly & complimentary' character. 'A very great change over a few years ago,' he observed proudly.[121]

At the beginning of May Dunning brought down his first budget. He reported a large surplus and another reduction in the sales tax. A tariff war with the United States was undesirable, but the government would not remain idle while American duties were raised. As a result, countervailing duties were threatened against the United States while duties levied on British imports were reduced. But the government's lack of confidence in the economic situation was becoming apparent. No estimate was given regarding revenues or expenditures for the coming year. The prime minister's rallying cry was closer to that of Sir John A. Macdonald than to the traditional Liberal position: 'Switch trade from U.S. to Britain, that will be the cry & it will sweep the country I believe.'[122] If the West expected a budget that reflected Dunning's Prairie background and bias, the region was sorely disappointed. Western members had to be content that there were more reductions than increases on items. The gap between the Ginger Group of Progressive radicals and the Liberal-Progressives was increased with an amendment put forward by the former group opposing protection and denouncing the increases to the British preference as inadequate. The amendment was defeated, and King was confident that it was the Liberal-Progressives who spoke for the West. The House was dissolved at the end of May, and an election set for 28 July 1930.

Mackenzie King entered the campaign confident of victory. The Liberal government had led the nation out of the mire and into prosperity. Although there were signs of economic trouble, he was sure the situation was manageable. Most of all, he believed the electorate would show its appreciation for the past nine years of solid administration. But the prime minister had badly miscalculated the situation. He underestimated his bases of support, particularly the West; his opponent, Richard Bedford Bennett; and the severity of the coming depression. The weaknesses in the Liberal party, meanwhile, were glaring. Moreover, the National Committee had not met since 1921. The prime minister had demonstrated little capacity for or enjoyment of the organizational side of politics, finding it 'undignified and almost sordid.'[123] 'Most of its functions, I take it,' King commented in 1928, 'have been superseded by the Ministers themselves.' In other words, his regional lieutenants had been painstakingly groomed, and they were expected to perform. In practice the federal party depended on the provincial organizations and federal ministers working through these bodies.[124] As usual, King dropped the organizational load on his faithful workhorse, Senator Andrew Haydon.

So much effort had gone into neutralizing the Progressives and reconstructing the Liberal party on the Prairies, yet that party still remained in a state of 'confusion.'[125] In reality the federal Liberals had spent all their energies on the Manitoba situation to no avail. There were no provincial Liberal governments in the West, and local party members continued to quarrel with the Progressives. The divisions in the provinces had not been bridged, even after King had brought the two most obvious candidates for regional lieutenant into the cabinet. As the prime minister was forced to admit, 'much remains to be done.'[126]

In Manitoba the Liberals were now 'in open revolt' against Ottawa's attempts to merge them with the Progressives. The Diehards were further incensed over not being consulted when Forke and Crerar, the two former Progressive leaders, were given new federal positions. The group felt dominated by the 'Ottawa Liberal Machine.'[127] The situation was no better in the other Prairie provinces. Alberta still remained without an effective federal minister, and Stewart was at '6's and 7's' with Brownlee.[128] In Saskatchewan the Gardiner and Dunning factions were squabbling; even the usually confident Gardiner was worried about the situation. Admitting that there would be 'a real fight in the West,' he also conceded that the region would require 'considerable attention.' Reports indicated that the most formidable Conservative organization the province had ever witnessed was up and running. The danger had to be realized in sufficient time to avoid the mistake of the provincial election – 'overconfidence.'[129]

By June King's confidence in western prospects was actually increasing. Dunning was 'much more hopeful' than he had been earlier of the outlook in Saskatchewan; moreover, the situation throughout Manitoba seemed to be improving. Reports suggested that Crerar was having success uniting the various groups. In early July the prime minister believed the Manitoba situation had finally been 'ironed out' and the two Liberal factions brought together.[130] 'From all that we can gather from surface indications and reports of organizers,' he wrote O.D. Skelton, 'the western situation is well in hand.' Liberal analysts estimated that Bennett's forces could gain perhaps three seats in Saskatchewan and one or two in Alberta. In Prince Albert everything seemed secure. Northern Saskatchewan, which would soon suffer from the fall in grain prices, was at the time still escaping the worst effects of the drought. Because John Diefenbaker had run against T.C. Davis in the provincial election, the federal organization nominated George Braden to oppose King. The Liberal executive indicated that Conservative efforts in the riding were 'useless.' C.H. McCann noticed a growing feeling of 'acquaintance' between King and his constituents and reported that the prime minister was viewed as 'a benefactor of the district.'[131]

Throughout the campaign King stood on the record of his government. Sound economic administration had ushered in prosperity, while the Dunning budget would ensure security in the difficult times ahead. But Bennett and the Conservatives were having success attacking the government's complacency and neglect. The Liberals, Bennett argued, had paid too little attention to the signs of economic difficulty and resulting unemployment. This argument had particular force in the West. Bennett claimed that the tariff concessions of the Dunning budget, which seemed hypocritical in their attempts to steal traditional Tory ground, would not be pursued by a Liberal government. The promises of the Conservative leader were unending: a session to provide jobs, protection for Canadian industries, security for agriculture, and an increase in imperial trade. 'Mackenzie King promises you conferences,' Bennett said. 'I promise you action. He promises consideration of the problem of unemployment; I promise to end unemployment. Which plan do you like best?'[132]

Unemployment and the competition in the dairy industry from New Zealand butter[133] crippled the Liberal campaign on the Prairies. King did not fully realize the extent of the unemployment problem or its potency as an issue until he reached the region.[134] Expecting the Dunning budget to produce western gratitude, he instead found himself on the defensive amid heckling over the unemployment question and the 'five cent speech.' King shrugged off the attackers as 'Tory organizers,' arguing that no provincial government had yet requested aid.[135] He attempted to highlight his background in labour issues. Western Liberals warned King that his strategy was not working against Bennett's direct promise to relieve the situation: 'This argument does not appeal to men with empty stomachs or empty pockets.'[136]

In Saskatchewan, with the Progressives supporting the provincial Conservative government, Liberals contested all but one of the twenty-one seats. The other two Prairie provinces witnessed more cooperation between Progressives and Liberals. In Manitoba Crerar successfully avoided three-cornered contests in all but two constituencies. Cooperation also seemed to be working in Alberta, where the Liberals sacrificed the field to Labour or UFA candidates in six constituencies and the Progressives reciprocated in four other ridings. None of the leading members of the Ginger Group in the province had Liberal opponents.[137] The problem in Alberta, however, ran too deep to be solved by some interparty cooperation. With no effective organization in the province, Liberals complained about their lack of propaganda outlets.[138] The situation always seemed 'confused.' At times a single organization would handle arrangements for both federal and provincial elections; at other times individual candidates were left on their own.[139] Relations with Premier Brownlee had deteriorated. King accused him of trying to shift the onus for lack of progress on unemployment onto Ottawa. After touring Alberta King complained that the province would remain one of the party's weakest links: 'Organization in Alberta is terrible. Stewart is worse than useless, is like an old woman, with no real control of situation. Things are much at 6's & 7's & we may lose in this province though thank Heavens there are not many seats to lose.'[140]

Throughout his tour, the unemployment problem plagued the prime minister. Finally he responded with indications that the federal government would pay dollar for dollar on public works. He noted, however, that such programs provided 'work & many who are talking don't want work.' If his reception in the West had dampened his confidence, in his optimistic moments King believed that Manitoba Liberals would probably lose only one or two seats, while in the other two provinces the party would maintain its present standing. He was sure Bennett had no appeal in the West. Indeed, King suggested there might be 'a real Liberal sweep.'[141]

In the general election of 1930 Mackenzie King's party was knocked from power. The Liberals won only eighty-seven seats and the Liberal-Progressives only three. Bennett's Conservatives took office with a total of 138 members. The picture was rounded out with the election of fifteen Farmer and Labour candidates and two Independents. The Conservatives, who held a comfortable majority of thirty, had broken through in every province. They certainly made in-roads on the Prairies, where their numbers increased from one to twenty-three, while the Liberals and Liberal-Progressives fell from thirty-two to eighteen seats. Liberal constituencies went from four to one in Manitoba; sixteen to eleven in Saskatchewan; and remained at three in Alberta. Although Mackenzie King won his seat in Prince Albert by a majority of 1192 votes, the Conservative candidate received 2310 votes to King's 1673 in the city and made strong gains in the traditional Liberal districts.[142] Both Crerar and Dunning were defeated. Some solace could be taken from the popular vote percentages, which gave 45.8 per cent to the Conservatives and 45.2 per cent to the Liberals; however, the fact remained that the election was a rout.

If losses in Quebec[143] came as the greatest shock, the numbers from the West were next in line. Searching for the bright side, King claimed to be 'glad' to see the Quebec and Saskatchewan 'blocs' broken and the party with a more even national distribution. Even so, he could not help note that the Saskatchewan result spelled destruction for the Liberal fortunes in the region. The overall defeat was blamed on the lack of organization and propaganda, followed by the New Zealand butter and unemployment issues. The 'five-cent speech,' King admitted, proved damaging because it was 'so contrary to my whole nature & spirit & action.' The loss of Crerar and Dunning was a severe blow; King remarked that it was 'perfectly terrible to have Stewart alone representing the West.'[144] Since Dunning had accepted the finance portfolio, his reputation had declined in the region, and his budget had been neither popular nor effective. Now out of office, he would accept a post with the Canadian Pacific Railway and turn to his eastern business interests. The ever-observant Dafoe did not believe that, after drawing pay from the CPR, Dunning could ever again represent a western constituency: 'Whether he realizes it or not he has made his choice for the present and perhaps all time.'[145] Dunning had become an easterner.

The Prairies were brimming with anti-Liberal sentiment. Westerners believed that federal immigration policies such as the Railway Agreement were tied to the unemployment problem, an issue for which Ottawa refused to take responsibility. At least half of the party's losses occurred in urban ridings, where most of the unemployed had drifted.[146] By November 1930, for example, 700 unemployed men would register in Prince Albert, and a flood of destitute people would continue entering the city from the rural districts.[147] As W.A. Buchanan, Liberal Senator and editor of the *Lethbridge Herald*, noted, 'undoubtedly unemployment and a certain amount of depression operated more against the Government out here than anything else.' Moreover, because the budget was so protectionist and the government's record in the West so mixed, neither could be featured in 'the foreground' of the campaign. Crerar agreed that the budget was simply too protectionist and ended up being 'more of a handicap than a help.' Not surprisingly, Gardiner saw the defeat as an inevitable result of too much compromising.[148]

In the months after the election the severity of the Depression along with the protectionist stance of the Bennett government convinced western Liberals that the Conservatives were in for difficult times. Crerar noted that Bennett's performance would at least allow Dunning's budget to be forgotten and again 'make the tariff issue' for the Liberal party. There was already a 'pretty definite reaction' against Bennett in the West that would 'gain momentum' until his government became 'the most unpopular in the nation's history.'[149] King agreed, saying he could not see how Bennett would 'hold the West & East together with tariff as the main issue.'[150] The election of a Tory government cemented the support of the *Free Press* for the Liberals. Dafoe made it clear he intended to 'carry on our own brand of warfare against Bennett.' He was not, however, impressed with King:

> I felt a good deal of exasperation over King's ... going off on a political adventure ... Mr. King's political sagacity all through the campaign and its antecedents was a minus quality but I rather look to him to show up well in Opposition. He may keep the party ship steering a straight course to a well-defined goal but I doubt whether he appreciates the magnitude of his task. I do not think his chances again of being Prime Minister are very good.[151]

King's biographer argues that the election of 1930 was a continuation of the trend back to the two-party system: 'Mistrust of the federal government had not disappeared from the prairies but Mackenzie King's efforts to placate the Canadian farmers had not been in vain. Regional dissatisfaction had been dissipated to the extent that no regional party had any vitality.'[152] But the reappearance of the traditional party system was to be shortlived. The Progressives had not disappeared; rather, they were in the process of changing shape, and their new form would prove even more dangerous to Prairie Liberalism. Western politics was in an unsettled state, and the Depression was to ravage the region more than any other. 'The farmer of the West is becoming somewhat red,' J.G. Ross warned, 'and I am afraid if the wrong lead happens to be given to him in the near future that most anything might happen.' If Mackenzie King feared the revival of the Progressive movement, Crerar noted a different threat, 'a sort of call to the Proletariat.' He was concerned that, 'in the present temper of the West,' a new left-wing message might get 'a considerable response.' Gardiner shrugged off the new threat. The Farmers were 'unsettled in their opinions' and lacked leadership. If Liberal remedies to the difficult times were offered, the 'new fangled political ideas' would dissipate, absorbed just like the Progressives.[153] Dafoe was not so sure. The radical agrarian element, while 'bewildered and disillusioned,' was not saying 'hereafter the Liberal party for us.' On the contrary, it seemed to have learned some lessons from the Progressive failure, and 'the spirit of 1921 may revive wilder than ever.' The Progressives had lacked one unanimous political philosophy and had based themselves on a populist appeal that suffered from severe provincial divisions. The same mistake would not be repeated. 'The Liberal party will have to swing pretty far to the left if it is to pick up the West,' Dafoe mused nervously.[154]

While Mackenzie King is often praised for defeating the Progressives and returning the West to the Liberal fold, the fact that the region was willing to move into the Conservative camp by 1930 can be seen as little other than failure. He was successful in absorbing the crypto-Liberals and in widening divisions among the Progressives, but the third party was not entirely defeated. Internal problems remained within the provincial Liberal parties, and it was finally clear that King had overestimated his hold on the region.

6

The Stiffer the Application, the Swifter the Cure, 1931–1935

Bennett has been sent to us as a scourge and the stiffer the application the swifter the cure. The deflation of Bennett stock throughout the West is remarkable.

J.W. Dafoe to Grant Dexter, 20 January 1931

The Depression brought the Prairie West to its knees. Falling grain prices, diminishing yields, and collapsing markets were joined by drought, crop disease, and insect plagues. Urban areas were beset by unprecedented levels of unemployment. The region had held the balance of power within the nation through much of the 1920s; by 1935 it was a debtor region. Political ramifications were inevitable. As politicians such as Mackenzie King grappled with broader national and international issues, the emphasis on region and province diminished. The revamping of federalism and the constitution, the crisis in capitalism and the beginning of a new economic order, and the lengthening shadows of dictatorship and the threats of world war relegated Prairie concerns to the background. The crude political reality was that as the region became less influential and, indeed, more burdensome, King's focus turned elsewhere: the West would never again receive the same attention from Ottawa. Meanwhile, the Depression and subsequent reaction of the federal government breathed new life into the third-party phenomenon. Prairie scepticism toward Ottawa had never disappeared; the rise of new protest movements, demonstrated a renewed search for alternatives. The nature of these movements, along with the changing relationship between Mackenzie King and the Prairie West, ensured them more longevity than had been enjoyed by the Progressives.

In his efforts to secure Liberal success in the Prairie West, Mackenzie King had periodically shifted his focus. During the 1920s he had looked to Saskatchewan as the beacon of hope for Prairie Liberalism. The province produced the most promising personnel; its Liberal party had won the battle against the Farmers; its organization had been described as 'perfect'; it housed the prime minister's constituency. Despite the debacle for the party with Gardiner's defeat in 1929, the Liberal tradition was reason for confidence that Gardiner would return to power in the next contest. With Saskatchewan seemingly 'safe,' King had shifted his focus to Manitoba in the period from 1926 to 1930. The province was viewed as the key to winning the battle against the Progressives; its most influential leaders shared King's compromising strategy; it housed the region's most powerful newspaper. With the Progressives in Ottawa all but neutralized, King believed that if their provincial forces could be brought on board, the West would be secure. He did not achieve the desired coalition in Manitoba, but by 1930 the Liberal leader was confident the province was under reasonable control. King did not believe that Bennett's victory was an indication of Tory strength in the West. To ensure a Liberal comeback, King next turned his attention to Alberta, the province where the party was most vulnerable.

Within Alberta lay the greatest failure of Prairie Liberalism. 'No one deplores more than I do the political situation as it affects the Liberals in Alberta,' King wrote. 'It seems to me there is more need of a searching diagnosis of causes and the application of the necessary remedies in Alberta than in any other province of Canada.'[1] Of course, a belated indication of concern, however genuine, would not be enough. The King governments had paid remarkably little attention to Alberta. The Liberal record in the province since 1921 was a disaster, and there had never been so much as a real glimmer of hope for the party throughout the decade. The result was that Mackenzie King, and the Liberal party for that matter, had to a large extent abandoned Alberta and placed their hopes on that province following Saskatchewan and Manitoba back to the fold. With the failure of this agenda, it was time for a more direct approach.

In the months following the general election, local Alberta Liberals were quick to inform their federal leader that they had been correct all along regarding the political leaning of Brownlee and the United Farmers of Alberta (UFA) government. While many of the party faithful had followed King's wishes and not opposed federal UFA candidates, Brownlee's provincial group had battled the Liberals. Although J.W.

McDonald was Liberal leader in Alberta, W.R. Howson was proving the most vocal member of the party. On the bright side, Howson noted that traditional party lines seemed to be returning because Bennett's victory had lured many Conservatives from the populist UFA ranks. The weakening of Brownlee's government in the face of the Depression could provide an impetus for a Liberal revival. Despite differences in strategy regarding the UFA, which had divided party members, Howson hoped that any desire for a provincial coalition had finally been abandoned. The past efforts of the Liberals in Ottawa, who had never understood Alberta politics, had only made matters worse. Now that both provincial and federal Liberals were in opposition, Howson called for a new era of dominion–provincial harmony. He was also pushing for a more radical party platform, even if its planks could not be carried out. Such a strategy seemed to have a special appeal in Alberta, where the UFA had entered government with a concrete program but carried through few of its promises. The people of Alberta, he argued, needed a 'rallying cry and the spirit and energy of evangelists.' His words were to prove more prophetic that he could have imagined.[2]

Mackenzie King was weary of hearing the same notes of optimism only to be drowned out by a chorus of defeat. He admitted an ignorance and helplessness when it came to the province's affairs: 'I confess I know so little about what is going on in Alberta at the present time that I hesitate to express any opinion as to the existing political situation.' The Liberal party seemed to be of the same cast as the Diehards of Manitoba and the Gardinerites of Saskatchewan, so King went on advancing the cause of compromise and the belief that the Alberta group was just being stubborn in refusing to forget past differences. He did not trust the advice of those on the scene, and past examples indicated that, to an extent, he was justified in this attitude. The situation in the province was made worse by serious personnel problems. When Robert Gardiner was appointed federal leader of the UFA, King heralded the decision because he believed 'at heart Gardiner is a sincere Liberal.' Federal and provincial members, meanwhile, continued to work in opposite directions. 'The party here,' J.A. Clarke complained, 'has disintegrated and has become a bunch of Kilkenny Cats, worse than ever in its history.'[3]

The situation in Manitoba in 1931, while relatively better than in Alberta, was by no means secure. Without the urgency for a provincial coalition, Liberals were now gearing up to fight as a separate party. In May even Crerar was indicating the impossibility of fusion and that it would be a 'mistake' for the Liberals to throw in their lot with Bracken.

Yet, by the following month he had again changed his mind. At the 1931 Liberal convention – one fragmented by the old rivalries for and against coalition – Dr Murdoch Mackay was chosen leader. The gathering and the resulting re-emergence of the old debate led Crerar to take a stand on the issue. If a choice had to be made, he was for coalition. Mackay's selection pleased Crerar, and he believed Bracken was anxious to cooperate. Several months later Crerar had again altered his opinion. Disgruntled with the provincial government's reaction to the Depression, he believed it was losing credibility with the populace. Unless a reorganization that included Liberals could considerably strengthen the government, coalition was undesirable.[4] As usual King maintained his opinion that cooperation against the Tories was desirable.

The federal Liberals had no relations with Anderson's coalition government in Saskatchewan. In the central Prairie province the strategy was more a matter of waiting for the Depression to take its course, thereby paving the way for the return of the Liberals. Gardiner's star was in the ascendant, and the period in opposition had allowed him to continue his manoeuvrings into the role of King's Prairie lieutenant, especially after Charles Dunning's departure from politics.

King's constituency of Prince Albert was now reason for some concern. The Liberal leader was becoming increasingly conscious that his absence from the riding was a handicap and source of ammunition for his opponents in Saskatchewan. He had come under scrutiny for the lack of attention given the constituency, and it was often pointed out that he showed interest only at election time. For his part, King attempted to offset such criticism by demonstrating the rewards of having the prime minister, or at least the party leader, as representative. Amid the pessimism and scepticism of the Depression, such arguments provided little assurance. 'Just how I am going to be able to have the good people of Prince Albert feel that I can represent them as effectively as one who may be living in the West has already begun to cause me some concern,' he noted. His campaign workers were informed that the role of party leader left King with little time to devote to the riding: loyalty to the constituency was overborne by duty to the nation. Warnings of another third party were also emerging from the riding. These, along with the aggressiveness of the recent Conservative campaign in Prince Albert, added to King's insecurity and fear of personal defeat.[5] When he had become the member for Prince Albert in 1925, 'King was well on his way to becoming one of the most travelled members in parliamentary history.' According to Gardiner, even Wilfrid Laurier had assessed the young politician as one who would not get elected in the same constituency twice.[6] Although the 1930 election had proven Laurier wrong, King was becoming apprehensive.

If the Prairie situation did not bode well for the Liberals, solace could at least be taken in the crumbling condition of the Conservative party. The Depression undercut any possibility of a long-term Tory break-through in the West, and reports confidently predicted disaster for Bennett at the next election.[7] The Liberals would have to do little other than sit back and observe the destruction. If the threat of Conservative victory had helped return J.W. Dafoe and the *Free Press* to Liberal ranks, the reality of Bennett's government secured their support. The editor admitted that he was leading the paper into full-scale war with Bennett. 'We never did a better stroke of work,' he proudly claimed, 'than when we made war on him from the day he took office making it clear to the world that we had no confidence in him or his programme.'[8] When the government brought down its budget in 1931, the contrast with the pre-ceding year was obvious. 'A very difft. scene than a year ago on the Dunning Budget,' King recorded, 'with drought in the West, there is a serious time ahead.' The Liberal leader was coming to realize just how kind the Fates had been: 'The nemesis that is following Bennett & his promises is amazing. Oh how grateful I am we went to the country when we did & are not in office today.'[9]

Mackenzie King could not help feeling smug. The Liberals had gov-erned Canada through prosperity and now the Conservatives were beset by depression. While briefly in Winnipeg at the beginning of 1932, he took 'immense satisfaction' in reminding the West that the region was largely responsible for Bennett's election.[10] In turn, westerners were quick to warn the Liberal leader not to be carried away by the same wave of confidence that had led to the 1930 defeat. Although the Depression was crushing the Conservatives, the result was not a dramatic rise in the popularity of the Liberals or Mackenzie King. Even Dafoe, who admitted that King was the most suitable leader in Canada, noted that 'it would not be correct to say that there is much enthusiasm for him.' His achieve-ments did not stand out in the public mind. To those on the political left, Dafoe remarked, King was in an even worse situation. Although he spoke the language of reform, left-wing progressives suspected 'he had at heart a strong dislike for them, and cherished the hope that the Liberals would be able to put them out of business.'[11]

Westerners also advised King to avoid partisanship. His speeches, 'filled with political attack,' would have little effect because the economic crisis had deepened Prairie scepticism and distrust of political parties.

The focus should remain on economics. According to T.A. Crerar it had to be remembered that the region was not populated by the 'political partisans' found in the East.[12] He also noted the increasing attractiveness of criticisms aimed at capitalism. The response to a challenger on the left should not be 'to shout at him as a dangerous agitator, but to survey our own structure and cure the defects. We have placed the emphasis altogether too largely on the materialistic side of life and not enough on things that have to do with the spiritual and cultural side of our existence.'[13] It is likely that King fully agreed with Crerar's analysis, and if the opportunity had presented itself he would probably have directed the Manitoban to *Industry and Humanity* for further enlightenment.

Although Mackenzie King found no problem focusing on the economy, he refused to believe that the Depression could not be solved by the same principles employed in the past. He was aware of the crisis in capitalism[14] and the debates surrounding ideas of inflationary spending and deficit financing, but he would experiment with new ideas only when success was reasonably assured. In the meantime he would hang on to the belief that past prosperity could be recreated through the old measures of fiscal restraint and balanced budgets. Tariff reduction was another economic policy that the Liberal leader would continue to seek throughout and even after the Depression. King would continue to believe that it 'encompassed most of Canadian politics.'[15] He was, of course, not the only one hanging on to the issue. Prime Minister Bennett was also wielding the tariff as the cure to Canada's economic woes. The Conservative tariff strategy contained the dismissal of the Tariff Advisory Board and a series of increases the likes of which had not been seen since John A. Macdonald's National Policy.[16] The continuation of the Depression only further convinced King that protectionism was failing.

Prairie Liberals agreed that Bennett's tariff policies were sealing his fate: 'The Tories have given us the key to the Citadel – it remains only for us to occupy the fort.' Nonetheless, westerners continued to maintain that Dunning's budget had surrendered Liberal principles on lower tariffs. King was again reminded that the region would not 'swing into the Liberal columns' out of mere opposition to the Conservatives. There would have to be constructive action, and this meant substantial tariff reductions. The third-party movements meanwhile were neglecting the tariff issue and emphasizing banking and currency problems.[17] The UFA members in Ottawa had responded to the government's tariff bill with a proposed amendment that the only solution to the Depression was the 'adoption of cooperative principles in production and distribution and by public control of credit.'[18] Some western Liberals supported the amendment (which was defeated), but the UFA members themselves had split on the tariff bill. Regardless, the tariff issue was diminishing in importance as the Depression thrust other issues to the forefront.

Despite King's desire to turn the tariff into the main issue, divisions remained within the Liberal party. The challenge for King was to form an effective strategy to oppose Bennett's high-tariff policies without furthering these divisions. At a time when the Depression was ushering in a new era of protectionism throughout the western world, the old protectionist–free trade gaps in the Liberal party were widening.[19] As a result, King decided to follow a cautious line of opposition. He was frustrated at the division and wanted to go after Bennett's high-tariff policy, but the threat to party unity was too risky. The party in opposition had also been weakened by the loss of such influential low-tariff supporters as Charles Dunning and T.A. Crerar. The Liberals would not aggressively advocate low tariffs because, according to King, 'to try to go that length today would be a great mistake – the country has not yet seen the evils of the protectionist measures already put thro.'[20] If King could avoid party dissension, the ravages of the Depression would destroy Bennett along with his tariff program.

Liberal hopes of avoiding controversy were soon dashed. Mackenzie King spent the latter half of 1931 attempting to clear himself and the party of the Beauharnois Scandal, in which the King government was accused of exchanging political favours for corporate gifts and donations.[21] Fortunately for the Liberals, the Depression played a large role in mitigating the political effects of the scandal, particularly in the West. The ire of the populace was so focused on the Bennett government and its handling of the economic malaise that the Liberals avoided the full impact. In Alberta the UFA government was attempting to use the scandal to revive itself, but the rural population had too many other things to worry about. In the 'final analysis' Beauharnois was proving 'pretty much of a dud,'[22] which did not provide the Tories with any consequent gains. Crerar did not believe that the scandal succeeded in calling the Liberal leader's personal integrity into question on the Prairies.

Nonetheless, the shame weighed heavily on Mackenzie King. He confessed that the party was in 'the valley of humiliation.'[23] After hearing rumours that 'Willie in the Valley'[24] was pondering resignation, Crerar attempted to soothe King's wounded pride: 'The unfortunate Beauharnois incident is fading into the background in the swiftly moving events around us.' Sensing that a change in leadership over the issue would be disastrous, Crerar increasingly found himself defending King.[25] J.W. Dafoe agreed that King was still 'the inevitable, and upon the whole the best leader for the next battle.'[26]

Although the scandal was overshadowed by the seriousness of the economic crisis, it did further Prairie convictions about the corruption of the traditional parties. Crerar had to admit that the damaging disclosures of the committee investigating the Beauharnois project had left their impression on the public mind, and 'a great many electors would be willing to consign both the old parties to the devil.'[27] After the scandal, King, who had never shaken off his fear of a third party on the Prairies, watched carefully for any sign of discontent leading to political action. He took comfort in the belief that any movement appearing at present would be a confession that the support given to Bennett in the last election was a mistake. It was an outstanding fact, he noted, that third parties always came into being under the Tories and disappeared under the Liberals. There had not been any under Mackenzie or Laurier, but they had appeared under Macdonald, Borden, and Meighen. While King still could not believe that, after all his efforts to defeat the Progressives, the region would once again turn to a third party, western Liberals were warning Ottawa to beware. According to J.J. Stevenson, a Liberal organizer from Prince Albert, 'At the present time the farmers of the West are just milling around and if they happen to find a leader with a good personality, ability and courage, to jump into the front ranks and take hold of the job I believe they will follow him, should they be successful it will mean our death-blow so far as the prairie west is concerned.' The sentiments were voiced from Prince Albert, where party organizers feared a revival of the Progressives. As usual, however, the 'ultra-radical element' was reported to be strongest in Alberta. UFA proposals for banking reform were receiving a sympathetic ear. King was being warned about the possibility of a 'Labour–Radical Farmer alliance' that would make 'a strong appeal.'[28]

Liberal fears became reality with the formation of the Co-operative Commonwealth Federation (CCF) in 1932. Mackenzie King's reaction differed markedly from that taken toward the Progressive Party in the early 1920s. The influence of the West in the nation was declining. Moreover, the Liberal leader was growing less patient with a region that he believed owed much to his party. He also believed it would be easier to oppose the CCF than the Progressives because of the former's declared socialist principles. The new movement was obviously not a group of misguided Liberals. The drive for reform, so inherent in the CCF phi-

losophy, touched a soft spot with King, but the approach was unacceptable. Whereas he had agreed with most Progressive aims, he clashed with
the CCF on the issue of inflation. Monetary policy had long been a
concern of the Alberta Progressives, who had played a leading role in the
formation of the new party. The desire for an inflationary policy was
being voiced across the Prairies; indeed, for many westerners, this had
replaced the tariff as the central issue in politics. While the price of wheat
had dropped to below 40¢ a bushel – the policies of the banks had
remained stable. For a debtor community, inflation offered hope. If
more money were put into circulation, it was argued, prices would rise.

Inflationary measures were far too radical for the Liberals in 1932, and
King had little doubt they would cause disruption within party ranks. 'I
fear we are going to have a difficult time in reconciling the views of some
of the members of our party on currency and credit problems,' he told
Crerar.[29] When the 1932 Conservative budget reflected the orthodox
desire to balance budgets, the Liberals responded with an amendment
that lower tariffs were the key to the return of prosperity. The Ginger
Group argued that a balanced budget and lower tariffs would not solve
unemployment or improve crop conditions. Instead the UFA members
proposed government control of the financial system. In caucus the
western Liberals were prepared to vote for the Progressive amendment,
but King appealed successfully for party unity. Although he would be
prepared to consider a central bank, he did not personally like the
idea.[30] Mackenzie King was finding himself out of tune with the new
western concerns.

The CCF had not yet made any impact at the provincial level, and the
Liberals looked for signs of their own improvement. The old issue of
coalition came to the forefront again in Manitoba early in 1932. Premier
Bracken was now advancing the cause of a union government, which
would even include the Conservatives, to deal with the province's disastrous financial situation. With Crerar's support, a letter was sent by the
government to the provincial Liberals requesting a coalition. Not surprisingly, the issue again split the party. The majority under Mackay agreed
to cooperate and commenced negotiations. The Diehards, who were
better organized than in previous years, reacted by appointing a central
committee with the goals of rejecting the proposal, electing separate
officers, and pushing for the replacement of Mackay as party leader. If
they failed to carry the next planned convention, they would form their
own party. At a convention held on 12 January 1932 the Liberals voted to
accept Bracken's invitation by a majority of approximately three to one.

The Liberals would unite with the United Farmers of Manitoba for the purpose of the upcoming provincial elections.[31] King, who was in Winnipeg in conjuction with the convention, was pleased with the state of affairs, noting 'how different the whole welcome & interest from first time I went to Winnipeg after becoming leader.'[32]

The Bracken government was reorganized immediately after the first session of the legislature in 1932. A joint organizational committee was established, but division plagued the process. The Diehards refused to accept the decision of the Liberal Association and took counter-measures. The Liberal League, headed by E.J. McMurray and Fred Hamilton, was organized with the declared objective of running its own candidates in all constituencies. Despite King's optimism, the break in the Manitoba Liberal party had finally occurred. Federal members would have to content themselves that the greater part of the Liberal party was linked with the Brackenites. According to Crerar, the support of the Liberal League was negligible in the traditional Diehard stronghold of Winnipeg and even weaker in the rural areas. Still, the situation was embarrassing.[33]

The election victory of Bracken's coalition led the federal Liberals to herald a successful conclusion to Liberal–Progressive division in Manitoba. King went so far as to claim that it would ensure a Prairie 'sweep' in the next federal election.[34] Such prognostications, however, rang hollow. Fusion had been gained only through an elimination of the Diehard element: while Progressives and Liberals were now united, the Liberal party itself was divided. There was more 'bitterness and vindictiveness' than ever before. If Mackenzie King had never accepted the Diehard attitude, he was not comfortable being at odds with the group. They were, he was forced to admit, the Laurier loyalists who had saved the party in 1917. While recognizing that the Bracken coalition would prove beneficial in the next federal campaign, King began to express concerns long harboured by the Diehards about the long-term survival of the Liberal party. With the lesson of the federal Progressives looming large, King pushed to have the Liberal Association in the province remain a 'separate entity,' despite the coalition. It would be 'fatal' to Manitoba Liberalism, he warned, to lose the identity of the party.[35]

A Liberal convention was also to be held in Alberta, and the party faithful were quick to warn King against a renewed push for fusion in their province. The 'experiment' in Manitoba, though interesting, would be impossible in Alberta. The upcoming convention was seen as important for other reasons. Stalwarts hoped it would bridge the divisions in the party and capitalize on the unpopularity of Bennett as well as Brownlee.

The path for a Liberal revival seemed open at last. Alberta Liberals had long felt that their federal counterparts were not providing their 'full support'; they now hoped that the gathering could be used to unite both branches of the party. For the first time, a request was made that King attend a provincial convention in Alberta. The federal leader replied that he was too busy.[36]

In February 1933 Mackenzie King gave a speech in Parliament that outlined Liberal policy. Reflecting what the president of the National Liberal Federation, Vincent Massey, called 'the new Liberalism,' it would be used as the platform for the 1935 election campaign. The caucus had met to hammer out a program acceptable to eastern and western Liberals, one that would serve as a rallying cry for party unity. King's speech called for tariff reductions increased British preferences, foreign trade agreements, a national commission to coordinate the administration of relief and to initiate work projects, and a balanced budget. The one radical departure was the proposal for a central bank.[37] The speech also outlined the Liberal approach to the Co-operative Commonwealth Federation. Whereas the Tories attacked the new movement, the Liberal leader pointed out that his party agreed with the CCF on many points. They shared similar aims; it was their solutions that differed. Certainly the Depression was pointing to 'defects and maladjustments in the system,' but the answer was not an entirely new order. The crisis was largely a product of morality, of 'the weaknesses and faults of human nature ... the greed of individuals.' The 'root cause' of the dilemma was a 'man-made Depression.'[38] In contrast to the new left-wing movement, the Liberals would become a middle-of-the-road party. The new strategy worried many western members, however, because the Prairie populace seemed prepared to give radical solutions a try. 'A good many decent people think the Liberal party have followed too much of a "middle of the road" policy,' Crerar informed King.[39] The West would have little tolerance for the Liberal leader's argument that the Depression reflected a crisis in morality.

The attitude of the CCF toward the Liberals further convinced King that the movement was not akin to the Progressives. Many in the West wished to see the Liberals take a sympathetic approach to the CCF so as not to alienate the disgruntled looking for quick solutions. Even if this was desirable, King argued, the CCF had made it impossible: 'To expect the leader of the Liberal party to support all the policies of another party which is doing what it can to undermine Liberalism, but has really nothing to give in return, would be carrying the idea of sympathetic cooperation too far.' Leading members of the new movement had declared their antagonism to the Liberal party to be as strong as that to the Tories and called for both to be destroyed. 'In the circumstances,' King noted, 'they cannot be regarded in any sense as allies.'[40]

It was only a matter of time before Prairie frustration manifested itself in King's own riding. King had been accused of ignoring his riding: he had no choice but to pay attention, however, when the Bennett government threatened the riding with redistribution in 1933.[41] Due to shifts in Saskatchewan's population patterns, the northern part of the province was to gain one seat at the expense of the southern area. According to T.C. Davis, the plan was to alter the boundaries of Prince Albert by excluding the 'predominantly Liberal' western section and adding a Tory eastern section. This eastern area was part of the constituency of the federal agriculture minister, Robert Weir, and the redistribution would therefore bring Weir and King into competition. Suddenly the Conservatives would have 'a fair chance of success.' If the changes had been made prior to the last election, they would have resulted in Liberal defeat by 618 votes rather than victory by 1192 votes.[42] King's increasing handicap in not being a resident of the area, it was argued, would 'result unfavourably' in a contest with Weir. For the first time he was advised to consider abandoning Prince Albert and running instead in what would be the new neighbouring riding of Rosthern.[43]

The Liberal leader seized the high moral ground, calling the redistribution an obvious gerrymander. Nothing would please him more than a battle with that 'hateful viperous' Weir, but as usual he claimed simply not to have the time. Personal defeat, he argued, was not at issue, although it would be highly embarrassing for the party. King did add that his 'heart' was 'very much in the problems of the West,' and he would be saddened if he had to leave Prince Albert.[44] When a plan was discussed between the Conservatives and Liberals to change the boundaries of Melville to shift Liberal votes toward Prince Albert, King refused, arguing that he would not consent to 'bettering' his own position 'where it involved a sacrifice of others,' in this case the aging W.R. Motherwell. Even when Bennett approached him privately to determine what he wanted done with the Prince Albert seat, King was confident he was fighting the good fight and refused to offer advice. He argued that if an honourable victory were not possible, then he would prefer defeat. The justice of the cause increasing his confidence, he doubted that Bennett would 'dare' gerrymander the constituency and face the wrath of public scrutiny for such a 'dastardly trick.'[45]

Morality was a poor match for anxiety. In the next several weeks King began to fear that redistribution would take place and would probably mean his defeat. Having never recovered from his earlier losses in North York, he was vulnerable to the ghosts of defeat that returned to destroy his confidence. His diary entry reflected his inner turmoil: 'I believe I shall win whatever they do, (tho' I may not).' The situation became so stressful that he claimed it made him 'feel like dropping out & devoting time to Literature. But for the Voices, & knowing it is their wish that I keep on, I wd be tempted to be indifferent.'[46] A meeting was held to determine if Motherwell would sacrifice Melville and run somewhere else, but he refused.[47] 'Motherwell has been a great disappointment this last few weeks,' King claimed. 'He has been selfish, exceedingly so.' The Saskatchewan members, preoccupied with their own situations, did not seem prepared to defend their leader's position in the House: 'What tires me most,' responded King, 'is the way our own men keep bartering to save themselves, regardless of principles which shld govern in a redistribution.'[48] As John Courtney notes, the federal redistribution of 1933 'provides a good instance of how King, feeling betrayed by colleagues and sensitive to the attacks of his opponents, imagined himself alone in fighting the good fight.'[49]

With King protesting the treatment of his riding, Bennett offered a compromise. The proposed northern boundary of Rosthern would be reduced and left in Prince Albert, while the southeastern corner of the riding would become part of Melfort. The compromise would maintain a block of Liberal votes for King while providing Conservative votes for Weir. While claiming it had not gone far enough, King accepted the proposal.[50] He believed he had held the high moral ground and – though confronted with a 'lack of chivalry' – had fought injustice 'in the open.' Bennett had made his determination clear, as far as King was concerned, to destroy his influence in Prince Albert, Saskatchewan, and the West.[51]

The redistribution left King more indecisive than usual over which course to take. With redistribution complete, King was considering abandoning Prince Albert to run in the new constituency of Rosthern, where victory seemed more assured.[52] However, by July, T.C. Davis was promising that, regardless of any redistribution, King would have no problem winning Prince Albert.[53] Anti-government sentiment was reaching a new high, and provincial by-elections pointed to Tory disaster.[54] Mackenzie King reconsidered, now determined to defend his riding, 'even if it seems probable that ... I will be encountering certain defeat.' Yet by the end of the summer he was once again complaining that if guarantees of victory could not be secured, he should be nominated in a riding where there was 'no doubt.' Rosthern would be acceptable if such a move would not be 'construed' as 'leaving the constituency ... for one entirely different and new.'[55] As late as March 1935 King was still expressing doubts about running again in Prince Albert. He seized on the issue of financial contributions as a rationale for giving up the riding. Outraged that constituency workers would ask him for financial support, even for his own campaign, King complained to Gardiner: 'I am prepared to let P.A. go if that is the spirit of the electorate there.'[56]

In 1933, with redistribution – if not King's intentions – settled, the Liberal leader prepared for a western tour. If the Depression was destroying the Conservatives, it was also deepening western distrust of the party system. The 'important task' of the Liberal party, Crerar counselled, was to restore the 'faith.'[57] King had been thinking of a Prairie trip as early as the summer of 1931. 'Will go West this year,' he had then nervously assured himself, 'I should be sure to go West this year – the West holds the key to the situation. Will be strong there all my life.'[58] The tour had been postponed in 1932 and then further delayed until after the Regina convention of the CCF in 1933.

The trip would allow King the opportunity to bolster his confidence regarding his relationship with the region. It would also be crucial in demonstrating that the Liberals were as prepared 'as any other party in Canada' to develop a radical program. The program would, of course, have to be 'practical' and in the interests of the entire nation.[59] Whereas the CCF had become the 'plaything and experimental ground of pseudo-intellectuals, monetary cranks, advocates of "Socialism in our time" and faddists who want to reconstruct the world and make over human nature,' the Liberals had monopolized the field of practical alternatives. Dafoe assured King that the tariff, which was being ignored by the CCF, could easily be made the 'decisive issue' in the West.[60] The farmers had also to be shown that Mackenzie King and the Liberal party cared for their plight and had developed policies to deal with the economic crisis. The Liberal leader was in full agreement, falling back immediately on his old western stance: 'The idea came that if Bennett uses Tariff as instrument of National policy to serve the Capitalist investor it can be used by Liberal Party to serve interest of the primary producers, agriculture etc. ... This is the place to attack the capitalist system, not by issuing paper money which will only serve to raise everything & wreck credit of country & abroad.'[61]

Mackenzie King toured the rural sections of the Prairie West, avoiding urban unemployment and radical labour unrest, and attempting to abate any enthusiasm for the CCF. His frustration with the region's radical tendencies was showing through. 'I can understand the resentment of the people against the action of the present administration and present intolerable conditions,' he admitted, 'but just why the swing ... towards the C.C.F. rather than towards the Liberal party ... I fail to see.' King pointed to his book, *Industry and Humanity*, as an indication of his personal commitment to social measures and evidence that he had been pushing for these issues long before the CCF: 'In a way I see this so strongly as almost to feel that I am but at the beginning of what I all along hoped might be my real life's work.'[62] But the years in government had diminished any popular notion of King as the reformer. 'King does not know the people,' W.A. Buchanan commented, 'does not really understand them, and then he seems also to have lost whatever he had at one time of the quality of fighting for the underdog.'[63] The decline of the Conservatives and rise of the CCF created the notion that the Liberals might become the party of the right. 'To my mind,' King wrote, 'that would be fatal to anything deserving of the name of Liberalism. We must continue to occupy the centre of the stage and the middle of the road as a people's party.' The Liberals would attempt to sail between 'Scylla and Charybdis.'[64]

The Manitoba situation, in the meantime, seemed to have improved. Because he viewed Winnipeg as a 'barometer' of the Prairie West, King took particular satisfaction in the atmosphere in that city, which he characterized as 'more congenial than at any previous time.'[65] Crerar reported that, although the CCF was not making substantial headway, increasingly their focus on banking problems was holding the public spotlight. For his part, Dafoe applauded King's rejection of the CCF and advised that in repudiating socialism he should make it clear that the new movement did not have a monopoly on 'programmes of social betterment and collective action.' There was a danger in taking a middle-of-the-road position because Canadian Liberalism would appear an 'arid political faith without works, subscribing to some kind of a nineteenth century conception of the policy of laissez-faire.'[66]

Despite his favourable impressions of Winnipeg, Mackenzie King was more comfortable in the rural areas, where he could avoid the still-simmering split in the Winnipeg Liberals as well as the urban unrest. He could not, however, avoid the drought. 'The sprinkling on the glass, with the dust made a greasy shield,' he observed while driving to Winkler. 'We went thro' a region where there had been crop failures in 3 successive seasons (to some extent) & where the grasshopper plague was very great, parts of growth being eaten to the ground till black earth shewed instead of golden grain.' At Winkler a group of Mennonites met the Liberal leader. King claimed that he was introduced as 'Moses who would lead the people out of the wilderness to the Promised Land.' Driving on a little further, he described a valley and lake as 'the promised land.'[67]

Mackenzie King continued his tour of the rural West, making frequent stops at picnics and the like. He visited his own riding of Prince Albert both on the way through and on the return trip. While in the constituency, King made a very rare stop at a reserve, where he spoke with 'two Indians.' His diary entry once again reveals his romantic perceptions: 'The sight of the women – bronzed & men swarthy & bright colours was quite appealing. It is to these men the continent belonged. Later I saw their tents & canoes by the river banks & thought of what it must mean to them to live so close to nature & how the spirit must reveal itself to them.'[68]

Yet Saskatchewan was more than fodder for King's romantic musings on those living close to the land. A federal by-election in the riding of Mackenzie was about to test the relative strength of the CCF and Liberals in the province. Not surprisingly, Jimmy Gardiner claimed that Saskatchewan would be the last Prairie province where the CCF would gain inroads. Other Liberals were more cautious, warning King to be wary. The Liberal leader viewed the by-election 'as likely to have more significance than anything else which may happen between now and the time of a general election.' A CCF victory would 'set the West on fire.'[69] When Gardiner led the Liberal forces to a decisive majority in Mackenzie on 23 October, King was elated. The result demonstrated, he claimed, that the CCF had 'not by any means captured the membership of the old Progressive party to the extent we have.'[70]

In Alberta, reports indicated that the radical movement was not abating and there was a very real threat of the CCF simply taking over from the UFA. On the other hand, the growing union between the UFA and CCF was forcing many former Conservatives back to their old party. Liberals hoped that with the UFA collapsing, the CCF still becoming established, and the Tories being tainted by Bennett's unpopularity, the Liberals would finally re-emerge at both the provincial and federal levels.[71]

Mackenzie King's strategy by 1934 was, quite simply, to avoid controversy. There was no need to come up with new solutions for the Depression because the Liberals could play upon the public's desire for stability.

Indeed, King did not believe new solutions were necessary. Instead he could concentrate on maintaining party unity while attacking as irresponsible Bennett's handling of the economic dilemma. The debates on the throne speech and budget were viewed as pre-election manoeuvrings. The Liberals opposed the extension of the Relief Bills as providing the government with a 'blank cheque.' The Conservatives by this time had reversed themselves on banking policy; in February 1934 they introduced legislation to establish the Bank of Canada. In order to prevent the government from dictating financial policy, the bank was to be run by private shareholders. King recognized that a privately owned central bank would never be accepted by his party, and western Liberals in particular, so he sought the middle ground. His solution was an institution with the majority of shareholders appointed by the government and the rest elected by private shareholders. When some members in caucus, such as Charlie Stewart, pushed for full government ownership and control, King put his foot down: 'I told them as leader I could not support state ownership of a bank ... Those who favoured State Socialism ought to be with the C.C.F.' The Liberals would stake out the 'middle of the road – with no quarter to Tories or State Socialists.'[72] In Parliament King simply pledged his party to the principle of a central bank without committing it for or against government control. As the debate continued over the next several months, the Liberal leader made his own position known but kept a tight lid on party division over the issue. The Liberals unanimously opposed Bennett's bill.[73]

The Liberal opposition tactics did not sit well with members from the Prairie West. Popular opinion in the region certainly supported stability in the midst of upheaval, but the effects of the Depression would not lead to a call for a return to the status quo. Western Liberals feared that radical sentiment was being underestimated by King's advisors, and the stance taken by the party was inadequate. The Conservative government proposed the Farmers' Creditors Arrangement Act to aid farmers who could no longer meet their mortgage obligations. The courts could not decide the mortgage amount that a farmer could meet. As Neatby points out, 'nobody opposed the legislation in the House but nobody was very optimistic about its effect.'[74] Neither the government nor the opposition seemed to have any direction on handling Prairie problems. Mackenzie King would have to return to his earlier ideas of reform and press for action through positive, aggressive leadership if he wanted to rebuild his western base.[75]

One issue in which the region was particularly interested was wheat marketing. Indeed, it replaced the tariff and inflationary schemes as the main Prairie issue,[76] and any party wishing success in the West would have to develop an acceptable position. In 1930 the pools had faced bankruptcy when the price of wheat crashed and the banks were dealt heavy losses. Prime Minister Bennett agreed to guarantee the banks against any loss, and John I. McFarland was appointed manager of the Central Selling Agency to dispose of its wheat holdings at the lowest possible loss to Ottawa. As the government became increasingly involved, McFarland held back wheat from the market in the hope that prices would rise. When this failed, he received authorization from the prime minister to buy futures in order to strengthen the market. By 1935 the total wheat and wheat futures held by the agency exceeded 200 million bushels. The government had assumed a huge financial liability with no legislative authority and had acquired a monopoly on the marketing of Canada's major export.

As the West showed increasing interest in the issue of wheat marketing, Tom Crerar sought to educate the Liberal leader. 'Of all the experiments in lunacy that Bennett has undertaken,' Crerar fumed, 'the red ribbon easily goes to his handling of the wheat situation.'[77] Despite failing crops in Canada, there was still a glut on the world market. The pooling experiment had been a dangerous risk that had been masked by stable prices during the 1920s. According to Crerar, the pools had made the first mistake in holding back wheat when the stability had been threatened, in order to await better prices. There had long been a push for a compulsory pool, particularly from Saskatchewan, and Crerar feared that the collapse would lead to an increased demand for a compulsory wheat board to ensure government control of marketing. It was, he believed, an idea that would become popular with the CCF.[78] If the Liberals did not take an aggressive stand, one way or the other, their position in the West would be placed further in jeopardy.

Mackenzie King was largely ignorant when it came to wheat marketing and had demonstrated little interest in the matter throughout his career. He was interested, however, in the ideological issue of government intervention in the economy. The most controversial issue of the 1934 session was the government's Natural Products Marketing Act, and if it were any indication of King's position on the government's role in the wheat economy, many western farmers were in for a shock. The bill was introduced in reaction to complaints emerging from British Columbia cooperatives that independent producers were dumping such perishables as strawberries on the market, thereby driving prices down. Appeals to the provincial government had led to action compelling the independent producers to conform to the cooperatives' grading and marketing regulations. After the provincial legislation was declared *ultra vires* by the courts, appeals were made to Ottawa. The resulting federal act would allow provincial marketing boards to act as federal boards as well. But it would also allow the federal government to control the production and sale of the majority of Canada's raw materials and foodstuffs. The CCF supported the bill, and in the Liberal caucus W.R. Motherwell fully endorsed the plan. Mackenzie King described it as 'a shameful measure' creating 'a lot of self-appointed soviets to manage affairs.' He attacked the bill in caucus as destroying the power of Parliament and in the House as endangering democracy.[79]

Whenever Liberal fortunes were in danger, Saskatchewan seemed to come to the rescue. On 19 June 1934 the Liberals wiped out the Anderson government in a provincial election in which not a single Conservative was elected. But, despite Liberal assurances that it was simply 'a return to old ways,' politics had changed in Saskatchewan.[80] In 1931 the United Farmers of Canada, Saskatchewan Section, had opted for direct political action, and in 1932 it had joined with the Independent Labour party to become the Farmer-Labour party. Two years later, the new party was already confident of victory. The 1934 campaign did not centre around the old issues of nationality and religion, but rather was dominated by the Depression. With cooperative government on its way out, there seemed a chance that the new party would deny the Liberals a majority. As a result, the contest was framed as a battle between liberalism and socialism. Although the Liberals easily won the contest, David Smith notes that, 'unlike the socialists, the Liberals did not yet appreciate that they were entering upon a permanent struggle.'[81]

Relations between Tory premier James Anderson and King had always been poor, so the federal leader was pleased to see the loyal Gardiner back in the premier's office. Since Charles Dunning's departure from politics, King had been seeking a new Prairie lieutenant. Gardiner's path to federal politics had been under construction for some time, and he came to Ottawa at the end of July for discussions. While he indicated a willingness to join the cabinet if the Liberals won the next contest, Gardiner remained bitter at having Dunning chosen over him in 1926. He informed King that he would first have to spend some time with his new government in Saskatchewan.[82] Despite the premier's manoeuvrings, Mackenzie King knew he had his man.

Meanwhile, W.R. Howson, who was now Liberal leader in Alberta, continued his efforts to form a stronger relationship between King and the province. Howson believed that Liberal success in the next provincial election looked 'exceedingly promising' and, if the present 'swing' continued, victory seemed assured. A victory, Howson reminded King, could only aid federal party fortunes. Of course the Alberta party would need a great deal more support from federal forces than had been received in the past: 'This is not a complaint,' Howson reassured King. 'It is merely a statement of fact.' For the first time it was hoped that Liberals at both levels would follow the same strategy. Howson believed that the CCF had to be strenuously opposed to aid in the final destruction of the UFA. He was fearful that King would handle the new party in the same conciliatory manner as the Progressives.[83]

Another of Howson's strategies involved the creation of a more unified, 'regional' Prairie Liberalism. The western Liberal parties had been divided in the past, first by the Union government then by the Progressives. With both threats to regional unity gone, the time seemed at hand not only to secure the future of the party in Alberta but in all of western Canada. Howson called for a western Liberal policy that would aid in the battle against the various 'isms' that Alberta 'bred in abundance.'[84] Late in the summer he began working to organize a gathering of Prairie Liberals.

Although Mackenzie King was pleased to see such energy and enthusiasm from the Alberta organization, he disagreed with Howson's approach. Reaction in other parts of the dominion to a western conference, he feared, would be 'unfortunate.' The West had always vocally opposed the dominance of the 'Quebec bloc'; the creation of a 'Prairie bloc' would receive equal opposition in the East. Personally, King did not trust sectional gatherings in any part of the country, believing they only bred national division. While there was nothing wrong with Liberals from the same region sticking together, meeting separately from the rest of the party was potentially troublesome. If King's response was somewhat discouraging, Howson at least expected his idea to receive a warm welcome from the most prominent Prairie Liberal, Jimmy Gardiner. He was wrong. Instead, Gardiner also viewed the scheme as potentially divisive, arguing that it was 'always a mistake to have Liberalism divided either into East or West, or by names which indicate divided opinion, whether they are applied to the East or to the West.' These responses angered Howson, who viewed them as another example of the federal party's typical lack of cooperation, and he made it clear that plans for the conference would proceed regardless. King was annoyed. He would not give a provincial party direct orders, but he did expect it to follow his advice. King informed Howson that if the Alberta Liberals were going to proceed with a conference, it must be made known that it was strictly an inter-provincial affair and 'in no way authorized either directly or indirectly from Ottawa.' A gathering of the western provinces, Howson was again warned, would be a 'fatal mistake.'[85]

Howson stuck to his guns, and the conference was held on 1 December 1934. Even though the event was attended by only Alberta Liberals, Howson reported to King that it was 'a magnificent success.' Despite his poor relationship with the prime minister, Howson continued to push for federal–provincial harmony. He had used potential federal gains in his province as an inducement to have King pay more attention, but to no avail: there was still a 'general impression' that the federal Liberals were 'very little interested' in Alberta. Playing on the federal leader's fear of third parties and the threat they posed to the entire region, Howson wrote to King: 'This province, as you are aware, has been the breeding ground of new movements, all of which have been detrimental to Liberalism. We originated the U.F.A., the C.C.F., the Farmer's Unity League, and are the protagonists in no small way of Socialism, Communism, and Social Credit. It is necessary to have an outstanding Liberal victory in both fields to cure this situation, and we need more definite assistance from Ottawa.' The response of Mackenzie King was typical: Alberta was receiving aid from the federal party 'in proportion to the size of its representation' in Parliament.[86]

Alberta Liberals may have been assuring success in the approaching provincial election, but signs augured ill. Social Credit – an economic policy popularized by Major C.H. Douglas and hammered into a political party by William 'Bible Bill' Aberhart – was stirring up strong agitation. True to its tradition, the province remained 'a hot bed for the propagation of new political ideas, especially anything connected with monetary reform.' Social Credit was described to King as a fanatical movement whose opposition to everything dubbed 'special interests' was solidifying popular support. The Depression seemed to be causing 'sound' people to listen to 'fairy tales.' By December 1934 King was receiving reports that the 'political pot' was 'beginning to boil.' The populace was more interested and active in a political campaign than had ever before been witnessed, and Social Credit was sweeping Alberta 'like a prairie fire.' Yet the following months brought conflicting views. There could be no question that the new movement was a 'dangerous factor.' It was obliterating the UFA and in most instances replacing it. Still, reports indicated that 'everything is up in the air.' Provincial Liberals were hopeful that the more time people had to consider Social Credit the more they would abandon it.[87]

In spring 1934 the UFA government had reluctantly decided to have evidence taken by the Legislature's Agricultural Committee on the Douglas System of Social Credit. Pressure for this gesture had come from many political directions, including W.R. Howson's own resolution on 10 February demanding an inquiry into Social Credit ideas. The 'hearings' demonstrated a split between Aberhart and Major Douglas, which the provincial Liberals assumed would lead to the rise of two rival Social Credit parties. Under the single-transferable vote system in Alberta, such an outcome would enable the Liberals to win the election. As John A. Irving has observed, 'Lulled into a false sense of security by their belief that the hearings had discredited Aberhart, the Liberals formed no conception, until nearly a year later, of the real strength of the Social Credit movement.'[88] Thus, instead of focusing on Social Credit, Howson led an attack against the UFA government. The provincial Liberal platform formulated at the convention on 3 December pledged the party, once in power, to take on Social Credit experts to aid in formulating policy. A Liberal government would also support a national bank. Howson was careful not to antagonize Aberhart because he wanted to secure Social Credit support after winning office. Charlie Stewart meanwhile was reporting that, although 'the lunatics were riding strong,' there was evidence of 'a falling away.'[89] The best one can say about Alberta, Crerar concluded from the conflicting reports, is that it was in a 'state of utter confusion.'[90] In reality, Alberta Liberals had waited so long for the disintegration of the UFA that, given the disastrous state of the Conservatives, they simply could not believe that another upstart radical movement could come along and snatch away office.

The provincial election in August 1935 resulted in William Aberhart's Social Credit sweeping to power. In essence, Social Credit simply replaced the United Farmers. The new movement broadened its appeal from an agrarian movement to one that represented what C.B. Macpherson calls the petit-bourgeois nature of Alberta.[91] There remained the emphasis on delegate democracy and opposition to the traditional two-party system. Social Credit rode the waves of western alienation, which had only increased in magnitude during the Depression. Unlike its predecessor, Social Credit offered solutions, usually very simple in nature, to the economic problems facing the debtor community. In the new age of technology, there was no reason for 'poverty in the midst of plenty.' The economic crisis was the result of a corrupt system dominated by eastern business interests. The new government would soon come to view the King Liberals as one of the corrupt tools of the eastern interests.

Mackenzie King was frustrated. He viewed the Alberta situation as resulting from the same condition that had plagued Liberalism in the province since he had become party leader: 'The result in Alberta is due to the absence of real leadership on the part of Liberals.'[92] The defeat also brought the frustrations of the provincial party to a boil. Aberhart 'was a "Man sent from God,"' Howson wrote King. 'What chance had any mere politician?' For fourteen years the UFA had painted the old-line parties as corrupt and villainous. Now 'Brother Aberhart' merely threw the farmers into the mix, 'so the U.F.A., Liberals and Tories were now in Alberta the direct descendants of His Satanic Majesty.' Howson warned King to take care in his dealings with Aberhart should the Liberals win the upcoming federal election. The Social Credit premier would seem friendly but would work to paint Ottawa as the villain: 'Get a picture of it – Premier Aberhart with large white wings, a harp and the Bible opened at the Prophecies, chatting with Premier King with black horns and a long graceful tail with an arrow on the end.' Although Howson realized his strongly worded letter would be somewhat of a shock to King, he could not curb his sarcasm: 'Possibly this is a new type of political letter for you to receive, but remember it comes from Alberta and we *are* different.' Federal hopes in the province were once again thrown into 'confusion.' Less than a year earlier, organizers were reporting that a large number of seats would go Liberal; now they were not calling any seat in the province secure.[93] King was thankful Alberta's 'weird business' and 'fanatical flame' were being kept within the bounds of that 'radical' province.[94]

By 1935 the wheat problem had forced its way onto centre stage. Even King was describing it as 'the largest question that Canada has to face.'[95] With the support of the pool representatives, Bennett was now attempting to pass the Grain Bill, creating a permanent board that would have sweeping powers and would control the marketing of all grains. The bill was generally popular on the Prairies, and any opposition would be viewed as a lack of sympathy for the western farmer. King, however, agreed with Crerar in opposing the bill because its compulsory features contradicted 'sound liberal principles.'[96] He would advance the 'Liberal attitude' that the state should regulate and control, but not participate in business. Examples such as the railways and banks, where private and state ownership worked side by side, were used to demonstrate the consistency of this approach.[97] J.W. Dafoe, who was also against the bill, reminded King that opposing the measure would be popular in Manitoba, where 'the pool has never been strong.' Alberta should not be a concern because it was in such a 'bedeviled' state. Saskatchewan, which was prejudiced against the Grain Exchange, would pose a problem.[98]

The Liberal strategy was to oppose not the bill but its permanent and compulsory nature. Disgruntled, many western Liberals continued to push for a permanent board. King was confident that if he could get these members to agree to his policy, the rest of the caucus would fall in line. Only in the West would a board with compulsory powers be popular, and he was relieved to have Gardiner, Dunning, Crerar, and Dafoe in agreement. It seemed 'inconceivable' that the Prairies would 'isolate themselves' over the issue and abandon the party that had 'always espoused the western cause.' But the situation was proving embarrassing. King's own government in 1922 had passed enabling legislation for the three Prairie provinces to create a wheat board. It was obvious the Liberals were now opposing this popular western policy.[99] In an attempt to delay the matter until agreement in caucus had been reached, King suggested that the government refer the bill to a special committee. Bennett found himself pressured into appointing such a committee. It decided that the powers of the bill were too broad and the compulsory features not necessary. The committee also reported that it was not necessary to have a board that would handle all grains, as opposed to just wheat. The result was the establishment of the Wheat Board, which would offer a minimum price to the producer, leaving farmers with the choice of selling their wheat to the board or to private grain dealers.

Western discontent reached its peak in the On-to-Ottawa Trek and Regina Riot in the summer of 1935. Frustration at the federal government's reaction to the unemployment situation led workers from the Relief Camps to stage a strike in Vancouver and then 'ride the rails' to take their message directly to Prime Minister Bennett in Ottawa. The trekkers grew in number as more unemployed men joined their ranks and jumped the boxcars along the CPR route through the southern Prairies. The trek was abruptly halted when the prime minister ordered the Royal Canadian Mounted Police to arrest the leaders in Regina, a decision that led to a riot.

Mackenzie King and his party responded cautiously to this emotionally charged event. Liberal opposition to Bennett's handling of the trek could foster the impression in Quebec that the party was sympathetic to communism. In Parliament King found it 'preferable' to allow J.S. Woodsworth to take the government to task. Although King obtained the correspondence between Gardiner and Bennett in order to become better acquainted with the issue, he avoided taking an active part in the debate. Privately, he noted that there was a sort of 'Nemesis' in the fact that the 'Tory' Bennett had 'incited' the riot in the 'Liberal' province of Saskatchewan. While King did not have any suggestions as to how the unemployment problem should have been handled, he did blame the Conservatives for the dilemma and the result.

The Liberal strategy of avoiding controversy while in opposition carried over into the federal election campaign of 1935. The party stressed co-operation and conciliation rather than policies, King rather than chaos. The rallying cry was that only the Liberals could offer a truly 'national' government. The one promise the Liberal leader did make involved tariffs. He continued to believe that the issue was crucial in gaining Prairie support. The populace was assured that a Liberal government would have a reciprocity agreement with the United States by the end of the year. As usual the party's tariff stand had to be moderated for eastern tastes, so on 4 September King made a speech in Halifax, indicating that he would remove Bennett's tariffs only 'gradually' and that a Liberal government would 'not injure any legitimate industry' by lowering tariffs, or take away from industry any of the protection provided prior to 1930.[100] While the speech shocked some Prairie Liberals, the tariff had lost much of its impact as an issue. Most members in the region realized the populace was more concerned with unemployment, banking and currency, railways, and wheat. King admitted that 'some of our friends in the West' were becoming 'a little panicky' about the absence of promises regarding unemployment and monetary reform.[101] He defended his position by pointing to the platform of 1933, which the party intended to follow and had been out-lined by caucus and the National Liberal Federation. His hands were tied: as party leader he was simply following party policy. Western Liberals were probably left wondering where this same commitment to platform prom-ises had been when it came to the platform of 1919.

Financing the campaign in the West was posing difficulties, but at least some semblance of Liberal organization had reappeared. In 1932, with the lesson of shady campaign contributions in the Beauharnois scandal looming large, King had seen to the replacement of the council of the National Liberal Organization Committee with the newly formed Na-tional Liberal Federation. Henceforth there would be some separation between the politicians and organizers. By the summer of 1932 Vincent Massey was made president of the federation, Norman Lambert became secretary, and Mackenzie King was relieved of any responsibility for publicity or finances. The vitality of the federation would depend on the provincial organizations. By 1935 Massey and Lambert were having problems both raising money on the Prairies and 'securing Toronto and Montreal money for the western provinces.' Alberta was viewed as a 'write-off in the eyes of the national party,' and the Saskatchewan machine was expensive to fund.[102] The reality of the situation could not be avoided. The federal party was simply not as concerned with winning the region as it had been in the past. The area was rife with discontent, and the populace was turning to radical alternatives. Mackenzie King was having increasing difficulty understanding and sympathizing with the western direction.

To suggest that the Liberals were confident about winning the election of 1935 is an understatement. King's western campaign was more concerned with grooming cabinet possibilities than orchestrating policies attractive to the region. In Manitoba he distanced himself further from the Diehard group that, after a brief upsurge, had faded to only a handful of embittered individuals. In March he had been warned that both E.J. McMurray and J.W. Wilton had made public addresses calling for a national convention to reconsider the question of leadership. In July King wrote R.F. McWilliams asking him to attempt to persuade J.W. Dafoe to run in the contest. Knowing that the Diehards would be furious at such a suggestion, he requested it be kept quiet for the time being.[103] Organization of the province was left to Crerar, who now faced some rivalry from Joe Thorson of Selkirk.[104] Premier Bracken gave the Liberals his full support throughout the campaign.[105]

The objective in Saskatchewan was to secure a regional advisor. King had been pressuring Charles Dunning to return to politics but, while he did wish to come back, he did not want to sacrifice his business opportunities. He was also aware that the West would object to his eastern affiliation and that Gardiner would view him as a rival. King planned on avoiding these obstacles by having Dunning as an eastern minister representing an eastern constituency. He had already concluded that, as Prairie lieutenant, Gardiner would be 'just as good as Dunning' and would 'command a larger following.' Moreover, there would be no question as to his loyalty. When the Saskatchewan premier was approached, King found him 'keener' than before: he 'seemed willing to come at once, leaving Davis as his successor.' The reaction pleased the Liberal leader, who saw that Gardiner 'would be a real strength.'[106]

By 1935 the expediency of winning western support had diminished, and so too had the importance of the Prince Albert constituency. All that remained was Mackenzie King's sentimental and romantic attachment to the riding he had represented longer than any other. While speaking in

Prince Albert, he had a vision: 'I seemed to see Prince Albert as one of the great cities of the future, and the vision of a statue of myself in one of its thoroughfares, as the one who had been its member for — years in the parliament of Canada. It seemed to me men might come to speak of me as Mackenzie King of Prince Albert, just as they speak of Chamberlain of Birmingham etc etc.'[107] While the Depression ensured King's victory in Prince Albert and allowed him to wax romantic about his attachment to the riding, it could not disguise the danger signs. Jubilant Social Creditors, fresh from victory in Alberta, 'poured' into the constituency, their cause further strengthened by an unofficial alliance with the Reconstruction party of Conservative renegade H.H. Stevens.[108] The campaign was demonstrating that the West did not reciprocate King's attachment, whether romantic or real. King knew that his cautious opposition to Bennett had not been popular on the Prairies at a time when the people were desperately seeking concrete solutions. The Depression had allowed the formation of the CCF, the Reconstruction party, and Social Credit – all of which were based in the West – as alternatives to traditional politics. 'I confess the situation does not look certain here,' he was forced to admit. 'There is a sort of apathy – an uncertainty in the minds of our own people of how things are going. – The people seem to forget & seem to want promises. Their new theories have bewildered them & they can't see a way out.' Instead of accepting any of the blame, he placed the onus onto the lack of leadership: 'We really need leaders (as a party) through the West, except Gardiner of Saskatchewan there is no one outstanding. The people are like a sheep without a shepherd.'[109]

His tour of Alberta only increased King's criticism of western leadership. He concluded from his first impressions of Aberhart that the most effective personalities were not being drawn into Liberal ranks. Describing the Social Credit premier as 'most cordial,' King wrote that the impression he left 'could not have been more favourable.' He looked like a 'good man.' King went so far as to invite Aberhart onto his speaking platform for that evening's election rally, but the premier declined. The Liberal campaign was emphasizing its ability to offer a national government by having the premier of every province join King on the platform. The plan was possible, of course, because no province had a Conservative government or even effective opposition that had survived the Depression's wrath. Except in Alberta, King would have success in bringing each premier onto the dais. When Charlie Stewart informed King as they were leaving the premier's office that W.R. Howson could not be located, the contrast between King's impression of the premier and the provincial

Liberal leader was acute: 'Think he may be drunk somewhere,' King recorded, 'Here is the whole story in a nut-shell. The Liberal Leader is a drunken unreliable lawyer of a blustering bull-dozing type, the Social Credit Leader, kindly, persuasive, clean living, most presentable etc – is it any wonder he won & the Liberals lost? The story I pray may be different in the federal field.' King then went on to meet the federal party candidates, concluding in turn that they were 'not a good average.' When Howson presided over the platform that evening, King was not impressed by his 'many rough jokes & references to drinking etc.' It was 'that gang,' he concluded, 'that ruins the party here.'[110]

On 14 October 1935 the Mackenzie King Liberals won a majority of historic proportions, with 178 members and almost 45 per cent of the popular vote. Manitoba returned fourteen and Saskatchewan sixteen Liberals from a combined thirty-six constituencies. In Alberta, only one Liberal was elected from the province's seventeen constituencies. By contrast, the Social Credit party, garnering half the vote, elected fifteen in that province. The party also managed to win two seats in Saskatchewan. The CCF elected seven, all west of Ontario. Indeed, the CCF received as many votes in Manitoba and Saskatchewan as the Tories. The Reconstruction party managed to elect only its leader, H.H. Stevens. The Conservative contingent was reduced to forty with one member from each of the Prairie provinces. In Prince Albert King was re-elected with 9087 votes; the Social Credit candidate finished second with 3185 votes.[111] Blair Neatby argues that the two-party system, almost re-established in 1930, was once again disrupted. In truth, it had never really returned. He is correct, however, in pointing out that 'the election results showed how deep the regional divisions had become.'[112]

When King looked to western representation in the new cabinet he had to consider the main Prairie Liberals: Gardiner, Dunning, Crerar, Motherwell, and Stewart. He was confident that if the first three were in the government, the farming interests would be 'pretty safely protected.'[113] The Alberta situation certainly did not pose any difficulties. King admitted to feeling a bit 'anxious' that Stewart did not win his seat, but there would be no finding him a safe riding outside the province this time. The Liberal leader was pleased, in fact, 'not to have to consider him.' Clearly any hopes of Alberta's 'return to common sense' had been dashed. 'Alberta will have to go unrepresented for a while & work out her own salvation,' King noted angrily. The province had 'isolated itself'; not to afford it cabinet representation was the only way to 'teach' it 'a lesson.' Albertans had long warned King not to lose faith in the province, that such action would only further isolate the area from central Canada, the federal government, and the Liberal party. After sixteen years, he was fed up. Mackenzie King had given up on Alberta.[114]

There was no doubt at the end of 1935 that Gardiner would come to Ottawa and serve as the main Prairie advisor. Since 1919 constant attempts by Mackenzie King to groom a suitable western lieutenant had failed to produce a loyal and effective general of the same ilk as Ernest Lapointe in Quebec. The Liberal leader had himself failed to be viewed as a Prairie defender, and by 1935 his stance was clearly marked as the protector of 'national unity.' His method of governing worked best by having the diverse areas of the nation represented by regional spokesmen who could be counted on for loyalty and who would bring specific concerns to the table. As prime minister, Mackenzie King would then serve as the negotiator among the various interests. The lack of an effective western spokesman, he believed, was largely responsible for the Liberal record in the West. He never seemed to realize that the Prairies could not always be treated as one region with one western Liberal commanding a following from all three provinces. Although he seemed at times to have come face to face with this reality, the implications were never embraced. To be fair to King, it should also be pointed out that many of the leading Liberals from the region had also failed to understand this essential fact. In addition, the area was changing, and the provincial differences were becoming increasingly marked. Regardless, the fact remained that in 1935 King was determined to have a strong Prairie lieutenant who could be looked upon to handle the discontent so evident in the region. Motherwell and Stewart had been inadequate regional advisors, and King had never liked or trusted Crerar. During the 1920s Dunning emerged as the probable candidate, but his exit from politics in 1930 and ensuing move into the Montreal business community put an end to these plans. Even before 1930 King had had his eye on Gardiner, but his attitude toward the Progressives and feud with Dunning had held him back. The quest for a Prairie general would finally come to an end in 1935, and King would never search again. With Gardiner in command of the region, western concerns would be left largely within his control. The result would lead Mackenzie King, and his government, to pay even less attention to the Prairie West.

Amid the complex array of considerations during the cabinet negotiations, the prime minister was astonished that the Dunning–Gardiner feud emerged as the major stumbling block. In assuming that, by having Dunning in the East, the dilemma would be solved, he had underestimated Gardiner's competitive tenacity. As soon as the Saskatchewan premier arrived in Ottawa for talks, Dunning became an issue. 'Gardiner's countenance at once took on a very strong and defiant look,' King noted. The premier went over Dunning's career, indicating that he had always 'taken the easy course' and been 'pretty selfish generally.' He had entered the recent campaign only in the late stages 'as a saviour of the situation in western Canada, when the battle itself had been won.' He always wanted 'to see how things were going to go before he would take any part.' Dunning had provided financial help to western candidates without Gardiner's knowledge so he could have 'a string on these men.' The premier even questioned Dunning's loyalty. Gardiner claimed he would have to 'think pretty carefully' before entering a government alongside his bitter rival.[115]

Mackenzie King realized Gardiner was going to 'fight with his back to the wall' and if possible use his own entry to keep Dunning out of cabinet. The prime minister countered that Dunning would come in only as an eastern minister. The 'field' in the West would be left to the regional lieutenant. In private, King agreed there was 'justification' for Gardiner's criticisms and that Dunning had been 'selfish, and very ambitious' and 'had not always played the game as he should.' His hope of avoiding the quarrel by separating the two men was, however, proving problematical.[116]

When it came to portfolio choices, Gardiner referred to an earlier conversation when he had indicated more of an interest in financial matters than agriculture. He did not want a 'minor' western portfolio while Dunning received a 'major' department. In fact, he felt 'just as able' for the finance portfolio. Yet King had witnessed Dunning's loss of western appeal when he stepped up to finance, and he was not about to have the same occur with Gardiner. The Saskatchewan politician had to be kept oriented toward a 'western' department. National revenue was suggested because it involved tariff regulations, customs, and taxes. King was confident Gardiner would be enticed because it 'really controlled the tariff situation.' The premier deflected the suggestion, arguing that he did not want to deal with the liquor business. A consolidated department that included immigration, colonization, forests, mines, parks, Indians, and territories was then suggested. King figured this department would have appeal because it concerned 'the matters of most concern to western Canada.' Once again Gardiner was unenthusiastic. The prime minister began to grasp that Gardiner wanted the prestigious finance portfolio. When asked if he enjoyed the confidence of the eastern business interests, he answered that he did, 'even more than Dunning.'[117]

As the negotiations dragged on, King became determined to have Dunning for finance and Gardiner for agriculture. The difficult times demanded a government of the best possible men, regardless of personal animosities. If Dunning could be convinced to enter the cabinet, he would be brought in. Although he may have been selfish and difficult to handle, King still believed he had impressive abilities and held 'great confidence' throughout the country. While Gardiner had financial skills, 'he was not yet known as a financial man by the country generally.' The finance portfolio was traditionally an eastern position, and although Dunning had held it, he was now regarded as an easterner. If Gardiner took finance, he could not serve as the western advisor. He would be in an awkward position when it came to dealing with the debt situation of the Prairie provinces. Dunning, on the other hand, 'would be in the position to act more independently in all these relationships.'[118] Gardiner again demonstrated his loyalty by indicating that, while Dunning's entry and hold on finance was not pleasing, he would accept the decision. His main objection, he argued, was Dunning's constant 'intriguing to get his own following in Saskatchewan; that he would be interfering in the administration of other people's affairs.' The prime minister again reminded Gardiner that the two men would be working in their 'own yards.' He feared that, if only one were invited into cabinet, their personal animosity could become a source of public embarrassment. For his part, Dunning handled the issue in his usual conciliatory manner. He agreed that, after not aiding in the campaign, he may not 'deserve recognition' and promised to leave Gardiner to handle the West.[119]

The discussion then returned to portfolio choices. King discussed the advantages of having Gardiner take immigration and resources, that it offered 'great patronage' and would 'keep him in touch with western Canada.' National revenue, while a more influential portfolio, was not really a possibility because the work would 'tie him down to Ottawa,' hampering plans to have him serve as Prairie advisor. It was evident, however, that Gardiner was willing to surrender his western influence to gain a more powerful portfolio. King sensed in his general attitude 'a desire to get closer contact with big interests, realizing a sort of political power in that connection.' He had 'the instincts of a political boss, and rather likes having a machine he can control.' In an attempt to keep his eyes focused on a western power base, King promised to 'back his wishes on western matters' and that Dunning would be thus informed.[120]

The issue of Gardiner's constituency choice also played a role in the discussions. He planned on taking over Motherwell's riding because the elderly politician was expected to retire. The position of lieutenant-governor of Saskatchewan had seemed a good position for Motherwell, but he was determined to battle for agricultural legislation and was now hesitant about leaving the House. In return for surrendering his constituency, he expected Gardiner to take the portfolio of agriculture and prevent it falling into Crerar's hands. Despite this additional pressure Gardiner made another attempt to gain a more powerful portfolio, suggesting railways. Once again King responded that this would weaken his position as a western advisor. Railways was to be with canals and water systems, and kept in eastern hands.

Manitoba representation in cabinet, while more clear-cut, was not without its problems. Crerar was the obvious choice, but personal antagonism affected the tone of the discussions. King claimed to be disappointed with Crerar's showing in his province and believed he had 'little hold' and had become 'ineffective.' The prime minister complained about the Manitoban's attachment to the Union government, the Home Bank, and the Grain Exchange. Ernest Lapointe agreed, and the two even went so far as to consider W.G. Weir as the province's representative. Later, when Lapointe suggested Dafoe for a cabinet position, King answered that he would be 'the very man.' If the *Free Press* editor would not enter the cabinet, King was hopeful he would become the minister to Washington. Dafoe, reached by telephone, was invited to join the government. While claiming to be 'touched' by the offer, he declined.[121] King pushed him to accept the Washington post to work on a reciprocity agreement 'to help towards securing what we have all striven for so long.' Dafoe promised to consider the proposal but later turned it down.[122]

Crerar met with King and requested the railway portfolio. The prime minister admitted to being 'abrupt' when he refused on the basis that, with the exception of Dunning and Lapointe (who happened to be at the discussions), no minister was to be returned to his previous department. When Crerar indicated that he was entitled to a 'major' portfolio, King's patience diminished even further. King and Lapointe had come to the conclusion that Crerar was not deserving of recognition because he had not even been in Parliament in the last session. There would be 'a good deal of opposition in taking him into the government at all.' When King told the Manitoban that Gardiner deserved 'a special obligation' due to his organizing work and service as premier of his province, it was Crerar's turn to disagree. He had been 'of no help but rather a hindrance' to the Liberals in Manitoba. Again the prime minister announced that both Gardiner and Crerar would be expected to take 'western' portfolios, and these included agriculture and the consolidation of interior and immigration. While continuing to push for railways, Crerar indicated a preference for the department handling natural resources. 'The truth of the matter is,' King noted, 'he has been more exacting than I expected he would be, and I feel more determined not to give him Railways.' Crerar had been 'most ineffective as the Minister of Railways when he held that portfolio.'[123] It was also likely that King was influenced by Charles Dunning. As Crerar's biographer observes, 'there had never been much love lost' between the two westerners. To a large extent, the antagonism reflected the differences in Manitoba and Saskatchewan Liberalism, just as the Dunning–Gardiner feud pointed to differences within the Saskatchewan party itself. The two men at least shared the Progressive heritage, but Dunning disliked Crerar's attachment to the Grain Exchange, while Crerar suspected Dunning of being sympathetic to the CPR and prejudiced against the national railway.[124]

When asked if there was any way of 'causing' Gardiner to take agriculture, Crerar suggested having Motherwell apply pressure from Saskatchewan. King phoned Motherwell, asking him to urge Gardiner to take agriculture. The pressure was applied, but Gardiner continued his efforts for a more influential portfolio and pushed again for trade and commerce. Although Motherwell had told him that his seat would not be available if the grain business were left to the East, Gardiner saw a way around the threat. He could take trade and commerce and handle grain from this department. He had no desire for the consolidated department of natural resources, referring to it as 'a sort of glorified Park's commission.'[125]

But the bartering was at an end. King had decided that agriculture would be held by a westerner and trade and commerce would go to the East. His first concern was having Gardiner as the western lieutenant: this meant accepting a western portfolio. The Saskatchewan politician was annoyed at having his ambitions checked. 'If they only wanted him for Agriculture in the east,' he told King, 'they could not think much of him, or did not want him very badly.' King was surprised that Gardiner and Crerar would even dare barter for more powerful positions: 'As I came back to my room I picked up a copy of "Animal Life" ... and felt it had something of significance for me. When I looked at its cover there was a picture of two peacocks on the limb of a tree, a large and a small one ... These two birds mean Crerar & Gardiner, with their respective vanities, each ambitious for high & higher office.' As for Gardiner, 'the little beggar is angling for one of the more important portfolios, and running the danger of getting out of his depth.'[126]

The two politicians made last-ditch attempts to improve their situations. If he was going to be forced into taking agriculture, Gardiner at least requested that Motherwell be appeased by having the Board of Grain Commissioners transferred from trade and commerce. Dunning did not believe this would be possible because agriculture dealt with production, and trade and commerce with distribution of sales. It was agreed that the supervision of the Wheat Board's operations would be placed under a subcommittee of council with Gardiner as a member. In the meantime he would be able to push for the transfer of the Board of Grain Commissioners. Crerar was called for one last meeting. While King pushed the importance of the western portfolios, Crerar continued to advocate railways. 'I told him,' King recorded, 'I simply could not give the matter further consideration; that I had reached the point where he must either take the portfolio or let someone else have it, but that I could not offer him anything else.' Crerar requested more time, but King's mind was made up – he would have to accept the new department of mines and resources once it was created.[127] Years later Crerar remembered that once the decisions were made, King told him that there would still be opposition to his coming from Manitoba. To Crerar, this was King's attempt to force him 'to beg for the job, and as far as I was concerned, I was doing no begging.'[128]

The cabinet negotiations pointed to future difficulties between Mackenzie King and his western representatives. His patience with the region had certainly diminished. Gardiner would serve as regional lieutenant, but he would have little influence in Manitoba. Crerar, who was to be the provincial minister, would not view Gardiner in any way as representative. Gardiner's influence in Saskatchewan would be unquestioned as long as Liberal fortunes remained strong, but the antagonism with Dunning could continue to pose problems. 'The antipathy of both Crerar and Dunning to Gardiner is an unpleasant feature,' King observed, 'and may make difficulties later on. Gardiner's loyalty to Liberalism and myself, and his organizing ability, are the strongest factors in his favour. He is not large-minded, and he has ambitions to be in touch with the big interests, and to create a machine. I can see this, and it is not in his favour. However, he is the man to get Alberta, as well as Saskatchewan, into line.'[129] Alberta was now being left to Gardiner, and King's hopes were pinned on the province not rejecting outside interference as Manitoba had done.

In the latter days of 1935 there was one 'western' situation that the new government had to deal with immediately – the Wheat Board. A cabinet wheat committee was formed that consisted of the ministers of mines and resources, trade and commerce, agriculture, and finance. Crerar and W.D. Euler made it clear that they favoured the elimination of Bennett's board. King believed that Gardiner, who had not yet returned to Ottawa, would be of the same opinion. Dunning and C.D. Howe, on the other hand, favoured keeping the board until the price of wheat increased. This way the Conservative creation, rather than the government, would have to carry the responsibility. The wheat committee was to discuss the situation and report to cabinet. King argued that caucus had previously agreed that the board would not be permanent, serving only to 'tide over an emergency situation.'[130] The decision to terminate the board certainly would not please the Prairie West.

In the meantime, advice from Alberta continued to warn the prime minister not to trust William Aberhart. During the federal campaign the premier had supported Bennett in his Calgary riding and had urged a Social Credit candidate to oppose King in Prince Albert. He was pushing Ottawa for assistance to refinance provincial debts; if he did not receive what he was requesting, provincial Liberals contended that he would use his radio broadcasts to blame the federal government. They further argued that, when Aberhart found it impossible to deliver on his electoral promises, he would blame Ottawa for obstructing his program. He would then likely move into the federal field in an attempt to achieve the necessary power to implement Social Credit.[131] To Mackenzie King these warnings seemed exaggerated. At the Dominion–Provincial Conference in December 1935 he found Aberhart willing to cooperate and work within the constitution. 'Aberhart's expression was a pleasing feature of the evening,' he reported after a dinner party. The prime minister even told Crerar that the Alberta premier should be brought into the Liberal camp and confidently prophesied that 'the next year or two will see the end of social credit.' He spent much of the conference talking with Aberhart, whom he 'liked personally' and for whom he 'felt real sympathy.'[132] He tried to convince himself that Alberta's independent approach to its creditors for the conversion of the interest charges on the provincial debt was 'timed inadvertently' and 'not intended to make trouble here.' The prime minister was pleased to have 'heard very little of Social Credit throughout the week.'[133] So far, he was prepared to give Aberhart the benefit of the doubt.

The atmosphere of the conference, in general, was cordial. It was, to a large extent, the same spirit of cooperation that prevailed throughout the recent campaign and had concluded with a massive Liberal rally at

Maple Leaf Gardens in Toronto, where eight of the premiers gave radio addresses from their home provinces offering support for the federal Liberal party. Assuredly, the premiers wished to avoid antagonizing the new government. In particular, the Prairie premiers could hardly afford to offend a federal government they were coming increasingly to rely upon for financial support. Under Bennett, Ottawa had reluctantly spent nearly $200 million on relief. The total debt was now $3 billion. But it was not enough. The western provinces were such poor credit risks that they could not borrow money because investors would not buy their bonds.[134] Although there would be no confrontations at the dominion–provincial gathering, disagreement was brewing beneath the artificial spirit of cordiality. Mackenzie King had no intention of altering the federal–provincial framework to place more financial responsibility on his government. Instead he had every intention of sticking to orthodox fiscal policies. After all, he had his own budget to balance. The premiers would leave Ottawa content that the new prime minister had at least accepted more responsibility for relief costs. A federal commission would be established to supervise these expenditures.

The years in opposition reflected a change in Mackenzie King's attitude toward the Prairie West. Expediency no longer forced him to pay special attention to Prairie concerns, and the Depression reduced the region's influence in the nation both economically and politically. The area was continuing to turn toward radical alternatives, but these were very obviously not movements that would easily be absorbed by the Liberal party. By 1935 King was coming to realize that he had never really understood the West. This realization was reflected in his changing attitude and diminishing sympathy. He was coming to settle comfortably into the role for which he would become known – the balancer of regional interests and the protector of national unity. Neatby gives King credit for leading the only national party in 1935, and this credit is well deserved. Mackenzie King had survived the restructuring of the Canadian party system, and the Liberals were securely back in office. But when it came to the condition of Liberalism on the Prairies in 1935, and King's original goals regarding the region and party, there was much less reason to congratulate the prime minister. What affinity he had felt with the region prior to the 1930s had all but disappeared. While in 1935 his attitude was still changing, the following years in office would make his new viewpoint only too obvious.

7

The Radical Has Left Us, 1936–1940

Gradually I see a re-alignment coming. The conservative party in the West is no longer a party. The radical has left us and is on his own in a third party. Those most anti-liberal in the conservative party will go into the third parties. I am alarmed about the future out here.

T.C. Davis to King, 7 April 1940

The period after 1935 would demonstrate just how much Mackenzie King's attitude toward and handling of the Prairie West had changed. Gone were the sympathies and affinities so commonly espoused; gone were the hopes that the region would serve as the base of a new Liberalism; gone was the idea that King was a 'spiritual westerner' who had found his home. When the prime minister looked west, he no longer saw the hopes and future of the nation. He saw an area stricken by drought and depression, unable even to pay its debts, and constantly begging the federal government – itself in a serious financial crisis – for relief. King no longer needed the region, not as he had in the past at any rate. But now the West needed the federal government. King had waited over fifteen years for the Prairie West to pass through its political crisis and become that Liberal base. He believed that his party had gone to considerable lengths to ensure western support. Now, even with the Conservatives almost completely destroyed on the Prairies, westerners were still inclined toward radical alternatives. Enough was enough. Throughout the remainder of his career the prime minister would demonstrate little more than frustration and impatience toward the area. This attitude would become manifest in his handling of Prairie Liberals and even of his western adviser. The Second World War would further shift the emphasis away from western issues.

As the continuing ravages of the Depression swept across the Prairies, the region increasingly looked to the federal government for aid. Only Ottawa could tax the more prosperous regions to help the others; only Ottawa could guarantee provincial loans and prevent default or even bankruptcy. But King's orthodox views kept him to 'limited objectives.' He was uncomfortable with the new demands placed upon the federal treasury, and while he had advocated a more interventionist state in his early career, the Depression forced the issue further than he was prepared to go. Increasingly, Mackenzie King would become a conservative among radicals. He was disdainful of Bennett's last-ditch efforts at increased federal intervention: 'King had interpreted the promises as irresponsible demagoguery, the new government activities as encroaching dictatorship, and the New Deal as unconstitutional.'[1] He had pulled the nation from recession in the early 1920s by reducing expenditures, balancing the budget, and lowering taxes to encourage business investment. His primary concern was securing the financial position of the federal government. The demands of the West would threaten these efforts.

Canada would be pulled from the Depression, King believed, through international trade and the cooperation of the provincial governments. In the end, he would receive neither. A minor trade agreement signed with the United States was only a 'gesture.'[2] Other countries insisted on maintaining their trade barriers. Meanwhile, the uncooperative attitude of some of the provinces, along with the desperate demands of others, indicated a serious crisis in dominion–provincial relations. The Dominion–Provincial Conference of December 1935 had increased federal relief grants as an interim policy and had set the wheels in motion for a National Employment Commission to establish a more efficient relief administration. There was talk of transferring certain taxation powers to the provinces and of a possible loan council so Ottawa could back provincial bond issues, thereby making it easier for the provinces to borrow money and reducing interest rates. King was convinced that Bennett's grants-in-aid to the provincial governments had encouraged extravagance and waste by offering them 'a blank cheque.' By spring 1936, although Finance Minister Charles Dunning was warning that the deficit for the fiscal year would be higher than expected, still more relief was needed. The projected deficit would be approximately $125 million, with federal relief costs above the expected $50 million level. 'The truth is,' King recorded in his diary, 'that not only municipalities and provinces are tending towards bankruptcy, many of them are already bankrupt, but that the Dominion itself will be in the same category if the wasteful practices which have become accepted in the last two years are continued.'[3] The prime minister responded by reducing federal aid below what was agreed to at the conference.

In January 1936 Dunning met with the provincial treasurers to talk about the ideas put forward at the conference. Again the loan council and the transfer of some indirect taxation powers were discussed. The proposals had unanimous agreement, or so it seemed. In the following months, amid the wake of Ottawa's reduction in aid to the provinces, the de facto power of the council became a source of friction. Whereas the provinces assumed they would have little difficulty in obtaining federal guarantees for credit, Ottawa was intent on attaching conditions. The issue immediately centred on the autonomy of the provincial treasuries. As Neatby points out, 'Dunning was not likely to endorse a provincial loan if he felt that the provincial government could exercise more rigid economies or could levy higher taxes.'[4] To the same extent, the premiers were not likely to surrender fiscal control to the arbitrary power of the federal government. Whereas Premier Duff Pattullo of British Columbia could approach private sources, thereby avoiding the demeaning necessity of turning to the council, Premier Aberhart of Alberta had no choice. A provincial debenture issue of $3 million would fall due on 1 April 1936.

Alberta requested a federal loan in March, but King persuaded his colleagues to insist that the province first agree to the dictates of the loan council. Aberhart refused the ultimatum, which he viewed as shameless blackmail and an outright attempt by Ottawa to gain control of Social Credit policies. If a province was applying for a loan but had not yet agreed to the conditions of the council, King argued in cabinet, it should be refused further advances even if it meant defaulting: 'It seems to me we have to face in Canada the possible default of provinces and municipalities & might as well do so sooner rather than later.' Jimmy Gardiner, and to a lesser extent T.A. Crerar, disagreed. The situation, of course, was facing primarily the West. While the men generally agreed with the fiscal approach of King and Dunning, their concern for the region was swaying their positions. In the end the cabinet decided to allow Alberta to default unless it came under control of the council.[5]

Dunning requested a clarification of Aberhart's position and intention. The premier answered that his province had not received enough details on the loan council to proceed, but he hoped 'the views of Alberta and the Dominion can be reconciled.' The finance minister, who saw through the delaying tactics, indicated he could not 'conceive that there would be any controversy over details.' The matter had been discussed previously, and everything had been clearly outlined.[6] The provincial treasurer from Alberta, Charles Cockcroft, had raised no objections to the council when it was first proposed. Yet to Aberhart it was a vehicle for federal domination and a way for Ottawa to interfere with the implementation of Social Credit. While the plan may have been discussed earlier, it had certainly not been made clear that Ottawa would demand such control over the process. If the loan were guaranteed first, the council could be discussed later. The premier then proposed a means of refinancing the loan without consulting the council. Dunning responded that this would provide the dominion with no effective means to control its own credit; there was no existing constitutional authority under which dominion subsidies could be pledged in this manner. 'Aberhart hopes, undoubtedly,' King remarked, 'to find a way out of government altogether by making an issue with the Dominion over its attempt to interfere with the autonomy of the provinces.'[7]

The premier continued to stall, the deadline for default approached, and Dunning's patience diminished. When asked again if he would agree to the loan council, Aberhart argued that he could not allow the future borrowing of the province to be controlled by Ottawa. The federal government responded by refusing his proposed refunding program, which would have used provincial bonds to meet the loan obligations. When the premier suggested that the dominion could meet the obligations and then allow Alberta to offer reimbursement from the natural resources settlement, Dunning again refused, this time on the basis that the settlement was already being used to offset debts presently owing.[8] Yet King did have some doubts, meanwhile, about allowing the province to default. He feared that the bankruptcy of Alberta might allow Aberhart to 'escape' from his 'obligations' and place the 'onus of failure' on the federal government. It would also set a bad precedent for the other Prairie provinces. The prime minister sought to have financial interests advance Aberhart the necessary funding to maintain the province's credit rating, but the scheme fell through.[9] On 1 April Alberta became the first province to default. By the end of the year it had defaulted on yet another maturing loan and had arbitrarily halved interest rates on all provincial bonds. Aberhart came to Ottawa in May to discuss the financial situation. King was now certain that the premier had no intention of cooperating with the dominion to find solutions but merely wished to stir up trouble.

Premier Patterson of Saskatchewan, in the meantime, was prepared to accept a loan council. The Liberal premier would have a more harmonious relationship with the federal government, especially with the influential Gardiner in cabinet. Saskatchewan was also in more dire financial straits. Despite the agreement, Gardiner and Crerar maintained their criticism of the council, arguing that the Western provinces should be free to borrow.[10] Graham Towers of the Bank of Canada feared that allowing Saskatchewan to default on a loan so soon after the Alberta failure would seriously jeopardize the nation's credit rating. Dunning and King agreed that the bank should finance the province's maturing obligations. They were both aware, however, that Aberhart would be sure to observe King's handling of the neighbouring province, and its Liberal government, for any sign of preferential treatment.

Despite Ottawa's position, King was never really comfortable with the loan council or the amendment to the British North America Act that would allow the transfer of indirect taxation powers from federal to provincial jurisdiction. Indeed, he was relieved when the the Conservative-controlled Senate voted down the amendments. But the budget of 1936 was also creating division. T.A. Crerar was advocating unorthodox measures. With King and Dunning planning on balancing the budget through increased revenues, Crerar was pushing a reduction in taxes. He argued that such a reduction would encourage economic activity, increase employment, and stimulate recovery. Despite the disagreement, Dunning's budget increased the sales tax as well as corporation taxes.

The West meanwhile was generally advancing a stronger role for the federal government as well as increased government intervention in society. Mackenzie King was brought into direct conflict with the region by maintaining his stance of protecting the federal treasury. The prime minister maintained his opposition to a federally sponsored unemployment insurance scheme, despite its popularity on the Prairies. Wrote King, '[I] pointed out that we were not a Tory party, nor a Socialist party, but a Liberal party, which stood for individual freedom and encouraging individual initiative and thrift. With respect to unemployment, we intended to meet it by getting men back to work, not to have in the State a trough for idle or worthless people to feed out of.'[11] The continual demands for social programs by the CCF led King to view such members as J.S. Woodsworth and Agnes Macphail as 'irresponsible.' They were 'developing from sincere radicals into clap-trap politicians of the cheapest variety.'[12] Yet before the next election, the scheme was in place. Whether King liked it or not, the role of the federal government in Canada was changing.

Aberhart's refusal to cooperate with the federal government had caused a rapid revision in King's attitude toward the Alberta premier. 'My opinion of him lessened considerably in conversation,' the prime minister recorded during the May meetings. With a premier who was determined to oppose Ottawa on almost every issue, the relationship between King and Alberta could only deteriorate: 'What a pathetic and indeed tragic picture it portrays ... I greatly fear that the pathos and the tragedy of the situation is only beginning to reveal itself.' The situation demanded a new strategy to handle the troublesome province. It was now particularly important to have a strong and united Liberalism in Alberta to provide a counterbalance to Aberhart, but the signs were not encouraging. Letters from disgruntled provincial Liberals continued to pour in complaining about the 'confused' situation. They argued that for twenty years the province had been suffering from 'exceedingly poor leadership.' If only proper command were provided, Alberta would somehow rise from its present 'morass.' Since the provincial organization could not be counted upon, the federal party would have to 'take the lead in this move.' All seemed agreed that 'someone with authority' had to 'take hold of the Alberta situation' and create an efficient organization. King, who sought to convince himself that federal intervention was a necessity, found no difficulty comparing Aberhart to the totalitarian leaders emerging in Europe: 'In the province of Alberta, a dictatorship of a kind no less dangerous to individual and collective liberty is rapidly gaining ground ... Unless the Liberal Party in the Province rises to its obligations as well as its opportunity ... no one can say how soon the last vestige of individual and collective freedom may disappear in Alberta.'[13]

As the relationship between Mackenzie King and the West changed, so also did his rapport with his constituency. Complaints were piling up in the riding office that Prince Albert was being treated no better by the King government than the Bennett government. The advantages of having the prime minister as representative now seemed insignificant. According to G.W.D. Abrams, with federal relief aid continually refused, 'it is not surprising that the patience of the citizens had worn thin, and the city unemployed were showing signs of serious unrest.' King demonstrated little concern for the plight of the unemployed, even in his home riding, where they had to suffer the additional burdens of particularly cold winters in 1936 and 1937. Relief workers even claimed that conditions in Prince Albert were the poorest in Saskatchewan.[14] Constituents felt that the prime minister avoided the area and that he was no longer concerned with advancing their interests. Liberal organizers continued to complain that he did not take an active enough interest in financing his own campaigns. Increasingly during the next four years, residents demonstrated a preference for a local representative who understood and voiced their concerns.

By 1937 the prime minister was being accused of using Prince Albert only for political convenience. 'I might state,' the chair of the riding's Liberal constituency association, J.W. Sanderson, wrote, 'there are some would-be trouble makers who are continuously trying to undermine you and the Liberal Party, with the statement that your only concern is to get elected and the only time this constituency sees you is when an election campaign is in progress.'[15] King, who expected the riding to understand his obligations, had little patience for these criticisms.[16] T.C. Davis played his role of mediator and attempted to explain the constituents' senti- ments: 'You are the Prime Minister of Canada and are representing Prince Albert, and naturally, your constituents have a rather exaggerated view of what you can do or should do for the constituency.'[17] Mackenzie King could point to what he had done for the riding in the past, but it was only too evident that he was no longer as concerned with Prince Albert, Saskatchewan, or the West as he once had been. The need to woo the Prairies had passed; concern was no longer focused on regional issues. King used events such as the signing of the Reciprocity Agreement, the meeting of the League of Nations, the Royal Coronation, and the Impe- rial Conference as reasons why he could not devote more time to Prince Albert.[18]

Western issues did occupy much of the cabinet discussions in 1936, but King, more often than not, found himself opposed to the region's position. When it came to the drought, the federal guarantees for loans, the tariff, the Bank of Canada, and the fixing of wheat prices, he sided with his eastern colleagues. His growing dislocation with the West was particularly evident in his persistent belief that the tariff remained the key to winning regional support. International trade was King's chosen route out of the Depression, and the trade agreement with the United States was, he believed, a major offering of reductions deserving of support. He was confident that the budget of 1936 demonstrated his good intentions and that 'the party has kept its promise in the matter of reducing duties on the instruments of production, and taking off the excess tariffs which Bennett had imposed.' Preoccupied with such issues, King could demonstrate a rather callous lack of concern for issues of immediate importance to westerners. King was aware of the desperate state of what was being called the 'dust bowl,' but his response was hardly helpful: 'It is part of U.S. desert area,' he observed coldly. 'I doubt if it will be of any real use again.'[19]

To make matters worse, the interest western Liberals did show for King's tariff policies was steeped in suspicion. After years of unfulfilled federal promises and vacillating policies, they questioned Dunning's stance and wondered whether he still held a 'western viewpoint' or if he was 'playing with the big interests.'[20] With eastern lobbyists constantly besieging the cabinet for tariff increases, and the prime minister's patience for the West deteriorating, Crerar was not convinced King would hold to reductions.[21]

Nationalization of the Bank of Canada was another issue that put distance between King and Prairie Liberals. While in opposition the party had promised to amend the Bank of Canada Act in favour of increased government control, and the prime minister was determined to be viewed as acting on his promises. Although Dunning was reluctant to reopen the question, King insisted that a majority of the bank directors should be appointed by the government. Some western members who did not believe this was enough advanced full government ownership. When they threatened to vote against the proposed amendment, King was annoyed and made it clear that caucus, not the House, was the place for debate.[22] In March 1938 the government nationalized the bank.

But it was the problem of the Wheat Board that most threatened King's relationship with the region. The Conservative government had established a price of 87.5¢ a bushel, which was above the open market price, to allow the board to acquire the bulk of the 1935 wheat crop. The government now held over 200 million bushels of wheat. Although the board was seen as a temporary measure, the Liberals had little choice but to accept the situation until that crop could be sold. For his part, King wanted the wheat sold and government intervention ended.[23] In contrast, pressure was mounting, particularly in Saskatchewan, for the continuation of the board.[24] When the board's chairman, John I. McFarland, disagreed with government intentions, he was abruptly dismissed and replaced by Winnipeg Liberal J.R. Murray. Jimmy Gardiner, as Prairie lieutenant, was expected to defend the government position in the House, and for a time he did just that. Much to King's delight, Gardiner and R.B. Bennett clashed over McFarland's stabilization policies in March 1936.[25]

The wheat situation improved that year as poor crops elsewhere in the world led to an increase in Canadian sales as well as an increase in the price. By August the open market price was higher than the board price.

King and Gardiner agreed that 'this was the time to get out ... If we do not get out of the price fixing now, we shall never be able to.' Dunning, who was also opposed to price fixing, reminded King that to eliminate the board may provide the CCF with a potent issue in the West. Annoyed that the finance minister would disagree with him, King blamed this stand on his 'regulation attitude ... Dunning does not like being over-ruled. – He has beneath all a nature that is "hostile," aggressive, & which causes antagonism. He also has a way of taking things in his own hands, and "telling" others what to do. Gardiner in most things has better judgement.'[26]

Debated in cabinet, the issues of price fixing and a minimum price for wheat ended up dividing the ministers into eastern and western factions. Gardiner began to support the 'western stand' on a minimum price alongside Crerar and Dunning. King believed it was best not to approve any price at present but leave the issue until the next session. In the meantime the government would work toward ending price fixing. When the majority in cabinet decided not to approve a minimum price, Dunning and Crerar were 'greatly disappointed,' believing 'a terrible mistake had been made.' Gardiner was also opposed to the decision but was prepared to 'face the situation.' When Murray of the Wheat Board was summoned before Cabinet to answer questions, he made a convincing argument that fixing the price would probably help wheat sales abroad while ending it would depress the market. At King's suggestion the cabinet adopted a compromise. The Wheat Board would maintain 87.5¢ as a floor price but would not accept any wheat unless the open market price fell below 90¢. A statement would also be issued that the government had appointed a royal commission to study the question of marketing. By not making use of the fixed price King hoped the argument for the necessity of the board would disappear. 'I felt we had better avoid unrest on the prairies at this time,' he recorded. 'It is what we prevent, rather than what we do that counts most in Government.'[27]

If avoiding unrest were King's goal, he failed to achieve it. The compromise was met by 'surprise, if not outright shock,' on the Prairies. The executive of the pools issued a statement, charging the government with denying the grain grower the right to deliver grain to the Wheat Board unless prices fell below 90¢. The efforts of organized agriculture to place the industry on a footing of economic equality, it was contended, had sustained 'a major reverse.' Liberal backbenchers from the West were under pressure from their constituents. The issue even created a rift between King and W.R. Motherwell, who had maintained his seat in Parliament after the 1935 election. The prime minister reacted to the vocal outcry by sending Gardiner and Crerar on western speaking tours to defend the policy.[28]

By the early months of 1937 the prime minister was aware of increasing discord in dominion–provincial relations. The provincial governments were emerging as Ottawa's major critics.[29] Although criticism was coming from across the nation, King believed the Prairie provinces were in the most danger of becoming 'isolated' and 'sectionalized.'[30] The stress placed on Canadian federalism by the Depression was being felt most clearly in the West. O.D. Skelton advised King that early and definite action had to be taken to control the developing chaos. The federal state was in danger of 'disintegrating,' and provincial governments were adopting 'an arbitrary and semi-Fascist attitude.' The 'increasing distrust of the East on the part of the Western provinces' had to be handled.[31] Mackenzie King believed the federal authorities were doing everything possible to deal with the malaise and the provincial governments were showing neither patience nor understanding.

This was certainly the case in Alberta, where discontent was not confined to the Social Credit party. Early in 1937 even provincial Liberals were joining the chorus of criticism, complaining that the King government discriminated against the province. A solution, they argued, lay in the appointment of one of their members to the cabinet. Alberta had remained relatively acquiescent in 1935 when the province was punished by exclusion from cabinet, but by 1937 it seemed almost impossible to argue that Ottawa was not being overly discriminatory. 'Everywhere I go in this Province,' W.C. Barrie reported, 'I meet the criticism, that Premier King, and Eastern Liberals are no longer interested in the liberal cause in Alberta.'[32] Some members were abandoning the party because Mackenzie King seemed intent on continuing to punish the province for its lack of support. 'When we get recognition from Ottawa for some of our well known Liberals I am all for organization,' one correspondent complained. 'Until we do our organization will not be touched.'[33] The prime minister, continuing what had become a vicious circle, replied that the situation would be remedied when Alberta voted Liberal.[34] He told J.A. MacKinnon, the only federal Liberal elected in the province, that Charlie Stewart had been treated favourably, and had been given a seat in Quebec after he failed to win one in Alberta, but such action would 'never occur again.' The province would be left 'entirely to herself' because it was 'the only way' to get the situation 'speedily cleared up.' The prime minister added that he had 'made quite plain to the Alberta people that I would not again attempt representation of their province in the Cabinet unless they were prepared to express confidence in me.'[35]

Despite King's indications to the contrary, a renewed effort was made in 1937 to reorganize both the provincial and federal Liberal parties in Alberta. The usual question surfaced over whether the provincial party should fight as a straight Liberal movement or cooperate with other groups. Previously, the option had been fusion with the governing United Farmers of Alberta; now it considered union with all groups opposed to Social Credit. The People's League, which had been formed as a vehicle for Social Credit opposition, called on all forces to unite against Aberhart. While it claimed to represent the Farmers, it had little cooperation from rural leaders and was more active in urban areas. The strength of Aberhart's party made coalition particularly attractive. Senator W.A. Buchanan began advising the prime minister that the only chance of defeating Social Credit lay in cooperation. The problem was that the straight Liberal group had opposed fusion with the UFA largely because of the latter's Tory elements. There would certainly be opposition to fusion with the Conservative party itself.

Mackenzie King's solution was to send in Gardiner to organize Liberalism at both levels. The minister of agriculture would not be given authority over patronage positions, but he was expected to lend his organizational talents and energy. Gardiner was fully prepared to wield his influence. He had been denied a more influential cabinet post; once in place as Prairie lieutenant, he would take full advantage. The difficulty for the West in the last fifteen years, he told Buchanan, his advisor for the south of the province, was that only Saskatchewan had stood up for Liberal principles – the others had been 'playing with every other wild organization that came along.' If the party were not up to 'the job that is obviously in front of them, the quicker they get out of the way and let someone else do it the better for everyone.' One of Gardiner's northern advisors, W.C. Barrie, reported that organizational work had 'gone to seed' and 'the decks had to be cleaned.'[36]

Jimmy Gardiner immediately set to work to end any talk of coalition, fusion, or cooperation. He argued that although a coalition could possibly defeat Aberhart, it would then 'break up,' and the province would be 'back into a worse mess than it is at the present time.' The most important thing, Gardiner argued, was to 'establish Liberalism firmly' in Alberta. The people were to emerge from the 'wilderness of isms' and 'cease building their hopes on the sands.' W.R. Howson, who was retiring, was leaving a relatively sound provincial organization. The problem was that federal organization was 'all but non-existent.'[37] Gardiner was determined to bring together the two completely separate associations. He also had to deal with a party dominated by lawyers seeking patronage and with a hostile north–south rivalry between Edmonton and Calgary.[38] The federal minister attended the provincial Liberal convention held at the beginning of June 1937. He discussed federal rehabilitation work and debt adjustment, but also attempted to play an influential role in the selection of a new leader. E.L. Gray seemed the most promising candidate, despite his inexperience. Nobody knew much about Gray other than that he had served as deputy minister of municipal affairs in Alberta and then as manager of the Eastern Irrigation District. Rather than an urban lawyer, he was a rural agriculturalist.[39] Gardiner noted that he was acceptable to all factions of the party; more importantly, he was 'a consistent Liberal.' His victory would provide 'the nearest thing to United Liberalism in Alberta that we have ever had in that Province.'[40] Prime Minister King was informed that the People's League was using the rumour of an early election in the province to 'stampede everyone' into its ranks. The league, Gardiner argued, was a Tory scheme that would attempt to use Gray and then 'deal with him later.'[41] Gardiner's suspicions were reinforced when the name of John McFarland, Bennett's chairman of the Wheat Board, became associated with the league.[42]

Opposition to the federal intervention was immediate. Liberals, mainly from the south of the province, who were advocating support of the People's League were furious when Gardiner 'laid down the law.' Straight Liberalism, they argued, had no chance against Social Credit. They pleaded with King to call off the Saskatchewan minister. Even Buchanan was now against Gardiner's intervention. Meanwhile, it became clear that E.L. Gray, whom Gardiner had touted as 'a consistent Liberal,' favoured cooperation against Aberhart. Alberta, he claimed, was 'greatly misunderstood by many people in Eastern Canada.' The province had turned against Liberalism in 1921; opposition to partisanship, along with a bitter dose of western alienation, had prevented its return. It was 'a Liberal province at heart,' Gray argued, but the dislike of 'partyism' meant that labels had to remain camouflaged. The new Liberal leader intended to have all people who believed in liberal principles work together. If the candidate could not go under the banner of 'straight' Liberalism, so be it. He advocated cooperation not fusion or unity, and he was frustrated that the press was misinterpreting his intentions. Yet, he had to admit that 'at the moment the political situation in the Province is quite confused.'[43] If Gray was confused, Mackenzie King was dumbfounded. Since 1919 he had been advocating cooperation in Alberta only to meet fierce opposition. Now he had sent Gardiner to advance the cause of straight Liberalism only to be once again at odds with provincial sentiment.

On 7 October 1937 Gray was elected to the provincial legislature in an Edmonton by-election as a 'fusion' candidate with the support of the Liberal and Conservative parties. While he defeated the People's League candidate, those advocating cooperation heralded his victory as an example of what could be achieved through united opposition to Social Credit. To those opposed to cooperation, Gray's declaration for 'an end to party politics' tolled the death knell for Liberalism in the province.[44] Gardiner had a different view. He had tolerated Gray's compromising attitude, but now that the by-election was over, he informed W.C. Barrie that 'activities in Alberta can be proceeded with in a little different manner from that followed recently ... We might just as well get down to our maximum number of liberals and start from there.'[45] The prime minister did not know which way to turn. Congratulating Gray on the victory, the prime minister fell back on his traditional support for cooperation. At least this way there seemed an opportunity to defeat the troublesome Social Credit government. 'Those who are opposed to the government's policies should leave no stone unturned in the effective organization of their forces,' King wrote.[46] He was particularly pleased to see a politician of Gray's calibre finally emerge: 'What the Liberal Party has needed, above all, in Alberta has been leadership.'[47] For his part, Gardiner gave no indication that he knew King was encouraging Gray toward coalition.

The federal budget of 1937 offered the prime minister some encouragement regarding the western situation. The economy was showing signs of improvement, with farm revenue and prices for farm products increasing in Alberta and Manitoba. The deficit forecast had decreased, and Mackenzie King believed his policy of fiscal restraint was working. The improvements, however, could not disguise the general discontent. Finding the session more tiring than usual, King was short-tempered with his colleagues. His ministers did not seem to share his concern with balancing budgets: after two years of holding the line on spending they were pushing for increases in their own departments. The western members were the most demanding. The region had become 'more radical,' and Prairie Liberals 'no longer seemed prepared to defend national policies or liberal principles.' Instead, according to Blair Neatby, they were pushing the prime minister 'to make concessions which were inconsistent with his views of sound administration but which seemed necessary to prevent an even more serious western revolt. What did the future hold when even western Canada, so long a fortress of Liberalism, seemed to favour a confrontation with eastern Canada?'[48]

Jimmy Gardiner, in particular, became the focal point of King's dwindling patience with the West. Although first conceived by the Bennett government in 1935, the Prairie Farm Rehabilitation Program was embraced by the minister of agriculture as the only workable solution to the problem of Prairie drought. Its immediate task was to promote the conservation of surface water resources on farms and to encourage practices designed to combat soil drifting. Not only did Gardiner embrace the program, he also took full advantage of its patronage powers to create the 'western empire' King had promised. As a result he became one of King's most troublesome ministers, one about whom the prime minister incessantly complained. While Ernest Lapointe was given almost free rein in Quebec, it seemed that the more Gardiner worked to fill his role of Prairie defender, the more his reputation diminished in King's eyes. The Saskatchewan minister, it must be noted, certainly did nothing to alleviate the situation. His uncompromising, aggressive, and competitive tenacity constantly aggravated the cabinet, only making the situation worse. King was involved in a bitter feud with Premier Mitchell Hepburn of Ontario, and Gardiner's close relations with the premier made the Prairie politician all the more suspect and subject to scrutiny. Gardiner even campaigned for Hepburn in the provincial election of October 1937. Although King felt fairly confident about his Prairie minister's loyalty, he believed that Gardiner was ambitious and would always support a winner.[49]

Meanwhile, western problems were multiplying. The ire of debt-plagued farmers was increasingly aimed at the lending institutions associated with the eastern 'big interests.' The anger, the nature of the criticisms, and the search for quick and apparent solutions increased support for Social Credit. Mackenzie King feared the Alberta experiment would spread to Saskatchewan and Manitoba.[50] Since the landslide election that had brought Aberhart to power in 1935, Alberta Liberals had warned Ottawa that the movement would not only spread to the other Prairie provinces but to the federal realm as well. 'My greatest alarm over the present conditions in Alberta,' W.M. Davidson claimed, 'is that Mr. Aberhart, failing to make headway in the province, may turn his entire campaign into the federal arena. With his power of organization and his present backing, that would be a serious threat if even present day depression continues.' Aberhart was threatening to place the provincial press, which strenuously opposed the Social Credit government, under licence. The growing chorus of opposition across the nation did not seem to be affecting the movement's appeal, and the premier shrugged off the criticism as an expected attack by the mouthpiece of the oppressive establishment. Federal Liberals were advised not to be lulled by reports that Social Credit was weakening; in fact it was probably gaining strength. Prime Minister King disapproved of such provincial legislation as the 1936 Reduction and Settlement of Land Debts Act, which retroactively cancelled all the interest owed on mortgages since 1932, but to intervene would only play into Aberhart's hands. The federal government would be tainted by the same criticism being hurled against all the banks and moneyed interests. Some Alberta Liberals wanted the premier confronted sooner rather than later. A 'firm stand' was required because Aberhart was prepared to 'knife the Federal Government on any and every possible occasion.'[51]

By 1937 western Liberals believed an opportunity to halt the spread of Social Credit had arrived. Talks encouraged by Gardiner between the Saskatchewan government and the mortgage companies in 1936 resulted in the cancellation of two years' mortgage interest in the drought areas, as well as the province's cancellation of two years of tax arrears and relief indebtedness. Ottawa added to the package by cancelling some $17 million in relief debts. Much the same was accomplished in Manitoba. The next year, with both provinces facing bankruptcy, the federal government had to decide whether to intervene to save the situation. A precedent had already been set, of course, when a loan was refused to Alberta. According to King, the cabinet 'was practically united' in opposition to more loans 'as simply sending good money after bad money.' Finance Minister Dunning, who had been opposed to bailing out Alberta, was now more concerned with the need to refund $300 million in federal bonds. Since much would depend on the credit rating of the federal government, he preferred not to have provincial governments default at this time. Graham Towers, the governor of the Bank of Canada, agreed. Western members added the incentive that the time was at hand to strike a blow at Social Credit. If the provincial governments were saved by Ottawa, they would receive ammunition against the Alberta movement at the same time. In contrast to Dunning, King argued in council that the nation's credit rating would be strengthened by showing the international financial community 'that we were ceasing to try to bolster up impossible situations.'[52]

In the end the cabinet decided to allow the banks to save the situation.

Dunning would lend money to Manitoba and Saskatchewan until his refunding operations were complete, but he still believed that in the long run the provincial administrations had to balance their own budgets. Part of the problem, he claimed, continued to be waste and extravagance. Gardiner found himself defending the western position, even though it went against his traditional liberal convictions. He began to push for an increase in the annual federal subsidies to the Prairie provinces.[53] Again Mackenzie King found himself opposing his Prairie colleagues. Eventually he reversed his stand and supported the measure, not out of sympathy for the region, but rather to avoid the increase of unrest: 'I think, it would be unfortunate to have repudiation become general throughout the West, and there is no saying where it might end.'[54] The Prairies had become a distant, deeply troubled region for King; his main concern was preventing it from falling completely into radical hands.

To counter inevitable charges of discrimination, financial assistance was also promised to Alberta following an investigation of its financial situation by the Bank of Canada. The press reports alleging discrimination were 'wholly unfounded,' King informed Aberhart. 'There has been and there is now no desire to discriminate between Alberta and other provinces. The principles applied in the case of Manitoba and Saskatchewan are equally applicable to Alberta.'[55] Privately, however, he was delighted to have manoeuvred Aberhart 'into a sort of cleft stick.' The premier would have to request an investigation of Alberta's finances, and this would enable the federal government 'to show wherein his methods have been different from those of the other two Provinces.'[56]

Although by early 1937 Canada was showing signs of recovering from the Depression, the spring and summer of that year were the driest on record and the Prairie drought continued. This combination of factors only fanned the crisis in dominion–provincial relations as well as unrest in the Prairie West. 'The disastrous conditions in the west,' Neatby argues, 'coming at a time when the end of the depression had seemed in sight, would almost certainly amplify the political protests from a region that was already bitter and disillusioned.'[57]

Mackenzie King wished to avoid a confrontation with the populist Social Credit and its charismatic leader. As far as he was concerned Social Credit was Aberhart's problem: he had no intention of interfering.[58] By September 1937 the premier was being pressured into more drastic action that would make confrontation with Ottawa inevitable. He had promised his electorate Social Credit measures within eighteen months of being elected, and the crop failure was complicating matters. The session of 1936 had left many Albertans disillusioned.

With the aid of an appointed Social Credit Board, and advice from Major Douglas himself, three bills were drafted to introduce Social Credit to the province. The first, the Credit of Alberta Regulation Act, would require all bank employees to be licensed and to sign an undertaking not to interfere with the property or civil rights of Alberta citizens. Because, according to the government, credit was a civil right, the implication was that licensed bankers would be obliged to lend money on terms that reflected the popular will. The bill also authorized the Social Credit Board to set up citizens' committees to supervise local bank operations. The other two bills were designed to prevent the courts from interfering: one denied unlicensed bankers any recourse to the courts; the other ruled out any attempt to challenge the validity of these acts in a court of law. The bills were quickly passed by the legislature. The two acts that denied recourse to the courts were clearly invalid and would certainly be ruled *ultra vires*. Moreover, the licensing legislation was an infringement on federal jurisdiction over banking. The problem for Ottawa was that the courts would take at least a full year to rule on the legislation; in the meantime the banking system would be in chaos. Aberhart would be able to implement his policies successfully and gain popularity by challenging the federal government. The alternative was federal disallowance. The provincial bill could be vetoed and there would no recourse for appeal.[59]

The use of disallowance had serious ramifications. It would allow Aberhart to argue that Ottawa was demonstrating its 'dictatorial' powers by denying his government a chance to fulfil its promises. 'I fear disallowance of the Banking legislation will be helpful to Aberhart,' W.A. Buchanan warned. 'Political consideration however must not be overlooked.'[60] Mackenzie King needed no such warning. While he had no doubt that the legislation was 'unquestionably ultra vires,' the use of disallowance may hinder 'matters in the long run.' Aberhart would make 'political capital' out of the controversy. Yet the threat to the federally chartered banks and the fact that the premier had thrown down the gauntlet allowed for little choice. The prime minister would not surrender to the provincial challenge and allow a situation that harked back to a time 'prior to the days of the Magna Carta.' He was personally opposed to such strong-arm measures as disallowance but found it his 'duty.'[61]

In an attempt to avoid the dilemma, King informed Aberhart that disallowance was being contemplated and advised him to refer the legislation to the Supreme Court before taking action. The premier responded by attacking the 'demagoguery' of the Canadian federal system. King tried to refute the premier's attempts 'to confuse the issue involved by references to financial tyranny or plutocratic opposition,' even though he was using similar charges against Aberhart.[62]

After the act was disallowed, Aberhart immediately called a special session of the legislature. Disallowance, he argued, was an outdated power that had to be opposed. The people of Alberta would continue to advance Social Credit regardless of Ottawa's defence of the financial system. Mackenzie King, a servant of the moneyed interests, was 'usurping' the province's right to an appeal.[63] A slightly modified Credit of Alberta Regulation Act was passed, but it would also be disallowed. To punish the banks for their opposition, Aberhart introduced a Bank Taxation Bill, which would impose a special levy on banks' paid-up capital and reserve funds. Convinced that the press's opposition to his measures reflected its status as the agent of the tyrannical interests, Aberhart formulated the Accurate News and Information Bill, which would require every newspaper in the province to divulge, on request, its source for any news item and to publish every official government statement in full.[64] At this point W.A. Buchanan, a newspaper owner from Lethbridge, pleaded with the prime minister for federal intervention. King did not hesitate in using the veto on this new 'confiscatory' legislation, although he recognized that the timing of the move might create an issue for the upcoming election in Saskatchewan.[65]

The onus, however, was on the lieutenant-governor of Alberta, who could direct that the bills be reserved for the consideration of the federal government. If Ottawa refused to give its explicit approval within a year, the legislation would not become law. King met with Gardiner and Alberta MP J.A. MacKinnon to discuss the situation. Much to his surprise, the prime minister was informed that the lieutenant-governor actually wished to dismiss the Aberhart ministry and ask Gray to form a government. King was strongly opposed to the wielding of such power: 'It is sheer madness. Action of the kind would almost certainly have repercussions in Saskatchewan which would cost the Liberals the election there, and might bring on a sort of civil war in Alberta.'[66] Aberhart responded by having the powers of disallowance and reservation tested before the Supreme Court. The three provincial bills would also be ruled upon.

The accusations of federal discrimination against Alberta reached fever pitch. In Parliament, Social Credit members argued that 'this discrimination is resented by the people of Alberta all the more because it comes as a culmination of many previous acts of discrimination against their province by this government.' Alberta's legislation had been disallowed while Quebec's controversial Padlock Law was left untouched.[67] The prime minister defended the government's position by indicating that, although he disapproved of the Padlock Law, it did not invade federal jurisdiction.[68] The justification was weak, however, and it was only too clear that the main difference was that one act had been passed by a government on the Prairies and the other by a government in Quebec.

Aberhart was now confronting King at every turn. He opposed both the formation of the Royal Commission on Dominion–Provincial Relations as well as its personnel, particularly J.W. Dafoe, because the members were harsh critics of Social Credit. The commission's sweeping mandate to recommend constitutional change was seen as one more example of federal domination. Ottawa, which had usurped Alberta's constitutional power, was now seeking to increase federal control in general. 'Both the personnel and terms of reference of the Commission,' Aberhart argued, 'rendered it useless for all practical purposes.' Changes to Canadian federalism should come through consultation with the provinces. 'I may say,' King responded, 'that there is no ground whatever for your implication of a connection between the announcement of the Commission's appointment and the disallowance of your recent legislation.'[69]

It seemed that the Alberta situation could hardly get any worse, but by 1938 Gardiner's interference in the province was also causing a serious commotion. The prime minister met with his minister of agriculture to discuss the situation, and despite the bitter reservations of the secretary for the National Liberal Federation, Norman Lambert,[70] the province was left to the Prairie lieutenant. King agreed to keep 'strictly to party lines.' He knew Gardiner had a tendency to be 'rightly Liberal' but believed that in this situation he was 'right on the whole.' When Gardiner's role in Alberta was discussed in cabinet, some members took exception to the interference. Yet King continued to support Gardiner's approach. When advised to pressure provincial Liberals to fall in line with the coalition movement, the prime minister refused, arguing that the Saskatchewan politician 'was on the right line.' Attempts at fusion, he responded using Gardiner's arguments, were disguised attempts by the Tories to get rid of Gray as provincial leader.[71]

Events in Alberta certainly seemed to support this contention. Following Gray's election to the legislature, the Conservatives began a renewed push for the disintegration of all parties and support for the People's League. Gray refused, clearly articulating the intention of the Liberal party to remain distinct. Gardiner congratulated the Liberal leader, confident that his faith in Gray had been vindicated. Yet, with division over the coalition issue remaining in party ranks, Gray was soon under considerable pressure. At an executive meeting in June 1938 he indicated that the issue of cooperation was best left to each local constituency. The People's League, meanwhile, had regrouped and reappeared under the leadership of McFarland as the Unity party.[72]

A federal by-election in East Edmonton on 21 March 1938 became the battleground for these forces. Gardiner, attempting to keep what he now viewed as Gray's pro-coalition provincial forces out of the campaign, called in his political machine from Saskatchewan. Just prior to the contest, Gray surprised everyone with a public address that attacked the People's League, the Unity party, as well as the provincial Conservative leader, D.M. Duggan, and advocated a straight Liberal platform.[73] This action, along with Gardiner's intervention and attitudes against coopera-tion, caused the Conservatives to oppose the Liberal candidate in the last week of the campaign. After the split in the anti–Social Credit vote allowed Aberhart's forces to win the federal seat, the Liberals emerged from the campaign divided and quarrelling. Gardiner was pleased that the defeat had finally placed the Liberals as the real opposition to Social Credit. The real fight, he argued, had not been against Aberhart but against coalitions, and the result, he claimed, 'very definitely kills the Unity idea.'[74] W.C. Barrie believed Gardiner had 'rendered a splendid service' to the Liberal cause. If only he could spend more time in the province, the party 'would have little to fear.'[75]

Nevertheless, there was little doubt that Liberalism in Alberta had received yet another setback. The intervention of the Saskatchewan minister, it was widely contended, had been a disaster. Resentment against his presence had played an important role in the by-election defeat. Gardiner's machine-style politics from Saskatchewan would not work in Alberta because the political traditions of the two provinces were simply too different. Alberta had long been punished by Mackenzie King for not voting Liberal. This punishment had taken the form of the province being left to 'stew in her own juice.' Yet even this was preferable to allowing the tenacious Saskatchewan minister 'to exercise the most vicious influence.' The result, Alberta Liberals feared, would be that Social Credit would easily maintain power at the provincial level and continue to send members to Ottawa.[76]

The prime minister had difficulty accepting that Gardiner had actually hindered the Alberta situation. Ultimately such a verdict would mean a return to the 'incessant strife' that had long plagued Alberta Liberalism.[77] Instead he blamed local Conservatives for ending any hopes of cooperation in the by-election by refusing to 'make way' for the Liberal candidate. The movement toward union was 'a disguised effort on the part of the Conservatives in the Province to get an ultimate control.' Yet eventually even King had to admit that having the campaign run by outsiders had operated against the Liberals.[78]

The incident revived demands that Alberta receive cabinet representation. 'We were disappointed when Mr. MacKinnon was not included in the cabinet of 1935,' one angry party member complained, 'our disappointment has grown since.' The province would not accept an outsider as its spokesman. Such a situation was breeding a 'feeling of apathy and resentment' that would 'eventually result in the obliteration of the Party.' W.C. Barrie was now indicating that popular resentment had reached the point where Alberta required its own cabinet minister, even if the representative had to work alongside Gardiner.[79] The minister of agriculture responded to the criticism by indicating that he had no problem with J.A. MacKinnon serving as the Alberta representative. The province, however, could hardly expect 'preferential' treatment based on its electoral record. Perhaps, he noted, it would be best to await the next election before receiving representation.[80]

Gardiner's failure was a bitter pill to swallow. 'I have been more disappointed with the efforts put forth in relation to political matters in Alberta during the past two years,' he confessed, 'than with any previous experience I have had.'[81] By year's end, MacKinnon was taken into cabinet as minister without portfolio. The prime minister had relented to the pressure and given Alberta representation.

The Alberta situation offered Mackenzie King one of his best lessons in handling the western region. As conditions in Manitoba had demonstrated in the late 1920s, Gardiner's interference in any province other than his own would prove destructive. The dynamics of Prairie Liberalism differed from province to province, yet King had persistently refused to acknowledge these differences or accept that his western advisor could not play the same role throughout the Prairies as Lapointe played in Quebec. When he learned that Social Credit could threaten the upcoming election in Saskatchewan, a 'distressed' King was finally prepared to admit that it had been a 'mistake' to send Gardiner into Alberta: in the future it would be better to leave Alberta to MacKinnon. In a rare instance of self-criticism, King seemed prepared to accept most of the blame for his decision.[82]

Prior to 1919 Mackenzie King had been in the forefront of changes that had seen the Canadian state play a more interventionist role in society. This position had provided him a close relationship with the Prairie region, which was in accord with much of that transition. Yet in the 1930s – with the winds of change blowing again and the West again at the forefront – King found himself in opposition, resisting the approach of the welfare state. Ultimately, however, he would be overwhelmed by demands for change. The budget of 1938 became the point of contention. Although the prime minister hoped to avoid controversial issues and maintain the emphasis on economic restraint and sound administration, the budget would mark the onset of a new era in Canadian fiscal policy. The national deficit was increasing, mainly due to the Prairie drought, and the costs of government were rising.

In January 1938, after making his usual proclamations in cabinet regarding responsible administration, King noted a lack of enthusiasm and support from his colleagues. Only Dunning seemed to share his attitude and approach. King accused the other ministers, who were frustrated by their meagre departmental budgets, of yielding 'to the socialistic and other trends of the times.'[83] Dunning informed the cabinet that there would be no tax reductions other than the tariff changes associated with another trade deal being negotiated with the United States. The ministers were told by King to reduce their expenditures. They all agreed to do their best, except for Crerar. The minister of mines and resources continued to argue that the budget could not be balanced simply by reducing costs. The answer had to come through increased revenues. Since higher taxes were impossible, the key lay in stimulating activity by injecting the economy with federal money. The other ministers had promised to work in King's desired direction, but several weeks later their projected departmental estimates indicated that their expenditures were increasing rather than decreasing. As budget day approached, the government came under heavy fire in Parliament for failing to deal with the impact of the 1937 western crop failure. Western Liberals were warning that the status quo was unacceptable: there was 'a rumble which may develop into a roar in the very near future if something is not done in a spectacular way.'[84]

Only Dunning was maintaining the line on a balanced budget; King himself was having second thoughts. An election was on the horizon, and he wanted to go to the people with a popular appeal. In April the prime minister named a cabinet committee to organize a program of public work projects. He justified his reversal by arguing that, at times, politics demanded reaction to situations as they developed: 'The world situation has headed the countries more and more in the direction of the extension of state authority and enterprise, and I am afraid Canada will not be able to resist the pressure of the tide.'[85] King would proceed slowly, resisting as much as possible, and only going as far as necessary. In the United States, President Franklin Roosevelt was calling for significant expenditures on emergency relief projects, but King believed he was going too far. Back in cabinet the committee appointed by the prime minister was also going too far and favouring what King called 'wasteful expenditures.'[86] Armed with the final report of the National Employment Commission, the minister of labour, Norman Rogers, was leading the charge toward deficit financing. Although the prime minister could ignore the recommendation that Ottawa assume full responsibility for unemployment relief, he could not ignore the widening divisions in cabinet. The dissension was not soothed until the cabinet agreed on a substantially increased estimate of expenditures for the year. The federal government was increasing spending during a recession. 'John Maynard Keynes,' Neatby claims, 'had come to Canada.'[87]

Mackenzie King, not fully recognizing the significance of the 1938 budget, described it as 'featureless.' Perhaps this term reflected his disappointment at being unable to include tariff reductions that were part of the trade negotiations with Great Britain and the United States, these concessions not being ready in time. Once again he promised that the next budget would include reductions.[88]

Western Liberals certainly did not see anything radical in the budget. Instead they focused their criticisms on the lack of tariff reductions. Charles Dunning had become a prime target of increasing regional antagonism toward the King government. The finance minister came under 'bitter' attack from Saskatchewan Liberals charging him with reversing the party's tariff policy. They accused him of becoming a Tory, yielding to his Montreal interests, and sacrificing any remaining western principles. During the budget discussions, Dunning had stood alone alongside King against the winds of change; the prime minister now came to the defence of his finance minister. Despite King's support Dunning was upset by the criticism, and he collapsed in the House during the budget debate. The ever-pragmatic King viewed Dunning's collapse as consistent with his hypochondria. He felt it was due more to emotional strain and fatigue than the heart problems the finance minister claimed. Nonetheless, he hoped that Dunning's condition would show the Western members the result of their endless gripes, and that, feeling remorse, they would ease up on their criticisms: 'My own feeling is that having secured a victim to satisfy their emotional strain, some of the Western members will now come a little more to their senses and in the end, we shall probably do better on the division than we otherwise would have done.'[89] The prime minister's reaction to Dunning's collapse may have been cold, but he was correct. When it came to the vote only one Liberal went against the budget.

Dunning would be absent from his office for most of the following year; he even threatened resignation on 1 August 1939. He told King that what had 'gnawed at his soul' in the last few years were the constant statements, attributed to Gardiner,' that he was 'standing in the way of the West receiving the assistance they [sic] should.' As the prime minister became increasingly impatient with the region, he had a similar reaction against Gardiner. The minister of agriculture had failed in Alberta, yet he was pushing for more influence in the cabinet: 'I really feel about Gardiner that he is more and more of a machine politician, and that Dunning was perhaps right in his estimate of his tendencies in that direction. My opinion of him is not what it was some time ago.'[90]

The Liberal party was changing by 1938 but so too were the Conservatives. In July R.B. Bennett retired. R.J. Manion became the new leader of a party that was desperate for unity, stability, and, most importantly, direction. Although the leadership decision would certainly not help the Conservatives on the Prairies, it was hoped that Manion, a Roman Catholic married to a French Canadian, could revive Tory fortunes in Quebec. The fact that both Meighen and Bennett had represented Prairie constituencies had done little to provide a genuine base for Tory support in the region. Having failed in the West, the Conservatives would turn their attention to making a breakthrough in Quebec. Manion's selection pleased King, who remained confident that the Bennett legacy would haunt the Tories for a long time. He concluded that 'Liberalism should be able to retain power in Canada for some years to come.'[91]

If Bennett's legacy might well plague the Tories, King had his own source of affliction – Aberhart. In March 1938 the Supreme Court issued its judgments on the Social Credit legislation, as well as the powers of disallowance and reservation, and they all favoured the federal position. A provincial government appeal of the decisions also lost. Aberhart then moved to challenge Ottawa on yet another issue. In 1937 the Social Credit legislation to cancel all interest on farm mortgages had been blocked by the courts. Now the premier introduced new legislation that would protect Alberta debtors from their creditors while at the same time levying a tax on the principal of any mortgages held by non-residents of the province. This measure was designed in part to extend the appeal of Social Credit to the other Prairie provinces, particularly Saskatchewan, where a provincial election was to be held in June. When the Alberta session ended, Aberhart and some of his colleagues entered the Saskatchewan campaign.

The federal Liberal party, with Gardiner directing the offensive, also took an active role, rallying behind the Patterson government. The prime minister, although convinced that the new Social Credit legislation would have to be disallowed, wanted to await the election results. The contest took on increased importance because it posed as the advance line in the war against Social Credit. 'To defeat Aberhart solidly in Saskatchewan at this time,' King noted, 'would do more to steady the whole of Canada than anything that has happened since our general election.'[92] The hopeless state of the Conservatives in the province was made more than obvious when eastern Tories, fearing the economic implications of a second Social Credit government, 'forsook' the provincial Conservative party and threw their financial support behind the Liberals.[93]

Amid the rush of outsiders into the campaign, the CCF party was almost forgotten. George Williams, the CCF leader, was rebuffed when he attempted to gain an alliance with Aberhart's Social Credit to defeat the Patterson Liberals. The rebuke was a blow to the CCF, but in the long term it served to bolster the party and ensure its survival. In the campaign of 1938 the party built its strength in the rural areas as well as among ethnic voters. It hammered the provincial government for failing to improve the economic situation, as had been promised in the last election, and for its ties to the federal Liberals. The intervention of Gardiner did not invoke much of a public outcry, however, particularly when Aberhart and his Social Credit ministers were travelling the province.

When the ballots were counted, only two Social Credit candidates were elected. The Liberals had won a stable majority. The result provided the prime minister with renewed confidence that disallowance was justified and that Social Credit could be confined to Alberta. But the victory also indicated a growing weakness of the Liberal forces in Saskatchewan. C.M. Dunn – a prominent Liberal, protégé of Gardiner, and heir to the organizational machine – was one of the Social Credit victims. Later that summer Dunn would again be defeated, this time by a CCF candidate in a Humboldt by-election. As David Smith concludes, the by-election was 'an astounding illustration of ineptitude on the part of the much-vaunted Liberal organization.'[94] The quasi-party system seemed unshakeable in Alberta as one-party dominance continued. By contrast, Saskatchewan remained true to a two-party alternative. The Conservatives had almost disappeared, and Social Credit had proved a passing fancy. The CCF was there to stay.

If Social Credit were again just an Alberta problem, wheat marketing was an issue that divided the entire region from the federal government. By the summer of 1938 the board had disposed of its crop holdings. With world production high, it was expected that prices would fall sharply. It was decision time for the government regarding Ottawa's role in wheat marketing. In the House, W.R. Motherwell repeated his embarrassing charges that the government had 'sterilized' the board. Opposition members smugly acknowledged his courage in denouncing his own party's position.[95] A royal commission had recommended a return to the open market, but Depression conditions made this difficult. Despite the growing chorus of western criticism, King and Gardiner could agree on the desire to eliminate the board and the fixed price. They disagreed, however, on the lengths to be taken to achieve such a feat. The other problem, of course, was convincing the West. In the face of what King admitted were 'exceptional circumstances,' the board would be continued for another year. When W.D. Euler led the charge in cabinet for a lower fixed price of 70¢ a bushel, Gardiner came to the defence of the Prairie farmer and pushed for 87½¢. King agreed with Euler that a high price, in effect, taxed the rest of the country to support the West. The eastern ministers were opposed to further subsidies for wheat. Yet, once again the threats of economic and political chaos in the west were too strong. The prime minister accepted the position that a higher price than 70¢ would have to be maintained.[96] A minimum price of 80¢, agreed to by Dunning, was adopted.

The government wished to restore marketing to the pools for the next year and thereby terminate the Wheat Board. According to Euler, the board represented 'class legislation of the worst kind ... confined to one class in one particular section of the country.'[97] Gardiner's strategy was to persuade the pools to revert to cooperative marketing under government guarantee. He planned to introduce a system whereby farmers would pay a one-cent per bushel levy on sold wheat, with the money being used as aid for failed crops. It would, in essence, provide insurance for wheat crop failure. The position reflected Gardiner's stand not just on wheat marketing but on western development. High wheat prices, he knew, would not be enough to solve the region's problems. Stability in the agricultural industry was essential, and this necessitated the rehabilitation of the drought areas and income guarantees that would then be joined by good prices: 'Gardiner's contribution to this complex progression of policy was to secure from his colleagues acknowledgement, grudgingly given by all but King, that grain was an essential industry, farming an endangered way of life worth saving, and the west a region deserving equal partnership with central Canada.'[98] Soon after the cabinet authorized his schemes, he was pushing the prime minister to transfer the entire wheat issue to the department of agriculture. Such a transfer would certainly raise the ire of Euler, the minister of trade and commerce.[99] The two had already determined their territorial struggle in cabinet. They butted heads late in 1937 when the Shaw Report, studying the marketing of agricultural products, was released before it was presented to cabinet. The report's findings reflected poorly upon Euler and his department. While the two ministers settled the disagreement over the report through a clearer definition of their respective 'orbits,' King believed Gardiner 'was pressing matters too far.'[100]

On 16 February 1939 Gardiner brought down his major policy statement in Parliament. He called for the government's involvement in the grain trade to revert from the Wheat Board to supervision of the grain exchange and encouragement for the creation of cooperative marketing associations or pools. The crop insurance plan would become an act of its own, and government intervention would occur only if the price of wheat fell below a guaranteed floor. As Neatby indicates, 'Gardiner was proposing that, barring an unexpected catastrophe, there would be no Wheat Board and no government support for the price of wheat.'[101] The statement touched off such a massive protest in the West that the minister of agriculture backed down, informing Mackenzie King that he was now prepared to recommend the continuation of the board in amended form.[102] These amendments would include a 60¢ initial payment and an acreage subsidy in areas of low yield. Gardiner's new proposals came before the cabinet on 16 March. He also managed to have some success in convincing the prime minister that the Canada Grain Act should be transferred from the department of trade and commerce to agriculture. King was being informed by western members that if the government did not ensure a 70¢ minimum price for wheat, 'the West would forget all we had done for them, and we could not hope to carry any seats there.' His response was a fair indication of the diminishing importance of Prairie support: 'Personally, I fear more and more that doing anything for the sake of winning at the polls is the utmost folly unless what is being done is, in itself, the right and the proper course to take regardless of political consequences.'[103]

The cabinet was split over wheat policy: 'Crerar decidedly of one view. Dunning, of another. Gardiner, of yet another. Euler opposed to all three. Ilsley unable to agree on any of the three.' Mackenzie King was exasperated: 'I frankly confess that while I thought I understood the problem at one time, I had now come [*sic*] so confused as to not be able to say what the consensus of view was, or to give any decision that seemed to be at all representative.' It was decided that Gardiner's amendments would be given a chance. King would rely on the minister of agriculture, who 'knows the West as well as anyone.' Regardless, the western reaction to the Wheat Board Amendment Act was just as pronounced as its response to the minister of agriculture's initial proposals. The Saskatchewan Wheat Pool circulated petitions urging the retention of the eighty-cent payment. It was argued that, because foreign markets were protected by tariffs and quotas, the Canadian Wheat Board was essential. Reports of regional dissatisfaction caused the issue to emerge again in cabinet. By that time, the prime minister was rapidly losing faith in his Prairie advisor: 'I am far from sure that Gardiner is right in believing that we can get Western Canada to accept favourably legislation which will reduce price to be guaranteed farmers for wheat from 80 cents as it is now under the Wheat Board to 60 cents. I am afraid this legislation if it carries will cost us many seats in Western Canada.' It seemed, he claimed, almost 'a sort of suicide' for Liberalism on the Prairies.[104] In the end, the cabinet accepted a compromise suggestion from Crerar of a 70¢ minimum price. Still, five western Liberals voted against the amended bill. The crop insurance scheme was passed in the form of the Prairie Farm Assistance Act. The government hoped that, aside from stabilizing farm income, the act would help alleviate regional discontent.

Although the government ended up bending toward the western position, Prime Minister King had surrendered the issue only grudgingly. The Prairie situation was frustrating, even irritating. The change in his western sympathies was also now evident when it came to dealing with the various delegations from the Prairies who in 1939 wished to present their specific concerns to the prime minister. As long as the delegations heaped glowing praise upon the government's record and demonstrated heartfelt gratitude for saving the region from the Depression, King was receptive. When criticism and requests for more aid were put forward, he quickly lost his patience. He pointed out that the government had to consider the interests of the entire nation, not just one region. As prime minister, he would go 'just as far' as he could 'in an effort to meet Western Canada ... but not a step further.' The Prairie populace would have to appreciate the record of past Liberal governments: 'This should be sufficient guarantee of our desire to meet the West without seeking to drive us into an impossible situation.'[105]

An expected election in 1939 was postponed by Canada's entry into the Second World War. Domestic issues, including the Liberal party's problems in western Canada, would be overshadowed by events in Europe. 'It is difficult to maintain an interest in politics during the war,' C.D. Howe admitted.[106] Prairie discontent led Prime Minister King to monitor the provincial situations closely for signs of what to expect in a federal contest. The Liberal party in Saskatchewan seemed solid, and the dissension and division in Manitoba was subsiding. In the Alberta election of March 1940, the Liberal, Conservative, and independent Labour parties merged and ran under the banner of Independents. According to J.A. MacKinnon, Social Credit had been weakened, but it was unlikely to translate into more Liberal seats. Instead the gains would probably go to the CCF, which had refused to cooperate with the Independents. The war, however, did seem to be boosting the federal Liberal's fortunes within the province, and MacKinnon wanted an immediate election to take advantage of this trend. 'There is a definite shift here to Mr. King,' he observed, 'as a sound, reliable and dependable leader in these troubled times.' Additional reports provided similar indications. The prime minister and his government were 'held in greater respect and higher esteem in Alberta than for many years past.' It had taken the war to impress upon the people 'the immeasurable value of wise and courageous leadership and able and sound administration.'[107]

As expected, the war dominated the federal election campaign of 1940. The timing of the election call was questionable until Ontario Premier Mitchell Hepburn carried his feud with Mackenzie King to new heights by moving a provincial resolution condemning Ottawa's war effort. The prime minister leaped at the opportunity to dissolve the House and call an election on the issue of confidence in the government to prosecute the war effectively. Mackenzie King was nervous about western prospects. He told the governor general at the end of January that the government would 'in Alberta, perhaps do better. In Saskatchewan not so well. Manitoba doubtful. We would lose something in the Prairies.'[108] Gardiner's information indicated that the Liberals should not expect the number of seats in Saskatchewan or Manitoba to change. Alberta representation could only improve, particularly if Social Credit support were actually declining and the CCF rising.[109]

The campaign tour across the Prairies at the end of February alleviated any anxiety the prime minister may have been experiencing.[110] Liberal prospects in Manitoba seemed better than expected. The second largest crop in Canadian history was creating optimism, and local grievances had been shelved in the midst of world war. Some seats were doubtful, but with such a large majority, losses had to be expected. Crerar told King that western opinion agreed with the calling of Hepburn's bluff. Although Crerar encountered scattered references to conscription on the Prairies, and some fear of the measure in the ethnic communities, he did not consider the issue as yet significant.[111] The outlook in the province was so positive that Norman Lambert described it as a 'political model.'[112] The only negative sign for the party was that the CCF was now seen as an active and dangerous threat.[113] After a speech in Winnipeg, King claimed to feel such a warm reception that 'on every side today, I received evidences of a sweep.' Liberal fortunes in Saskatchewan remained sound, but the machine was expensive to maintain and campaign funds were no longer as accessible. Gardiner informed King that at least one-third of the money would have to come from the central office.[114] Since his appointment as minister without portfolio, J.A. MacKinnon had been reporting that prospects in Alberta were improving. Still, high prices and unemployment were continuing to pose problems, and the province would have to rely completely on outside help to fund the campaign. The prime minister was informed by outside organizers that reliable information regarding Alberta's prospects, as usual, was difficult to obtain. The blurring of federal and provincial issues would augment Social Credit's influence in the general election.[115] As Grant Dexter, a journalist with the *Winnipeg Free Press*, observed, while MacKinnon was optimistic, caution was necessary. His political judgment had 'not yet been blooded.'[116] Overall, Mackenzie King expected to lose only minimal ground on the Prairies.[117]

Given conditions in Prince Albert, the prime minister was more concerned with his riding than ever before. The area had seen its worst years of the Depression in 1937 and 1938, with northern Saskatchewan finally falling prey to the drought. The much improved crop in 1939 would not wipe out the effects of nine years of Depression.[118] King, admitting that his constituents had been very considerate in not making demands on his time, noted that a trip was now imperative because he had not visited the area since the last election. Upon visiting the riding, his doubts about being re-elected and his guilt for the long absence increased. He attempted to assure himself that the visit was a 'sort of intimate personal one which helped to bring my constituents and myself closer together.'[119]

In the election on 26 March 1940 the Liberals were easily returned with a majority government of 181 seats. The Conservatives won only 40, the

Social Credit 10, the CCF 8, and the independents and others 6. Only in the four western provinces did the government fail to win a majority of the popular vote. Still, King's party won 15 out of 17 seats in Manitoba, 12 of 21 in Saskatchewan, and 7 of 17 in Alberta. The prime minister was again returned in Prince Albert, but his majority was noticeably reduced – he defeated the National Unity candidate by only 774 votes. 'It has been by a miracle that I did not lose,' he admitted when the results were known.[120] Amid prospects of war contracts, the urban vote went Liberal, while the rural vote went National Unity. T.C. Davis reported that the causes of King's near defeat were 'first and foremost lack of proper organization' and second 'the unholy alliance' between Social Credit and Conservatives. 'This combination,' he noted, 'nearly proved disastrous.' There was no doubt that the anti-Liberal vote was moving into third parties.[121]

There were no major changes to western cabinet representation after the election. Some general portfolio shuffling took place, and when W.D. Euler was appointed to the Senate, J.A. MacKinnon was given trade and commerce. He would chair the wheat committee, which had lost another member when C.A. Dunning retired prior to the election to be replaced in finance by Layton Ralston. J.L. Ilsley moved to finance in July after defence minister Norman Rogers was killed in an air crash and Ralston accepted the vacant portfolio.

The years from 1935 to 1940 demonstrated the changes in the relationship between the Liberal party of Mackenzie King and the Prairie region. As Reg Whitaker has observed, 'after 1935 the Liberals never regained the level of electoral support which they had enjoyed after the [first] war. They were generally weaker in the West than in any other part of the country.'[122] The Depression was the main catalyst for this change. The crisis increased the pace of western decline in the nation and consequently the region's willingness to turn to radical alternatives. When the same old Liberal party with the same old politicians returned to power, they found themselves increasingly out of step with western issues. Mackenzie King could continue to harp on about the tariff; Jimmy Gardiner about straight Liberalism; Tom Crerar about open market conditions; and Charles Dunning about fiscal responsibility; but these no longer constituted the major concerns of the Prairie West. Gardiner and Crerar could at least remain in accord with their bases of support on some issues and alter their positions on others, but King was now completely at odds with the region. He found himself opposed to the West at every turn.

8

Viewing the Mountains without
Scaling the Hills, 1941–1950

Intensive organization has placed the C.C.F. in a very commanding position in Western Canada ... It is freely admitted from all schools of thought that you have carried on a war effort of a very high order, but western opinion views the mountains without seeming to realize the necessity of the regimentation required to scale the hills.

F. McRae to King, 14 July 1944

The war years marked the height of Mackenzie King's career. Although there were doubts that the prime minister was a strong enough leader for such a military crisis, he emerged from the war with a united country that had doubled its gross national product and increased its budget ten-fold in five years. Political victories followed on the heels of the economic and military successes as the Liberal party won two more elections under his leadership. He surpassed Robert Walpole in holding power longer than any statesman in the English-speaking world. In 1948 the reins of leadership were handed over to King's successor, and the party would maintain power for another nine years. During the 1940s King was heralded for implementing major steps toward the welfare state and for preserving French-English unity in the face of a conscription crisis that had smashed the party in 1917. His success was perhaps best demonstrated by the attitude of J.W. Dafoe, the arch-western spokesman, who had undergone a reversal in his estimation of the prime minister. 'My relations with King have never got to the point of warm friendship,' the editor wrote in 1943, 'but they have been close enough to give me an impression, which grows with every contact, that there is more to this man than I have thought.' In reaction to critical press reports, Dafoe informed J.A. Stevenson that the 'systematic disparagement and belittlement of everything he has done has vexed me to the point that I have become somewhat of a partisan on his behalf – something I never was previously.'[1]

But the period from 1941 to 1950 also witnessed the continued decline, if not the ultimate collapse, of the Liberal party in the West. Canada was changing, and so too were politics on the Prairies. The transition from an agricultural to an industrial economy and from a rural to an urban population became increasingly apparent and highlighted the shift in political emphasis from the West to central Canada. Domestic issues were neglected as the government focused on the war. The two domestic problems that did receive attention were conscription in Quebec and Premier Mitchell Hepburn's revolt in Ontario. In the past King had been remarkably successful in adapting to the changing times, remaining abreast of political transition, and holding on to office. He succeeded in achieving the same results during the 1940s. His party responded to the new demands placed upon federalism as well as to the shift toward the welfare state. By the end of King's tenure in office, the 'government party' was firmly entrenched. But in the process both Mackenzie King and his party lost the support of the Prairie West. The Liberals in each of the three provinces had failed to pass on the torch to a new generation. Gardiner and Crerar were still expected to deliver the support of their provinces, but their influence was clearly waning. The successes of the Second World War period disguised the true state of Prairie Liberalism.

As Canada entered its third year of war, the trend toward centralized federalism moved along at a furious pace. Although the recommendations of the Rowell–Sirois Commission on dominion–provincial relations had been delivered in the middle of February 1940, they were withheld until after the general election. They called upon Ottawa to assume the burden of provincial debts, relief, and income taxes. Premier Aberhart of Alberta had refused to submit a brief to the commission or to accept its eventual recommendations. Manitoba's reaction was quite the opposite. As Morton points out, the announcement of the commission had been 'greeted with satisfaction, almost with jubilation, in Manitoba, for it seemed to be a tacit acknowledgment of the province's claim that the western provinces had been the victims rather than the beneficiaries of national policies and that the constitutional allocation of responsibilities and revenues had become intolerable.'[2] Premier Bracken, along with Crerar in cabinet, petitioned the prime minister to implement the findings and to call a conference to discuss the report. Mackenzie King preferred to wait until the war was over and then employ the findings in postwar reconstruction. The matter, however, could not be delayed. The wartime need for greater federal control and increased revenue, particularly in the areas of direct taxation, pushed the cabinet to consider the findings immediately. A dominion-provincial conference was called for January 1941. King was personally suspicious of the 'financial interests' pushing the implementation of the report and alarmed by the increase in federal control. The situation created by the war, however, demanded action.[3]

The conference erupted into an expected battle between Ottawa and the more affluent provinces, with Premiers Hepburn of Ontario and Pattullo of British Columbia attacking the government's efforts. Aberhart of Alberta also joined the assault against federal intervention. Bracken of Manitoba pressed the claims of the poorer, 'have-not' provinces. Godbout of Quebec,[4] Macmillan of Nova Scotia, and McNair of New Brunswick remained sceptical of the report's recommendations, while Campbell of Prince Edward Island and Patterson of Saskatchewan were prepared to accept change in the federal–provincial relationship. Despite the prime minister's failure to win provincial cooperation, he would implement change. Ottawa would impose heavy wartime taxes, and any province agreeing to surrender its income, corporation, and succession taxes would receive in compensation an annual payment equal to its previous revenue from these fields. After the cabinet accepted the scheme, the Dominion–Provincial Taxation Agreement Act became part of the 1942 budget.[5]

Despite the continuing state of discord in dominion–provincial relations, the war did seem to cause a change in Aberhart's attitude toward King. The premier claimed to desire a new spirit of cooperation between Alberta and Ottawa, and promised to aid fully in the war effort. However, a superficial aura of wartime unity could not mask continuing complaints of discrimination. In October 1941 the premier complained that the regulations imposed by the Canadian Broadcasting Corporation (CBC) were discriminatory. The federal Liberals, by contrast, were being allowed more freedom. According to Aberhart, it was only his 'friendship' with the prime minister that impelled him even to bring up the issue at all. The letter was even signed 'your friend in Alberta.' In March of the following year Aberhart requested that King pursue the matter of extending the province's boundaries northward. When the two men had earlier discussed the issue, Aberhart had reminded the prime minister of Alberta's cooperative efforts of late.[6] After years of frustration and poor relations with the province, Mackenzie King was unlikely to respond in kind.

At the same time, King's support of Gardiner in the cabinet was dwindling. The minister of agriculture battled relentlessly in defence of western issues, but as usual the position being advanced was also aimed at increasing his own influence. Gardiner's ambition became intertwined with Prairie incentives, and his general unpopularity within cabinet often obstructed progress. King noticed that Gardiner's relations with most of his colleagues, including those from the West, were strained. The minister's position on Prairie issues, though 'right,' was often 'over-ruled' because he was 'always so tenacious of his own point of view that others, while respecting his motives, feel that they themselves must show a greater amount of tenacity than might otherwise be necessary,' noted King.[7] The minister of agriculture demanded complete control of the many facets of his department, from production to sales; as Grant Dexter indicated, 'wheat is his baby.' Gardiner certainly resented Crerar's wielding any influence. 'You people in Manitoba don't grow wheat in quantity any more,' he told Dexter. 'You represent the trading, the marketing interest. You are all grain exchange people, whether you realize it or not.'[8] Gardiner was also bitterly resisting Ilsley's efforts to take responsibility for controls on agricultural products away from his department. With public opinion growing anxious about the increased powers of the government, King often complained about Gardiner's selfish handling of his portfolio and strong-arm dealings with fellow ministers. 'Jimmy has been desperately unpopular with the cabinet at large for some time,' Dexter reported to Dafoe. 'Ralston once remarked to me that Jimmy was the most difficult colleague he had ever known.'[9] Gardiner and western issues became indistinguishable, and King's attitude hardened toward both. The war only exacerbated the situation. Agricultural matters for the prime minister, 'if not peripheral, were secondary ... and their importance decreased as the war dragged on and military questions grew more pressing.'[10] He had no patience for ministers jockeying for power during such a crisis.

King's opinion of Crerar was also deteriorating. According to the prime minister he seemed to lack the proper concern and understanding for the 'common' Canadian and was 'losing his grip' on his province as well.[11] Nonetheless the Manitoba politician held such a prominent role during the war that King could not help but view him as more than a provincial or regional politician. His experience in the First World War made Crerar the only federal minister to serve in both wartime cabinets. Deputy chairman of the all-powerful war cabinet, he had been considered for the defence portfolio in 1939. When the British government requested a Canadian minister to travel to London at the beginning of November 1939 and discuss the dominion's capacity to provide money and resources, King sent Crerar. He attempted to convince the British that they had an obligation to buy Canadian wheat and to offer a good return to the Prairie farmer. Although Britain had been purchasing on the world market at a price that was well below the Canadian level, the mother country was prepared to buy from Canada if a decent price was obtained. Britain suggested a target of 70¢ a bushel; Crerar declined and requested a guaranteed supply for twelve months at 93.5¢ or until 1 July 1941 at one dollar. The request was refused, and the question remained unresolved with Britain continuing to buy on the open market. In May 1940 the British agreed to purchase fifty million bushels at 82.5¢.[12] Gardiner accused Crerar of 'torpedoing' his control of wheat through the Department of Agriculture because the Manitoban had 'a lot of fixed ideas in his head which he got in the last war.'[13] Crerar's traditional belief in open markets for wheat was altered when he recognized the very real threat of a Europe dominated by Germany. He began to consider a long-term contract with Britain, something Gardiner had been advocating for months. Such an idea, however, was rejected by cabinet. With the fall of France, the estimation of the two westerners proved correct. Continental markets closed, futures prices declined, and the wheat surplus increased.[14]

The war also gave Gardiner the opportunity to rise above the label of regional politician. Since the 1940 election he had been manoeuvring to gain the finance department or, if this proved impossible, at least to raise the status of agriculture. His ambition and tenacity were well known. While returning to Canada from a trip to Britain late in 1940, Gardiner's ship was threatened by a German pocket battleship. 'Damn lucky for the pocket battleship that it escaped,' Dexter noted sarcastically.[15]

The Saskatchewan politician was asked by King to consider surrendering agriculture and accepting the portfolio of national war services. While he was not the prime minister's first choice for the new department, which would administer the recent National Resources Mobilization Act, his impressive organizational skills and appetite for work rendered him a suitable candidate. The position would offer Gardiner 'a broad national constituency rather than a particular regional bias' and would also mean a place on the influential war committee that was directing the nation through orders-in-council. As the minister of mines and resources, and senior privy councillor, Crerar was presently the only westerner on the committee. Although King wanted

Gardiner to relinquish agriculture, an alternative candidate could not be located, so he took on both portfolios.[16]

The new department was not 'high in the ministerial pecking order,' and cabinet friction resulted as Gardiner attempted to expand its influence. He made a direct bid to have responsibility for the Wheat Board and the Agricultural Supplies Board transferred from trade and commerce to national war services. He had not been pleased when W.D. Euler had control of these responsibilities, and J.A. MacKinnon's appointment was little better. Neither, according to Gardiner, knew anything about wheat. Although from Alberta, MacKinnon represented the 'urban professional' group that had always dominated the province's Liberal party. The request for the board's transfer was denied by an advisory committee on economic policy. Mackenzie King quickly became dissatisfied with Gardiner's juggling of his two departments. After being scolded by the prime minister in January 1941, the Saskatchewan minister threatened to resign if he did not get his way on matters within his jurisdiction. King believed Gardiner had 'got his head turned' from holding both portfolios: 'He is really falling in between the two. He is adopting Euler's tactics of being unpleasant with every colleague who disagrees with him and trying to get his way by a ruthless forcing of the situation, sometimes in a very underhanded manner.'[17] A difference of opinion over the coordination of the department's publicity caused a breach that led to further misunderstanding and finally, in June 1941, to Gardiner's resignation from war services.

To his credit, Gardiner's achievements as wartime minister of agriculture were impressive. Although the administration and policies of the Wheat Board remained within the department of trade and commerce, the quagmire of agricultural marketing, along with King's ignorance on the subject, did at least allow the minister to maintain some status in cabinet. By contrast, his experience with the Department of National War Services was a 'failure' and 'clear demotion' that undoubtedly injured his reputation and removed him from the influential war committee.[18] 'Gardiner's run in a Hepburn–Hitler direction,' King recorded. 'What he does not see is [the] extent to which he is prejudicing his own future in the eyes of his colleagues who will have some say on the ground of who is to succeed myself.'[19] King's lost confidence in his Prairie lieutenant would never be regained.

Gardiner's waning fortunes reflected those of his region. The indisputable importance of agriculture in wartime could not disguise the decline of the West. The region's main industry 'assumed greater political visibility' but 'declined in relative importance in the Canadian economy.'[20] The war, while restoring prosperity, was aggravating the contrast between the farming and non-farming sectors of the economy: the returning prosperity was not being felt equally.[21] Nonetheless, Gardiner battled on in an attempt to defend the Prairie farmer.

In March 1941 the cabinet was discussing the need to have western farmers decrease their wheat acreage and grow alternative grains to avoid a surplus. Canadian farmers were to be paid for summer fallowing or planting coarse grains as opposed to wheat. Mackenzie King, who was not comfortable with limiting produce, acknowledged that Prairie income had to be maintained 'to avoid the Western situation getting completely out of hand at the time of war.'[22] Crerar was opposed on the basis that the reduction would cause a myriad of other problems, including increasing surpluses in other areas.[23] Gardiner's concern was to increase the income of wheat farmers, defending them against what he perceived as the biases of other ministers. A compromise was reached that involved the introduction of delivery quotas, maximum quotas, and wheat acreage reduction payments. There would also be a two-price system for wheat: the domestic price was increased through a millers' processing tax, with the proceeds to accrue to the farmers.[24]

The trend toward increased federal control and restriction resulted in the organization of the Wartime Prices and Trade Board, the Wartime Industries Control Board, and the Foreign Exchange Control Board. Prime Minister King remained uncomfortable with the new federal powers, including increased taxes as well as the controls on the marketplace, but he fell in line with the dominant cabinet position. He was alarmed by Ilsley's sweeping proposals for price control and the effects of a freeze to check spiralling inflation. Representing discontented farmers, H.H. Hannan, the president of the Canadian Federation of Agriculture, complained to King that the freeze discriminated against agriculture because the industry, after a decade of depression, was not yet on par with other sectors of the economy. Prices were just beginning to rise, with farmers finally feeling the benefits.[25] Gardiner was in agreement. It was becoming apparent that attempts at wheat acreage reduction were problematic. If the amount of wheat being produced decreased, so did the farmers' income. To make matters worse, those in the Palliser's Triangle could grow little other than wheat. Gardiner, seeing that the Wartime Prices and Trade Board's aim to reduce inflation ran counter to his own overriding desire to see prices rise, would come to clash repeatedly with the organization. Because of his protests against the government policy of wage and price controls, grain farmers received a bonus of $20 million, which when added to other incentives, brought their goal of one dollar a bushel wheat close to reality. The cabinet also agreed that no ceiling would be placed on the domestic price for wheat.[26]

The wartime restrictions and controls were damaging Liberal fortunes in the West. The region felt that it was being ignored when it came to representation on the boards, and that these boards were being administered without regard for popular government. The general perception was that the agencies were dominated by judges and lawyers, while labour, small business, and farming interests were excluded. They were run by 'dictators within their own field.'[27] The desperate state of the war in the first several years was also crippling morale. Western party members appealed to the prime minister to visit their region and stay as long as possible. Aside from any political gains to be made, King's presence was required to aid morale and the military recruiting campaign. He was told not to 'shrink at this time from allowing yourself to be dramatized a bit, more conspicuously and picturesquely as Canada's wartime leader. There is a feeling ... that you have somewhat lost your touch with the people of the west.'[28] King blamed the opposition press and the conscriptionist movement[29] for his declining popularity. He reiterated his usual argument, that national obligations prevented him from visiting the region.

A western tour was finally undertaken in the summer of 1941 to promote the government's recruiting drive and stave off the demands for conscription. As Dexter noted, King 'kind of figures he hasn't lost the old curves and means to give the west a real whirl.'[30] But the prime minister was shocked by the hostile reception and blamed the reaction on the region's support for conscription.[31] According to J.L. Granatstein, 'organized opinion in the West seemed to be all out for conscription and all out against Mackenzie King.'[32] In Saskatchewan, the government's wheat policy was under fire. The primary features of the policy at the outbreak of war had been the Wheat Board's guaranteed initial payment of seventy cents along with acreage payments in circumstances defined by the Prairie Farm Assistance Act. The problem was that the acreage payments were proving insufficient compensation and western wheat producers were not able to take advantage of wartime prosperity.[33] The wheat pools were arguing that the government incentives were merely an attempt to keep the price of wheat down and the farmers from entering real prosperity. Since his retirement from cabinet in 1935, W.R. Motherwell had become increasingly sceptical of Ottawa's handling of the West. Gardiner received reports that he was attending pool meetings and claiming that the government's agricultural policies were revamped at election time to 'clutch the throat' of the voter.[34]

Reports from Prince Albert were also pessimistic. Since 1939 complaints had been circulating that a few prominent Liberals in the constituency were 'being permitted to become rich out of the War.' Criticism of the King government had become commonplace. Saskatchewan Liberals were genuinely worried because 'the campaign of slander' had become 'intensified to an almost unbelievable extent.'[35] Support for the war effort had initially been enthusiastic in the urban areas of the province, and when the Department of Transport had taken over the Prince Albert municipal airport in January 1940, the mayor had predicted that one hundred aircraft and more than one thousand Royal Canadian Air Force personnel would be stationed in the city. These prospects were deflated soon after the federal election, when the government announced that only an elementary flyer-training school comprising 217 people would be established.[36] King responded by demonstrating what had become a token concern for constituency affairs. Prince Albert became a link in the British Commonwealth Air Training Plan and in March 1941 became home to an Air Observer School. In November Jack Sanderson, the Liberal organizer and constituency manager for Prince Albert, paid the prime minister a visit, requesting he push to have runways and additional air training schools constructed in the riding. King agreed that 'Prince Albert is entitled to both.' Later that day, he took up the matter with the minister of national defence for air, 'Chubby' Power, 'who also promised to go into it carefully,' effectively delaying action on the issue. The prime minister, noting that the constituency was pressing to be recognized 'as a military district,' claimed to be doing everything possible 'to have its interests fully considered.'[37]

Although the search for the salvation of the Liberal party continued in Alberta, the war only confirmed King's lack of interest in the province. Despite occasional calls for another attempt at federal organization, the provincial party was now left to deal with the hopeless situation on its own. It was conceded that 'no amount of overhauling' would be sufficient. 'I do not know what can be done,' J.B. Howatt wrote, 'but surely to God there is somebody in Ottawa that has some sense enough to size this situation up to realize we shall either be a Social Credit Government or what is worse, a C.C.F. Government after the next election if somebody does not beat some sense into the damn fool Liberal executive of this Province.'[38] Party prospects were left to J.A. MacKinnon, but his ignorance of agricultural issues diminished his already weak influence in cabinet and much of Alberta's organization was still left to Gardiner.

A provincial election was held in Manitoba on 22 April 1942 and, despite the withdrawal of the CCF, the Bracken coalition won fifty of fifty-five seats. By this time Bracken had been premier for almost nineteen years, yet his recent stand in favour of implementing the Rowell–Sirois report had pushed his popularity to new heights. His 'non-partisan' government swept the contest on a platform of postwar planning and agriculture. He had emerged from the Depression as 'the recognized spokesman and leader of the West ... the voice of western Canada, the one man who best represented the needs, interests, and ambitions of the prairie provinces.' With Bracken in control and the Liberals supporting coalition, Mackenzie King felt confident that Manitoba was secure. Although the premier had maintained his Progressive affiliations, King was confident that he was a disenchanted Liberal like so many others from the province. It was hoped he would eventually join the federal cabinet, and the support he had given the Liberals back in 1935 seemed an indication he was coming King's way. The Depression had certainly left Bracken disenchanted with the Prairie situation. The problem was that by the late 1930s he was also 'disenchanted with King's protracted style.'[39]

Early in 1942, Arthur Meighen's return to politics came to an abrupt end when he was defeated in a by-election in York South, Ontario, by the CCF candidate. The Conservatives, searching for a new leader, turned to John Bracken. The party needed someone who was associated with agriculture and could attract the rural vote; someone who could draw disaffected Liberals away from King and offer a firm alternative to the CCF; someone who could do what Bennett had accomplished in 1930. Bracken had no real desire to enter federal politics or become associated with either of the traditional parties. Yet King's anti-conscriptionist policies and the Tory party's appeal to his sense of duty convinced him, in the end, to accept the leadership. The party agreed to his condition of acceptance and changed its name: John Bracken became leader of the Progressive Conservative party in December of 1942. The 'voice of western Canada' was now commanding the Tory forces.[40]

Jimmy Gardiner was not surprised by the move. He prided himself on his ability to detect disguised Conservatives, and had always claimed that Bracken was Tory blue. He had, of course, levied this particular charge against most of the Progressive movement. By contrast, T.A. Crerar was outraged at the premier's defection: 'in his view, Bracken had betrayed the Liberal party and the people of Manitoba, to say nothing of political friends like himself who had given the Manitoba premier their support over the years.'[41] Mackenzie King, although surprised by the leadership move, was pleased nonetheless. It was certainly preferable to the return of his arch-nemesis, Arthur Meighen. The change in party labels, he believed, was nothing more than absurd hypocrisy. Bracken's selection, King wrote, had been the 'worst choice' possible for the Tories.[43] King believed that the decision would also 'take the steam out of the C.C.F.,' which he felt had become popular in the West only because of the collapse of Tory opposition.[43] Yet while the Conservatives might make gains on the Prairies, they would suffer in the rest of the nation. This, King could accept.

By 1942 there was good reason to believe that the Conservatives would take Prairie seats away from the Liberals. With farmer delegations descending on Ottawa to such an extent that the situation was 'reminiscent of the seige of 1910,' King's concern about western conditions had increased.[44] After the prime minister, along with Jimmy Gardiner, had met with the delegations to discuss wheat policy, King realized that his reputation in the region had been severely damaged. He was careful to note the reaction of westerners, and he made a token effort to convince himself that he was still fighting to defend their interests in 'considering the rights of the producers before those of the trade.' He claimed the West still held his 'sympathies.'[45] On 9 March 1942 it was announced that the initial payment for wheat would be increased from seventy to ninety cents.

Despite King's earlier assessment that the Tories would hurt the CCF in the west, the third party continued to claim ground. In an about face, King claimed not to be surprised: Meighen's defeat to the socialist party in York South 'was bound to be looked upon as prophetic as well as significant.' Any government during wartime, the prime minister argued, was almost certain to suffer defeat in the postwar period due to wartime taxes and restrictions. The only way to avoid such a fate was through proper organization. The Liberals were suffering because, while the government was concerned with winning the war, the CCF was concerned with grooming an effective organization. The upsurge also seemed to indicate that Gardiner's influence was diminishing even in Saskatchewan. The next election in the province would be a 'battle.' If the province fell, the Liberals would lose their traditional bastion of strength in the region. According to Gardiner, two matters were making it 'impossible' for the Liberals to gain western support: wartime controls, especially price levels on grain, and the National War Services Board, which in 1942 had drafted 'almost everyone off the farm.' It was one of the rare occasions when Jimmy Gardiner and Robert Forke were in agreement. There was a growing discontent among farmers, Forke informed King, 'because of the arbitrary manner in which your Government was dealing with farm problems without consulting the people who produce the agricultural wealth of this country.'[46]

Bracken's departure to federal politics had left the Manitoba Liberals in the lurch. The provincial party had been 'too long submerged in Brackenism.' While 'the old guard' had almost entirely disappeared, the survivors were no longer in tune with provincial sentiment, nor did they wield any influence. There was no 'new blood' to replace the previous generation of Liberals. 'New names and new faces won't help if they spring from a generation outdated, with a philosophy outmoded in the popular mind,' Manitoba Liberal L.A. Mutch informed King. The party at both levels had been declining since 1935. The two previous federal elections had been won due to the weakness of the Tories under Bennett and Manion, rather than the strength of the Liberals under King. The emerging CCF seemed the only alternative attuned to the people's temperament and concerned with western issues. 'Your personal place is secure in history,' Mutch bluntly warned the prime minister. 'Your place in 1945 is not.'[47] King admitted to being 'terribly worried' about both the Manitoba situation and the CCF threat.[48]

Mackenzie King and his party were showing the strain of war and the many years in office. 'This is the end of an era,' Dexter noted. The government, composed of 'burnt out men,' had 'lost its constructive power.' By 1943 the prime minister feared that the political scene would again become dominated by minority governments and coalitions. The wave of popularity that had surrounded the Liberal government in the 1940 election had dissipated; the cabinet was reduced to internal dissension; and the party no longer seemed to have 'the gumption to go out and fight the CCF.'[49] If King's government went to the polls at present, westerners argued, it would be 'hopelessly defeated.' Prairie Liberalism was in the 'doldrums, helplessly being sniped at by every political adventurer who covets the office of Government.'[50] Even Gardiner admitted that there was not a single safe seat left in the entire region.[51]

On the bright side, the Prairie provinces produced a good harvest in 1943; the wheat crop was just under the historic yield of 1929. The heavy yield, along with the brutally harsh winter, did create other problems, such as a choked elevator system and a resulting demand for government cash advances on farm-stored grain. The advances were avoided when the United States considerably increased its Canadian wheat purchases. With wartime demand increasing, the fixed price would rise to $1.20. The year also marked the final phase in the transformation of Liberal wheat policy. After years of resisting the pools and demands for government intervention, the King government surrendered to the creation of a compulsory wheat board. By autumn the concern about surpluses that had forced government action in 1941 was replaced by 'a scramble to meet rising demand.' To avoid an increase in wheat prices as well as threats to the treasury and wage and price policies, the government gave the Wheat Board a monopoly. Crerar returned to his position as defender of the open market, arguing that the action was too drastic, but the cabinet was against him.[52] It was doubtful, however, whether the reversal on wheat marketing or the improving conditions could produce a parallel reversal in Prairie Liberalism.

Unlike the governing Liberals, who were preoccupied with the war, the other political parties were certainly prepared to take advantage of the nation's sagging morale and general sentiments of insecurity. The CCF, which had been pressing for increased social services for years, was campaigning on the need to prepare for postwar reconstruction. Politicians sensed the popular insecurity that stemmed from fears of a recurrence of the postwar recession of the early 1920s or, worse yet, a return to more recent depression conditions. According to J.L. Granatstein, 'Social Welfare legislation, fundamentally conservative in intent, could help dampen down this unrest; it could cushion the shocks of peace; it could help re-elect the Liberal Party and thus maintain the free-enterprise economy against the assaults from the left.' The Progressive Conservatives also continued to change with the times. John Bracken officially committed the party to social security, full employment, collective bargaining, and medical insurance. Only the Liberal Party seemed 'left out.' Critics argued that the party was too concerned with running the war.[53] While the Marsh Report indicated a willingness to study social problems and even ponder solutions such as increased social security, the wartime demands were too pressing for attention to be focused on reconstruction. Instead King turned critics to *Industry and Humanity* – written at a time when few others were pondering such radical action – as evidence of his reforming spirit.[54]

The need for change in party direction was pressed on the prime minister when the CCF went from zero to thirty-four seats in the Ontario provincial election of 4 August 1943. Five days later the Liberals lost four federal by-elections: two of the seats were in Quebec, lost to the Labour-Progressive party and the Bloc Populaire Canadien; the other two were in Manitoba and Saskatchewan at the hands of the CCF. The losses indicated the growing resentment against the government in Quebec and the increasing influence of the Left in the West. Grant Dexter labelled them the 'good-bye elections.' The Canadian Institute of Public Opinion added to the shock by reporting that at the national level the CCF had the support of 29 per cent of the population while the Liberals and PCs trailed with 28 per cent each.[55] The popularity of the government had tumbled from its 1941 high of 55 per cent.[56] Not wanting to be 'alarmist,' W.A. Buchanan nonetheless admitted to being very concerned. 'From all that I hear and all that I sense ... if an election was to be held now or in the near future, the C.C.F. might very well sweep all the western provinces.'[57]

The Liberal party had to be reorganized and revitalized. The machinery was in poor condition: after the 1940 campaign the National Liberal Federation had virtually 'ceased to exist.' The presidency passed through several people's hands while the NLF sat moribund.[58] Organization on the Prairies was in an even worse state. 'The Liberal position in Western Canada is becoming more hopeless every day,' one Liberal organizer reported. There was a dominant impression that many of the Liberals involved in organization were out only to make personal gains. More often than not, party officials blamed the miserable situation on the war. The Liberals had to show that they were not entirely preoccupied with events abroad. 'There is only one reason for the decline in the liberal fortunes,' Gardiner's son wrote King, 'and that is the people are beginning to feel that the liberals have no more interest in them.'[59]

The rise of the CCF prompted Mackenzie King to act on his reforming impulse that had sat dormant since 1919. He returned to the realm of social security to ponder again such schemes as health insurance, family allowances, old-age pensions, and veterans' allowances. These proposals would go hand in hand with unemployment insurance, which had already been implemented in 1940. According to the prime minister, the Liberals had to keep in touch with the working classes and farmers to avoid the danger of being eliminated altogether and of allowing the CCF to steal Liberal ground.[60] He blamed the 'reactionaries' in his government for having 'smothered almost to death the tender green shoots of real liberalism.'[61] Party members such as Ian Mackenzie and Jack Pickersgill pushed for action 'without delay.' Promises would be 'useless' – the government would be judged on 'concrete, tangible evidences of action.'[62] Crerar, however, was holding the traditional Liberal fort in espousing individual initiative, and King was annoyed at his refusal to follow party direction.[63]

On 11 January 1944 the cabinet approved the establishment of three new departments: Reconstruction, National Health and Welfare, and Veterans Affairs. J.L. Granatstein characterizes the throne speech as 'a landmark in the development of the social-security state in Canada.' The government pledged itself to social insurance and promised family allowances, health insurance, old-age pensions, and a floor price for farm staples.[64] Yet these initiatives were still just promises, and the prime minister was already infamous for making empty promises. The Liberals might be able to steal the CCF thunder in the rest of the nation, but the party's strength would not be so easily sapped in the West.

This was certainly the case in Mackenzie King's riding. Senator J.J. Stevenson had been monitoring Prince Albert for King since the summer of 1943, and the prognosis was not good. The senator, when asked to report frankly on whether the seat could be won, replied that, while the majority would be reduced, victory was still probable. This was not enough assurance for the prime minister, who seemed uncertain about contesting the riding again. He admitted that his lack of time and money given to the riding organization was proving destructive. In searching for a scapegoat, he noted that the constituency had been 'allowed to drift.' Several key organizers had died, T.C. Davis had gone to Ottawa in 1940 as Gardiner's deputy minister in war services, and prominent Liberals such as Jack Sanderson had been accused of profiting from government contracts. King voiced a faint hope: 'It may be that in some way I shall come through in the end.'[65]

Although the Prairie stronghold of Saskatchewan was under seige, Gardiner refused to believe his province was rejecting Liberalism. Saskatchewan had maintained the Liberal faith throughout the Progressive assault. Why would it abandon the fort now? But as King had already admitted, the CCF was different from the Progressives. Western alienation encompassed more than the farmers. The CCF appealed to the Labour movement and the intelligentsia; it offered a home to the ethnic groups who had previously boarded with the Liberals. But for Gardiner, as for King, the problem was not so deeply rooted. There was no barrier to the appeal of Liberalism in the West – there was simply a problem with organization. As a result of the unofficial political truce created by the war, other parties had gained the opportunity to build their forces. The Liberal organizations, on the other hand, had been disrupted. To make matters worse, local members in Saskatchewan were not facing up to the CCF challenge and seemed instead to be abandoning the field. The party, 'exhausted' after a decade of drought, depression, bankruptcy, and third-party challenges, had 'jumped at the chance to call a halt to politics.' Gardiner's successor, W.J. Patterson, had even gone so far as to suggest a union government. The provincial leaders obviously did not share the federal minister's passionate belief in the Liberal cause.[66] 'Everybody has gone on a holiday since you and Mr. Davis left the Govt.,' one correspondent wrote. Gardiner blamed the situation on the apathy of the provincial party in the face of the impressive growth of the CCF: that party's 'supporters had principles they believed in and on which they would not compromise, and they volunteered their abundant energies to convince the voters that these principles were sound. In other words they acted the way Gardiner thought Liberals should act.'[67]

As the war dragged on, Ottawa's interventionist policies and multitude of wartime regulations continued to hinder party prospects. The wheat pools had turned against the Liberals, and the CCF was taking full advantage of the situation. As the government lost by-elections in Saskatchewan, such as the one in Humboldt in 1943, Gardiner noted that the party was apathetic, while the CCF was 'coming of age.' He was disgusted when local Liberals actually joined the criticism of federal policies. The machine that Gardiner had spent decades tuning was no longer running smoothly.[68] Personally, although the minister of agriculture shared the public concern about price controls and wage freezes, he viewed such measures as necessary. Ultimately he would stand by his party and leader. In so doing, he would become part of the 'government party' that was rapidly losing ground in his region.

The seriousness of the situation reached new heights in the provincial election of 15 June 1944, when the CCF stormed Saskatchewan with forty-seven of fifty-two seats and two-thirds of the overseas vote. As Granatstein puts it, the result was 'enough to frighten even the sturdiest of Liberals.' Indeed, R.J. Deachman noted that the campaign had a particularly 'disturbing' element to it. The Liberals finally realized that the CCF popularity was no temporary upsurge that would just as quickly disappear.[69]

Because they had expected Gardiner's forces to withstand the CCF assault, federal Liberals were left reeling and groping for answers in the aftermath. Even though he was in Ottawa, it was generally conceded that the federal minister maintained control of the provincial organization. All Gardiner could do, however, was attribute the defeat to Liberal apathy. The party had done 'nothing between elections' and never went 'near the public.' The Liberals were now perceived as the defender of big business and no longer concerned with the common people. Gardiner claimed that the Patterson government had 'proved worse than useless as an ally' and had not aided his efforts at organization.[70] Members of the provincial party, meanwhile, were not prepared to sit idly by while all the blame was thrust on their shoulders. 'For once I think that even Mr. Gardiner's analysis leaves much to be desired,' J.E. Doerr informed King. The Liberal machine that ran both provincial and federal parties had become old and the demand for change overwhelming. The candidates were the same men who had appeared 'time and time again' before the electorate throughout the past thirty-four years. There were few openings and opportunities for new blood, and this had 'dampened the enthusiasm of other ambitious men.' As a result, Patterson's government had 'lost touch with the people.' Filled with 'autocrats,' it was held 'in contempt' by the public.[71] Any connection with the federal party only made matters worse. The CCF had even won the Prince Albert provincial riding.[72]

There can be little doubt that the war hampered the traditional power of the Liberal organization in Saskatchewan. Control of patronage was largely lost to Gardiner as the wartime agencies assumed additional responsibilities and created a new bureaucracy. Contracts were removed from the influence of the old party organization. Decisions were made quickly without attention to the Liberal establishment. The result was the appearance 'almost overnight, of an autonomous organizational structure immune and often insensitive to the effect of its policies on intricate and mature party relations.'[73] It was, however, the impressiveness of the CCF organization that spelled the defeat for the provincial Liberals in 1944. In many ways the CCF learned the tricks of the trade from the long-entrenched Liberals and simply beat them at their own game. Yet the CCF was more than a formidable organization – it was a new party with a new ideology to offer the Saskatchewan electorate. The emergence of a socialist alternative sent the Liberal party into the wilderness in search of its own roots. For years the party had stood as the reform option in the province. The Liberals prided themselves on being the defender of the farmer against the interests, the common man against big business. Now, the party had tackled the CCF head on, had based its campaign on attacking socialism. Yet clearly the electorate was unconvinced by Liberal onslaughts against the evils of the socialist and communist bogey. Indeed, 'the heedless way the Liberals campaigned against the CCF ...

indicated their loss of touch with public opinion.' Whereas the federal party moved to steal the CCF thunder, the Saskatchewan Liberals stood in opposition, and there they would remain for many years. Furthermore, Liberal candidates were older than previously, and fewer of them were farmers.[74] Party losses were not confined to the rural areas, however, but spread dramatically to the cities as the CCF became the champions of the Labour movement.

Mackenzie King claimed not to be surprised by the defeat. He blamed Hepburn's record in Ontario and the rise of the CCF in that province for providing the movement an impetus in Saskatchewan. Patterson was also the subject of scrutiny because he had added to the dilemma by 'unduly' prolonging his term in office. He was 'heavy, lethargic and less idealistic' than the CCF leader, Tommy Douglas, who was 'a man of high ideals ... a better leader in the minds of the rural people.'[75] The Liberal party in the province had lost its 'active leadership,' had 'gone a little to seed.' Inevitably, King's wrath also came down on Gardiner for losing his hold and being viewed 'too much as a machine politician.' When the cabinet discussed the results, and some of the blame was aimed at federal policies, King protested by defending his record on Prairie issues. The government was advancing the agricultural industry by negotiating reciprocal trade agreements with the United States.[76]

If the Saskatchewan defeat spelled trouble for the Liberals, it was 'a major catastrophe' for the Progressive Conservatives. The attempt to refashion Tory hopes around the choice of Bracken as leader was obviously failing.[77] The election made it clear that, while the Saskatchewan populace wanted change, they did not want the Progressive Conservative party. The eastern interests who had pushed Bracken into the leadership on the belief he would carry the Prairies 'must be feeling rather blue,' Crerar noted.[78]

King tried to convince himself that the CCF winning the Prince Albert provincial seat did not 'concern' federal politics.[79] At the dinner celebrating his twenty-fifth anniversary as leader, the prime minister stated his intention to run again in his constituency of Prince Albert after the war.[80] Nonetheless, the Saskatchewan results became the final straw for many federal Liberals who felt the time had come for the prime minister to abandon his western riding. There seemed no need for the captain to go down with the sinking ship, and on 13 July 1944 Gardiner was approached by some of his colleagues to persuade King to run in the riding of Ottawa East. But Mackenzie King's sentimental attachment to the constituency had become remarkably strong. He told Gardiner that

Prince Albert had offered its seat at a time of need and had returned him on many occasions. The executive, free to choose a local candidate, had always remained faithful. He would now return that loyalty, win or lose.[81]

Despite the prime minister's determination, reports from the riding executive became increasingly negative. The CCF's powerful organization was in full operation throughout the province. If an election were held in 1944, the situation in Prince Albert would be 'hopeless.' King was again requested to visit the constituency to bolster his own prospects. Almost out of habit, he provided his usual apologies for having to decline. Senator Stevenson was now equally pessimistic. During three weeks spent travelling throughout the riding, he had not met a single person who believed King could be re-elected: 'There is a terrible change in the West and now with the C.C.F. in power in Sask. they are all up on their toes and rearing to go ... I would strongly advise you to take a seat in Prince Edward Island as this is rotten here and I am afraid cannot be saved ... I am sorry to have to report this but I am telling you exactly how I find things and I want to see you run in a sure seat as it would be a calamity for the country if you were defeated ... to say the least the situation here looks dark.'[82] Regardless, King remained determined to run in Prince Albert, 'come what may.' Privately, he complained about the situation and placed most of the blame on local organizers. He pointed to reports that members of the executive had been profiting from war contracts.[83] At a time when he was obliged to sacrifice all his time to winning the war and could not 'cultivate' his own political interests, others were profiting from personal greed. If his constituency could not be looked after by others, he sulked, then he would just have to face defeat. The party would have to deal with the consequences, because such a defeat would certainly mean his retirement from politics.[84]

Some signs of optimism were now at least emerging from Manitoba. Crerar's most recent report on Liberal prospects was certainly more hopeful than the previous year's. The only problem was that the improved situation was resulting more from PC and CCF losses than Liberal gains. It would, as a result, be temporary. Bracken's personal prestige had 'distinctly waned,' and the fact that he was not yet holding a seat in Parliament was lessening his impact as Progressive-Conservative leader. The CCF success in Saskatchewan was attracting considerable notice, but its failures in Alberta, Quebec, and New Brunswick had set the movement back. King pushed for a changing of the guard in Manitoba. Convinced that Crerar's 'political usefulness' was 'completely gone,' he believed that the province would need new representation. The prime minister was resentful that the Manitoba minister had not offered more support during the conscription crisis. Although he had sided with King in 1942, he had reluctantly opposed him in 1944. This stance would almost cost him a promised Senate appointment. King believed that Crerar was 'quite unpopular' with the Manitoba members and no longer wielded any 'real influence.' The minister's 'set of friends' belonged 'to a past generation.'[85] In fact, most of them were dead.

By February 1945, when King decided that Crerar would 'have to be dropped,' the minister had already indicated that he did not wish to run again. Federal Liberal hopes in Manitoba were coming to centre on a new generation of provincial party members. Bracken had been replaced at the head of the provincial government by Stuart Garson, and his coalition again won power in the election of 1945, capturing forty-three of fifty-five seats. Since Bracken's exit, Crerar had been attempting to convince the new premier – a known Liberal – to abandon the coalition label and make the government a straight Liberal ticket. Much to Crerar's chagrin, Garson maintained the 'non-partisan' nature of the coalition by indicating that it would not involve itself with either federal party.[86] Mackenzie King, meanwhile, was eyeing Garson for his cabinet. The problem was convincing him to join. The premier felt he could make a 'larger and better contribution' by remaining in his position. In leaving Manitoba he would be accused of being a 'time server.' Moreover, the example of Bracken provided no incentive to abandon the secure office of premier. He had 'fallen heir' to a 'legacy' of coalition government, and any move to break it would probably bring ruin to the Liberal party in the province.[87] If he was in any doubt, the state of Liberal popularity in the West sealed the premier's decision.

In Alberta, party officials were again petitioning the prime minister for federal aid and, in particular, the help of federal cabinet ministers. Social Credit had campaigned against the abuses of capitalism and was now maintaining office against the threat of socialism. The struggle for actual Social Credit policies had all but disappeared with the death of Aberhart in 1943. The deeply etched sentiments of western alienation remained, but, given the socialist challenge, the Alberta business community was now convinced that Premier Ernest Manning was on its side. For Social Credit, the CCF calls for increased government ownership and control simply led the party to be hurled into the same pit as the evil financiers of central Canada. The Liberal party did not know where to turn. King offered no solutions, but one thing was clear – Alberta could not turn to Ottawa.

The long-delayed federal election was to be held immediately following the conclusion of the war in Europe. The theme of the campaign
would be that Mackenzie King was the only man with sufficient experience to lead the nation through the troubled times ahead.[88] Although it
was remarkably reminiscent of previous campaign themes, it seemed
logical to expect the victory in Europe to provide the Liberals with a
substantial boost. Other party notables were not so sure. Chubby Power
was convinced an election had to be held prior to war's end while the
attention of the populace remained riveted to the task at hand. Angus
Macdonald agreed that Liberal prospects were dim and that the service
vote would reject Mackenzie King for the lack of support given the
military.[89] The twin pillars of Liberal support – Quebec and Saskatchewan – were crumbling, and organization through the National Liberal
Federation had come to naught. The prime minister was more optimistic
that the stock of the government was increasing. Its war record certainly
seemed commendable. Wartime restrictions had caused damage, but the
populace was now looking to reconstruction policies, and the move into
the realm of social services was proving successful. Prairie Liberals,
however, were not so certain that it would be enough to salvage the party
in their region: 'People seldom vote out of gratitude. Therefore, although the war record does not condemn the present Government,
neither does it assure their [sic] re-election. The war record if it were bad
could alone defeat them – but being good it *alone cannot* re-elect them.'[90]

If Mackenzie King were confident about victory at the polls in 1945, he
was uncertain about the West and anxious about his own seat. With
reports from Senator Stevenson indicated that there was 'no hope of
winning,' King now admitted it was probably 'inadvisable' to 'court
defeat.' He began to prepare justifications in the event that he abandoned the riding. His endangered position would assuredly be employed
as a campaign issue, and the Conservatives would ask the electorate
whether it wished to support a party with a defeated leader. 'The outside
world,' King wrote, 'might never understand my being beaten by thousands possibly in Prince Albert ... It would hardly be a fitting close to my
career.' Defeat would also deny the prime minister the opportunity to
deal with postwar reconstruction. Given these considerations, he now
indicated that 'it would be better that I should run in some other
constituency.' He considered the riding of Prince in Prince Edward
Island, the constituency he had briefly represented in 1919. The riding of
North Waterloo, Ontario, where he had first been elected, was attractive,
but so many years had passed that his ties to the area had been severed.

Russell County and Ottawa East were other Ontario ridings that posed possibilities, and their locations would eliminate the same criticism that he had faced in Prince Albert about not representing a riding where he was a resident. Still, the nagging guilt of abandoning Prince Albert, the only constituency King could ever really call his own, was troubling.[91]

King, aware that the chances in Prince Albert were remote, hoped that, if he contested the riding, the situation would improve during the campaign. The jubilance of victory in the war could provide the necessary boost in his popularity, and early in the year reports indicated that the situation was indeed improving. Gains were being made in the northern part of the constituency, while prospects in the south were at least looking brighter. Although the urban areas would have to improve, it seemed some headway was being made. It was now reported that King could be re-elected, as long as the Conservatives nominated a candidate and the anti-government vote was split.[92] Gardiner, urged by his eastern colleagues to convince King to seek election elsewhere, personally wished to see the prime minister contest the Saskatchewan seat. Liberal fortunes in the West, and the province in particular, were in dire straits and bailing out could prove the deathblow. With King still considering running, Gardiner informed his chief that success was indeed attainable. The prime minister was pleased by the vote of confidence and troubled that many of his other ministers did not seem as concerned with his possible defeat. MacKinnon, 'no doubt like others, took it for granted that I might be defeated in P.A., but would find a constituency elsewhere immediately after. I told him on no consideration would I seek a seat elsewhere if I were defeated; that would mark the completion of my life in Parliament.'[93]

On 17 February Stevenson provided an update. Admitting that he had earlier found the situation 'hopeless,' the senator noted that, with the organization up and running, the momentum seemed to be rolling King's way. The people were already beginning to find dissatisfaction with the provincial CCF government. Such discontent, however, would not be enough. The Tories would almost certainly combine with the CCF in an attempt to defeat the prime minister. Stevenson advised him to run in Russell and not risk personal defeat.[94] On 21 March 1945 Mackenzie King met with the president of the Prince Albert Liberal organization as well as Senator Stevenson. M.I. Humphries explained that, despite a brighter outlook, there were still real possibilities of defeat. The rural vote seemed to be swinging back toward the Liberals, but the urban vote was solidly CCF. The CCF candidate had a long-standing reputation among the local farming community and, with the aid of the provincial organization, he was playing on the impatience of the working classes toward federal wartime wage controls as well as the CCF promises of social security, medical care, and a national housing plan.[95] The 'foreign' vote in the city was also solidly CCF. Humphries indicated that if the prime minister could just spend a few days in his riding, 'they would feel very sure' of victory. This, King explained, was 'out of the question.' He would be out of the country for almost a month attending a meeting of the United Nations in San Francisco. Not only would there be no possibility of attending the nomination meeting, he would be able to make no more than one speech in the constituency throughout the campaign.[96]

With the Liberal cabinet and caucus pushing the prime minister to change ridings, the time had come to make a final decision. The desperate Saskatchewan members pleaded with him to remain and fight for the party in what had always been the Prairie stronghold. If Prince Albert were abandoned, wrote Wilfrid Gardiner, Jimmy Gardiner's son, 'the death blow would be signed for the present and also perhaps for the future ... Half my faith in the Liberal Party would go if I felt the Leader would forsake those who have helped him in the past for the province of Ontario which has continually knifed him in the back.' But T.H. Wood advised King to run in Ontario because the Prince Albert situation looked too uncertain. A poll done in 1944 indicated that the Liberals would receive 900 fewer votes in the city of Prince Albert than in 1940. King's 1940 majority in the entire constituency had been only 750 votes.[97]

At the beginning of April Mackenzie King indicated that he had decided not to run for re-election in Prince Albert and that he was prepared to accept the nomination for Russell.[98] He discussed his decision in a gathering of Liberal members. Led by Walter Tucker, who made what King described as a 'passionate, powerful and deeply moving speech,' the Saskatchewan members pleaded to have the prime minister reconsider. They argued that the Tories would accuse him of being 'afraid to run in Saskatchewan' and of abandoning the West. King admitted to feeling 'a real physical pain in my heart at the thought of severing a connection with a constituency of which I had been the member for nearly 19 years.' The meeting had a considerable impact – by its close he had again changed his mind. 'In the light of what had been said ... it was quite clear that I should not leave P.A. ... The Tories would make the most of my leaving the West as a sign of lessening the party's chances there.' King's desperate desire for a sense of belonging outweighed even his fear of personal defeat. Reached by phone, an elated Humphries was informed of the decision. He felt there would be a battle but believed victory was possible.

The prime minister could now relax a little. The decision was no longer weighing on his mind; the course had been set. He congratulated himself on his resiliency: 'It ought to put the metal into the men who will be responsible for my running in P.A. ... I believe my readiness to run in Saskatchewan will help the party tremendously and certainly the public will appreciate it. If I am defeated there will be pretty much a tremendous revulsion of feeling against defeating a P.M. who has been as faithful to his task and carried the country through the war as I have these last 5 or 6 years.'[99] On 7 May the riding executive was informed that Mackenzie King would allow his name to go before the nominating convention.[100] The decision would, he told himself, 'cause the people there to respond to what is a chivalrous attitude toward the constituency and the faith that I have in them.'[101]

Nonetheless, King's anxieties continued throughout the campaign. When the trip to San Francisco seemed to end any possibility of even visiting the riding, his concerns reappeared. Early on he had claimed that going to Prince Albert 'was my last hope and last straw for success there.' Failure to do so would 'almost certainly ... mean that I could not be elected.' King's optimism increased again, however, with the conclusion of the war in Europe. 'I have felt today for the first time that I might win,' he recorded on 5 May. 'Tonight I believe I shall win that constituency. This victory in Europe is going to help immensely in the campaign.' He did manage to visit the riding briefly and make one speech. His CCF opponent, E.L. Bowerman, did not seem to be a strong candidate, especially when contrasted to King and his wealth of experience: 'I find ... that the people have been following my work and career with interest and that they have in mind the service that I have rendered during the period of the war. Indeed there has been nothing seen or heard today which makes me feel that there is not a decidedly friendly feeling toward myself, and a certain sense of pride in my representation of the constituency.'[102]

In the general election of 11 June 1945, Mackenzie King believed the Liberals would make some gains in Alberta, maintain their position in Saskatchewan, and lose perhaps a couple of seats in Manitoba.[103] He expected a majority and he received it, but only by the barest of margins. The Liberals won 127 seats, the Conservatives 68, the CCF 29, and the Social Credit 13. The Liberals won 41.3 per cent of the popular vote, the Conservatives 28.5, and the CCF 14.7. If the prime minister were surprised by the small majority, he was dumbfounded by the outcome on the Prairies. The frustration aimed at wartime constraints, the uncertainty of postwar reconstruction, and the discontent over conscription all affected the western vote, but the gulf that was growing between the Liberal party and region could not be disguised. The party held on to nineteen seats, a drop of twenty-five. Nowhere was the slide more obvious than in Saskatchewan. Andrew McNaughton was defeated in Qu'Appelle, and Gardiner barely salvaged his seat by a slim margin of twenty-eight votes.[104] The Liberals lost ten of their twelve seats, while the CCF won eighteen. King, admitting that the Saskatchewan results were a 'mystery,' was completely taken aback by 'so general a defeat.'[105] Gardiner, in particular, would suffer 'sustained permanent injury to his political reputation and prowess.'[106] Although the prime minister would blame poor organization for the Prairie situation, those who had worked the region offered a more alarming prognosis.[107] 'It would be easy to say that better organization and a little more work would have changed the result,' one Manitoba Liberal observed. 'I do not believe that this is true ... I think we polled all the support we had.'[108] Despite holding on to ten of seventeen Liberal seats in Manitoba, King was furious that Garson and the Liberal members of his provincial government had not identified themselves openly with the federal party. In Alberta, MacKinnon and one other Liberal retained their seats. Except for MacKinnon's efforts, King admitted, 'the province has been left alone.'[109]

As was so often the case, the situation facing Mackenzie King in the West was mirrored in the Prince Albert constituency. On election night, learning that the CCF was leading, the prime minister was prepared to face defeat: 'When I really felt I was defeated, I felt a little outbreak of perspiration for the moment, but that was hardly noticeable and soon passed away. It was like a tiny shock.' Humphries phoned later to report that King was leading by 300 to 500 votes. However, the military results had yet to come in, and the CCF was waiting for them before conceding defeat. King felt 'fairly well assured of having been returned.' The soldier vote would not be known for at least a week. In the meantime, he tried to convince himself that, after winning the constituency, he could not possibly lose to the service vote. Obviously he hoped the bitterness of the conscription crisis had been lost amid the victory celebrations: 'It is literally true that no man in Canada has done more or as much for members of the service as I have. This is the irony of the situation.'[110]

On 19 June the prime minister was informed that he had been defeated. His majority of 263 votes in the civilian canvas was not the equal of the CCF majority in the service vote – E.L. Bowerman had a majority of 129. King used the war to rationalize the defeat: 'Throughout the period of the last Parliament, my time was given unreservedly to the work of government – to the problems of war, to preparation for the period of transition from war to peace and to the meeting of postwar problems ... I was not seeking to win elections at a time when I regarded the winning of the war as the first duty of every citizen, myself most of all. This made it impossible for me to be in the constituency on more than one or two occasions in the course of the past five years.' He comforted himself that his near victory was remarkable in light of the general defeat in Saskatchewan. In thanking the executive for the hard-fought battle and the years of service, King indicated that he wished to make it out to Prince Albert to thank his organizers personally. The severance with the constituency, he promised, would prove 'more apparent than real.' The truth, however, was not long in coming. When the prime minister was invited to open the Prince Albert Fair, he declined due to other obligations.[111] He became the member for Glengarry, Ontario.

The contest of 1945 would be the last general election Mackenzie King would fight. For the next several years Jimmy Gardiner continued his role as Prairie lieutenant and attempted to 'recoup the losses.' Yet all the signs indicated that the Liberal party would not soon regain strength in the West. Gardiner combed the province for potential candidates; few emerged. In 1946 W.J. Patterson stepped down as provincial leader in Saskatchewan. The ensuing contest for the leadership between E.M. Culliton and Walter Tucker demonstrated that relations between Ottawa and Regina were becoming strained. Tucker was viewed as more of a 'reforming' Liberal, and therefore perhaps more fit to meet the CCF challenge. However, he was also perceived as a 'Gardiner man,' and 'an unprecedented hostility toward Ottawa pervaded the provincial party's deliberations.'[112] Although Tucker was ultimately chosen as leader, Gardiner's efforts were now unwelcome, even in Saskatchewan. Over the next several years the provincial party became increasingly opposed to his control of federal patronage positions. By the summer of 1947, he was perceived by many as a political liability. The foundations of the Liberal fortress had collapsed completely. Tucker was even anxious to prevent Gardiner from making one of his partisan speeches at a provincial convention because he did not want it to appear that the minister of agriculture was directing policy. According to Ralph Maybank, 'everybody without any exception whatever in the party in Saskatchewan is dead against Gardiner.'[113] King confessed to reading reports about the

Saskatchewan situation 'with feelings of dismay.' He had not realized that
Liberal fortunes were at 'so low an ebb.' The party's situation, he noted,
was 'really tragic.'[114]

In the Saskatchewan provincial election of 1948 the Liberals could not
ignore their federal counterparts. Their internal weaknesses forced them
into a position where they were 'totally dependent upon Ottawa for
assistance.'[115] The dependency provided the CCF with ample ammunition that the party was the puppet of Jimmy Gardiner. To make matters
worse, when the coalition issue emerged regarding joint Liberal-Progressive candidates, Gardiner's traditional stand was opposed by Walter
Tucker. The provincial party had little choice, however, and followed the
federal directive opposing coalition. The result, Tucker claimed, 'may
have defeated the Liberals in 1948.'[116] When the votes were counted the
Liberals increased their representation from five to nineteen seats, but
their popular vote fell to an all-time low of 31 per cent. The CCF
maintained power and took advantage of the reappearing breach between the federal and provincial Liberals. The traditional Liberal base in
the province – small businessmen and independent farmers as well as the
ethnic groups – had been completely undercut by the CCF. In the
meantime the Liberals had become associated with an unsympathetic
government in Ottawa. The minister of agriculture was at least pleased
with the increase in seats, and King believed the result had 'put a militant
spirit into the Party of which it has been in great need.'[117] The federal
election of 1949 seemed to heighten the possibility of a Liberal resurgence in the province. The party won fourteen seats and its popular vote
climbed to 44 per cent, the highest since 1930. It was, however, just a lull
in the storm and 'marked the end, not the beginning.' As David Smith
has noted, 'the political world Gardiner had controlled for so long was
about to change and would pass from view in the fifties.'[118]

Such was also the case in cabinet, where the Prairie lieutenant's influence and reputation underwent even further decline. While he continued to formulate wheat policy, the breach between the West and the
Liberal party was glaring.[119] During the war Gardiner had been successful in contractual negotiations with the British Ministry of Food, and he
saw no reason why similar contracts could not be negotiated for wheat. A
Canada–United Kingdom Wheat Contract was pursued in the summer of
1946, with Gardiner aggressively leading the way. He believed that the
trend during the war for negotiations to be conducted on the basis of
'gentlemen's agreements' could continue. With MacKinnon's acquies-
cence, Gardiner had exploratory talks with the British on the subject of a

wheat deal before seeking authority from cabinet. He even broke away from his usual precedent of discussing wheat policy initiatives with the western farm producers.[120] Gardiner took matters almost completely into his own hands. A four-year contract was negotiated that would see a fixed price for wheat set at $1.55 for the first two years, along with floor prices of $1.25 and $1.00 for the third and fourth years. Opposition began to develop over the contract's implicit assumption that wheat prices would fall in the next several years. Tying Canadian wheat exports to the British market, the deal also flew in the face of planned agreements with the United States.

On 19 June 1946 King claimed that, while the contract offered stability to Canadian farmers, it contained 'elements which are in the nature of a great gamble.' It could also 'destroy' opportunities to pursue freer trade with the United States and the establishment of 'an ultimate world price of wheat.' Amid reservations, the prime minister confessed that Gardiner had proceeded in such an arbitrary fashion that 'no one knows what he is saying.'[121] T.A. Crerar, who was in the Senate, also demonstrated his opposition to the deal.[122] Despite the opposition, the agreement was announced on 25 July. It would work in conjunction with a five-year pool. The debate over the contract continued to rage over the next four years, particularly between the pools and the grain exchange. In the end, it had to be admitted that the contract cost the government money when farmers were reimbursed because of the rising price of wheat on the international market. Gardiner always claimed in his defence that the British had not kept to the spirit of the agreement and that a 'have regard to' clause for the last two crop years should have ensured that they take into account any discrepancy between the world price and what they paid after 1945.[123] But the justification could not repair the damage done to his reputation. The fiasco was symptomatic of what had become the relationship between King's government and the farmers of western Canada. Ottawa had created a compulsory wheat board, albeit partly due to western pressure, but the result was that the federal government alone received all the Prairie criticism for any unfavourable wheat policy.

Early in 1947, after Gardiner learned that the Glengarry constituency might be eliminated in redistribution, he suggested that King again consider running in Prince Albert. The executive, he added, was 'anxious' for the prime minister to do so, and the constituency could be made 'perfectly secure.' King did not hesitate in responding: 'Nothing would induce me to run in Prince Albert again.' When M.I. Humphries asked him to use his influence for an increase in the number of customs offices, an enlargement of public buildings, and the construction of a dam and bridge in Prince Albert, the response was equally revealing: 'I pointed out to him, I could hardly be expected to help to further the riding when it had defeated me but indicated I was not letting that influence my judgement.' King promised to do what he could but his lack of interest in the affairs of his old riding was all too apparent.[124]

Mackenzie King's final dealings with Manitoba were indicative of the frustration he felt over the way the West was responding to his government and leadership. Organization continued to receive blame for much of the problem, and he did not see how it would be rectified when there were no younger Liberals emerging to lead the way. 'None of the young Liberals are prepared to put time or money into an organization or to seek to find the latter,' he observed. 'The older Liberals have lost or are losing their interest in the future of the party.' Stuart Garson, an obvious candidate to lead party efforts in Manitoba, as well as to become the representative in Ottawa, was in no hurry to break his coalition and enter a government that was not strong in the region. Federal by-elections in the West were not encouraging. 'It makes me sad to see the Liberal party begin to disintegrate,' Mackenzie King mourned. In December 1946 he again approached Garson to enter the cabinet but was refused.[125] It was not until November 1948, after King had retired, that Garson would enter the federal cabinet as minister of justice. According to Maybank, the premier's move to the federal field 'would turn out to be a distinct disadvantage' because the provincial Liberals would suffer for abandoning the popular tradition of non-partisanship established by Bracken.[126] The appointment, however, would have little overall impact on federal party fortunes in the region. King's party, with or without Garson, had little western appeal.

The efforts continued in Alberta to have the federal party aid Liberalism in the province. A brief postwar revival was led by J. Harper Prowse, who was selected leader of the party in 1947. Like his predecessors, Prowse and his small caucus worked to promote cooperation with Ottawa. Organizational work was carried on 'simultaneously' on the basis that the two levels were not 'severable.' Any separation, it was argued, would be a confession of a lack of support and confidence. At first, J.A. MacKinnon responded to the renewed efforts with enthusiasm. Prowse, along with the provincial party president, John Stambaugh, were regularly consulted on patronage matters, so as to provide the Liberals in Alberta with a reward and incentive system. By 1950 these cooperative efforts, like all the others, had collapsed. MacKinnon's successor as

Alberta spokesman in cabinet was George Prudham, who became minister of mines and technical services. The federal minister as well as the government in Ottawa were seen by provincial Liberals as too friendly with the oil industry, which for its part was perceived as too friendly with the Social Credit government of Ernest Manning. In Ottawa federal party members complained that their provincial counterparts were embarrassing some very large and influential investors through their opposition to the Manning government. In the years after 1950, the division increased, and the old complaint surfaced that federal Liberals were 'on stilts, above and beyond the provincial organization.'[127]

After much delay, Mackenzie King announced a leadership convention for August and his retirement for mid-November 1948. With Louis St Laurent, the 'unofficial' hand-picked successor, the party tradition of alternating between anglophone and francophone leaders was to be honoured. Yet St Laurent was not an enthusiastic candidate. According to Grant Dexter he was being carried along on the enthusiasm of Quebec, after the prime minister had 'practically told those people that St. Laurent was the natural man to succeed him.'[128] King was angered when he learned that Gardiner intended to contest the leadership. In King's view the minister of agriculture was 'an outsider, a man from the hinterlands in a party which ... never had a leader from outside central Canada.'[129] Aware that Gardiner coveted the office, King swore 'he will never be P.M.' When Dexter reported that Gardiner had threatened to make it difficult for anyone to stand in the way of his winning the leadership, King became even more adamant: 'It is amazing to me that any man should be working toward securing the position of leadership for himself. I doubt if Gardiner would ever get the support of the Party.' He agreed with his eastern colleagues that the Saskatchewan politician did not have the necessary 'sort of presence and manner' and that he was 'too autocratic.'[130] A strategy was developed to have a number of leading cabinet ministers, including Howe, Abbott, Claxton, Martin, Chevrier, and Garson, enter the contest and then withdraw while making known their support for St Laurent.[131]

Throughout the leadership campaign Mackenzie King maintained the stance that he was neutral and would play no role in choosing a successor. Never believing that Gardiner would carry the convention, he nonetheless worried that he might create 'serious division in the ranks of the Party.'[132] Gardiner's organizational skills and ambitious drive did cause some in the party hierarchy to consider him a threat.[133] It was estimated that MacKinnon would deliver the Alberta delegates. Manitoba would support mainly St Laurent (although Crerar would second Chubby Power's nomination) but other prominent Liberals from the province would deliver some following to the agriculture minister. Saskatchewan would go solidly Gardiner. In the Maritimes, Gardiner would place second behind Ilsley, the most popular Liberal in the region, while some sections of Ontario would also support him. Quebec would be solidly for St Laurent and British Columbia would give half its support to Gardiner. Not wanting to start 'a war' in Saskatchewan, Walter Tucker would support Gardiner. Tucker admitted that the agriculture minister had treated him poorly in the past and that only St Laurent could hold a national government together. When Colin Campbell came out for Gardiner, King claimed it was 'the same combination that some years ago met with Hepburn to which Gardiner was a party and were going to try to oust me. A machine group.' Such 'an exceedingly dangerous' prospect was conveniently enough to force him into making his support for St Laurent known: 'It would be difficult for me if matters got too far to refrain from letting the party know for whom I stand ... The interest of the country may demand a final word. I am letting it be known through other sources just how I feel about the importance of St. Laurent being chosen.'[134] Gardiner's appeal to the delegates at the convention led King to break his own rule of 'neutrality,' and he voted on the first ballot in full view of the press.[135]

The Second World War had renewed the Canadian obsession with French–English relations. Despite Gardiner's attempt to challenge what King considered party orthodoxy – that the leadership alternate between French and English candidates – the domination of central Canada won out. The Prairie West was neither 'populous nor powerful enough' to pose a serious challenge to the 'entrenched might' of Quebec and Ontario.[136] Louis St Laurent was selected as leader of the Liberal party on the first ballot with 848 votes, while Gardiner received 323 and Power 56. As Norman Ward and David Smith acerbically note, 'Thus Gardiner learned at first hand what the statistics of the Department of Agriculture had revealed for some time: there were more Canadians who were not farmers than who were.'[137] King admitted that 'the fact that the West is so strongly Gardiner will operate against him in the other provinces.' When speaking to the delegates, the prime minister had difficulty even alluding to the strength Gardiner had always brought to the party. In a spirit of vindictiveness strong even for Mackenzie King, he recorded that 'somehow or another something kept saying to me he had been really shameful in his whole behaviour. I did not think there was any need to mention his name at this time. I thought he quite deserved the lesson he was getting.'[138]

The 1948 leadership convention was supposed to make some form of recommendation to restore Liberal organization across the nation, but 'like most of the proceedings of the convention it then disappeared from history.'[139] The leadership contest, David Smith asserts, not only limited Gardiner's political fortunes; with the choice of St Laurent, it 'adversely affected Liberal sympathies in the west.'[140] King had told St Laurent 'that unless there was some evidence of radicalism from our party in Western Canada we would lose the whole West.'[141] The words were token advice, and King knew there was little chance of the already elderly 'Uncle Louis' responding to the challenge. The party would continue the trends of the previous decade. The shift that had been gradually occurring for decades was now evident in the details. Gardiner was consulted on little of the reconstruction work centred on dominion–provincial relations. When a shuffling of office space took place on Parliament Hill, agriculture was moved from the hub of administration. It was indicative of the department's 'displacement in the galaxy of federal portfolios.'[142]

Jimmy Gardiner returned to his post as minister of agriculture in St Laurent's new government and to his political base in Saskatchewan. But the two men never really got along. In the federal election of 27 June 1949 the Liberals won a resounding victory and the Prairies fell in line with the national trend by returning thirty-one of fifty-three seats. The situation, however, was becoming increasingly clear. As Ward and Smith note, 'The decline of the Liberals in Saskatchewan presaged ... a decline of national Liberalism even if the federal party continued to win a majority of the seats in Parliament.' The fact that Gardiner was forced increasingly into the role of Prairie defender in these years demonstrated the continuing shift in government sympathies. He was viewed as a machine politician and, as such, an anachronism by those in his own party. His battle for the Saskatchewan dam in the 1950s demonstrated this shrinking sympathy as well as the declining influence of the region and its arch-defender. Gardiner had always maintained his faith that at least with Mackenzie King in office, great western development schemes were possible. With St Laurent, however, there was 'not the same understanding of western needs.'[143] The prime minister became wary when both the minister of agriculture and Tommy Douglas's CCF provincial government were pushing for the dam. The irony in having Gardiner and the socialists lumped together merely highlighted the growing antagonism between the Liberal government in Ottawa and the region. 'Ultimately, without the support of the national leader ... the Liberals coasted into decline in the west.'[144]

Gardiner, who feared political indifference toward the West on behalf of the federal party, saw an equally dangerous sentiment in Saskatchewan. A concern with constituency rather than party matters was replacing the partisan enthusiasm where it had once been strongest. The party system no longer functioned with grass-roots organization, partisan press, and acknowledged patronage. Revolutions in communication and transportation were altering political campaigning just as they were transforming farming. The federal and provincial organizations would no longer cooperate. The quagmire of leadership that had long plagued the Alberta and Manitoba parties was appearing in Saskatchewan by 1952. The federal minister of agriculture moved to influence the provincial leadership selection in 1954, but this time he did not get his way.[145] In the last decade of his career, even Gardiner's supremacy in organizational matters was seriously challenged.[146]

Mackenzie King would not live to see the final collapse of the Liberal party in the Prairie West. He died on 22 July 1950. Although St Laurent kept the party in office until 1957, the transition of power to 'Uncle Louis' was reflective of the 'Government Party' that had become complacent in office. The Prairie West, traditionally viewed as a Liberal region, was the first to abandon the party. 'How long and by what means,' David Smith asks, 'could the Liberals keep the farmers' allegiance, once the party had signalled a shift in interest away from its agrarian base outside of central Canada?'[147] In essence, he answers the question: 'If central Canadians were united on a position, prairie Liberals must inevitably lose.'[148] Ironically it would be King's long-standing opponent in Prince Albert, John Diefenbaker, who would orchestrate a Conservative revival in the West and, as the 'Prairie native son,' sweep the Liberals from office in 1957.

Conclusion

It has been argued that 'the Diefenbaker transformation of the electoral map in 1957–8 had a much more deadly effect upon the Liberals in the West than in any other region of the country.'[1] While this was undoubtedly the case, the decline of Prairie Liberalism began long before the election of 1957 or the selection of Louis St Laurent as leader in 1948. These events were merely the final stages in a process that had been ongoing at least since 1935 and, to a considerable extent, well before.

The demise of the Liberal party in the West occurred mainly in the Age of Mackenzie King. From the beginning of his career, King had worked to maintain party strength in what was traditionally perceived as a Liberal region. He failed. The primary cause was perhaps inevitable and far beyond the control of one politician or party: Canada was changing from a rural-agricultural to an urban-industrial nation. The accompanying transition of political influence from the Prairies to central Canada coincided with the entrenchment of the Liberals as the 'Government Party' in Ottawa. The new national Liberalism became increasingly less appetizing in a region that became increasingly alienated.

As the West diminished in national importance, so did the initial emphasis Mackenzie King placed on the region and therefore the sympathy he held for its concerns. In his later years, Jimmy Gardiner would remember King as a western sympathizer, but his view was tempered by nostalgia and a favourable comparison to Louis St Laurent and Lester Pearson. Prairie support was essential when King became party leader in 1919, and he became 'the spiritual westerner' to gain that support. It was then played off against Quebec to win the party national representation and King a stronger hold on the leadership. He worked to placate the region when its political influence was at its height, and succeeded in keeping it within Liberal reach just long enough for the Depression to force it back to the party in a desperate condition. King's perceptions of the Prairies inevitably proved idealistic and altered accordingly as time passed. His ignorance of western issues, and the entire region for that matter, gradually became obvious. 'Oddly enough,' Jack Pickersgill notes, 'for the aspiring leader of a country in which the main industry was still agriculture, King showed little interest and less understanding of the farming community, its grievances and its aspirations ... He never developed any ideas of his own about agricultural policy.' Pickersgill remembered a comment by R.J. Deachman that 'the reason the Chief never understood the farmers was that he had never known the feel of barnyard manure oozing up between the toes of his bare feet.'²

To hold power after 1926 the Liberal party had to bolster its strength in central Canada. The West became increasingly expendable. A weakened, less influential region would not receive the same attention – particularly set within the trend toward centralization necessitated by a depression and world war – and any remnants of Liberal strength would disappear. King returned to his favourite role as 'Laurier's successor' and, with another conscription crisis, to the necessity of placating Quebec. As the realities and necessities of governing a nation of diverse regions emerged, and the political influence of the West declined, Mackenzie King shed his western sympathies accordingly. The decline of Prairie Liberalism, therefore, paralleled the decline of the West in Canada.

King's handling of the region can be seen through several microcosms: his relationship to his Prince Albert constituency; his policies and attitudes toward the diverse array of western issues such as the tariff, freight rates, the Hudson Bay Railway, natural resources, and the wheat board; and his dealings with western leaders. They all demonstrate that after the threat of the agrarian revolt had passed, King's attention and sympathy were directed less to western concerns.

Perhaps more than anything else, a study of Mackenzie King and the Prairie West highlights the complex relationship between province and region. The three Prairie provinces shared political, economic, and social concerns, as well as a sense of regional alienation, but each also possessed its own distinct characteristics. These distinctions increased with time. A comparison of the Liberal parties in the Prairie provinces reveals what has been called a 'somewhat bewildering kaleidoscope of differences.'³ Mackenzie King never fully came to terms with this essential fact. Whereas the United Farmers would storm Alberta and Manitoba, they would never gain office in Saskatchewan. Yet even in that province the party had to adapt to changing conditions in order to survive. It did, and through the first half of the century Saskatchewan ranked second only to Quebec as the Liberal stronghold in the nation. But perhaps this, in itself, is revealing. It was questionable how long Mackenzie King and the party could appease such contrasting bases of support. Choices would have to be made, and the ramifications were inevitable. Saskatchewan would remain loyal to King and the Liberals until the alternative offered by Tommy Douglas and the CCF proved too alluring. With the collapse of Saskatchewan, Prairie Liberalism was doomed.

Manitoba, on the other hand, had a strong Liberal base, but internal division plagued the party. The breach of 1917 took decades to heal and remained a festering wound while the province was further divided between an urban group in Winnipeg and the various rural groups. Although King would be quite successful at absorbing Manitoba leadership into his cabinet and destroying federal Progressivism, coalitions and 'non-partisanship' would complicate the situation and prevent a Liberal breakthrough.

Alberta, meanwhile, could not have been more politically different from Saskatchewan. The story of the Liberal party in this province is dismal. Mackenzie King never gained any ground in Alberta, instead meeting with an unending series of failures. From the beginning of King's career the province refused to support the Liberals and was always prepared to show its resentment against the two traditional parties and its deep-rooted sense of western alienation by taking chances on radical alternatives such as the UFA and Social Credit. To make matters worse, the party was split by a rivalry between Edmonton and Calgary factions. King, who always placed the blame on local Liberals, was highly critical of party organization and leadership. He reacted by 'punishing' the province with inadequate cabinet representation. If the poor state of organization and leadership did merit the prime minister's criticism, the situation also reflected the failure of his strategy. The lack of Liberal advisors led King to be more ignorant of affairs in Alberta than those in either of the other two Prairie provinces. His attempts to treat it with the same strategy used in either Manitoba or Saskatchewan failed. Punishing Alberta, however, only served to further convince the province to send its support elsewhere.

The postwar era would witness the continuing, and even more rapid, destruction of the Liberal party on the Prairies, or what David Smith has called 'the regional decline of a national party.' An even greater insensi-

266 Mackenzie King and the Prairie West

tivity to western concerns along with increased moves toward centralization and an obsession with Quebec, the constitution, and separatism, further weakened Liberals' appeal to western voters. The individual provinces, distinct from party control in Ottawa, became the spokesmen for western discontent. The 1970s and the resource boom would point to a resurgence in western prosperity, but its effects would be much more long-standing in Alberta than in either Saskatchewan or Manitoba. The result, again, would highlight the provincial differences within the region. Regardless, there would be no resurrection of Prairie Liberalism.

Notes

Abbreviations

GAI   Glenbow Alberta Institute
NAC   National Archives of Canada
PAA   Provincial Archives of Alberta
PAM   Provincial Archives of Manitoba
QUA   Queen's University Archives
SAB   Saskatchewan Archives Board
UMA   University of Manitoba Archives
UML   University of Manitoba Libraries

Introduction

1 David Smith, *The Regional Decline of a National Party: Liberals on the Prairies* (Toronto, 1981)
2 David Smith, *Prairie Liberalism: The Liberal Party in Saskatchewan, 1905–1971* (Toronto, 1975), Smith *Regional Decline of a National Party*, and Norman Ward and David Smith, *Jimmy Gardiner: Relentless Liberal* (Toronto, 1990)

1: In Search of the New Jerusalem, 1874–1919

1 Gerald Friesen, *The Canadian Prairies: A History* (Toronto, 1987) 92
2 Ibid., 303
3 Douglas Owram, *Promise of Eden: The Canadian Expansionist Movement and the Idea of the West, 1856–1900* (Toronto, 1980) 5, 149, 165
4 Friesen, *Canadian Prairies*, 303
5 R. Douglas Francis, *Images of the West* (Saskatoon, 1989) 107

6 Gerald Friesen, 'Studies in the Development of Western Canadian Regional Consciousness, 1870–1925' (PhD diss., University of Toronto, 1973) 1; Journalists, novelists, and poets such as P.G. Laurie, Ralph Connor, Robert Stead, Robert C. Edwards, and J.W. Dafoe, for example, encouraged these images. For a full discussion see Friesen, 'Studies in the Development,' 109.

7 Stephen Leacock, preface to *My Discovery of the West: A Discussion of East and West in Canada* (Toronto, 1937)

8 The West was a 'liberal' frontier relative to the East, but was 'conservative' relative to the American frontier. This led to a 'duality of conservatism and reform' that came to characterize Prairie political thinking. Owram, *Promise of Eden*, 138, 144–5

9 Friesen, 'Studies in the Development,' 123

10 Owram, *Promise of Eden*, 219

11 *William Lyon Mackenzie King Diaries* (Toronto, 1973) 22 June 1895

12 Ramsay Cook, *The Regenerators: Social Criticism in Late Victorian English Canada* (Toronto, 1985) 169

13 Richard Allen, *The Social Passion: Religion and Social Reform in Canada, 1914–1928* (Toronto, 1973) 3

14 Friesen, *Canadian Prairies*, 351

15 King Diaries, 19 June 1898

16 Cook, *The Regenerators*, 211

17 King Diaries, 22 February 1900; 24 August 1897; 14 February 1898; 31 October 1911

18 Ibid., 28 April 1903

19 Ibid., 26 April 1903

20 Ibid., 13 January 1914

21 NAC, William Lyon Mackenzie King Papers, MG 26, J1, reel 1919, vol. 22, King to H.B. Cowan, 23 April 20268–9, 1914

22 King Diaries, 5 March 1899; 13 February 1904; 26 April 1903; 22 April 1907; 24 September 1897

23 William Lyon Mackenzie as quoted in E.K. Brown, 'Mackenzie King of Canada,' *Harper's* (January 1943) 193

24 J.W. Pickersgill, 'Mackenzie King's Political Attitudes and Public Policies: A Personal Impression,' in *Mackenzie King: Widening the Debate*, ed. John English and J.O. Stubbs (Toronto, 1978) 16

25 W.L.M. King, introduction to *Industry and Humanity* (Toronto, 1947) xviii–xix

26 King Papers, reel 1905, vol. 6, 5414–15, King to Walter Scott, 11 December 1906; reel 1906, 5609, W.G. Walker to King, 12 December 1906

27 R. MacGregor Dawson, *William Lyon Mackenzie King: A Political Biography, 1874–1923* (Toronto, 1958) 85

28 King, *Industry and Humanity*, 11
29 King Diaries, 11 July 1899; 23 January 1900; 27 January 1900; 11 July 1899; 12 July 1899
30 Friesen, *Canadian Prairies*, 221
31 W.L. Morton, *The Progressive Party in Canada* (Toronto, 1950) 1–4
32 King Diaries, 20 April 1922
33 Friesen, *Canadian Prairies*, 188
34 The debate was initially set out in such works as Vernon C. Fowke's *The National Policy and the Wheat Economy* (Toronto, 1957). More recently it has been the subject of debate among economic historians such as John Dales and Kenneth Norrie. See Dales, 'Some Historical and Theoretical Comment on Canada's National Policies,' in *Canadian History since Confederation*, ed. B. Hodgins and R. Page (Georgetown, ON 1972), and Norrie, 'The National Policy and the Rate of Prairie Settlement: A Review,' in *The Prairie West: Historical Readings*, ed. R. Douglas Francis and Howard Palmer (Edmonton, 1992).
35 Dawson argues that 'to Taussig must be given the credit for conforming and consolidating King's belief in the theory of free trade.' Dawson, *King*, 73
36 King Diaries, 13 December 1897; 22 April 1907
37 Friesen, *Canadian Prairies*, 191
38 Alan F. Turner, 'W.R. Motherwell: The Emergence of a Farm Leader,' *Saskatchewan History* 11, no. 1 (1958): 100
39 King Diaries, 8 April 1922
40 Friesen, 'Studies in the Development,' 133
41 Morton, *Progressive Party*, 5
42 See Friesen, *Canadian Prairies*, 332–3.
43 David Laycock, *Populism and Democratic Thought on the Canadian Prairies, 1919–1945* (Toronto, 1990) 21–3
44 Ibid., 25
45 Morton, *Progressive Party*, 35–40
46 As quoted in Friesen, 'Studies in the Development,' 164
47 Fowke, *National Policy*, 154–6
48 C.B. Macpherson, *Democracy in Alberta: Social Credit and the Party System* (Toronto, 1953) 8–9. See also V.C. Fowke, *Canadian Agricultural Policy: The Historical Pattern* (Toronto, 1946), and Fowke, 'Royal Commissions and Canadian Agricultural Policy,' *Canadian Journal of Economics and Political Science* 14, no. 2 (1948): 163–75.
49 King Papers, reel 1918, vol. 21, 19538A–A2, J.A. Stevenson to King, 25 June 1913; 19538A3–7, King to Stevenson, 4 July 1913
50 As quoted in Morton, *Progressive Party*, 20

51 As quoted in Fowke, *National Policy,* 66
52 King Diaries, 18 January 1911
53 Fowke, *National Policy,* 161–2
54 King Diaries, 29 February 1912
55 Morton, *Progressive Party,* 25–6
56 Ibid.
57 King Papers, reel 1920, vol. 23, 21394–4, Laurier to King, 24 April 1914
58 Ibid., reel 1935, vol. 44, 38933, King to Sydney Fisher, 13 April 1919
59 King Diaries, 15 May 1917
60 King Papers, reel 1920, vol. 24, 21794, King to J.H. Munro, 27 April 1914
61 *Grain Growers' Guide,* 2 August 1916, 5
62 King Diaries, 13 October 1911; 26 October 1911
63 King Papers, reel 1916, vol. 19, 17468–70, Sydney Fray to King, 6 January 1912
64 King Diaries, 13 October 1911; 26 October 1911
65 John Herd Thompson, *The Harvests of War: The Prairie West, 1914–1918* (Toronto, 1978) 59
66 J.E. Rea, 'The Wheat Board and the Western Farmer,' *The Beaver* (February–March 1997): 15–16
67 Ibid., 16
68 Paul Craven, *'An Impartial Umpire': Industrial Relations and the Canadian State, 1900–1911* (Toronto, 1980) 38
69 King, *Industry and Humanity,* 85, 528
70 Morton, *Progressive Party,* 59
71 UMA, John Wesley Dafoe Papers, MSS 3, box 1, file 6, Dafoe to T. Cote, 18 December 1917
72 R.A. Wardhaugh, 'Cogs in the Machine: The Charles Dunning–Jimmy Gardiner Feud,' *Saskatchewan History* 48, no. 1 (spring 1996): 21–2
73 Dafoe Papers, file 4, Dafoe to Augustus Bridle, 14 June 1921
74 King Diaries, 3–6 October 1917
75 Dafoe Papers, box 2, file 5, Dafoe to Sydney Fisher, 20 August 1915
76 Friesen, 'Studies in the Development,' 308
77 Friesen, *Canadian Prairies,* 366
78 Dafoe Papers, box 1, file 4, Dafoe to Augustus Bridle, 14 June 1921; box 3, file 4, Dafoe to C. Sifton, 21 July 1919
79 Friesen, *Canadian Prairies,* 366
80 QUA, T.A. Crerar Papers, 2117, series II, box 63, Crerar to J.A. Glen, 19 June 1919
81 J.E. Rea, *T.A. Crerar: A Political Life* (Montreal, 1997) 27
82 Dafoe Papers, box 1, file 4, Dafoe to Augustus Bridle, 14 June 1921

83 Crerar Papers, series II, box 64, Crerar to Michael Clark, 18 July 1919
84 Dafoe Papers, box 4, file 4, Dafoe to Clifford Sifton, 21 July 1919
85 Dawson, *King*, 277
86 See Friesen, *The Canadian Prairies*, and A. Ross McCormack, *Reformers, Rebels, and Revolutionaries: The Western Canadian Radical Movement, 1899–1919* (Toronto, 1977).
87 This is, of course, a generalization that does not necessarily apply to every labour organization in the East. As James Naylor has correctly pointed out in *The New Democracy: Challenging the Social Order in Industrial Ontario, 1914–1925* (Toronto, 1991), there was a broad range of working-class ideologies, and each group of workers responded according to their particular regional experience. Still, if generalizations are to be made, the western unions were more radical, or at least were perceived as such.
88 Craven, *'An Impartial Umpire'*, 133–4
89 King Papers, reel 1934, vol. 43, 37626, King to G.E. Brown, 26 September 1919
90 Morton, *Progressive Party*, 78
91 Dawson, *King*, 292
92 As quoted in David Smith, *Prairie Liberalism: The Liberal Party in Saskatchewan, 1905–1971* (Toronto, 1975) 78
93 King Diaries, 18–22 February 1919
94 Dawson, *King*, 299
95 Crerar Papers, series II, box 63, Crerar to F.S. Jacobs, 28 June 1919
96 Dafoe Papers, box 4, file 4, Dafoe to Clifford Sifton, 21 July 1919
97 Crerar Papers, series II, box 64, Crerar to Michael Clark, 18 July 1919
98 As quoted in Peter Regenstreif, 'The Liberal Party of Canada: A Political Analysis' (PhD diss., Cornell University, 1963) 343
99 See Laycock, *Populism and Democratic Thought*, 19–22
100 Morton, *Progressive Party*, 79
101 Such as the right of association; a living wage; an eight-hour day; a weekly day of rest; the abolition of child labour; the principle of representation of labour; an adequate system of insurance against unemployment, sickness, maternity, dependence in old age, and other situations. Dawson, *King*, 299–302; Morton, *Progressive Party*, 80
102 Dafoe Papers, box 4, file 4, Dafoe to Clifford Sifton, 21 July 1919
103 Crerar Papers, series II, box 64, Crerar to Michael Clark, 18 July 1919
104 Dawson, *King*, 307
105 Morton, *Progressive Party*, 81
106 John W. Lederle, 'The Liberal Convention of 1919 and the Selection of Mackenzie King,' *Dalhousie Review* 27, no. 1 (April 1947): 85

107 As quoted in Morton, *Progressive Party*, 78
108 Bruce Hutchison, *Mackenzie King: The Incredible Canadian* (Toronto, 1953)
4
109 Dafoe Papers, box 4, file 4, Dafoe to Clifford Sifton, 21 July 1919
110 As quoted in Cook, *The Regenerators*, 213

2: Following Phantoms, 1919–1921

1 *William Lyon Mackenzie King Diaries* (Toronto, 1973), 21 October 1919
2 NAC, W.L.M. King Papers, MG 26, J1, reel 1933, vol. 42, 37089, W.W. Andrews to King, 10 August 1919
3 Ibid., reel 1936, vol. 45, 39751–2, F.C. Hamilton to King, 28 August 1919
4 *Grain Growers' Guide*, 20 August 1919, 1741
5 King Papers, reel 1933, vol. 42, 36890–1, J.E. Adamson to King, 25 August 1919
6 King Diaries, 27 October 1919
7 King Papers, reel 1937, vol. 47, 41398–400, King to T. Mcmillan, 26 November 1919
8 Ibid.
9 Ibid., reel 1936, vol. 46, 40101–2, King to A.E. Hill, 25 November 1919
10 Ibid., reel 1937, vol. 47, 41398–400, King to T. Mcmillan, 26 November 1919
11 Ibid., 41393, King to T. Mcmillan, 16 August 1919
12 Ibid., reel 1933, vol. 42, 36791–806, 'The Liberals and the Farmers,' article for the *Grain Growers' Guide*, 22 November 1919
13 Ibid., 41393, King to T. Mcmillan, 16 August 1919
14 QUA, Norman P. Lambert Papers, series I, box 1, J.A. Stevenson to Lambert, 16 August 1919
15 King Papers, reel 1938, vol. 48, 41858, E.S. Miller to King, 25 November 1919
16 Ibid., reel 1936, vol. 46, 39951–2, Hugh Mackenzie to Andrew Haydon, 31 December 1919
17 Ibid., 40101–2, King to A.E. Hill, 25 November 1919
18 King Diaries, 27 October 1919
19 King Papers, reel 1935, vol. 44, 38962–3, 'Document discussing policy to avoid three-way contests'
20 Ibid., reel 1937, vol. 47, 41379–80, King to N.T. Macmillan, 25 September 1919
21 Ibid., vol. 48, 41739–41, King to W.M. Martin, 5 September 1919
22 Ibid., 41736, W.M. Martin to King, 16 August 1919; 41742, Martin to King, 8 September 1919

23 As quoted in David Smith, *Prairie Liberalism: The Liberal Party of Saskatchewan, 1905–1971* (Toronto, 1975) 77–8

24 UMA, J.W. Dafoe Papers, MSS 3, box 1, file 4, Dafoe to Borden, 29 September 1917

25 King Papers, reel 1938, vol. 48, 41983–4, W.R. Motherwell to W.M. Martin, 25 August 1919; reel 1939, 41991–4, Motherwell to Martin, 10 September 1919

26 Ibid., reel 1937, vol. 48, 41748–9, W.M. Martin to King, 30 September 1919

27 King Diaries, 7 October 1919

28 Ibid., 8–9 October 1919

29 W.L. Morton, *The Progressive Party in Canada* (Toronto, 1950) 82

30 King Papers, reel 1938, vol. 48, 41858, E.S. Miller to King, 25 November 1919

31 Smith, *Prairie Liberalism*, 79

32 King Papers, reel 1935, vol. 45, 39442–3, W.G.A. Gourlay to C.M. Goddard, 27 September 1919

33 Ibid., reel 1937, vol. 48, 41738, W.M. Martin to King, 3 September 1919; 41746, Martin to King, 29 September 1919; 41747, King to Martin, 8 October 1919; 41750, King to Martin, 8 October 1919; 41759, Martin to King, 17 November 1919; 41764, Martin to King, 11 December 1919

34 King Diaries, 25 February 1920; 28 February 1920

35 Morton, *Progressive Party*, 98

36 King Diaries, 23 April 1920

37 King Papers, reel 1941, vol. 54, 46504–6, J.G. Gardiner to King, 1 March 1920

38 Ibid., reel 1943, vol. 55, Motherwell to King, 26 February 1920. For a full discussion of Gardiner's attitude toward the Progressives see Norman Ward and David Smith, *Jimmy Gardiner: Relentless Liberal* (Toronto, 1990).

39 King Papers, reel 1936, vol. 46, 39951–2, Hugh Mackenzie to Andrew Haydon, 31 December 1919

40 Ibid., reel 1944, vol. 57, 49472–3, A.N. Bannerman to King, 29 April 1921

41 Ibid., reel 1937, vol. 47, 41349–53, A.M. McLeod to King, 28 November 1919

42 Ibid., reel 1936, vol. 46, 39951–2, Hugh Mackenzie to Andrew Haydon, 31 December 1919

43 David Laycock, *Populism and Democratic Thought in the Canadian Prairies, 1910–1945* (Toronto, 1990) 20–1, 69

44 King Papers, reel 1941, vol. 53, 46140–1, King to L.G. de Veber, 6 December 1920

45 King Papers, reel 1936, vol. 45, 39797, Arthur C. Hardy to King, 19 August 1919; vol. 46, 39951–2, Hugh Mackenzie to Andrew Haydon, 31 December 1919

46 Ibid., reel 1941, vol. 53, 45426–9, J.R. Boyle to King, 28 June 1920
47 Ibid., reel 1937, vol. 47, 40768, King to Rodolphe Lemieux, 20 December 1919
48 Ibid., 40100, A.E. Hill to King, 18 November 1919
49 Smith, *Prairie Liberalism*, 32–3; see also William Brennan, 'Press and Party in Saskatchewan, 1914–1929,' *Saskatchewan History* 27 (1974): 81–94.
50 King Papers, reel 1937, vol. 47, 41349–53, A. McLeod to 28 King, November 1919
51 Ibid., reel 1936, vol. 45, 40101–2, King to A.E. Hill, 25 November 1919
52 Ibid., 47586–8, A. McLeod to King, 27 March 1920
53 Ibid., reel 1938, vol. 48, 41860–1, E.S. Miller to King, 24 December 1919
54 Ibid., reel 1939, vol. 51, 43829, Walter Scott to King, 3 November 1919
55 Ibid., reel 1938, vol. 48, 41739–41, King to W.M. Martin, 5 September 1919
56 Ibid., 46728–30, Andrew Haydon to [first name unknown] Locke, 9 March 1920; 46761–2, Memorandum of the National Liberal Organization Committee, 12 May 1920
57 Ibid., 46812–3, Andrew Haydon to King, November 1920
58 Canada, House of Commons, *Debates*, 1 June 1920, 2981–94
59 King Diaries, 18 January 1920
60 Dafoe Papers, box 4, file 4, Dafoe to Clifford Sifton, 10 November 1920
61 King Diaries, 18 January 1920
62 *Grain Growers' Guide*, 21 July 1920, 8, 10–11
63 King Papers, reel 1941, vol. 53, 46104–6, R.J. Deachman to King, 16 June 1920; 46140–1, Deachman to King, 23 July 1920
64 Ibid., reel 1943, vol. 55, 47768–70, King to Violet Markham, 29 December 1920
65 Ibid., reel 1941, vol. 53, 46108–9, King to R.J. Deachman, July 1920
66 Dafoe Papers, box 4, file 4, Dafoe to Clifford Sifton, 10 November 1920
67 W.C. Kennedy, rather than Charles Murphy and C.P. Graham, would go from Ontario. King Papers, reel 1942, vol. 55, 47270–2, King to Rodolphe Lemieux, 3 September 1920
68 King Diaries, 8 October 1920; 21 October 1920
69 Ibid., 12 October 1920
70 Ibid., 22 October 1920; 25 October 1920
71 King Papers, reel 1944, vol. 57, 49472–3, A.N. Bannerman to King, 29 April 1921
72 Ibid., reel 1951, vol. 67, 57978–9, Lewis Stubbs to Andrew Haydon, 17 January 1921
73 Ibid.
74 King Diaries, 31 October 1920; 2 November 1920; 3 November 1920

75 Ibid., 2 November 1920
76 Ibid., 9 November 1920
77 Dafoe Papers, box 4, file 4, Dafoe to Clifford Sifton, 10 November 1920
78 Ibid.
79 'Mr. King and the West,' *Free Press*, 3 November 1920
80 King Diaries, 22 November 1920; 5 February 1920
81 King Papers, reel 1943, vol. 55, 47768–70, King to Violet Markham, 29 December 1920
82 King Diaries, 12 January 1921; 21 February 1921
83 King Papers, reel 1944, vol. 58, 49485–6, J.R. Boyle to King, 21 February 1921
84 Ibid., 49863–6, J.R. Boyle to King, 13 August 1921
85 QUA, T.A. Crerar Papers, 2117, series III, box 97, Crerar to A.K. Cameron, 2 July 1921
86 King Papers, reel 1946, vol. 60, 51857–8, King to F. Ford, 10 October 1921
87 King Diaries, 13 September 1921
88 King Papers, reel 1944, vol. 57, 49724, King's private secretary to J.J. Bildfell, 20 September 1921
89 King Diaries, 14 November 1921
90 Crerar Papers, series II, box 107, Crerar to [first name unknown] Lyon, 9 December 1921
91 King Diaries, 6 September 1921
92 King Papers, reel 1946, vol. 59, 51198, King to George De Buse, 10 August 1921
93 Ibid., MG 26, J5, Speeches, reel 1985, vol. D3, 1502–9, King's speech at Edmonton, 6 October 1920
94 *Debates*, 19 May 1921, 3613–4
95 As quoted in R. MacGregor Dawson, *William Lyon Mackenzie King: A Political Biography, 1874–1923* (Toronto, 1958) 351
96 King Papers, reel 1950, vol. 66, 56904, J.A. Robb to King, 3 October 1921
97 Ibid., reel 1948, vol. 63, 54180–1, King to Rodolphe Lemieux, 9 September 1921
98 Gerald Friesen, *The Canadian Prairies: A History* (Toronto, 1987) 335
99 King Papers, reel 1944, vol. 58, 49869–72, J.R. Boyle to King, 9 September 1921
100 Ibid., reel 1945, vol. 58, 50103–4, W.A. Buchanan to King, 10 December 1921
101 Ibid., reel 1947, vol. 61, 52673–83, George Hagle to King, 21 September 1921
102 Ibid., 51038A–A17, O.E. Culbert to King, 12 December 1921

103 King Diaries, 14 November 1921
104 C.B. Macpherson, *Democracy in Alberta: Social Credit and the Party System* (Toronto, 1953) 26–7
105 Smith, *Prairie Liberalism*, 87–9
106 King Papers, reel 1950, vol. 65, 65868–71, W.R. Motherwell to King, 1 July 1921
107 King Diaries, 3 September 1921
108 King Papers, reel 1950, vol. 65, 55862–5, W.R. Motherwell to King, 17 January 1921
109 Ibid., reel 1946, vol. 60, 52172–3, Jimmy Gardiner to King, 5 September 1921
110 Smith, *Prairie Liberalism*, 91–2
111 Dafoe Papers, box 4, file 4, Dafoe to Clifford Sifton, 7 December 1921
112 King Papers, reel 1948, vol. 62, 53755–6, J.F. Kilgour to King, 10 December 1921
113 Dafoe Papers, box 4, file 4, Dafoe to Clifford Sifton, 14 October 1921
114 King Papers, reel 1950, vol. 66, 56907–8, W.D. Robb to King, 17 October 1921
115 Ibid., 56914, King to J.A. Robb, 22 October 1921
116 King Diaries, 11 November 1921
117 *Grain Growers' Guide*, 10 November 1920, 5
118 Dafoe Papers, box 1, file 4, J.W. Dafoe to Augustus Bridle, 14 June 1921
119 UML, Sir Clifford Sifton Papers, reel 735, J.A. Stevenson to J.W. Dafoe, 16 September 1921
120 Frederick W. Gibson, 'The Cabinet of 1921,' in *Cabinet Formation and Bicultural Relations*, ed. F.W. Gibson. Studies of the Royal Commission on Bilingualism and Biculturalism (Kingston, 1970) 74
121 King Diaries, 26 November 1921
122 King Papers, reel 1947, vol. 61, 53105, King to Andrew Haydon, 13 December 1921
123 King Diaries, 10 December 1921
124 As quoted in Dawson, *King*, 355
125 King Diaries, 8 December 1921
126 Gibson, 'Cabinet of 1921,' 74
127 King Papers, reel 1947, vol. 61, 53105, King to Andrew Haydon, 13 December 1921
128 Ibid., 53120, Haydon to King, 14 December 1921
129 King Diaries, 14 December 1921
130 As quoted in Gibson, 'Cabinet of 1921,' 81
131 Dafoe Papers, box 12, file 4, Cliford Sifton to Dafoe, 8 December 1921
132 Ibid., box 4, file 4, Dafoe to Sifton, 19 December 1921

133 Ibid., box 12, file 4, Sifton to Dafoe, 14 December 1921
134 As quoted in Gibson, 'Cabinet of 1921,' 86
135 High protectionists from Ontario and the Maritimes such as George
     Graham, D.D. McKenzie, and E.M. Macdonald were being proposed for
     cabinet. The Gouin group was advocating six ministers from Quebec,
     including the protectionists Rodolphe Lemieux and J.A. Robb. See
     Gibson, 'Cabinet of 1921,' for a full discussion.
136 Only W.C. Kennedy of the Ontario Liberals remained opposed to
     Progressives in cabinet, and Fielding strongly endorsed the alignment.
     Béland, Lemieux, and Gouin preferred Ontario to Prairie Progressives
     and favoured Drury over Crerar, but they were all prepared to give the
     plan support.
137 Dawson, *King,* 364
138 King Diaries, 14 December 1921
139 Ibid., 19 December 1921
140 Ibid., 20 December 1921
141 As quoted in Gibson, 'Cabinet of 1921,' 88
142 King Diaries, 21 December 1921
143 See Gibson, 'Cabinet of 1921,' 91–2
144 King Diaries, 24 December 1921
145 Ibid., 20 December 1921
146 Dafoe Papers, box 12, file 4, Clifford Sifton to Dafoe, 30 December 1921
147 Lambert Papers, series I, box 1, Lambert to J.D. Atkinson, 31 December
     1921
148 *Grain Growers' Guide,* 3 September 1919, 12
149 Crerar Papers, series III, box 97, Kirk Cameron to Crerar, 28 December 1921

3: Belling the Cat, 1922–1924

 1 NAC, W.L.M. King Papers, MG 26, J1, reel 2245, vol. 76, 63127, Andrew
    Haydon to King, 27 March 1922
 2 QUA, T.A. Crerar Papers, 2117, series II, box 79, Crerar to H.B. Mitchell,
    10 June 1922
 3 As quoted in R. MacGregor Dawson, *William Lyon Mackenzie King: A
    Political Biography, 1874–1923* (Toronto, 1958) 387
 4 King Papers, reel 2246, vol. 78, 64171, King to [first name unknown]
    Landry, 6 February 1922
 5 Ibid., reel 2248, vol. 82, 66921, T.C. Norris to King, 28 April 1922
 6 Ibid., reel 1945, vol. 58, 51038A–A17, O.E. Culbert to King, 12 December
    1921. 'I think the so-called Progressives are going back rather than forward

in public favour. There are notes of dissatisfaction cropping up here and there and the enthusiasm seems, to a great extent, to have worn off.' Reel 2242, vol. 70, 59799–800, J.R. Boyle to King, 9 June 1922

7 Ibid., reel 1945, vol. 58, 50666–7, H.H. Christie to King, 9 December 1921
8 Ibid., reel 2247, vol. 80, 65673–4, E.J. McMurray to King, 29 June 1922
9 Ibid., reel 2268, vol. 116, 88760–2, McMurray to King, 28 May 1924
10 *William Lyon Mackenzie King Diaries* (Toronto, 1973) 29 October 1920
11 King Papers, reel 2250, vol. 86, 69600–2, J.G. Turgeon to King, 4 March 1922
12 Ibid., reel 2242, vol. 70, 59825–7, King to J.R. Boyle, 18 December 1922
13 Ibid., reel 2251, vol. 89, 70781–4, King to G. Bell, 16 July 1923
14 Ibid., reel 2242, vol. 70, 59825–7, King to J.R. Boyle, 18 December 1922
15 Dawson praises Fielding for this initiative and argues that 'it also showed that this desire had not been advocated merely as an aid in the elections but had become a continuing element in Liberal policy.' Fielding's actions in the House regarding the tariff would seem to indicate that the gesture lacked any real commitment. Dawson, *King*, 383–4
16 As quoted in ibid., 387
17 UMA, J.W. Dafoe Papers, MSS 3, box 1, file 4, Dafoe to W.A. Buchanan, 6 December 1923
18 Peter Regenstreif, 'The Liberal Party of Canada: A Political Analysis' (PhD diss., Cornell University 1963) 346–7
19 King Diaries, 5 February 1922
20 Dafoe Papers, box 4, file 4, Dafoe to Clifford Sifton, 11 July 1922
21 J.E. Rea, 'The Wheat Board and the Western Farmer,' *The Beaver* (February–March 1997): 18–19
22 See Paul Craven, *'An Impartial Umpire': Industrial Relations and the Canadian State, 1900–1911* (Toronto, 1980).
23 King Diaries, 15 March 1922
24 Rea, 'The Wheat Board,' 19. See John Kendle, *John Bracken: A Political Biography* (Toronto, 1979).
25 C.F. Wilson, *A Century of Canadian Grain* (Saskatoon, 1978) 183
26 King Diaries, 20 April 1922
27 King Papers, reel 2248, vol. 82, 66914–8, T.C. Norris to King, 10 March 1922
28 Ibid., reel 2242, vol. 70, 59842–4, J. Bracken to King, November 1922
29 Ibid., reel 2245, vol. 76, 62707–12, King to Herbert Greenfield, 20 February 1922
30 Ibid., reel 2244, vol. 73, 61639–46, Charles Dunning to King, 10 April 1922
31 King Diaries, 17 November 1922
32 Ibid., 16 November 1922
33 Ibid., 28 April 1922; 16 November 1922

34 Dawson, *King,* 447
35 King Diaries, 26 April 1922
36 All quotes are from Dawson, *King,* 392.
37 Bruce Hutchison, *Mackenzie King: The Incredible Canadian* (Toronto, 1943) 55
38 King Diaries, 8 April 1922
39 House of Commons, *Debates,* 4 May 1922, 1435
40 King Diaries, 8 April 1922
41 Dafoe Papers, box 4, file 4, Dafoe to Clifford Sifton, 6 May 1922
42 King Papers, reel 2256, vol. 98, 76587–91, Duncan Marshall to King, 21 February 1923
43 Ibid., reel 2247, vol. 80, 65759–60, R.F. McWilliams to King, 1 September 1922
44 Ibid., reel 2248, vol. 82, 66926–9, King to T.C. Norris, 25 July 1922
45 Ibid., reel 2246, vol. 79, 65205–6, King to [first name unknown] McCullach, 17 October 1922
46 King Diaries, 17–22 September 1922
47 As quoted in Dawson, *King,* 413
48 *Maclean's Magazine,* 1 December 1922, as quoted in J.E. Rea, *T.A. Crerar: A Political Life* (Montreal, 1997) 97
49 King Diaries, 11 November 1922
50 Ibid., 12 November 1922
51 King Papers, reel 2253, vol. 93, 73599–600, Herbert Greenfield to King, 2 January 1923; 73658–61, Greenfield to King, 29 December 1923
52 King Diaries 4 April 1923; 12 April 1923; 21 April 1923
53 As quoted in Dawson, *King,* 455
54 King Papers, reel 2252, vol. 92, 72531–6, Charles Dunning to King, 27 July 1923
55 Ibid., vol. 91, 72012–4, S.K. Colquhuon to King, 26 April 1923
56 SAB, Charles Avery Dunning Papers, M6, J.B. Musselman to C.A. Dunning, 9 June 1922
57 See William Brennan, 'C.A. Dunning and the Challenge of the Progressives: 1922–1925,' *Saskatchewan History* 22 (1969): 1–12
58 *Regina Morning Leader,* 6 October 1923
59 King Papers, reel 2252, vol. 92, 72531–6, Charles Dunning to King, 27 July 1923; David Smith, *Prairie Liberalism: The Liberal Party in Saskatchewan, 1905–1971* (Toronto, 1975) 176–8
60 King Papers, reel 2252, vol. 92, 72531–6, Dunning to King, 27 July 1923
61 Ibid., 73084–5, Jimmy Gardiner to King, 18 December 1923
62 Wilson, *Century of Canadian Grain,* 229

63 Rea, 'The Wheat Board,' 19–21
64 Dafoe Papers, box 4, file 4, Dafoe to Clifford Sifton, 12 March 1923
65 As quoted in Dawson, *King*, 450
66 This stand toward increased dominion autonomy had been apparent in the Chanak, Lausanne, and Halibut Treaty issues.
67 Dafoe Papers, box 4, file 4, Dafoe to Clifford Sifton, 12 September 1923
68 Ibid., box 1, file 4, Dafoe to W.A. Buchanan, 6 December 1923
69 King Papers, reel 2266, vol. 113, 86689–94, King to Peter Larkin, 25 January 1924
70 Ibid., reel 2256, vol. 97, 76319, R.F. McWilliams to King, 10 December 1923
71 King Diaries, 5 December 1923
72 Peter Regenstreif, 'A Threat to Leadership: C.Λ. Dunning and Mackenzie King,' *Dalhousie Review* 44 (April 1964): 274
73 King Papers, reel 2269, vol. 120, 90994–1000, G.W. Sahlmark to King, 7 January 1924
74 Ibid., reel 2262, vol. 106, 82425–31, J.R. Boyle to King, 4 January 1924
75 King Diaries, 3 January 1924
76 King Papers, reel 2266, vol. 113, 86271–4, J.F. Kilgour to King, 26 February 1924
77 Ibid., reel 2260, vol. 105, 81054–6, J.G. Turgeon to King, 11 December 1923

4: The Angels on Side, 1924–1926

1 UMA, J.W. Dafoe Papers, MSS 3, box 4, file 4, Dafoe to Clifford Sifton, 12 March 1923
2 *William Lyon Mackenzie King Diaries* (Toronto, 1973) 10–11 January 1924
3 QUA, T.A. Crerar Papers, 2117, series II, box 79, Crerar to J.A. Glen, 29 January 1924
4 NAC, W.L.M. King Papers, MG 26, J1, reel 2266, vol. 113, 86562–3, King to Ernest Lapointe, 30 May 1924
5 Ibid., reel 2261, vol. 107, 82450–1, King to John Bracken, 29 January 1924
6 King Diaries, 4 January 1924
7 King Papers, reel 2268, vol. 116, 88705–9, John Bracken to King, January 1924
8 King Diaries, 3 January 1924
9 King Papers, reel 2266, vol. 113, 86562–3, King to Ernest Lapointe, 30 May 1924
10 Ibid., reel 2294, vol. 164, 118748–51, King to L.A. Taschereau, March 26, 1926.
11 King Diaries, 25–6 February 1924; 6 January 1924
12 Dafoe Papers, box 4, file 5, Dafoe to Clifford Sifton, 13 February 1924

13 King Diaries, 6 January 1924

14 Ibid., 27 February 1924; 18 March 1924

15 Dafoe Papers, box 4, file 5, Dafoe to Clifford Sifton, 3 April 1925

16 King Diaries, 22 March 1924

17 Ibid., 10 April 1924

18 H. Blair Neatby, *William Lyon Mackenzie King: The Lonely Heights, 1924–1932* (Toronto, 1963) 17–18

19 King Diaries, 10 April 1924

20 Ibid.

21 Ibid., 13 April 1924

22 King Papers, reel 2264, vol. 110, 84315–16, Charles Dunning to King, 23 April 1924

23 'One forgets that the early explorers made their way to the Canadian West by the Straits & Hudson's [*sic*] Bay, that the waters that touch the northern part of Manitoba are Atlantic Ocean waters, that the Middle West of U.S. as well as Canada may find a profitable water route there. The fact that there is so much propaganda against it, by Montreal interests make me feel C.P.R. fears that competition.' King Diaries, 9 April 1924

24 As quoted in Roger Graham, *Arthur Meighen: And Fortune Fled* (Toronto, 1963) 334–5

25 Crerar Papers, series II, box 79, Crerar to A.K. Cameron, 1 August 1924

26 Neatby, *Lonely Heights*, 24–30

27 Ibid., 26

28 King Diaries, 21 October 1924

29 King Papers, reel 2267, vol. 116, 88645–56, A.M. McLeod to King, 23 February 1924

30 King Diaries, 3 October 1924

31 King Papers, reel 2267, vol. 116, 88658–60, A.M. McLeod to King, 8 August 1924

32 King Diaries, 4 October 1924; Crerar Papers, series III, box 97, Crerar to Kirk Cameron, 15 October 1924

33 Dafoe Papers, box 4, file 4, Dafoe to Clifford Sifton, 3 April 1925

34 *Leader* (Regina), 1 November 1924

35 King Papers, reel 2265, vol. 110, 84871–3, Jimmy Gardiner to King, 15 November 1924

36 King Diaries, 24 October 1924; 27 October 1924

37 King Papers, reel 2265, vol. 110, 84875–7, King to Jimmy Gardiner, 31 December 1924

38 Crerar Papers, series II, box 79, Crerar to A.K. Cameron, 23 October 1924

39 King Papers, reel 2264, vol. 109, 84057–9, Fred L. Davis to King, 28 November 1924

40 King Diaries, 6 December 1924; 18 December 1924
41 King Papers, reel 2265, vol. 110, 84875–7, King to Jimmy Gardiner, 31 December 1924
42 House of Commons, *Debates*, 18 June 1925, 4438
43 King Diaries, 27 February 1925; 7 March 1925. The revised Australian agreement came into effect in October.
44 Ibid., 9 July 1925; 18 August 1925; 25 February 1924
45 King Papers, reel 2279, vol. 136, 101344–7, N.T. Macmillan to King, 23 May 1925
46 King Diaries, 18 August 1925; 9 July 1925
47 King Papers, reel 2279, vol. 136, 101049–51, King to I.A. Mackay, 23 November 1925
48 Ibid., reel 2275, vol. 129, 97167–71, Charles Dunning to King, 22 August 1925
49 King Diaries, 23 October 1925
50 Neatby, *Lonely Heights*, 66
51 Herbert Marler, Vincent Massey, and W.E. Foster were brought in. G.H. Boivin replaced Bureau.
52 Neatby, *Lonely Heights*, 68
53 As quoted in W.L. Morton, *The Progressive Party in Canada* (Toronto, 1950) 237
54 King Papers, reel 2274, vol. 127, 95864–8, T.A. Burrows to King, 14 August 1925
55 Dafoe Papers, box 4, file 5, Dafoe to Clifford Sifton, 3 April 1925
56 King Papers, reel 2284, vol. 146, 107709–11, M.G. Walker to King, 1 August 1925; reel 2285, vol. 147, 108202–3, A.M. Young to King, 5 December 1925
57 Ibid., reel 2276, vol. 131, 98136–8, King to F.C. Hamilton, 16 November 1925
58 Ibid., reel 2275, vol. 128, 96456–7, J.A. Clarke to King, 14 August 1925
59 King Diaries, 29 September 1925
60 King had sat for North York (the constituency that defeated him in 1917) since December 1921.
61 Neatby, *Lonely Heights*, 74
62 King Diaries, 30 October 1925
63 UML, Clifford Sifton Papers, reel 598, 164649, D.N. Cooper to Sifton, 24 October 1925; 164650, Sifton to Cooper, 30 October 1925; 164664–5, R.J. Cromie to Sifton, excerpt from editorial in *Vancouver Sun*, 14 November 1925
64 Kirk Cameron wrote Crerar suggesting that King should resign the leadership, have George Murray replace him, and accept the High Commissionership in London. Murray would gain eastern support while Dunning would

provide support from the West. Ernest Lapointe and P.J.A. Cardin would have to push such action to ensure Quebec support. Crerar Papers, series III, box 97, Kirk Cameron to Crerar, 3 November 1925

65 Peter Regenstreif, 'A Threat to Leadership: C.A. Dunning and Mackenzie King,' *Dalhousie Review* 44 (April 1964) 353

66 Dafoe Papers, box 4, file 5, Dafoe to Clifford Sifton, 20 November 1925

67 Sifton Papers, reel 598, 164633–8, T.A. Burrows to Sifton, 20 November 1925

68 'I agree with you that King has shown grave defects in leadership; I agree with you that his leadership today is probably the heaviest liability the Liberal party has, but I come back again to the question, – what is the alternative?' Crerar Papers, series III, box 97, Crerar to Kirk Cameron, 26 February 1926

69 As quoted in Regenstreif, 'Threat to Leadership,' 353–4

70 Neatby, *Lonely Heights*, 88

71 King Papers, reel 2281, vol. 140, 103712–4, H.W. Wood to King, 27 November 1925

72 Dafoe Papers, box 4, file 5, Dafoe to Clifford Sifton, 5 December 1925

73 'I think,' Dafoe wrote, King is 'of the same mind as he was in the last parliament, that if a couple of Progressives would come into the government everything would be lovely.' Dafoe Papers, box 2, file 5, Dafoe to Robert Forke, 16 November 1925

74 As quoted in Neatby, *Lonely Heights*, 90

75 Ibid., 89

76 King Diaries, 16 November 1925

77 King Papers, reel 2275, vol. 129, 97221–8, King to Charles Dunning, 19 December 1925

78 King Diaries, 4 November 1925; 13 November 1925

79 King Papers, reel 2280, vol. 137, 102179–80, King to C.R. Mitchell, 26 November 1925

80 Ibid., reel 2292, vol. 160, 115939–41, A.H.S. Murray to King, 12 February 1926

81 Ibid., reel 2276, vol. 130, 97661–3, King to Jimmy Gardiner, 3 December 1925

82 See R.A. Wardhaugh, 'Cogs in the Machine: The Charles Dunning–Jimmy Gardiner Feud,' *Saskatchewan History* 48, no. 1 (spring 1996): 20–9.

83 David Smith, *Prairie Liberalism: The Liberal Party in Saskatchewan, 1905–1971* (Toronto, 1975) 80

84 Norman Ward and David Smith, *Jimmy Gardiner: Relentless Liberal* (Toronto, 1990) x

85 Ibid., 41
86 Smith, *Prairie Liberalism*, 154
87 Ward and Smith, *Gardiner*, 41
88 GAI, interviews of Jimmy Gardiner by Una Maclean Evans, 29 December 1961–6 January 1962
89 King Diaries, 31 January 1926
90 GAI, interviews of Jimmy Gardiner by Una Maclean Evans, 29 December 1961–6 January 1962
91 King Papers, reel 2288, vol. 153, 111770–1, Jimmy Gardiner to King, 8 March 1926; See Wardhaugh, 'Region and Nation: The Politics of Jimmy Gardiner,' *Saskatchewan History* 45, no. 2 (fall 1993): 24–36.
92 As quoted in Ward and Smith, *Gardiner*, 60–1
93 King Diaries, 2 January 1926
94 King Papers, reel 2280, vol. 137, 102187–8, C.R. Mitchell to King, 16 December 1925
95 Ibid., reel 2276, vol. 131, 98530–5, Andrew Haydon to King, 23 November 1925
96 Ibid., reel 2289, vol. 154, 112575, A.B. Hudson to King, 10 February 1926
97 Neatby, *Lonely Heights*, 95
98 Dafoe Papers, box 2, file 5, Dafoe to Robert Forke, 16 November 1925
99 Neatby, *Lonely Heights*, 98
100 Ibid., 99–100
101 King Papers, reel 2289, vol. 156, 113308–13, King to P.C. Larkin, 17 February 1926
102 'We decided in Council we would seek *open* cooperation with Progressive Labor & Indept, who have given us support.' King Diaries, 15 January 1926; 18 January 1926
103 Ibid., 19 January 1926
104 Neatby, *Lonely Heights*, 78
105 King Diaries, 11 January 1926; 7–8 January 1926
106 Morton, *The Progressive Party*, 247
107 See R.A. Wardhaugh, 'A Marriage of Convenience? Mackenzie King and Prince Albert Constituency,' *Prairie Forum* 21, no. 2 (fall 1996): 177–200.
108 G.W.D. Abrams, *Prince Albert: The First Century, 1866–1966* (Saskatoon, 1966), 224, 227–8, 255, 266
109 King Diaries, 15 January 1926
110 Ibid., 3 February 1926; King Papers, reel 2288, vol. 152, 111164–5, King to Charles Dunning, 16 February 1926
111 King Papers, reel 2285, vol. 147, 108202–3, P.M. Anderson to King, 22 January 1926

112 Ibid., reel 2288, vol. 152, 111164–5, King to Charles Dunning, 16 February 1926

113 King Diaries, 16–22 February 1926

114 W.A. Waiser, *Saskatchewan's Playground: A History of Prince Albert National Park* (Saskatoon, 1989) 26

115 King Diaries, 12 May 1926

116 Waiser, *Saskatchewan's Playground*, 28

117 King Diaries, 6 February 1926

118 Crerar Papers, series III, box 97, Crerar to Kirk Cameron, 26 February 1926

119 King Papers, reel 2286, vol. 149, 109487–91, T.A. Burrows to King, 29 May 1926; reel 2287, vol. 151, 110566–8, T.A. Crerar to King, 16 April 1926; reel 2291, vol. 158, 114591–2, A.M. McLeod to King, 24 April 1926

120 King Diaries, 15 June 1926

121 Ibid., 18–21 June 1926

122 Ibid., 3 August 1926

123 'I may say that I have been able to understand and to some extent sympathize with the insurgent Progressives. Like them I have only been able to bring myself to give the Government a hand by contemplating the probabilities of the Conservatives coming into power.' Dafoe Papers, box 4, file 5, Dafoe to Clifford Sifton, 19 February 1926

124 King Diaries, 18 August 1926

125 King Papers, reel 2287, vol. 151, 110574–6, T.A. Crerar to King, 14 September 1926

126 Neatby, *Lonely Heights*, 163

127 King Papers, reel 2289, vol. 154, 112366–7, F.C. Hamilton to King, 22 September 1926; 112622, A.B. Hudson to King, 20 September 1926

128 Dafoe Papers, box 4, file 5, Dafoe to Clifford Sifton, 26 October 1926

129 King Diaries, 6 August 1926

130 King Papers, reel 2287, vol. 151, 110718–19, W.M. Davidson to King, 28 April 1926

131 Ibid., reel 2293, vol. 163, 118326–8, G.P. Smith to King, 19 April 1926

132 Neatby, *Lonely Heights*, 164–5

133 King Diaries, 10 August 1926; 16 August 1926

134 Abrams, *Prince Albert*, 270

135 Neatby, *Lonely Heights*, 169

136 Dafoe Papers, box 5, file 5, Dafoe to John Willison, 17 September 1926

137 King Papers, reel 2289, vol. 154, 112619–21, A.B. Hudson to King, 18 September 1926

138 Crerar Papers, series II, box 80, Crerar to A.K. Cameron, 2 September

1925; Crerar to Charles Dunning, 15 September 1926; Crerar to Cameron, 15 September 1926

139 Dafoe Papers, box 2, file 8, Dafoe to W.D. Gregory, 17 September 1926; Crerar to J.C. Lewis, 4 August 1926

140 King Diaries, 20 September–4 October 1926

141 V.C. Fowke, 'Royal Commissions and Canadian Agricultural Policy,' *Canadian Journal of Economics and Political Science* 14, no. 2 (1948): 172, 174

142 Gerald Friesen, *The Canadian Prairies: A History* (Toronto, 1987) 304, 313

5: Leaving the Plough in the Furrow, 1927–1930

1 Bruce Hutchison, *Mackenzie King: The Incredible Canadian* (Toronto, 1953) 25, 80

2 *William Lyon Mackenzie King Diaries* (Toronto, 1973) 31 March 1928; 4 November 1928

3 Ibid., 29 April 1927; H. Blair Neatby, *William Lyon Mackenzie King: The Lonely Heights 1924–1932* (Toronto, 1963) 200. See also George F. Henderson, 'Mackenzie King the Farmer,' *Up the Gatineau* 20 (1994): 15–21.

4 Neatby, *Lonely Heights*, 196

5 King Diaries, 28 July 1928

6 For a full discussion, see W.A. Waiser, *Saskatchewan's Playground: A History of Prince Albert National Park* (Saskatoon, 1989) 25–30

7 NAC, W.L.M. King Papers, MG 26, J5, reel 2295, vol. 167, 121019–22, T.C. Davis to King, 17 June 1927

8 Waiser, *Saskatchewan's Playground*, 31

9 King Papers, reel 2296, vol. 168, 121580–1, H.J. Fraser to L.C. Moyer, 26 February 1927

10 Ibid., reel 2298, vol. 171, 123580–4, King to Charles Macdonald, 11 June 1927

11 Neatby, *Lonely Heights*, 231

12 QUA, T.A. Crerar Papers, 2117, series III, box 97, Crerar to Kirk Cameron, 12 October 1927

13 John Kendle, *John Bracken: A Political Biography* (Toronto, 1979) 63–4; Crerar Papers, series II, box 80, Crerar to Kirk Cameron, 4 July 1927

14 King Papers, reel 2298, vol. 172, 123861, R.F. McWilliams to King, 14 January 1927

15 Ibid., reel 2296, vol. 168, 121702–3, Jimmy Gardiner to King, 11 April 1927. According to Kendle, Robson's name was put forward for the leadership just fifteen minutes before nominations closed. The Liberals favouring coalition believed Robson also desired fusion and he swept the floor.

Kendle, *Bracken*, 64; SAB, James Garfield Gardiner Papers, S-1.137, reel 5, 8312–13, Gardiner to H.A. Robson, 21 September 1927. Gardiner was aware that Bracken came from a Tory family, and this augmented his belief that most Progressives were disguised Conservatives.

16 As quoted in Kendle, *Bracken*, 65
17 King Papers, reel 2299, vol. 174, 125555–7, H.A. Robson to King, 23 April 1927
18 Gardiner Papers, reel 5, 7719–21, Gardiner to W.R. Motherwell, 10 April 1926; 7765–8, Gardiner to Charles Stewart, 17 March 1926
19 As quoted in Gordon Unger, 'James G. Gardiner: The Premier as a Pragmatic Politician, 1926–1929' (MA thesis, University of Saskatchewan, 1967) 51
20 Crerar Papers, series III, box 97, Crerar to Kirk Cameron, 18 May 1927
21 King Papers, reel 2296, vol. 168, 121506–7, R. Forke to King, 20 August 1927
22 Ibid., reel 2299, vol. 174, 125575–8, H.A. Robson to King, 30 June 1927
23 Ibid., reel 2303, vol. 181, 129730–6, Jimmy Gardiner to King, 17 January 1928
24 Crerar Papers, series II, box 80, Crerar to Kirk Cameron, 4 July 1927
25 King Papers, reel 2298, vol. 172, 123864–5, R.F. McWilliams to King, 3 September 1927
26 King Diaries, 27 February 1928
27 King Papers, reel 2303, vol. 181, 129737–41, King to Jimmy Gardiner, 5 March 1928
28 King Diaries, 27 February 1928
29 David Smith, *Prairie Liberalism: The Liberal Party in Saskatchewan, 1905–1971* (Toronto, 1975) 108
30 King Papers, reel 2296, vol. 168, 121723, Jimmy Gardiner to King, 23 August 1927. For a full discussion see the following MA theses at the University of Saskatchewan: William Calderwood, 'The Rise and Fall of the Ku Klux Klan in Saskatchewan' (1968); Patrick Kyba, 'The Saskatchewan General Election of 1929' (1964); Gordon Unger, 'James G. Gardiner: The Premier as a Pragmatic Politician, 1925–1929' (1967); see also Patrick Kyba, 'Ballots and Burning Crosses: The Election of 1929' in Norman Ward and Duff Spafford, eds., *Politics in Saskatchewan* (Don Mills, ON, 1968) as well as Smith, *Prairie Liberalism*
31 John Herd Thompson and Allen Seager, *Canada, 1922–1939: Decades of Discord* (Toronto, 1985) 130–1
32 King Papers, reel 2302, vol. 180, 129007–8, T.C. Davis to W.D. Euler, 25 January 1928; reel 2296, vol. 168, 121728–31, King to Jimmy Gardiner, 30 August 1927

33 Thompson and Seager, *Canada*, 131
34 *Grain Growers' Guide*, 1 December 1927, 11; 1 March 1928, 8; 1 June 1928, 15, 17
35 Neatby, *Lonely Heights*, 245
36 King Diaries, 16 February 1928; 11 February 1928
37 *Grain Growers' Guide*, 15 March 1928, 7
38 King Diaries, 17 March 1928; 16 May 1928
39 King Papers, reel 2303, vol. 179, 128328–9, John Bracken to King, 24 January 1928; 128332–5, King to Bracken, 20 February 1928
40 Neatby, *Lonely Heights*, 246–9
41 As quoted in G.W.D. Abrams, *Prince Albert: The First Century, 1866–1966* (Saskatoon, 1966) 271
42 King Diaries, 4 May 1928
43 King Papers, reel 2302, vol. 180, 129018–21, King to T.C. Davis, 14 May 1928
44 Ibid., reel 2305, vol. 186, 133080–1, T. Robertson to King, 17 June 1928
45 King Diaries, 3 July 1928
46 King Papers, reel 2302, vol. 179, 128324–5, John Bracken to King, 10 January 1928
47 Neatby, *Lonely Heights*, 249–50
48 King Diaries, 3 July 1928
49 King Papers, reel 2302, vol. 179, 128326–7, King to John Bracken, 28 February 1928
50 King Papers, reel 2307, vol. 189, 134839, L. Stubbs to King, 2 March 1928
51 Neatby, *Lonely Heights*, 252
52 Neatby, on the other hand, argues that one reason for King's procrastination on the Manitoba resource transfer was because any concessions to Bracken would be resented by the provincial Liberals. Ibid.
53 As quoted in Kendle, *Bracken*, 69–70
54 King Papers, reel 2306, vol. 186, 133146–51, H.A. Robson to King, 18 May 1928; 133139–42, Robson to King, 21 April and 1 May 1928; 133143–5, King to Robson, 19 May 1928; reel 2302, vol. 179, 128340–2, John Bracken to King, 15 June 1928
55 As quoted in Kendle, *Bracken*, 68
56 King Papers, reel 2306, vol. 186, 133117–18, H.A. Robson to King, 4 January 1928
57 King Diaries, 22–3 March 1928; 20 April 1928
58 Ibid., 3 July 1928
59 Ibid., 4–6 July 1928; Lapointe continued to represent the eastern contention that any gains made by the West had to receive the support of the other provinces, which may also wish to put forward claims of their own.

60 Neatby, *Lonely Heights*, 254–5; King Diaries, 10 July 1928

61 King Diaries, 8 July 1928

62 Ibid., 5 August 1928; 10 August 1928

63 Waiser, *Saskatchewan's Playground*, 34–5

64 King Diaries, 13 December 1928

65 King Papers, reel 2305, vol. 186, 133241–2, G.H. Ross to King, 29 March 1928

66 Ibid., reel 2308, vol. 191, 136625–7, Joseph A. Clarke to Andrew Haydon, 8 May 1929

67 *Grain Growers' Guide*, 15 March 1929, 8

68 King Papers, reel 2308, vol. 192, 136727–8, King to T.A. Crerar, 23 September 1929; reel 2309, vol. 194, 137771–3, King to Jimmy Gardiner, 22 April 1929

69 As quoted in Kendle, *Bracken*, 82–3

70 Ibid., 94; PAM, John Bracken Papers, MG 13, I2, box 4, folder 1929, file coalition 1929–36, Bracken to H.A. Robson, 6 March 1929

71 As quoted in Kendle, *Bracken*, 95

72 King Papers, reel 2309, vol. 193, 136831–5, J.W. Dafoe to King, 23 February 1929; 136837–8, Dafoe to King, 2 March 1929

73 Ibid., reel 2323, vol. 201, 142074–80, King to H.A. Robson, 4 March 1929; reel 2309, vol. 193, 136831–5, J.W. Dafoe to King, 23 February 1929; reel 2308, vol. 191, 136082–3, E. Brown to King, 2 March 1929; 136263–9, King to D. Cameron, 13 March 1929; reel 2311, vol. 198, 139944–9, E.J. McMurray to King, 27 March 1929

74 Kendle, *Bracken*, 68, 96

75 King Papers, reel 2309, vol. 194, 138016–36, Thomas Taylor to King, 15 March 1929

76 Kendle, *Bracken*, 97

77 King Papers, reel 2309, vol. 194, 138016–36, Thomas Taylor to King, 15 March 1929

78 Ibid., vol. 193, 136839–42, J.W. Dafoe to King, 9 March 1929; vol. 194, 137767–70, Jimmy Gardiner to King, 20 March 1929

79 Ibid., reel 2315, vol. 205, 144878–81, J.W. Wilton to King, 20 March 1929

80 King Diaries, 19 March 1929

81 King Papers, reel 2308, vol. 191, 135823–6, E.D.R. Bisset to King, 23 March 1929

82 Kendle, *Bracken*, 98

83 King Papers, reel 2307, vol. 190, 135233–5, Manitoba Liberals to King, n.d.; reel 2315, vol. 205, 144885–8, J.W. Wilton to King, 19 April 1929

84 Ibid., reel 2313, vol. 201, 142074–80, King to J.A. Robb, 4 March 1929

85 Ibid., reel 2309, vol. 194, 137758–9, Jimmy Gardiner to King, 3 January 1929

86 C. Frank Steele, *Prairie Editor: The Life and Times of Buchanan of Lethbridge* (Toronto, 1961) 54

87 King Diaries, 7 June 1929

88 King Papers, reel 2309, vol. 193, 136952–5, T.C. Davis to King, 9 September 1929; reel 2313, vol. 201, 141715, G.C. Porter to King, 19 September 1929; reel 2314, vol. 204, 143888–90, G. Spence to King, 18 July 1929

89 King Diaries, 23 October 1929; 6 November 1929; 7 November 1929

90 King Papers, reel 2318, vol. 212, 149349–52, W.R. Howson to Charles Stewart, 3 February 1930; 149360–2, King to Howson, 24 October 1930

91 Neatby, *Lonely Heights*, 296

92 King Diaries, 1 November 1930

93 Ibid., 26 November 1929

94 Gardiner Papers, reel 10, 17610–2, King to Jimmy Gardiner, 29 October 1929

95 J.W. Dafoe, for example, was angered with Dunning's drive to have the Hudson Bay terminal at Churchill rather than Nelson. 'There is a great big question mark in my mind against the said Mr. Dunning. I am beginning to wonder if ... in getting Dunning he [King] was getting the biggest double-crosser in the business.' Dafoe Papers, box 2, file 2, Dafoe to G. Dexter, 4 August 1927; 'Charlie will have to get over this idea that he can play the drill-sergeant; and make everybody perform the evolutions that he desires; or he will suffer complete political shipwreck.' Dafoe to Dexter, 12 April 1927

96 King Diaries, 4 November 1929; 22 November 1929

97 King Papers, reel 2308, vol. 192, 136736–40, T.A. Crerar to King, 30 November 1929; 136742–5, King to Crerar, 3 December 1929

98 King Diaries, 30 December 1929

99 Ibid., 9–13 December 1929 .,

100 King Papers, reel 2309, vol. 193, 136974–5, T.C. Davis to King, 12 December 1929; reel 2315, vol. 206, 145230–4, J.T.M. Anderson to King, 17 January 1930

101 King Diaries, 9 December 1929

102 King Papers, reel 2315, vol. 206, 145235–40, King to J.T.M. Anderson, 7 February 1930

103 King Diaries, 6 March 1930; 11 December 1929

104 Ibid., 14 December 1929

105 Neatby, *Lonely Heights*, 298

106 As quoted in Kendle, *Bracken*, 105–6

107 King Diaries, 31 December 1929
108 Neatby, *Lonely Heights*, 301
109 Gerald Friesen, *The Canadian Prairies: A History* (Toronto, 1987) 384–5
110 Neatby, *Lonely Heights*, 305
111 G.F. Wilson, *A Century of Canadian Grain* (Saskatoon, 1978) 239
112 House of Commons, *Debates*, 24 April 1922, 1073
113 King Papers, reel 2316, vol. 207, 146026–8, King to John Bracken, 8 January 1930
114 King Diaries, 26 February 1930
115 Ibid., 25 July 1930
116 House of Commons, *Debates*, 3 April 1930, 1225–8
117 Neatby, *Lonely Heights*, 323
118 King Diaries, 11 February 1930; 11 April 1930
119 King Papers, reel 2318, vol. 212, 148988–9, A.E. Darby to R.J. Deachman, as quoted in Deachman to Andrew Haydon, 17 March 1930
120 Ibid., reel 2319, vol. 213, 149952–4, T.P. King to W.L.M. King, 5 February 1930; reel 2320, vol. 215, 151189–94, N.T. Macmillan to King, 11 March 1930
121 King Diaries, 25 April 1930
122 Ibid., 9 April 1930
123 Neatby, *Lonely Heights*, 328
124 See Whitaker, *The Government Party: Organizing and Financing the Liberal Party of Canada* (Toronto, 1977).
125 Neatby, *Lonely Heights*, 330
126 King Diaries, 12 May 1930
127 King Papers, 2319, vol. 213, 149952–4, T.P. King to King, 5 February 1930
128 King Diaries, 12 May 1930
129 King Papers, reel 2317, vol. 210, 148246, Jimmy Gardiner to King, 19 May 1930
130 King Diaries, 28–30 June 1930; 1 July 1930
131 King Papers, reel 2323, vol. 221, 155148–50, King to O.D. Skelton, 14 July 1930; reel 2319, vol. 214, 150539–45, C.H. McCann to King, 6 February 1930
132 As quoted in Neatby, *Lonely Heights*, 334
133 Canadian dairy producers had begun to compete with products from New Zealand. The Conservatives criticized the admission of New Zealand butter, claiming it was destroying Canada's dairy industry.
134 Neatby, *Lonely Heights*, 336
135 King Diaries, 3 July 1930
136 King Papers, reel 2320, vol. 215, 151152–5, A.M. McLeod to King, 20 June 1930

137 Neatby, *Lonely Heights*, 337
138 Ibid., reel 2317, vol. 209, 147112–4, T.A. Crerar to King 10 June 1930; reel 2316, vol. 208, 146664–7, K.A. Blatchford to King, 12 September 1930
139 Peter Regenstreif, 'The Liberal Party of Canada: A Political Analysis' (PhD diss., Cornell University 1963) 245
140 'Stewart is no good as a minister, or organizer ... He has no suggestion as to what is best to do. He himself should have arranged it all.' King Diaries, 3 July 1930
141 Ibid., 10–11 July 1930; 28 July 1930
142 Abrams, *Prince Albert*, 312
143 The Liberals lost twenty-one seats in Quebec.
144 King Diaries, 20 September 1930; 29 July 1930; 2 August 1930
145 Dafoe Papers, box 2, file 2, Dafoe to Grant Dexter, 3 November 1930
146 Neatby, *Lonely Heights*, 340
147 Abrams, *Prince Albert*, 312
148 King Papers, reel 2316, vol. 207, 146160–1, W.A. Buchanan to King, 5 August 1930; reel 2317, vol. 209, 147162–9, T.A. Crerar to King, 7 November 1930; vol. 210, 148268–71, Jimmy Gardiner to King, 10 November 1930
149 Ibid., reel 2317, vol. 209, 147162–9, T.A. Crerar to King, 7 November 1930
150 King Diaries, 3 August 1930
151 Dafoe Papers, box 2, file 2, Dafoe to Grant Dexter, 8 August 1930; box 3, file 7, Dafoe to D.A. McArthur, 7 October 1930
152 Neatby, *Lonely Heights*, 341
153 King Papers, reel 2321, vol. 219, 153990–1, J.G. Ross to King, 27 November 1930; reel 2317, vol. 209, 147162–9, T.A. Crerar to King, 7 November 1930; vol. 210, 148268–71, Jimmy Gardiner to King, 10 November 1930
154 Dafoe Papers, box 2, file 2, Dafoe to Grant Dexter, 3 November 1930

6: The Stiffer the Application, the Swifter the Cure, 1931–1935

1 NAC, W.L.M. King Papers, MG 26, J1, reel 2326, vol. 227, 158592–4, King to W.R. Howson, 19 December 1931
2 Ibid., reel 2324, vol. 224, 156843–4, K.A. Blatchford to King, 10 March 1931; reel 2316, vol. 207, 146160–1, W.A. Buchanan to King, 5 August 1930; reel 2318, vol. 212, 149358–9, W.R. Howson to Charles Stewart, 9 September 1930; reel 2326, vol. 227, 158588–91, Howson to King, 13 December 1931. The same sentiments for a more radical platform were voiced by most Alberta Liberals who sensed the mood of the province. 'I sometimes feel that it would be to our advantage as a party to take a rather pronounced stand a little more to the leftward,' W.A. Buchanan wrote. Reel 2328, vol. 231, 161640–1, Buchanan to King, 7 July 1932

3 Ibid., reel 2316, vol. 208, 146683–4, King to J.A. Clarke, 30 December 1930; 161216–17, King to G.H. Webster, 28 January 1931; reel 2325 vol. 225, 157290–3, J.A. Clarke to G.P. Graham, 13 November 1931

4 Ibid., reel 2325, vol. 225, 157341–4, T.A. Crerar to King, 4 May 1931; 157351–3, Crerar to King, 29 June 1931; reel 2326, vol. 227, 158975–8, King to W.J. Lindal, 19 April 1931; reel 2325, vol. 225, 157363–6, Crerar to King, 7 October 1931

5 King Papers, reel 2326, vol. 228, 159154–6, King to Charles McDonald, 14 January 1931; reel 2328, vol. 231, 161107–12, W.A. Tucker to King, 1 January 1931

6 Norman Ward and David Smith, *Jimmy Gardiner: Relentless Liberal* (Toronto, 1990) 55

7 King Papers, reel 2325, vol. 225, 157586–8, T.C. Davis to King, 16 July 1931

8 UMA, J.W. Dafoe Papers, MSS 3, box 2, file 2, Dafoe to G. Dexter, 20 January 1931

9 *William Lyon Mackenzie King Diaries* (Toronto, 1973), 1 June 1931; 24 June 1931; 1 July 1931

10 Ibid., 12 January 1932

11 Dafoe Papers, box 3, file 9, Dafoe to V. Massey, 7 December 1931

12 King Papers, reel 2325, vol. 225, 157341–4, T.A. Crerar to King, 4 May 1931

13 King Papers, vol. 184, Crerar to King, 2 September 1931

14 'The capitalistic system to-day is under fire, it is on trial, it is being investigated; and I hope, indeed I believe, it is being modified.' House of Commons, *Debates*, 16 June 1931, 2668

15 H. Blair Neatby, *William Lyon Mackenzie King: The Lonely Heights, 1924–1932* (Toronto, 1963) 344

16 Ibid., 350

17 King Papers, reel 2325, vol. 225, 157642, R.J. Deachman to King, 5 May 1931; reel 2328, vol. 231, 161640–1, W.A. Buchanan to King, 7 July 1932

18 As quoted in Neatby, *Lonely Heights*, 364

19 Ibid., 356–7

20 King Diaries, 2 June 1931

21 The scandal involved disclosures of close connections between the Liberal government and the Beauharnois syndicate, which had been given the contract for a diversion to the St Lawrence River. The details of the scandal are discussed in T.D. Regehr, *The Beauharnois Scandal: A Story of Canadian Entrepreneurship and Politics* (Toronto, 1990)

22 King Papers, reel 2329, vol. 234, 163385–6, J. Boyd McBride to King, 3 June 1932

23 House of Commons, *Debates*, 30 July 1931, 4709

24 QUA, T.A. Crerar Papers, series III, box 119, Charles Murphy to Rodolphe Lemieux, 5 February 1932

25 King Papers, reel 2325, vol. 225, 159357–62, T.A. Crerar to King, 2 September 1931; Crerar Papers, series III, box 98, Crerar to Kirk Cameron, 31 August 1931; King Papers, reel 2325, vol. 225, 157363–6, Crerar to King, 7 October 1931; Crerar Papers, series III, box 95, Crerar to Cameron, 2 November 1931

26 Dafoe Papers, box 2, file 2, Dafoe to G. Dexter, 20 November 1931

27 Crerar Papers, Crerar to Kirk Cameron, 31 August 1931

28 King Papers, reel 2328, vol. 231, 161096–97A, A.F. Totzke to King, 4 February 1931; 161098–100, King to Totzke, 9 February 1931; J5, Speeches, reel 2799, vol. 33D, 19258–61, 12 January 1932; reel 2328, vol. 231, 160889–92, J.J. Stevenson to King, 19 January 1931; vol. 232, 161946–7, Crerar to King, 4 January 1932

29 H. Blair Neatby, *William Lyon Mackenzie King: The Prism of Unity, 1932–1939* (Toronto, 1976) 30; as quoted in Neatby, *Prism of Unity*, 31

30 King Diaries, 1 February 1933

31 John Kendle, *John Bracken: A Political Biography* (Toronto, 1979) 115–18, 120–2

32 King Diaries, 14 January 1932

33 King Papers, reel 2328, vol. 231, 161954–5, T.A. Crerar to King, 8 March 1932; vol. 232, 161959–61, Crerar to King, 6 June 1932

34 King Diaries, 18 June 1932

35 King Papers, reel 2328, vol. 232, 161963–7, T.A. Crerar to King, 22 August 1932; reel 2329, vol. 233, 162605–13, King to Jimmy Gardiner, 10 September 1932; reel 2330, vol. 235, 163609–11, Norman McKay to King, 4 July 1932; reel 2331, vol. 237, 164854–7, King to J.T. Thorson, 22 August 1932

36 Ibid., reel 2329, vol. 234, 163385–6, J. Boyd McBride to King, 3 June 1932; reel 2331, vol. 237, 164896–7, G.H. Van Allen to King, 23 May 1932; 164898–9, King to Van Allen, 1 June 1932

37 Neatby, *Prism of Unity*, 34–8

38 House of Commons, *Debates,* 27 February 1933, 2492–2512

39 King Papers, reel 2328, vol. 232, 161946–7, T.A. Crerar to King, 4 January 1932

40 Ibid., reel 3672, vol. 195, 166036–8, King to C.A. Dunlop, 8 July 1933; 166041–2, King to E.L. Dunn, 5 October 1933

41 For a full discussion see John C. Courtney, 'Mackenzie King and Prince Albert Constituency: The 1933 Redistribution,' *Saskatchewan History* 29 (winter 1976): 1–13.

42 House of Commons, *Debates,* 22 May 1933, 5276–7

43 King Papers, reel 3672, vol. 195, 165802–3, T.C. Davis to King, 28 January 1933
44 Ibid., 165804–5, King to Davis, 2 February 1933
45 King Diaries, 12 May 1933; 17 May 1933
46 Ibid., 12 May 1933; 17 May 1933
47 The member for Last Mountain, Harry Butcher, would stand aside for Motherwell, probably be taken into the Saskatchewan cabinet until Motherwell died, and then return to the seat. Motherwell refused but was prepared to accept a Tory map that joined a portion of Butcher's constituency with Melville. Ibid., 18 May 1933
48 Ibid., 27 May 1933; 22–3 May 1933
49 Courtney, 'King and Prince Albert,' 13
50 Ibid., 11
51 King Papers, reel 3674, vol. 198, 168541, King to T. Robertson, 14 June 1933
52 King Diaries, 27 May 1933
53 Ibid., 14 June 1933; King Papers, reel 3672, vol. 195, 165855–6, T.C. Davis to King, 14 July 1933
54 A provincial by-election in Kinistino, which contained parts of all three of the proposed federal constituencies, provided further evidence of declining Tory fortunes. King Papers, reel 3672, vol. 196, 166338–9, Jimmy Gardiner to King, 24 May 1933
55 Ibid., vol. 195, 166346–7, King to Jimmy Gardiner, 10 June 1933; vol. 196, 166219–22, King to C. Fleury, 29 August 1933
56 King Diaries, 23 March 1935
57 King Papers, reel 3672, vol. 195, 165688–9, T.A. Crerar to King, 30 June 1933
58 King Diaries, 21 August 1931
59 King Papers, reel 3674, vol. 197, 168087–8, King to H. Moyle, 26 June 1933
60 Dafoe Papers, box 3, file 3, Dafoe to King, 15 June 1933; box 4, file 2, Dafoe to Newton Rowell, 28 July 1931
61 King Diaries, 20 July 1933
62 King Papers, reel 3672, vol. 195, 165119, King to H.A. Allen, 9 June 1933; reel 3674, vol. 198, 168680, King to Norman Rogers, 18 March 1933
63 Dafoe Papers, box 6, file 6, W.A. Buchanan to Dafoe, 11 July 1934
64 King Papers, reel 3673, vol. 197, 167631–3, King to Ian Mackenzie, 14 November 1933; reel 3674, vol. 197, 167879, King to A. Massey, 31 March 1933
65 King Diaries, 21 July 1933
66 King Papers, reel 3672, vol. 195, 165979–80, T.A. Crerar to King, 15 May 1933; 165726–7, J.W. Dafoe to King, 8 August 1933

67 King Diaries, 22 July 1933
68 King Diaries, 20 July 1933
69 King Papers, reel 3674, vol. 198, 168526–31, N. Robertson to King, 8 June
   1933; reel 3672, vol. 196, 166327, King to Jimmy Gardiner, 25 March 1933
70 Neatby, *Prism of Unity*, 47
71 King Papers, vol. 195, 165436, W.A. Buchanan to King, 4 July 1933; reel
   3674, vol. 198, 168472–3, D.E. Riley to King, 2 March 1933
72 King Diaries, 1 March 1934
73 Neatby, *Prism of Unity*, 54–5
74 Ibid., 57
75 King Papers, reel 3677, vol. 201, 171956–9, G.G. McGeer to King, 21 June
   1934; 172163–4, E.J. McMurray to King, 27 January 1934
76 J.E. Rea, 'The Wheat Board and the Western Farmer,' *The Beaver* (February–March 1997): 23
77 As quoted in J.E. Rea, *T.A. Crerar: A Political Life* (Montreal, 1997) 168
78 King Papers, reel 3675, vol. 199, 170109–12, T.A. Crerar to King, 8 January
   1934
79 Neatby, *Prism of Unity*, 58–9
80 David Smith, *Prairie Liberalism: The Liberal Party in Saskatchewan, 1905–1971*
   (Toronto, 1975) 199
81 Smith, *Prairie Liberalism*, 217
82 King Diaries, 31 July 1934
83 King Papers, reel 3676, vol. 200, 170835–6, W.R. Howson to King, 2 June
   1934
84 Ibid., 171050–1, W.R. Howson to King, 30 August 1934
85 Ibid., 171054–6, King to W.R. Howson, 30 August 1934; vol. 199, 170745,
   Jimmy Gardiner to King, 9 October 1934; vol. 200, 171057–9, Howson to
   King, 19 September 1934; 171060–1, King to Howson, 24 September 1934
86 Ibid., 171065–6, W.R. Howson to King, 27 December 1934; 171072, King to
   W.R. Howson, 2 January 1935
87 King Papers, reel 3678, vol. 202, 173582–3, Charles Stewart to King,
   28 September 1934; reel 3679, vol. 204, 174836–8, W.A. Buchanan to King,
   4 May 1935; 173573, Stewart to King, 9 August 1934; reel 3677, vol. 202,
   173904–6, D.E. Reily to King, 11 December 1934
88 John A. Irving, *The Social Credit Movement in Alberta* (Toronto, 1959) 93
89 King Papers, reel 3678, vol. 202, 173582–3, Charles Stewart to King,
   28 September 1934
90 Crerar Papers, series III, box 98, Crerar to Kirk Cameron, 18 May 1935.
91 C.B. Macpherson, *Democracy in alberta: Social Credit and the Party System*
   (Toronto, 1953) 93

92 King Diaries, 23 August 1935
93 King Papers, reel 3679, vol. 206, 177287–91, W.R. Howson to King, 4 September 1935; reel 3681, vol. 207, 178280–2, J.B. McBride to King, 26 August 1935; reel 3683, vol. 210, 181039, J.H. Brown to King, 10 July 1935
94 King Diaries, 23 August 1935
95 Ibid., 7 June 1935
96 King Papers, reel 3679, vol. 205, 175499–505, T.A. Crerar to King, 19 June 1935
97 King Diaries, 12 June 1935
98 King Papers, reel 3679, vol. 205, 175622–4, Dafoe to King, 29 June 1935
99 King Diaries, 2 March 1935; 10 June 1935; 19 June 1935; 13 June 1935
100 King Papers, reel 3679, vol. 205, 176387–8, F.O. Fowler to King, 7 September 1935
101 As quoted in Neatby, *Prism of Unity*, 120
102 Reginald Whitaker, *The Government Party: Organizing and Financing the Liberal Party of Canada* (Toronto, 1977) 68, 73
103 King Papers, reel 3679, vol. 205, 175684–5, T.C. Davis to N. Lambert, 1 March 1935; reel 3682, vol. 208, 179621–2, King to R.F. McWilliams, 15 July 1935
104 Crerar owned a farm in Thorson's riding and had previously contemplated running there. Rea, *Crerar*, 170
105 PAM, John Bracken Papers, MG 13, I2, box 2549, file 1, 8 October 1935
106 King Diaries, 10 June 1935; see also Ward and Smith, *Gardiner*; King Diaries, 23 July 1935.
107 King Diaries, 24 September 1935
108 G.W.D. Abrams, *Prince Albert: The First Century, 1866–1966* (Saskatoon, 1966) 320–1
109 King Diaries, 19 September 1935
110 Ibid., 25 September 1935
111 Abrams, *Prince Albert*, 321
112 Neatby, *Prism of Unity*, 122–3
113 The cabinet negotiations are discussed in detail in King's Diaries, 14–22 October 1935.
114 Ibid., 14 and 17 October 1935
115 Ibid., 18 October 1935
116 Ibid.
117 Ibid.
118 Ibid., 19 October 1935
119 Ibid.
120 Ibid.

121 Dafoe Papers, box 2, file 1, J.W.Dafoe to Wallace Dafoe, 26 November 1935
122 King Diaries, 18 October 1935
123 Ibid., 17 and 21 October 1935
124 Rea, *Crerar*, 171–2
125 King Diaries, 21 October 1935
126 Ibid., 23 October 1935
127 Ibid., 22 October 1935
128 As quoted in Rea, *Crerar*, 172
129 King Diaries, 21 October 1935
130 Ibid., 31 October 1935
131 King Papers, reel 3684, vol. 211, 181650–2, G.H. Ross to King, 4 December 1935
132 King Diaries, 9 December 1935; 13 December 1935
133 King Papers, reel 3684, vol. 211, 181654, King to G.H. Ross, 23 December 1935
134 Neatby, *Prism of Unity*, 149

7: The Radical Has Left Us, 1936–1940

1 H. Blair Neatby, *William Lyon Mackenzie King: The Prism of Unity, 1932–1939* (Toronto, 1976) 155
2 Ibid., 153
3 *William Lyon Mackenzie King Diaries* (Toronto, 1973) 4 April 1936
4 Neatby, *Prism of Unity*, 158
5 King Diaries, 18 March 1936
6 NAC, W.L.M. King Papers, MG 26, J1, reel 3687, vol. 215, 185287, Charles Dunning to William Aberhart, 20 March 1936; 185288, Aberhart to Dunning, 21 March 1936; 185289, Dunning to Aberhart, 23 March 1936
7 King Diaries, 17 March 1936
8 King Papers, reel 3687, vol. 215, 185293, Charles Dunning to William Aberhart, 26 March 1936; 185294, Aberhart to Dunning, 27 March 1936; 185295, Dunning to Aberhart, 30 March 1936; 185296, Aberhart to Dunning, 30 March 1936; 185297, Dunning to Aberhart, 30 March 1936
9 W.L.M. King Diaries 28 March 1936; 30 March 1936
10 Ibid., 25 April 1936
11 Ibid., 14–15 May 1936; 23 June 1936; 22 April 1936
12 Ibid., 7 April 1936
13 King Papers, reel 3687, vol. 215, 18748, King to R.J. Deachman, 11 April 1936; reel 3689, vol. 220, 189002–3, P.M. Lee to King, 18 January 1936; reel

3687, vol. 215, 185438–9; J.S. Courper to King, 7 May 1936; reel 3694, vol. 228, 196086–8, King to W.W. Sharpe, 14 November 1936

14 G.W.D. Abrams, *Prince Albert: The First Century, 1866–1966* (Saskatoon, 1966) 321–3

15 King Papers, reel 3729, vol. 242, 207718–9, J.W. Sanderson to King, 21 October 1937

16 'My position can only be linked to that of a captain of a ship on a strong sea. I can leave my post here, and travel to other parts for personal or political reasons, but cannot do so without the certain knowledge that some matter of peace or war necessitating an immediate decision, which the Prime Minister alone can give in the name of the country, may come up in the course of that absence.' Ibid., 207720–1, King to Sanderson, 30 October 1937

17 Ibid., reel 3687, vol. 215, 185702–3, T.C. Davis to King, 15 April 1936

18 Ibid., reel 3742, vol. 266, 226044–7, King to Omer Demers, 3 July 1939

19 King Diaries, 30 April 1936; 19 August 1936

20 King Papers, reel 3693, vol. 225, 194169–70, J.G. Ross to King, 20 April 1936

21 UMA, J.W. Dafoe Papers, MSS 3, box 7, file 5, T.A. Crerar to Dafoe, 4 March 1936

22 King Diaries, 26 April 1936

23 Ibid., 31 October 1935

24 King Papers, reel 3689, vol. 219, 188201–2, J.F. Johnston to King, 14 July 1936

25 King Diaries, 25 March 1935

26 Ibid., 19 August 1936; 27 August 1936

27 Ibid., 25–7 August 1936

28 G.F. Wilson, *A Century of Canadian Grain* (Saskatoon, 1978) 529

29 Neatby, *Prism of Unity*, 186

30 King Diaries, 20 January 1937

31 As quoted in Neatby, *Prism of Unity*, 187

32 King Papers, reel 3723, vol. 231, 198513–14, W.C. Barrie to King, 5 January 1937

33 SAB, J.G. Gardiner Papers, S-1.137, reel 21, 48573–5, C.F. Connolly to W.C. Barrie, 16 August 1936

34 King Papers, reel 3723, vol. 231, 198514, King to W.C. Barrie, 13 January 1937; King Diaries, 18 December 1936

35 King Diaries, 2 December 1936; 15 December 1936

36 Gardiner Papers, reel 20, 48504, W.C. Barrie to Jimmy Gardiner, 18 January 1936

37 Ibid., reel 21, 49729–30, Gardiner to W.A. Buchanan, 31 August 1936; reel

20, 48504, W.C. Barrie to Gardiner, 18 January 1936; reel 19, 41333–5, Gardiner to T.D. Leonard, 8 October 1937; reel 21, 49801–5, Gardiner to Buchanan, 17 November 1937; 48572, W.C. Barrie to C.F. Connolly, 18 August 1936; 50489, W.R. Howson to Gardiner, 29 January 1936

38 Norman Ward, 'Hon. James Gardiner and the Liberal Party of Alberta, 1935–1940,' *Canadian Historical Review* 56, no. 3 (September 1975): 305

39 Ibid., 311

40 King Papers, reel 3725, vol. 234, 201362–6, Jimmy Gardiner to King, 28 May 1937

41 Gardiner Papers, reel 19, 43125–7, Gardiner to King, 17 November 1937

42 Ward, 'Gardiner,' 310

43 King Papers, reel 3730, vol. 243, 208974–6, G.H. Steer to King, 25 March 1937; reel 2724, vol. 232, 199503–4, W.A. Buchanan to King, 26 August 1937; reel 3725, vol. 234, 201711–12, E.L. Gray to King, 1 December 1937

44 Ibid., reel 3724, vol. 233, 199676–7, C.E. Campbell to King, 12 October 1937

45 Gardiner Papers, reel 21, 48747–8, Gardiner to W.C. Barrie, 9 October 1937

46 King Papers, reel 3729, vol. 241, 206923–4, King to D.E. Riley, 12 October 1937

47 Ibid., reel 3725, vol. 235, 201713–14, King to E.L. Gray, 10 December 1937

48 Neatby, *Prism of Unity*, 195

49 King Diaries, 3 October 1937

50 'If false political theories and doctrines continue to be applied and remain unexposed in Alberta, they may sweep over into other provinces more rapidly than we expect.' King Papers, reel 3694, vol. 228, 196086–8, King to W.W. Sharpe, 14 November 1936

51 Ibid., reel 3686, vol. 214, 184539, W.M. Davidson to W.A. Buchanan, 2 April 1936; 184569–70, Buchanan to Jimmy Gardiner, 2 September 1936; 184551–2, Buchanan to King, 16 May 1936

52 King Diaries, 15 December 1936

53 Neatby, *Prism of Unity*, 198–9

54 King Diaries, 4 January 1937; 8 January 1937

55 King Papers, reel 3723, vol. 231, 198154, King to William Aberhart, 19 February 1937

56 King Diaries, 22 February 1937

57 Neatby, *Prism of Unity*, 225

58 Ibid., 226

59 Ibid., 227–8

60 King Papers, reel 2724, vol. 232, 199498–9, W.A. Buchanan to King, 6 August 1937

61 King Diaries, 5–6 August 1937

62 King Papers, reel 2724, vol. 232, King to William Aberhart, 17 August 1937

63 Ibid., 198171–2, William Aberhart to King, 17 August 1937

64 Neatby, *Prism of Unity*, 229–30

65 King Diaries, 18 May 1938

66 Ibid., 19 May 1938

67 House of Commons, *Debates*, 1 February 1938, 95–100. In 1937 Premier
    Maurice Duplessis brought in the Act Respecting Communist Propaganda,
    which made it illegal to use a house to propagate communism. On order, a
    house could be locked up if the attorney general believed the act to be
    broken. The legislation was extremely subjective, providing the government
    with sweeping powers.

68 King Diaries, 6 July 1938

69 King Papers, reel 3731, vol. 245, 209894–5, William Aberhart to King, 9
    September 1938; reel 3723, vol. 231, 198182–5, Aberhart to King, 26 August
    1937; 198187–9, King to Aberhart, 2 September 1937

70 Lambert handled federal party finances; this function brought him into
    conflict with Gardiner in both Saskatchewan and Alberta.

71 King Diaries, 10 September 1937; 28 October 1937; 21 December 1937

72 Ward, 'Gardiner,' 314–17

73 King Papers, reel 3735, vol. 254, 216353–6, C. McLaurin to King, 26 April
    1938

74 Gardiner Papers, reel 21, 48793–4, W.C. Barrie to Gardiner, 29 March 1938

75 King Papers, reel 3731, vol. 245, 210145–6, W.C. Barrie to King, 2 April 1938

76 Ibid., reel 3734, vol. 251, 214536–9, J.B. Howatt to King, 23 March 1938

77 King Diaries, 21 December 1937

78 King Papers, reel 3734, vol. 252, 214540–1, King to J.B. Howatt, 29 March
    1938

79 Ibid., 214713–5, D.R. Innes to King, 5 February 1938; reel 3735, vol. 253,
    215430–2, E. Litchfield to King, 5 April 1938; 215993–4, J.P. McIsaac to
    King, 8 August 1938

80 Gardiner Papers, reel 21, 48774–5, Gardiner to W.C. Barrie, 13 January 1938

81 As quoted in Norman Ward and David Smith, *Jimmy Gardiner: Relentless
    Liberal* (Toronto, 1990) 220

82 King Diaries, 15 April 1938

83 Ibid., 12 November 1937

84 As quoted in Neatby, *Prism of Unity*, 252

85 King Diaries, 1 April 1938

86 Ibid., 5 May 1938

87 Neatby, *Prism of Unity*, 249–55

88 King Diaries, 8 June 1938; 22 June 1938

89 Ibid., 22 June 1938
90 Ibid., 22 June 1938; 11 August 1939
91 Ibid., 7 July 1938
92 Ibid., 8–9 June 1938
93 Neatby, *Prism of Unity*, 266
94 David Smith, *Prairie Liberalism: The Liberal Party in Saskatchewan, 1905–1971* (Toronto, 1975) 240
95 Wilson, *Century of Canadian Grain*, 558
96 King Diaries, 23 June 1938; 26 July 1938
97 As quoted in Wilson, *Century of Canadian Grain*, 527
98 Ward and Smith, *Gardiner*, 253–4
99 Wilson, *Century of Canadian Grain*, 586–9
100 King Diaries, 16 December 1937
101 Neatby, *Prism of Unity*, 306–7
102 Wilson, *Century of Canadian Grain*, 592–4
103 King Diaries, 20 March 1939
104 Ibid., 21 March 1939; 5 April 1939
105 Ibid., 24 April 1939
106 King Papers, reel 4570, vol. 289, 244458, C.D. Howe to King, 30 July 1940
107 Ibid., reel 4571, vol. 297, 246090, J.A. MacKinnon to A.D.P. Heeney, 5 March 1940; reel 4575, vol. 305, 252062–3, J.H. Sissons to King, 11 October 1939
108 King Diaries, 27 January 1940
109 King Papers, reel 3743, vol. 267, 227063–5, Jimmy Gardiner to King, 15 July 1939
110 J.L. Granatstein, *Canada's War: The Politics of the Mackenzie King Government, 1939–1945* (Toronto: 1975) 90
111 J.E. Rea, *T.A. Crerar: A Political Life* (Montreal 1997) 198–9
112 Ibid.
113 King Papers, reel 3748, vol. 276, 233608–12, C.G. Power to King, 18 July 1939
114 Reginald Whitaker, *The Government Party: Organizing and Financing the Liberal Party of Canada* (Toronto, 1977) 118
115 King Papers, reel 3746, vol. 272, 230681–2, J.A. Mackinnon to King, 31 July 1939; reel 4571, vol. 291, 1246085, Mackinnon to King, 23 February 1940; reel 3746, vol. 272, 230675–7, Mackinnon to King, 18 July 1939; reel 3748, vol. 276, 233608–12, C.G. Power to King, 18 July 1939
116 As quoted in Frederick W. Gibson and Barbara Robertson eds., *Ottawa at War: The Grant Dexter Memoranda, 1939–1945* (Winnipeg, 1994) 46
117 King Diaries, 29 February 1940
118 Abrams, *Century of Canadian Grain*, 329–32
119 King Diaries, 29 February 1940

120 Ibid., 15 May 1940
121 King Papers, reel 4568, vol. 286, 242326–7, T.C. Davis to King, 7 April 1940
122 Whitaker, *Government Party*, 346

8: Viewing the Mountains without Scaling the Hills, 1941–1950

1 UML, J.W. Dafoe Papers, MSS 3, box 1, file 4, Dafoe to E.K. Brown, 12
  January 1943; box 5, file 5, Dafoe to J.A. Stevenson, 12 February 1942
2 W.L. Morton, *Manitoba: A History* (Toronto, 1957) 431
3 J.L. Granatstein, *Canada's War: The Politics of the Mackenzie King Government,*
  1939–1945 (Toronto, 1975) 167–8
4 Adélard Godbout and the Quebec Liberals had defeated the troublesome
  Union Nationale of Maurice Duplessis with the 'help' of Ernest Lapointe
  and the Quebec MPs.
5 Granatstein, *Canada's War*, 173–4
6 NAC, W.L.M. King Papers, MG 26, J1, reel 4860, vol. 299, 253557, William
  Aberhart to King, 6 October 1940; reel 6804, vol. 321, 271872E–E1,
  Aberhart to King, 26 March 1942
7 *William Lyon Mackenzie King Diaries* (Toronto, 1973) 2 March 1942
8 As quoted in Frederick W. Gibson and Barbara Robertson, *Ottawa at War:*
  The Grant Dexter Memoranda, 1939–1945 (Winnipeg, 1994) 15, 21
9 Dafoe Papers, box 8, file 2, G. Dexter to Dafoe, 3 January 1941
10 Norman Ward and David Smith, *Jimmy Gardiner: Relentless Liberal* (Toronto,
  1990) 265
11 King Diaries, 22 May 1940
12 Granatstein, *Canada's War*, 64
13 As quoted in Gibson and Robertson, *Ottawa at War*, 15, 21
14 J.E. Rea, *T.A. Crerar: A Political Life* (Montreal, 1997) 200
15 As quoted in Gibson and Robertson, *Ottawa at War*, 91.
16 King suggested Patterson, but Gardiner was opposed because the Saskatchewan premier did not have an agricultural background. Ward and Smith,
  Gardiner, 238
17 King Diaries, 9 January 1941
18 Ward and Smith, *Gardiner*, 237–46
19 King Diaries, 9 January 1941
20 Ibid., 254–5
21 Ward and Smith, *Gardiner*, 254–5
22 King Diaries, 11 March 1941
23 Rea, *Crerar*, 201
24 Ward and Smith, *Gardiner*, 256
25 Granatstein, *Canada's War*, 180–3

26 Ward and Smith, *Gardiner*, 257–8
27 As quoted in Ward and Smith, *Gardiner*, 279
28 King Papers, reel 4865, vol. 311, 262507–10, D.A. McNiven to King, 28 June 1941
29 King Diaries, 30 May 1940
30 As quoted in Gibson and Robertson, *Ottawa at War*, 173
31 King Diaries, 27 June 1941
32 Granatstein, *Canada's War*, 203
33 G.F. Wilson, *A Century of Canadian Grain* (Saskatoon, 1978) 719
34 SAB, J.G. Gardiner Papers, S-1.137, reel 20, 43713–6, D.A. McNiven to Gardiner, 17 October 1941
35 King Papers, reel 4871, vol. 319, 270862–6, Walter Tucker to King, 15 April 1941
36 G.W.D. Abrams, *Prince Albert: The First Century, 1866–1966* (Saskatoon, 1966) 332–3
37 King Diaries, 5 November 1941
38 King Papers, reel 6804, vol. 321, 272177–8, B. Avxier to J.A. MacKinnon, 24 September 1942; reel 6807, vol. 325, 278873–4, J.B. Howatt to MacKinnon, 23 September 1942
39 John Kendle, *John Bracken: A Political Biography* (Toronto, 1979) 181–3
40 Ibid., 183–6
41 Rea, *Crerar*, 215
42 King Diaries, 9–11 December 1942
43 As quoted in Gibson and Robertson, *Ottawa at War*, 393
44 Wilson, *Century of Canadian Grain*, 732
45 King Diaries, 5 March 1942; 26 February 1942
46 King Papers, reel 6805, vol. 323, 273958–60, King to W.R. Davies, 3 September 1942; reel 6806, vol. 324, 275661–2, H.R. Fleming to King, 4 September 1942; reel 7037, vol. 340, 292875–6, Jimmy Gardiner to King, 14 August 1943; 292908–9, Robert Forke to King, 1 February 1943
47 Ibid., reel 7042, vol. 347, 299730–46, L.A. Mutch to King, 27 August 1943
48 King Diaries, 6 October 1942
49 As quoted in Gibson and Robertson, *Ottawa at War*, 446
50 King Papers, reel 7034, vol. 337, 289610–18, J.J. Bench to King, 23 September 1943
51 Gibson and Robertson, *Ottawa at War*, 433
52 Rea, *Crerar*, 216–17
53 Granatstein, *Canada's War*, 250–2
54 King Papers, reel 6811, vol. 332, 284020, King to A. Roebuck, 29 October 1942
55 Granatstein, *Canada's War*, 265

56 Peter Regenstreif, 'The Liberal Party of Canada: A Political Analysis' (PhD diss., Cornell University, 1963) 139–40

57 King Papers, reel 7034, vol. 337, 289975, W.A. Buchanan to King, 31 August 1943

58 Granatstein, *Canada's War*, 252

59 King Papers, reel 7035, vol. 338, 290176, J.G. Campbell to King, 9 November 1943; reel 7037, vol. 340, 292896–7, J.W. Gardiner to King, 23 October 1943

60 King Diaries, 11 February 1944

61 As quoted in Gibson and Robertson, *Ottawa at War*, 441

62 As quoted in Granatstein, *Canada's War*, 266–7

63 Rea, *Crerar*, 221–4

64 Granatstein, *Canada's War*, 274, 276

65 King Diaries, 9 June 1943; 2 March 1944; 4 March 1944

66 Ward and Smith, *Gardiner*, 269–72

67 Ibid., 274

68 As quoted in ibid., 272, 274–8

69 Granatstein, *Canada's War*, 284; King Papers, reel 7049, vol. 358, 310586–7, R.J. Deachman to King, 23 June 1944

70 As quoted in Ward and Smith, *Gardiner*, 284, 285

71 King Papers, reel 7050, vol. 358, 310891–3, J.E. Doerr to King, 30 June 1944

72 Abrams, *Prince Albert*, 346

73 Ward and Smith, *Gardiner*, 281

74 David Smith, *Prairie Liberalism: The Liberal Party in Saskatchewan, 1905–1971* (Toronto, 1975) 252, 248, 250

75 King's first meeting with Premier Douglas reflected his desire to see younger men emerging as Liberal leaders in the West: 'I confess I was very pleased to see Douglas looking so young and enthusiastic about his work.' King Diaries, 24 July 1944

76 Ibid., 16 June 1944; 29 June 1944

77 Kendle, *Bracken*, 211

78 QUA, T.A. Crerar Papers, 2117, series III, box 105, Crerar to G. Dexter, 17 June 1944

79 King Diaries, 16 June 1944

80 Granatstein, *Canada's War*, 287

81 King Diaries, 13 July 1944

82 King Papers, reel 7051, vol. 361, 313115–17, M.I. Humphries to King, 20 July 1944; 313122–6, King to Humphries, 2 September 1944; reel 7059, vol. 375, 326443–6, J.J. Stevenson to King, 14 July 1944

83 King Diaries, 26 July 1944; 9 June 1943

84 King Papers, reel 7060, vol. 377, 328519–20, King to T.W. Wood, 26 March 1944

85 King Diaries, 14 January 1944; 1 January 1945; 1 February 1945
86 PAM, Stuart Garson Papers, MG 13, J1, box 2358, file 9, T.A. Crerar to Garson, 5 January 1943; box 2356, file 6, Garson to J.W. Pickersgill, 12 November 1945
87 King Papers, reel 7050, vol. 360, 312260–1, J.A. Glen to King, 20 December 1944
88 Granatstein, *Canada's War*, 403
89 Ibid., 383–6
90 King Papers, reel 7049, vol. 357, 310003–10, T.A. Crerar to King, 18 September 1944; reel 9874, vol. 382, 342203, S. Hansen to Jimmy Gardiner, 21 February 1945
91 King Diaries, 8 February 1945
92 King Papers, reel 9874, vol. 382, 343199–200, G.J. Matte to Jimmy Gardiner, 19 February 1945
93 King Diaries, 15 February 1948
94 Ibid., 17 February 1945
95 Abrams, *Prince Albert*, 349
96 King Diaries, 21 March 1945
97 King Papers, reel 9874, vol. 382, 342232–3, Wilfrid Gardiner to King, 5 April 1945; reel 9887, vol. 397, 359631–2, T.H. Wood to King, 6 April 1945
98 King Diaries, 29 March 1945; 3 April 1945
99 Ibid., 5 April 1945
100 King Papers, reel 9875, vol. 384, 343949, King to M.I. Humphries, 7 May 1945
101 King Diaries, 7 April 1945
102 Ibid., 12 April 1945; 5 May 1945; 7 May 1945; 19 May 1945
103 Ibid., 9 June 1945
104 The CCF levied accusations of vote tampering, and an inquiry eventually confirmed the charge. The tampering had been done, however, with the intent of discrediting Gardiner. Ward and Smith, *Gardiner*, 286
105 King Papers, reel 9783, vol. 380, 340720–1, King to W.L. Davies, 6 July 1945
106 Ward and Smith, *Gardiner*, 287
107 'Nothing could better illustrate the effect of organization and propaganda than the position of the Prairie provinces.' King Diaries, 18 June 1945
108 King Papers, reel 9174, vol. 111, 370705–9, L. Mutch to King, 26 October 1946
109 King Diaries, 24 May 1945; 12 June 1945
110 Ibid., 11 June 1945; 16 June 1945
111 King Papers, reel 9875, vol. 384, 343962–4, King to M.I. Humphries, 19 June 1945; 343984–7, King to Humphries, 7 July 1945

112 Smith, *Prairie Liberalism*, 254
113 PAM, Ralph Maybank Papers, MG 14, B35, box 5, file 90, Diary, 29 June 1947
114 King Papers, reel 11045, vol. 433, 395344, King to T.C. Wood, 7 March 1947
115 Smith, *Prairie Liberalism*, 259
116 As quoted in ibid., 259
117 King Diaries, 25 June 1948
118 Ward and Smith, *Gardiner*, 291
119 Wilson argues that, while Gardiner was 'de facto wheat policy maker,' the influence of his fellow ministers served to counter his 'sanguine incursions' against the treasury. Wilson, *Century of Canadian Grain*, 788, 846
120 Ibid., 867
121 King Diaries, 19 June 1946
122 Wilson, *Century of Canadian Grain*, 864
123 Ward and Smith, *Gardiner*, 266–7
124 King Diaries, 11 February 1948; 18 March 1948
125 Ibid., 17–22 October 1946; 16 December 1946
126 Maybank Papers, box 5, file 91, Diary, 27 January 1948
127 As quoted in David Smith, *The Regional Decline of a National Party: Liberals on the Prairies* (Toronto, 1981) 62–3
128 QUA, Grant Dexter Papers, series I, box 5, Diary, 2 June 1948
129 Reginald Whitaker, *The Government Party: Organizing and Financing the Liberal Party of Canada* (Toronto, 1977) 177
130 King Diaries, 30 May 1946; 17 October 1946; 13 March 1947
131 Whitaker, *Government Party*, 177
132 King Diaries, 23 March 1948
133 Dexter Papers, series I, box 5, Diary, 27 July 1948
134 King Diaries, 4 August 1948
135 Whitaker, *Government Party*, 178
136 Ibid.
137 Ward and Smith, *Gardiner*, 298
138 King Diaries, 5 August 1948; 7 August 1948
139 Whitaker, *Government Party*, 179
140 Ward and Smith, *Gardiner*, 293
141 King Diaries, 14 June 1945
142 Ward and Smith, *Gardiner*, 297
143 As quoted in ibid., 312
144 Ibid., 315
145 'Hammy' Macdonald, a former Conservative and the only coalition candidate to win a seat in 1948, became leader. Smith, *Prairie Liberalism*, 265

146 Ibid., 300, 305
147 Ibid., 296
148 Ward and Smith, *Gardiner*, 293

Conclusion

1 Reginald Whitaker, *The Government Party: Organizing and Financing the Liberal Party of Canada* (Toronto, 1977) 379–80
2 J.W. Pickersgill, 'Mackenzie King's Political Attitudes and Public Policies: A Personal Impression,' in *Mackenzie King: Widening the Debate*, ed. John English and J.O. Stubbs (Toronto, 1978) 19
3 Whitaker, *Government Party*, 379–80

Bibliography

Primary Sources

Glenbow Alberta Institute, Calgary

Interviews of Jimmy Gardiner by Una Maclean Evans, 29 December–6 January
    1961–2

National Archives of Canada, Ottawa

C.D. Howe Papers, MG 27 III, B 20
William Lyon Mackenzie King Papers, MG 26, J1, Primary
    Correspondence Series
William Lyon Mackenzie King Papers, MG 26, J5, Speeches
Liberal Party of Canada Papers, MG 28 IV 3
C.G. Power Papers, MG 27 III, B 19
Records of Boards, Offices, and Commissions, RG 36
Records of the Department of Agriculture, RG 17
Records of the Department of the Interior, RG 15
Records of the Federal–Provincial Conferences, RG 47
Records of the Privy Council Office, War Cabinet
Committee, RG 2, 7C
Records of Royal Commissions, RG 33

Provincial Archives of Alberta, Edmonton

Premier's Papers, 1921–55, 69.289

Provincial Archives of Manitoba, Winnipeg

John Bracken Papers, MG 13, I2
Executive Council, Premier's Office, Office Files, 1921–58, GR 43
Stuart S. Garson Papers, MG 13, J1
Ralph Maybank Papers, MG 14, B35
T.C. Norris Papers, MG 13

Queen's University Archives, Kingston

G.F. Chipman Papers
Thomas Alexander Crerar Papers, 2117
Grant Dexter Papers
Charles Avery Dunning Papers
Norman P. Lambert Papers

Saskatchewan Archives Board, Saskatoon

Charles Avery Dunning Papers, M6
James Garfield Gardiner Papers, S-1.137
W.M. Martin Papers, M4
W.R. Motherwell Papers, M12
W.J. Patterson Papers, R-79
W.A. Tucker Papers

University of Manitoba Archives, Winnipeg

John Wesley Dafoe Editorials Collection
John Wesley Dafoe Papers, MSS 3

University of Manitoba Libraries, Winnipeg

Sir Clifford Sifton Papers

Newspapers

Calgary Herald
Edmonton Bulletin
Edmonton Journal
Grain Growers' Guide
Regina Morning Leader

Prince Albert Herald
Reginal Daily Star
Regina Leader Post
Winnipeg Free Press

Published Primary Sources

Canada House of Commons. *Debates.*
Cook, Ramsay, ed. *The Dafoe–Sifton Correspondence, 1919–1927.* Altona, MB: D.W. Friesen, 1966
Dafoe, J.W., and W.L. Morton, eds. *The Voice of Dafoe.* Toronto: Macmillan, 1945
King, W.L.M. *Industry and Humanity: A Study in the Principles Underlying Industrial Reconstruction.* 1917. Reprint, Toronto: Macmillan, 1947
Power, C.G., and Norman Ward, eds. *The Memoirs of Chubby Power.* Toronto: Macmillan, 1966
William Lyon Mackenzie King Diaries. Toronto: University of Toronto Press, 1973

Secondary Sources

Abrams, G.W.D. *Prince Albert: The First Century, 1866–1966.* Saskatoon: Modern Press, 1966
Allen, Richard. 'The Social Gospel as the Religion of the Agrarian Revolt.' In *The Prairie West: Historical Readings,* edited by D. Francis and H. Palmer, 439–50. Edmonton: Pica Pica Press, 1985
– *The Social Passion: Religion and Social Reform in Canada, 1914–1928.* Toronto: University of Toronto Press, 1973
Bell, Edward. *Social Classes and Social Credit in Alberta.* Montreal: McGill-Queen's University Press, 1993
Betke, Carl F. 'The United Farmers of Alberta, 1921–1935.' In *Society and Politics in Alberta,* edited by Carlo Caldarola, 14–32. Toronto: Methuen, 1979
Bickle, Ian. *Turmoil and Triumph: The Controversial Railway to Hudson Bay.* Calgary: Detselig, 1995
Bocking, D.H. 'Premier Walter Scott: His Early Career.' *Saskatchewan History* 13, no. 2 (1960): 81–99
Brennan, William. 'The "Autonomy Question" and the Creation of Alberta and Saskatchewan.' In *The New Provinces: Alberta and Saskatchewan, 1905–1980,* edited by H. Palmer and D. Smith, 43–63. Vancouver: Tantalus Research, 1980
– 'C.A. Dunning and the Challenge of the Progressives, 1922–1925.' *Saskatchewan History* 22, no. 1 (winter 1969): 1–12
– 'C.A. Dunning, 1916–1930: The Rise and Fall of a Western Agrarian Liberal.'

In *The Developing West: Essays on Canadian History in Honor of Lewis H. Thomas*, edited by John E. Foster, 243–70. Edmonton: University of Alberta Press, 1983

– 'Press and Party in Saskatchewan, 1914–1929.' *Saskatchewan History* 27, no. 1 (winter 1974): 81–94

Britnell, G.E. *The Wheat Economy.* Toronto: University of Toronto Press, 1939

Britnell, G.E., and V.C. Fowke. *Canadian Agriculture in War and Peace.* Stanford, CA: Stanford University Press, 1962

Byrne, T.C. *Alberta's Revolutionary Leaders.* Calgary: Detselig, 1991

Caldarola, Carlo. 'The Social Credit in Alberta, 1935–1971.' In *Society and Politics in Alberta*, edited by Carlo Coldarola, 33–48. Toronto: Methuen, 1979

Cook, Ramsay. *The Politics of J.W. Dafoe and the Free Press.* Toronto: University of Toronto Press, 1963

– *The Regenerators: Social Criticism in Late Victorian English Canada.* Toronto: University of Toronto Press, 1985

Courtney, John C. 'Mackenzie King and Prince Albert Constituency: The 1933 Redistribution.' *Saskatchewan History* 29 (winter 1976): 1–13

Craven, Paul. *'An Impartial Umpire': Industrial Relations and the Canadian State, 1900–1911.* Toronto: University of Toronto Press, 1980

Dawson, R. MacGregor. *William Lyon Mackenzie King: A Political Biography, 1874–1923.* Toronto: University of Toronto Press, 1958

Donnelly, Murray. *Dafoe of the Free Press.* Toronto: Macmillan, 1968

Eager, Evelyn. 'The Conservatism of the Saskatchewan Electorate.' In *Politics in Saskatchewan*, edited by Norman Ward and Duff Spafford, 1–19. Don Mills ON: Longmans, 1968

Elliot, David R., and Iris Miller. *Bible Bill: A Biography of William Aberhart.* Edmonton: Reidmore Books, 1987

Elton, David K. 'Alberta and the Federal Government in Historical Perspective, 1905–1977.' In *Society and Politics in Alberta*, edited by Carlo Caldarola, 108–30. Toronto: Methuen, 1979

English, John, and J.O. Stubbs, eds. *Mackenzie King: Widening the Debate.* Toronto: Macmillan, 1978

Ferns, H.S., and Bernard Ostry. *The Age of Mackenzie King: The Rise of the Leader.* London: Heinemann, 1955

Ferguson, G.V. *John W. Dafoe.* Toronto: Ryerson Press, 1948

Fergusson, Bruce. *Rt. Hon. W.S. Fielding: The Mantle of Howe.* Windsor, NS: Lancelot Press, 1970

– *Rt. Hon. W.S. Fielding: Mr Minister of Finance.* Windsor, NS: Lancelot Press, 1971

Finkel, Alvin. *The Social Credit Phenomenon in Alberta.* Toronto: University of Toronto Press, 1989

Flanagan, Thomas, and Martha Lee. 'From Social Credit to Social Conservatism: The Evolution of an Ideology.' In *Riel to Reform: A History of Protest in Western Canada,* edited by George Melnyk, 182–97. Saskatoon: Fifth House, 1992

Foster, F.L. 'J.E. Brownlee: A Biography.' PhD diss., Queen's University, 1981

Fowke, V.C. *Canadian Agricultural Policy: The Historical Pattern.* Toronto: University of Toronto Press, 1946

– *The National Policy and the Wheat Economy.* Toronto: University of Toronto Press, 1957

– 'Royal Commissions and Canadian Agricultural Policy.' *Canadian Journal of Economics and Political Science* 14, no. 2 (1948): 163–75

Francis, R. Douglas. 'Changing Images in the West.' In *The Prairie West: Historical Readings,* edited by D. Francis and H. Palmer, 629–49. Edmonton: Pica Pica Press, 1985

– *Images of the West.* Saskatoon: Western Producer Prairie Books, 1989

Friesen, Gerald. *The Canadian Prairies: A History.* Toronto: University of Toronto Press, 1987

– 'The Prairies as Region: The Contemporary Meaning of an Old Idea.' Unpublished paper, 15 December 1991

– 'Studies in the Development of Western Canadian Regional Consciousness, 1870–1925.' PhD diss., University of Toronto, 1973

Gibbins, Roger. 'Regionalism in Decline: 1940 to the Present.' In *Riel to Reform: A History of Protest in Western Canada,* edited by George Melnyk, 215–23. Saskatoon: Fifth House Publishers, 1992

Gibson, Fred, ed. *Cabinet Formation and Bicultural Relations.* Studies of the Royal Commission on Bilingualism and Biculturalism. Kingston: Queen's Printer, 1970

Gibson, Frederick W., and Barbara Robertson, eds. *Ottawa at War: The Grant Dexter Memoranda, 1939–1945.* Winnipeg: Manitoba Record Society, 1994

Glassford, Larry. *Reaction and Reform: The Politics of the Conservative Party under R.B. Bennett, 1927–1938.* Toronto: University of Toronto Press, 1992

Graham, Roger. *Arthur Meighen, A Biography: The Door of Opportunity.* Toronto: University of Toronto Press, 1960

– *Arthur Meighen, A Biography: And Fortune Fled.* Toronto: University of Toronto Press, 1963

– *Arthur Meighen, A Biography: No Surrender.* Toronto: University of Toronto Press, 1965

Granatstein, J.L. *Canada's War: The Politics of the Mackenzie King Government,*
1939–1945. Toronto: Oxford University Press, 1975
– *The Ottawa Men: The Civil Service Mandarins, 1935–1957.* Toronto: University
of Toronto Press, 1982
Gray, James. *R.B. Bennett: The Calgary Years.* Toronto: University of Toronto
Press, 1991
Hall, D.J. 'T.O. Davis and Federal Politics in Saskatchewan, 1896.' *Saskatchewan*
History 30, no. 1 (winter 1977): 56–62
Henderson, George F. 'Mackenzie King the Farmer.' *Up the Gatineau* 20 (1994):
15–21
– *W.L. Mackenzie King: A Bibliography and Research Guide.* Toronto: University of
Toronto Press, 1998
Hoffman, George. 'The 1934 Saskatchewan Provincial Election Campaign.'
Saskatchewan History 36, no. 2 (spring 1983), 41–57
– 'The Saskatchewan Farmer–Labor Party, 1932–1934: How Radical Was It at
Its Origin?' *Saskatchewan History* 28, no. 2 (fall 1975): 52–64
Hutchison, Bruce. *Mackenzie King: The Incredible Canadian.* Toronto: Longmans,
Green, 1953
Irving, John A. *The Social Credit Movement in Alberta.* Toronto: University of
Toronto Press, 1959
Kendle, John. *John Bracken: A Political Biography.* Toronto: University of Toronto
Press, 1979
Kyba, Patrick. 'Ballots and Burning Crosses.' In *Politics in Saskatchewan*, edited
by Norman Ward and Duff Spafford 105–23. Don Mills, ON: Longmans,
1968
Laycock, David. *Populism and Democratic Thought in the Canadian Prairies, 1910 to*
1945. Toronto: University of Toronto Press, 1990
Leacock, Steven. *My Discovery of the West: A Discussion of East and West in Canada.*
Toronto: n.p., 1937
Lederle, John W. 'The Liberal Convention of 1919 and the Selection of
Mackenzie King.' *Dalhousie Review* 27, no. 1 (August 1947): 85–92
McCormack, A. Ross. *Reformers, Rebels, and Revolutionaries: The Western Canadian*
Radical Movement, 1899–1919. Toronto: University of Toronto Press, 1977
Macpherson, C.B. *Democracy in Alberta: Social Credit and the Party System.* To-
ronto: University of Toronto Press, 1953
McGregor, F.A. *The Fall and Rise of Mackenzie King, 1911–1919.* Toronto:
Macmillan, 1962
Melnyk, George, ed. *Riel to Reform: A History of Protest in Western Canada.*
Saskatoon: Fifth House Publishers, 1992
Milnor, Andrew. 'The New Politics and Ethnic Revolt, 1929–1938.' In *Politics in*

Saskatchewan, edited by Norman Ward and Duff Spafford, 151–77. Don Mills, ON: Longmans, 1968

Morton, W.L. 'The Bias of Prairie Politics.' In *Historical Essays on the Prairie Provinces*, edited by Donald Swainson, 289–300. Toronto: McClelland and Stewart, 1970

– *The Progressive Party in Canada*. Toronto: University of Toronto Press, 1950

Neatby, H. Blair. *William Lyon Mackenzie King: The Lonely Heights, 1924–1932*. Toronto: University of Toronto Press, 1963

– *William Lyon Mackenzie King: The Prism of Unity, 1932–1939*. Toronto: University of Toronto Press, 1976

Norrie, Kenneth. 'The National Policy and the Rate of Prairie Settlement: A Review.' In *The Prairie West: Historical Readings*, edited by R. Douglas Francis and Howard Palmer, 237–56. Edmonton: University of Alberta Press, 1992

Owram, Doug. *Promise of Eden: The Canadian Expansionist Movement and the Idea of the West, 1856–1900*. Toronto: University of Toronto Press, 1980

Pickersgill, J.W., and D.F. Forster. *The Mackenzie King Record*. Vol. 3. *1945–1946*. Toronto: University of Toronto Press, 1970

– *The Mackenzie King Record*. Vol. 4. *1946–1947*. Toronto: University of Toronto Press, 1970

Rea, J.E. *T.A. Crerar: A Political Life*. Montreal: McGill-Queen's University Press, 1997

– 'T.A. Crerar and the Progressive Challenge.' In *Swords and Ploughshares: War and Agriculture in Western Canada*, edited by R.C. McLeod, 223–38. Edmonton: University of Alberta Press, 1993

– 'The Wheat Board and the Western Farmer.' *The Beaver* (February–March 1997): 14–23

Regehr, T.D. *The Beauharnois Scandal: A Story of Canadian Entrepreneurship and Politics*. Toronto: University of Toronto Press, 1990

Regenstreif, Peter, S. 'The Liberal Party of Canada: A Political Analysis.' PhD diss., Cornell University, 1963

– 'A Threat to Leadership: C.A. Dunning and Mackenzie King.' *Dalhousie Review*, 44 (April 1964): 272–89

Reid, Escott M. 'The Saskatchewan Liberal Machine before 1929.' In *Politics in Saskatchewan*, edited by Norman Ward and Duff Spafford, 93–104. Don Mills ON: Longman, 1968

Rolph, William Kirby. *Henry Wise Wood of Alberta*. Toronto: University of Toronto Press, 1950

Sinclair, Peter R. 'Class Structure and Populist Protest: The Case of Western Canada.' In *Riel to Reform: A History of Protest in Western Canada*, edited by George Melnyk, 198–214. Saskatoon: Fifth House Publishers, 1992

Smith, David. 'James G. Gardiner: Political Leadership in the Agrarian
Community.' In *Swords and Ploughshares: War and Agriculture in Western
Canada*, edited by R.C. McLeod, 203–22. Edmonton: University of Alberta
Press, 1993
– *Prairie Liberalism: The Liberal Party in Saskatchewan, 1905–1971*. Toronto:
University of Toronto Press, 1975
– *The Regional Decline of a National Party: Liberals on the Prairies*. Toronto:
University of Toronto Press, 1981
– 'Western Politics and National Unity.' In *Riel to Reform: A History of Protest in
Western Canada*, edited by George Melynk, 43–60. Saskatoon: Fifth House
Publishers, 1992
Spafford, Duff. 'The "Left Wing" 1921–1931.' In *Politics in Saskatchewan*, edited
by Norman Ward and Duff Spafford, 44–58. Don Mills ON: Longmans, 1968
– 'The Origin of the Farmers' Union of Canada.' *Historical Essays on the Prairie
Provinces*, edited by Donald Swainson, 254–66. Toronto: McClelland and
Stewart, 1970.
Steele, Frank C. *Prairie Editor: The Life and Times of Buchanan of Lethbridge.*
Toronto: Ryerson Press, 1961
Taylor, Jeff. *Fashioning Farmers: Ideology, Agricultural Knowledge, and the Manitoba
Farm Movement, 1890–1925*. Regina: Canadian Plains Research Center, 1994
Thomas, L.G. *The Liberal Party of Alberta, 1905–1921*. Toronto: University of
Toronto Press, 1950
– 'The Liberal Party in Alberta, 1905–21.' *Canadian Historical Review* 28
(December 1947): 411–27
Thomas, L.H. 'The CCF Victory in Saskatchewan, 1944.' *Saskatchewan History*
34, no. 2 (winter 1981): 1–16
Thomas, Lewis H. *William Aberhart and Social Credit in Alberta*. Toronto: Copp
Clark, 1977
Thompson, J.H. *The Harvests of War: The Prairie West, 1914–1918*. Toronto:
McClelland and Stewart, 1978
Thompson, J.H., and Allen Seager. *Canada, 1922–1939: Decades of Discord.*
Toronto: McClelland and Stewart, 1985
Turner, Allen R. 'W.R. Motherwell and Agricultural Education, 1905–1918.'
Saskatchewan History 12, no. 4 (1959): 81–96
– 'W.R. Motherwell: The Emergence of a Farm Leader.' *Saskatchewan History*
11, no. 1 (1958): 94–103
Unger, Gordon. 'James G. Gardiner and the Constitutional Crisis of 1929.'
Saskatchewan History 23, no. 2 (1970): 41–9
– 'James G. Gardiner: The Premier as a Pragmatic Politician, 1926–1929.' MA
thesis, University of Saskatchewan, 1967

Vajcner, Mark Eric. 'The Public Career of Stuart Garson: The Manitoba Years.'
MA thesis, University of Manitoba, 1993
Waiser, W.A. *Saskatchewan's Playground: A History of Prince Albert National Park.*
Saskatoon: Sixth House Publishers, 1989
– 'Hon. James Gardiner and the Liberal Party of Alberta, 1935–40.' *Canadian Historical Review* 56, no. 3 (September 1975): 303–22
Ward, Norman, and David Smith. *Jimmy Gardiner: Relentless Liberal.* Toronto:
University of Toronto Press, 1990
Ward, Norman, and Duff Spafford, eds. *Politics in Saskatchewan.* Don Mills, ON:
Longmans, 1968
Wardhaugh, R.A. '"Awaiting the Return of Common Sense": Mackenzie King
and Alberta.' *National History* 1, no. 3 (winter 1997–8): 262–71
– 'Cogs in the Machine: The Charles Dunning–Jimmy Gardiner Feud.'
Saskatchewan History 48, no. 1 (spring 1996): 20–9
– 'The "Impartial Umpire" Views the West: Mackenzie King and the Search for
the New Jerusalem.' *Manitoba History* 29 (spring 1995): 11–22
– 'James Gardiner, Land Policy, and Dominion–Provincial Relations.' MA
thesis, University of Saskatchewan, 1990
– 'A Marriage of Convenience? Mackenzie King and Prince Albert Constitu-
ency.' *Prairie Forum* 21, no. 2 (fall 1996): 177–200
– 'Region and Nation: The Politics of Jimmy Gardiner.' *Saskatchewan History*
45, no. 2 (fall 1993): 24–36
Whitaker, Reginald. *The Government Party: Organizing and Financing the Liberal
Party of Canada.* Toronto: University of Toronto Press, 1977
Wilson, G.F. *A Century of Canadian Grain.* Saskatoon: Western Producer Prairie
Books, 1978

Index

Hudson, A.B., 53, 62–8, 82, 85, 89, 94, 102, 106, 108, 110, 123, 145–6
Hudson Bay Railway, 78, 89, 99–100, 101, 108, 115, 122, 125, 130, 131, 137, 264
Hull House, 9
Humboldt by-elections: of 1938, 223; of 1943, 245
Humphries, M.I., 251, 252–3, 254, 257–8
Hutchison, Bruce, 79

Icelanders, 14
Ilsley, J.L., 226, 229, 233, 236
immigration, 74, 115–16, 134, 136, 137, 138, 160
Imperial Conferences: of 1923, 89–90; of 1926, 142; of 1931, 155
Independent Labour party, 181
Indians, 6, 7, 11, 178
industrialization, 6, 7, 8, 9, 127, 231, 263

Kennedy, D.M., 120
Kennedy, W.C., 62
Keynes, J.M., 221
Kilgour, J.F., 92
King, J.H., 84
King, William Lyon Mackenzie: on agriculture, 49, 129; on bankruptcy of Prairie provinces, 201, 202, 213–14; on Bennett, 161, 167; cabinet negotiations, of 1921, 61–8; —, of 1935, 190–6; on CCF, 170–1, 173–4; on Chanak crisis, 82–3; on Depression, 154, 167–8, 178–99, 205–6; on disallowance, 215–17; on Farmers (and Progressives), 12–13, 36, 37–43, 47, 53–5, 58–60, 61–8, 73, 81–3, 89–91, 93–4,

96–8, 104, 109–10, 112, 116, 119, 128, 134, 140, 143, 144–5, 153, 161–2, 170; 'five-cent' speech, 154–5, 158, 160; on freight rates, 17, 79–81, 100–1, 103–5; on Hudson Bay Railway, 78, 89, 99–100; imperial conference of 1923, 89–90; *Industry and Humanity*, 25, 168, 177, 242; on labour issues, 9–13, 17, 25, 29, 32, 74; leadership, 49–50, 70, 73–4, 77, 90–1, 96, 110, 111, 125, 169–70, 173; leadership convention, of 1919, 9, 30–4; —, of 1948, 259–61; on monetary policy, 171, 173, 179; on national bank, 206; on natural resources question, 15, 75–7, 83–4, 96, 137, 139, 140–2, 144, 148, 149, 152–3; on On-to-Ottawa Trek, 186–7; on party organization, 72, 149, 151, 157, 160; perceptions of Prairies, 4, 6–8, 10–11, 13–14, 23, 34–5, 36, 37, 51, 72, 103, 118, 129, 142, 154, 178, 188–9, 264; philosophy of, 8–9, 25; platform of 1919, 38–9, 69, 79, 98; on Prairie constituency, 23–4; on Prince Albert constituency, 117–18, 123–4, 130–1, 138, 142, 166–7, 174–6, 188–9, 228, 247–8, 250–5, 257–8; on radicalism, 20, 29–30, 177; and social gospel, 10–11, 25; on socialism, 12, 38, 179, 220; on tariffs, 15–16, 22–3, 56–7, 84–6, 97, 103, 106, 108, 115, 137, 143, 155, 156, 168–9, 173, 176, 187; on unemployment, 136, 138, 154–5, 158–9, 173, 203, 204; university career of, 9; on Wall Street crash, 153; western speaking tour, of

tariffs, 15, 18, 20, 21–2, 28, 29, 32, 49,
50, 56–7, 63, 66, 73, 78–9, 84–6, 96,
97–100, 105–6, 107, 111, 115, 117,
119, 122, 125, 130, 137, 143, 155,
156, 158, 161, 168–9, 171, 173, 176,
180, 187, 200, 205, 206, 220, 221,
226, 264
Tarr, Edgar, 110
Taussig, Frank William, 16
taxation, 29, 97, 130, 137, 143, 156,
200, 201, 203, 220, 231–2
Taylor, Thomas, 146–8
Thorson, Joe, 188
Towers, Graham, 203, 213
Toynbee, Arnold, 9, 13
Trudeau, Pierre Elliott, 3
Tucker, Walter, 252, 255, 256, 260
Turgeon, J.G., 72, 92
Turgeon Commission, 142, 143, 148,
152

unemployment, 136, 137, 138, 154,
158–9, 160–1, 163, 186–7, 198, 200,
203, 204, 221, 228
Union government, 25, 26, 27–8, 31,
39, 40, 43, 48, 51, 57, 64, 71, 72,
135, 194
United Farmers of Alberta. See
Farmers
United Farmers of Canada, Saskatch-
ewan Section, 181
United Farmers of Manitoba. See Farm-
ers
United Farmers of Ontario, 44, 52, 68
United Grain Growers, 88
United Nations, 252, 253
United States, 18, 21, 25, 29, 33, 78,
143, 155, 156, 187, 200, 205, 220,
221, 247, 257
Unity Party, 218
urbanization, 6, 7, 8, 127

Vancouver Strike (1935), 186

Wall Street crash, 153–4
Walpole, Robert, 230
war cabinet, 233
war committee, 234
Wartime Elections Act, 29, 48, 71,
135
Wartime Industries Control Board,
236
Wartime Prices and Trade Board,
236–7
Weir, Robert, 174–6
Weir, W.G., 194
welfare state, 22, 230, 231, 242–4
Wetaskiwin constituency, 117
Wheat Board, 24–5, 57, 74, 88,
179–81, 185–6, 187, 196–8, 206–8,
210, 224–7, 235, 237–8, 242, 264
wheat committee, 196–7
wheat pools, 57, 88, 120, 154, 180,
185–6, 207, 224, 225, 226, 242, 245,
257
wheat prices, 17, 18, 24, 48, 79, 129,
153–4, 158, 163, 171, 180, 205,
206–8, 224–7, 233–4, 236–7, 240,
241–2, 257
Wilton, J.W., 188
Winkler, 177–8
Winnipeg Electric Company, 144
Winnipeg General Strike, 29
Winnipeg Grain Exchange, 24, 57,
74, 88, 154, 186, 194, 257
Wood, Henry Wise, 46, 111
Wood, James A., 130
Wood, T.H., 252
Woodsworth, J.S., 98, 115, 121, 186,
203

York South federal by-election
(1942), 239–40

Ross - 11/06 (Lundgren)